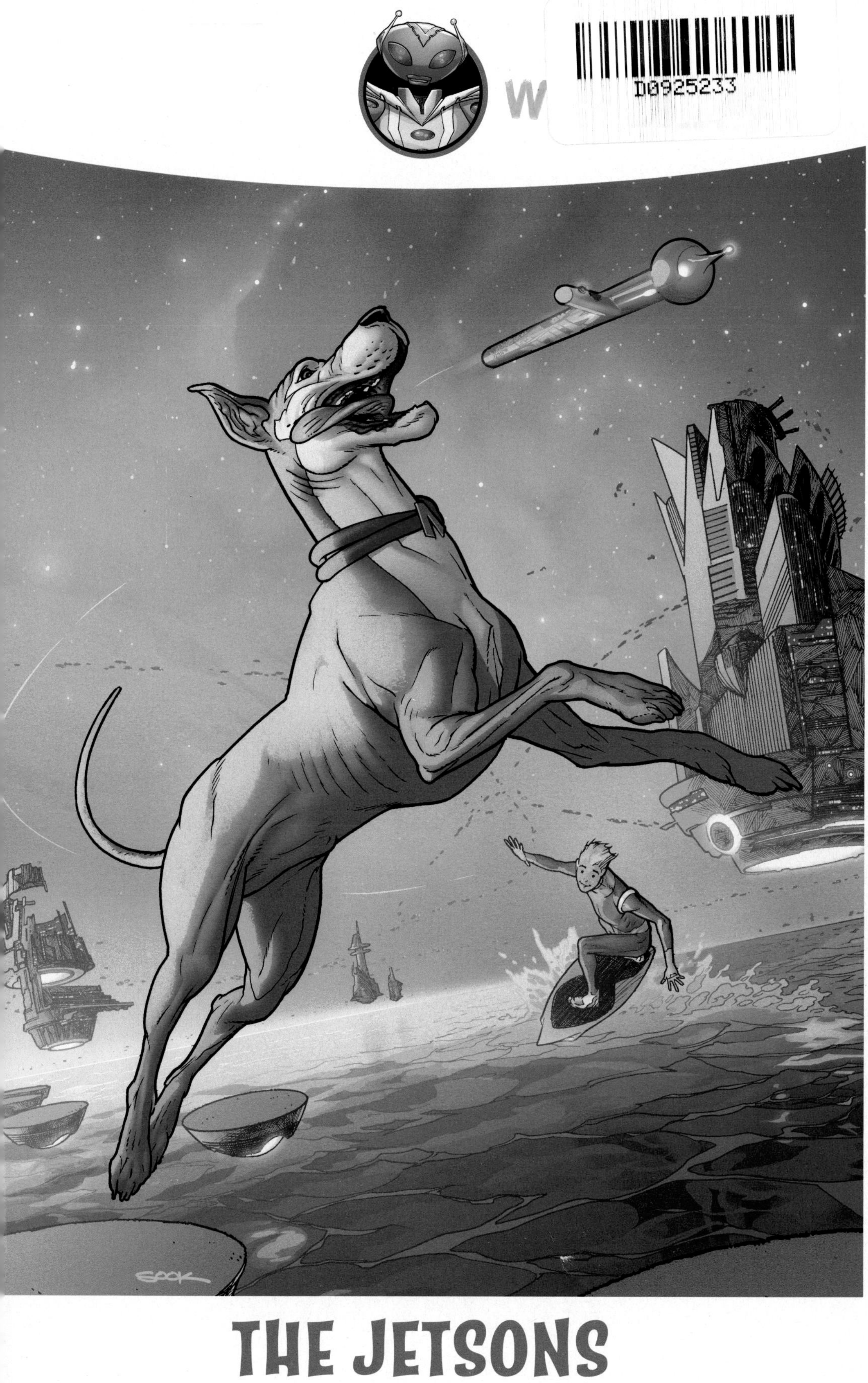

THE JETSONS

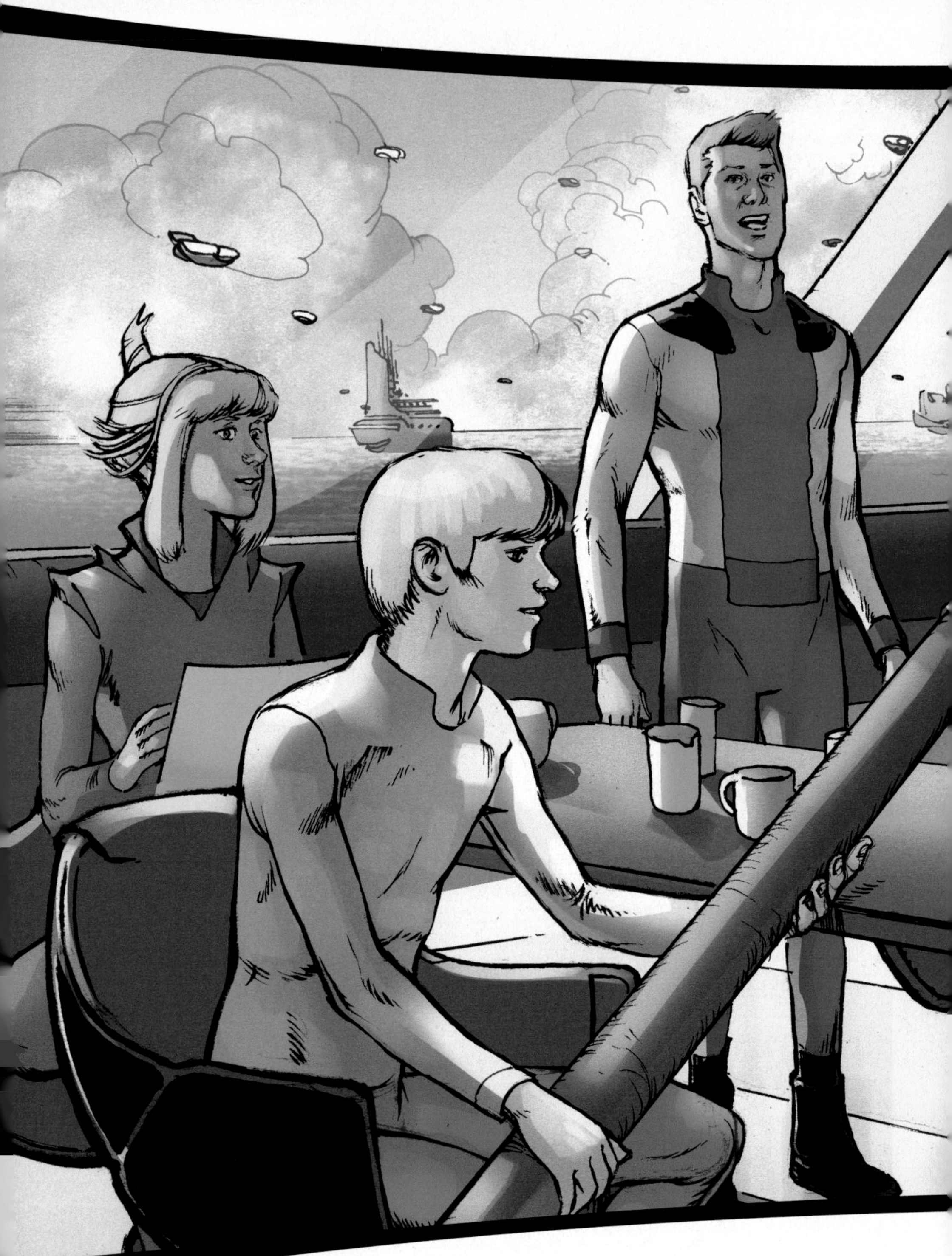

THE JETSONS

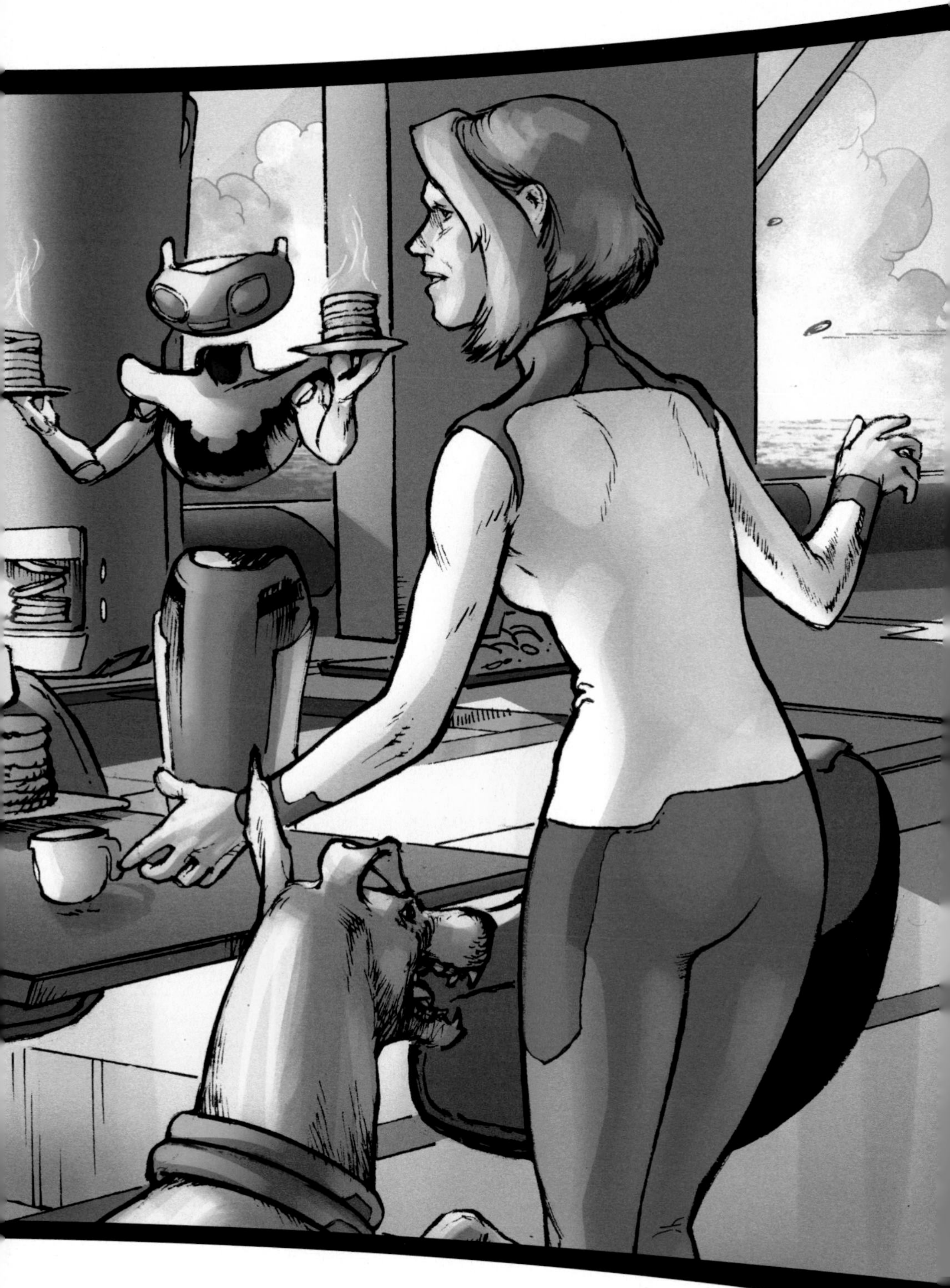

JIMMY PALMIOTTI writer **PIER BRITO** artist
ALEX SINCLAIR colorist **DAVE SHARPE** letterer
AMANDA CONNER and **PAUL MOUNTS** series and collection cover artists

PROLOGUE by
JIMMY PALMIOTTI and **AMANDA CONNER** writers
PIER BRITO artist **ALEX SINCLAIR** colorist **MICHAEL HEISLER** letterer

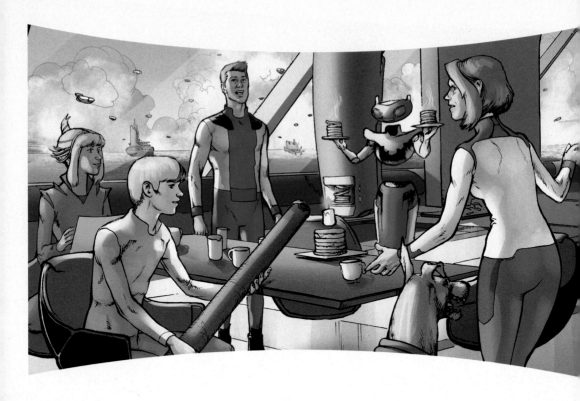

JOEY CAVALIERI Editor - Original Series
BRITTANY HOLZHERR Associate Editor - Original Series DIEGO LOPEZ, MICHAEL McCALISTER Assistant Editors - Original Series
JEB WOODARD Group Editor - Collected Editions ERIKA ROTHBERG Editor - Collected Edition
STEVE COOK Design Director - Books DAMIAN RYLAND Publication Design

BOB HARRAS Senior VP - Editor-in-Chief, DC Comics
PAT McCALLUM Executive Editor, DC Comics

DIANE NELSON President DAN DiDIO Publisher JIM LEE Publisher GEOFF JOHNS President & Chief Creative Officer
AMIT DESAI Executive VP - Business & Marketing Strategy, Direct to Consumer & Global Franchise Management
SAM ADES Senior VP & General Manager, Digital Services BOBBIE CHASE VP & Executive Editor, Young Reader & Talent Development
MARK CHIARELLO Senior VP - Art, Design & Collected Editions JOHN CUNNINGHAM Senior VP - Sales & Trade Marketing
ANNE DePIES Senior VP - Business Strategy, Finance & Administration DON FALLETTI VP - Manufacturing Operations
LAWRENCE GANEM VP - Editorial Administration & Talent Relations ALISON GILL Senior VP - Manufacturing & Operations
HANK KANALZ Senior VP - Editorial Strategy & Administration JAY KOGAN VP - Legal Affairs JACK MAHAN VP - Business Affairs
NICK J. NAPOLITANO VP - Manufacturing Administration EDDIE SCANNELL VP - Consumer Marketing
COURTNEY SIMMONS Senior VP - Publicity & Communications JIM (SKI) SOKOLOWSKI VP - Comic Book Specialty Sales & Trade Marketing
NANCY SPEARS VP - Mass, Book, Digital Sales & Trade Marketing MICHELE R. WELLS VP - Content Strategy

THE JETSONS

Published by DC Comics. All new material Copyright © 2018 Hanna-Barbera. All Rights Reserved. Originally published in single magazine form in THE JETSONS 1-6, BOOSTER GOLD/THE FLINTSTONES SPECIAL 1. Copyright © 2017, 2018 Hanna-Barbera. All Rights Reserved. The stories, characters and incidents featured in this publication are entirely fictional. DC Comics does not read or accept unsolicited submissions of ideas, stories or artwork.

DC Comics, 2900 West Alameda Ave., Burbank, CA 91505. Printed by LSC Communications, Kendallville, IN, USA. 6/1/18. First Printing. ISBN: 978-1-4012-8025-3

Library of Congress Cataloging-in-Publication Data is available.

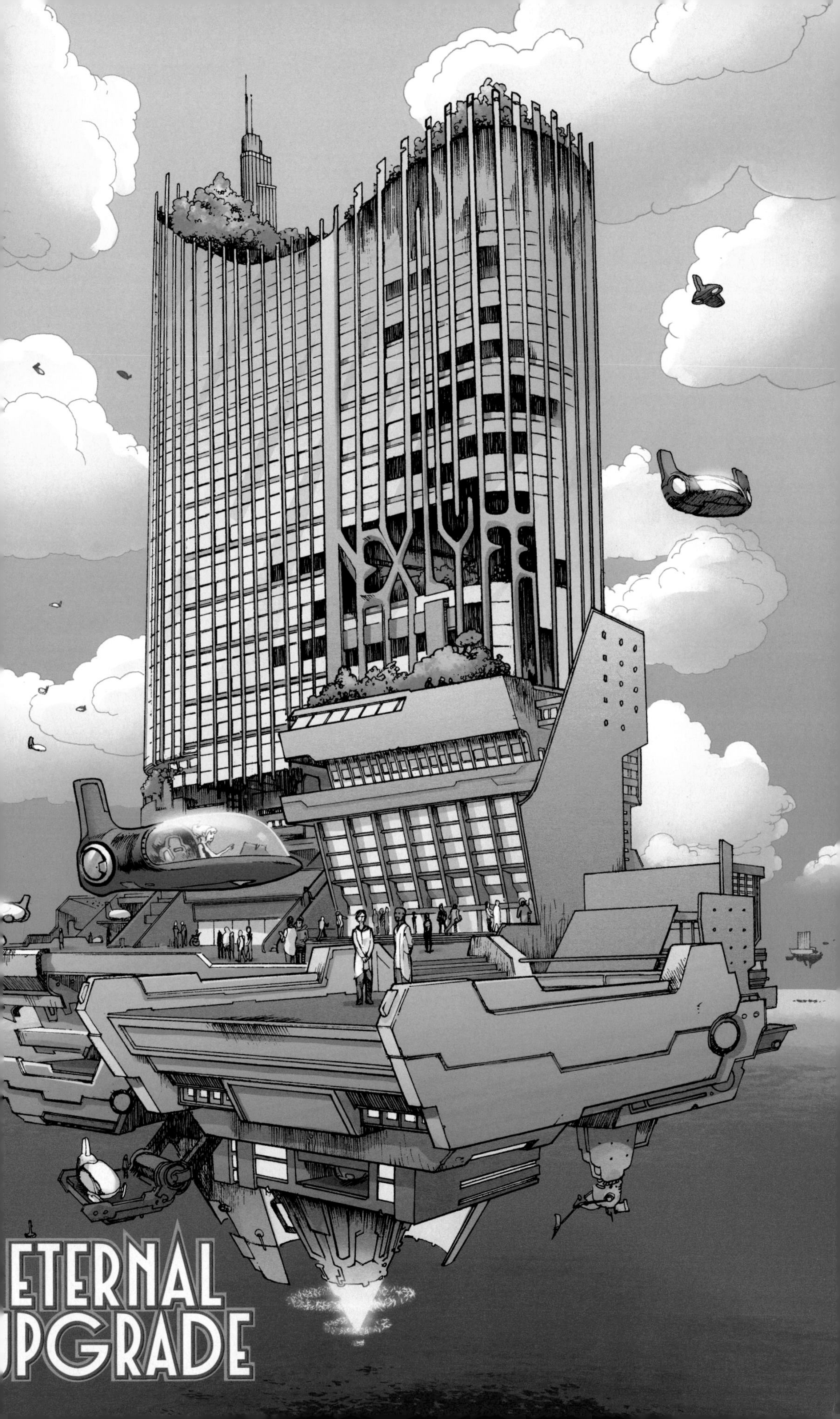
NEXUS
ETERNAL
UPGRADE

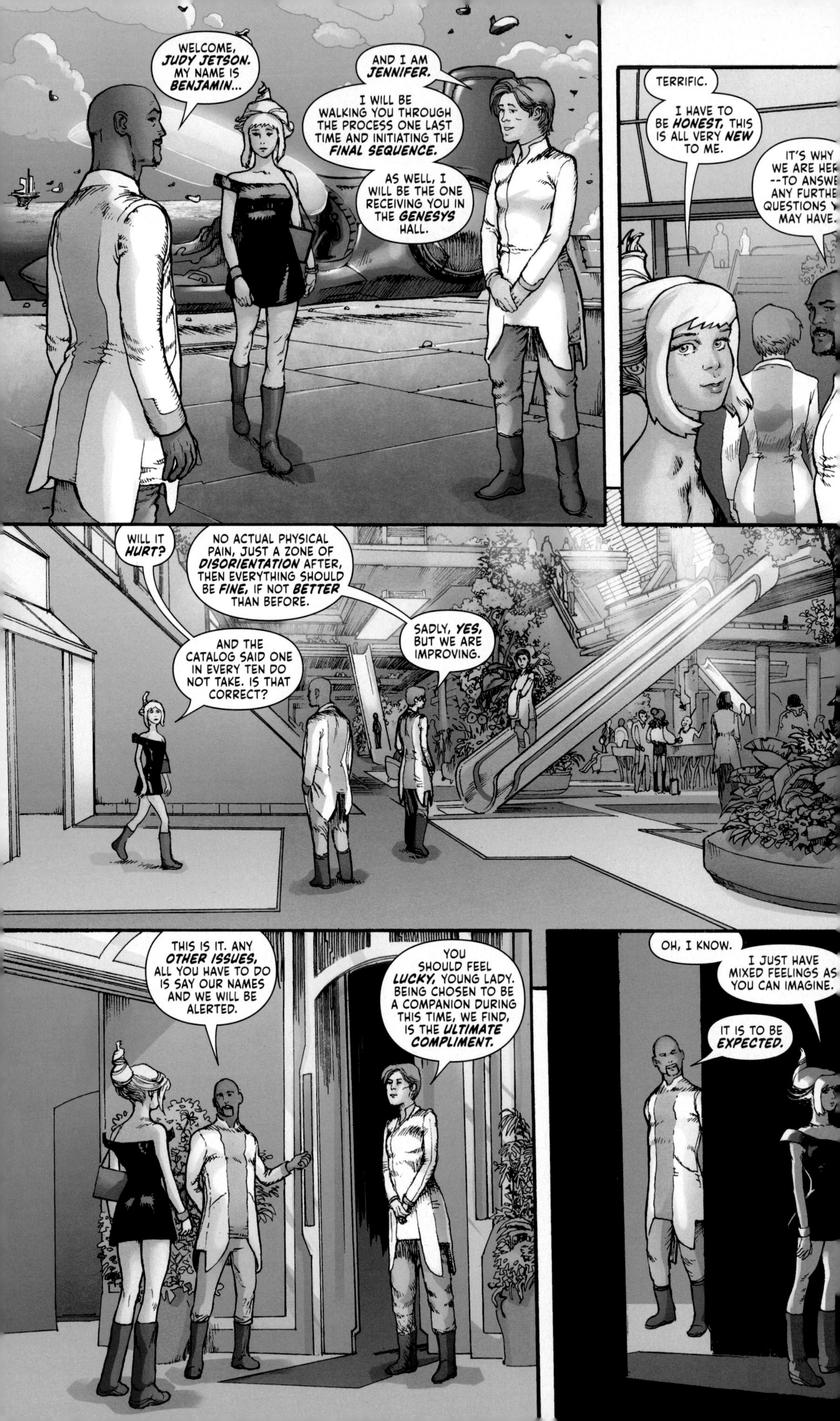
WELCOME, JUDY JETSON. MY NAME IS BENJAMIN...
AND I AM JENNIFER.
I WILL BE WALKING YOU THROUGH THE PROCESS ONE LAST TIME AND INITIATING THE FINAL SEQUENCE.
AS WELL, I WILL BE THE ONE RECEIVING YOU IN THE GENESYS HALL.
TERRIFIC.
I HAVE TO BE HONEST, THIS IS ALL VERY NEW TO ME.
IT'S WHY WE ARE HER --TO ANSWE ANY FURTHE QUESTIONS MAY HAVE.
WILL IT HURT?
NO ACTUAL PHYSICAL PAIN, JUST A ZONE OF DISORIENTATION AFTER, THEN EVERYTHING SHOULD BE FINE, IF NOT BETTER THAN BEFORE.
AND THE CATALOG SAID ONE IN EVERY TEN DO NOT TAKE. IS THAT CORRECT?
SADLY, YES, BUT WE ARE IMPROVING.
THIS IS IT. ANY OTHER ISSUES, ALL YOU HAVE TO DO IS SAY OUR NAMES AND WE WILL BE ALERTED.
YOU SHOULD FEEL LUCKY, YOUNG LADY. BEING CHOSEN TO BE A COMPANION DURING THIS TIME, WE FIND, IS THE ULTIMATE COMPLIMENT.
OH, I KNOW.
I JUST HAVE MIXED FEELINGS AS YOU CAN IMAGINE.
IT IS TO BE EXPECTED.

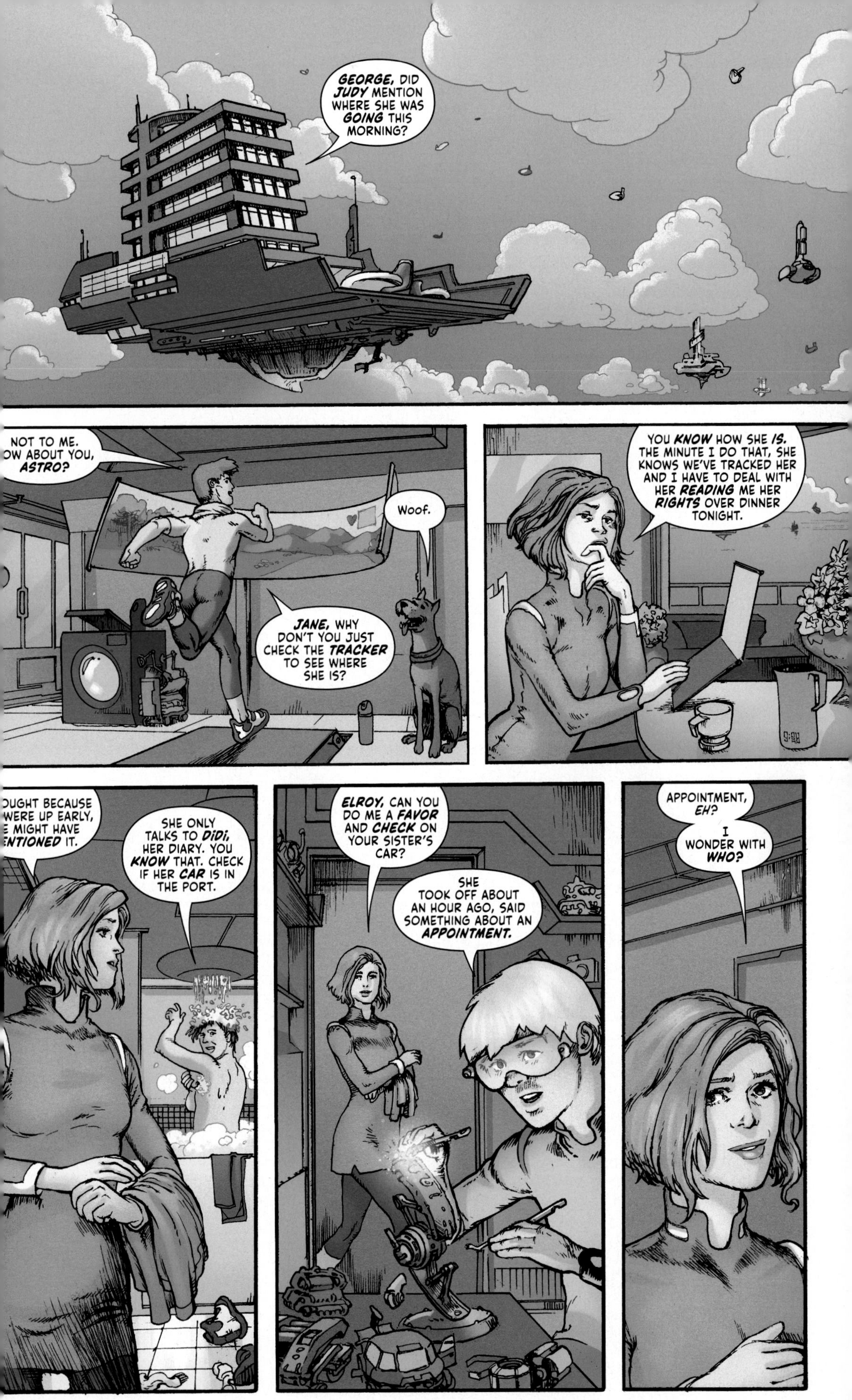
GEORGE, DID JUDY MENTION WHERE SHE WAS GOING THIS MORNING?
NOT TO ME. OW ABOUT YOU, ASTRO?
Woof.
JANE, WHY DON'T YOU JUST CHECK THE TRACKER TO SEE WHERE SHE IS?
YOU KNOW HOW SHE IS. THE MINUTE I DO THAT, SHE KNOWS WE'VE TRACKED HER AND I HAVE TO DEAL WITH HER READING ME HER RIGHTS OVER DINNER TONIGHT.
OUGHT BECAUSE WERE UP EARLY, E MIGHT HAVE ENTIONED IT.
SHE ONLY TALKS TO DiDi, HER DIARY. YOU KNOW THAT. CHECK IF HER CAR IS IN THE PORT.
ELROY, CAN YOU DO ME A FAVOR AND CHECK ON YOUR SISTER'S CAR?
SHE TOOK OFF ABOUT AN HOUR AGO, SAID SOMETHING ABOUT AN APPOINTMENT.
APPOINTMENT, EH?
I WONDER WITH WHO?

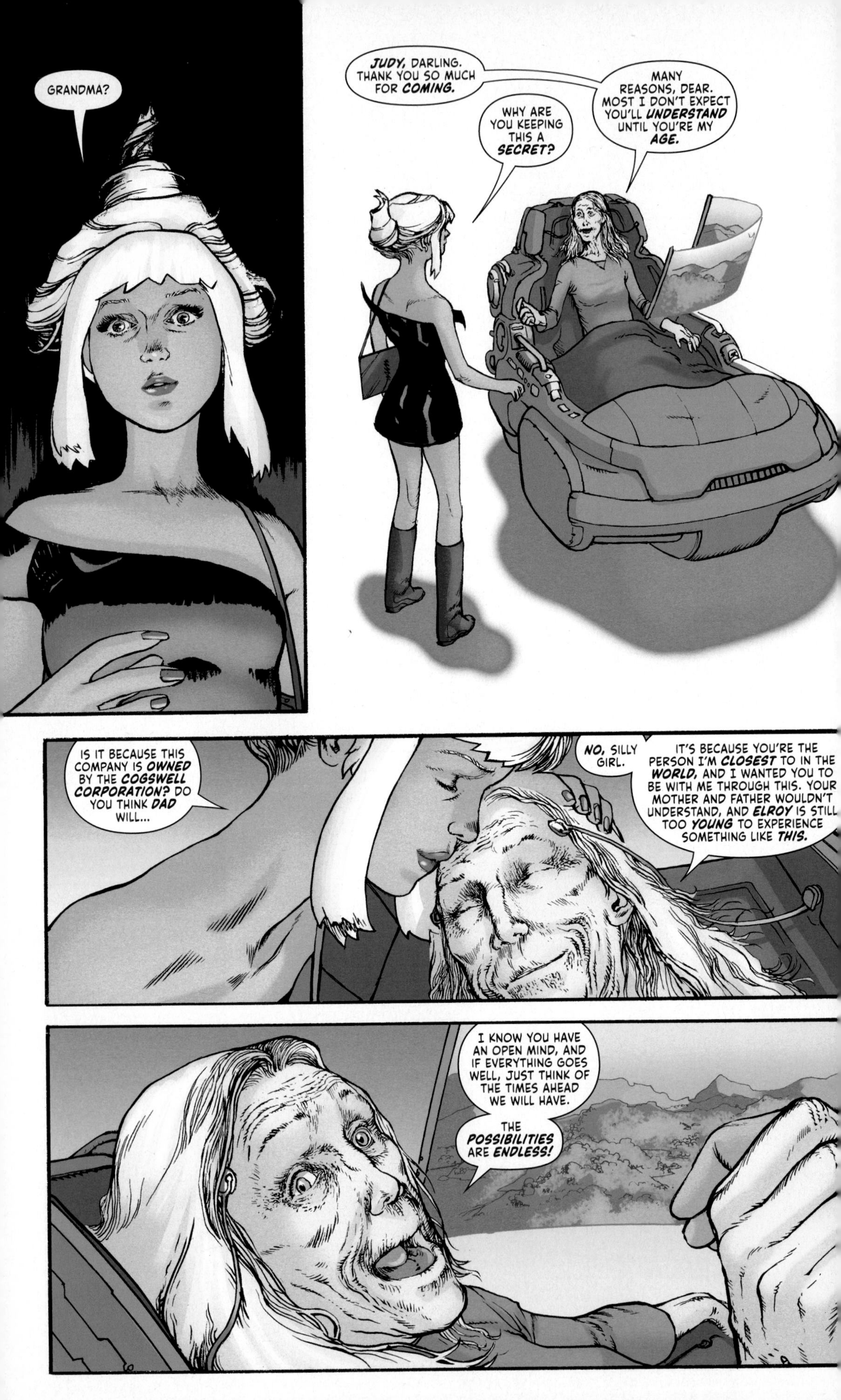
GRANDMA?
JUDY, DARLING. THANK YOU SO MUCH FOR COMING.
WHY ARE YOU KEEPING THIS A SECRET?
MANY REASONS, DEAR. MOST I DON'T EXPECT YOU'LL UNDERSTAND UNTIL YOU'RE MY AGE.
IS IT BECAUSE THIS COMPANY IS OWNED BY THE COGSWELL CORPORATION? DO YOU THINK DAD WILL...
NO, SILLY GIRL.
IT'S BECAUSE YOU'RE THE PERSON I'M CLOSEST TO IN THE WORLD, AND I WANTED YOU TO BE WITH ME THROUGH THIS. YOUR MOTHER AND FATHER WOULDN'T UNDERSTAND, AND ELROY IS STILL TOO YOUNG TO EXPERIENCE SOMETHING LIKE THIS.
I KNOW YOU HAVE AN OPEN MIND, AND IF EVERYTHING GOES WELL, JUST THINK OF THE TIMES AHEAD WE WILL HAVE.
THE POSSIBILITIES ARE ENDLESS!

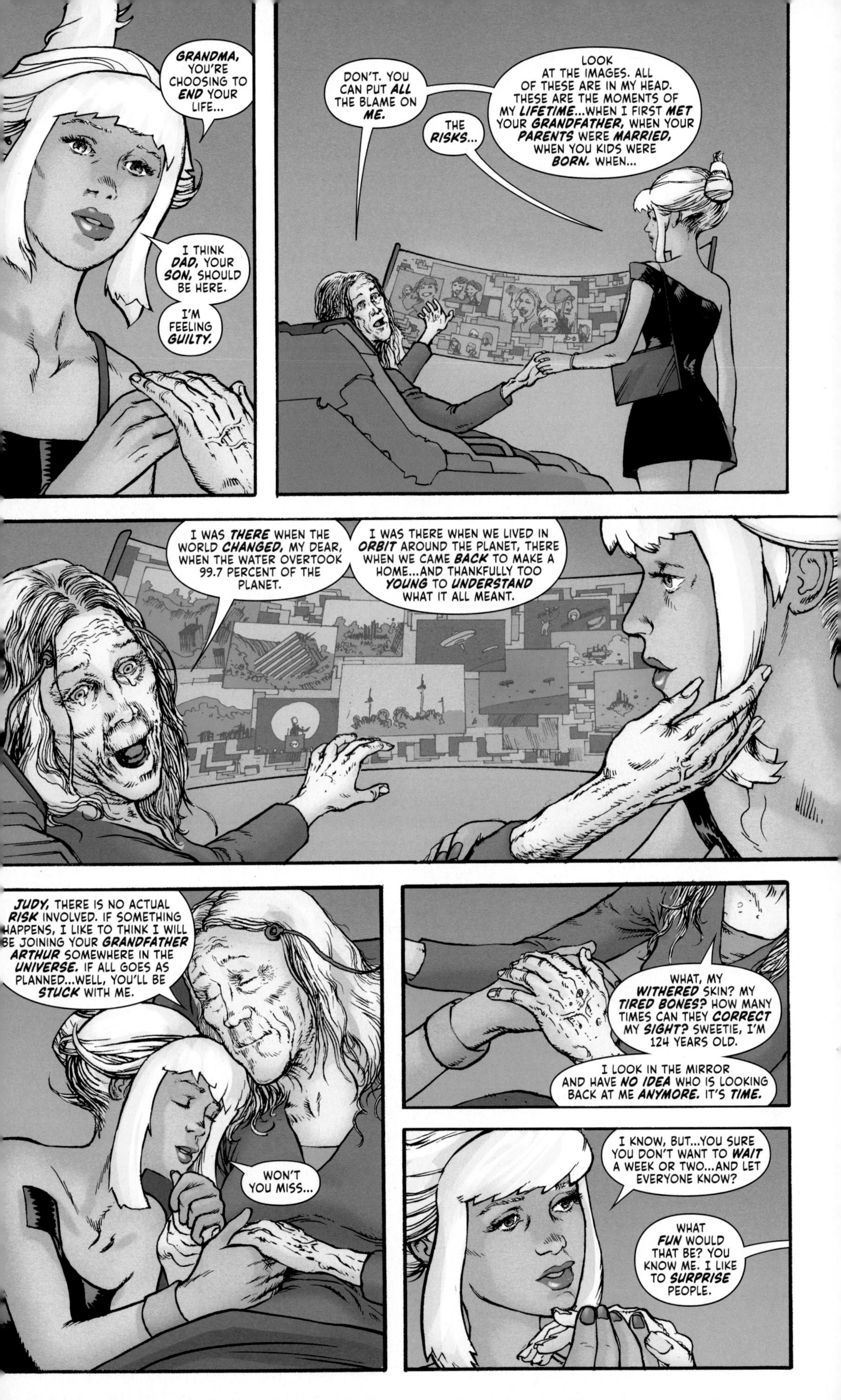
GRANDMA, YOU'RE CHOOSING TO END YOUR LIFE...
I THINK DAD, YOUR SON, SHOULD BE HERE.
I'M FEELING GUILTY.
DON'T. YOU CAN PUT ALL THE BLAME ON ME.
THE RISKS...
LOOK AT THE IMAGES. ALL OF THESE ARE IN MY HEAD. THESE ARE THE MOMENTS OF MY LIFETIME...WHEN I FIRST MET YOUR GRANDFATHER, WHEN YOUR PARENTS WERE MARRIED, WHEN YOU KIDS WERE BORN. WHEN...
I WAS THERE WHEN THE WORLD CHANGED, MY DEAR, WHEN THE WATER OVERTOOK 99.7 PERCENT OF THE PLANET.
I WAS THERE WHEN WE LIVED IN ORBIT AROUND THE PLANET, THERE WHEN WE CAME BACK TO MAKE A HOME...AND THANKFULLY TOO YOUNG TO UNDERSTAND WHAT IT ALL MEANT.
JUDY, THERE IS NO ACTUAL RISK INVOLVED. IF SOMETHING HAPPENS, I LIKE TO THINK I WILL BE JOINING YOUR GRANDFATHER ARTHUR SOMEWHERE IN THE UNIVERSE. IF ALL GOES AS PLANNED...WELL, YOU'LL BE STUCK WITH ME.
WON'T YOU MISS...
WHAT, MY WITHERED SKIN? MY TIRED BONES? HOW MANY TIMES CAN THEY CORRECT MY SIGHT? SWEETIE, I'M 124 YEARS OLD.
I LOOK IN THE MIRROR AND HAVE NO IDEA WHO IS LOOKING BACK AT ME ANYMORE. IT'S TIME.
I KNOW, BUT...YOU SURE YOU DON'T WANT TO WAIT A WEEK OR TWO...AND LET EVERYONE KNOW?
WHAT FUN WOULD THAT BE? YOU KNOW ME. I LIKE TO SURPRISE PEOPLE.

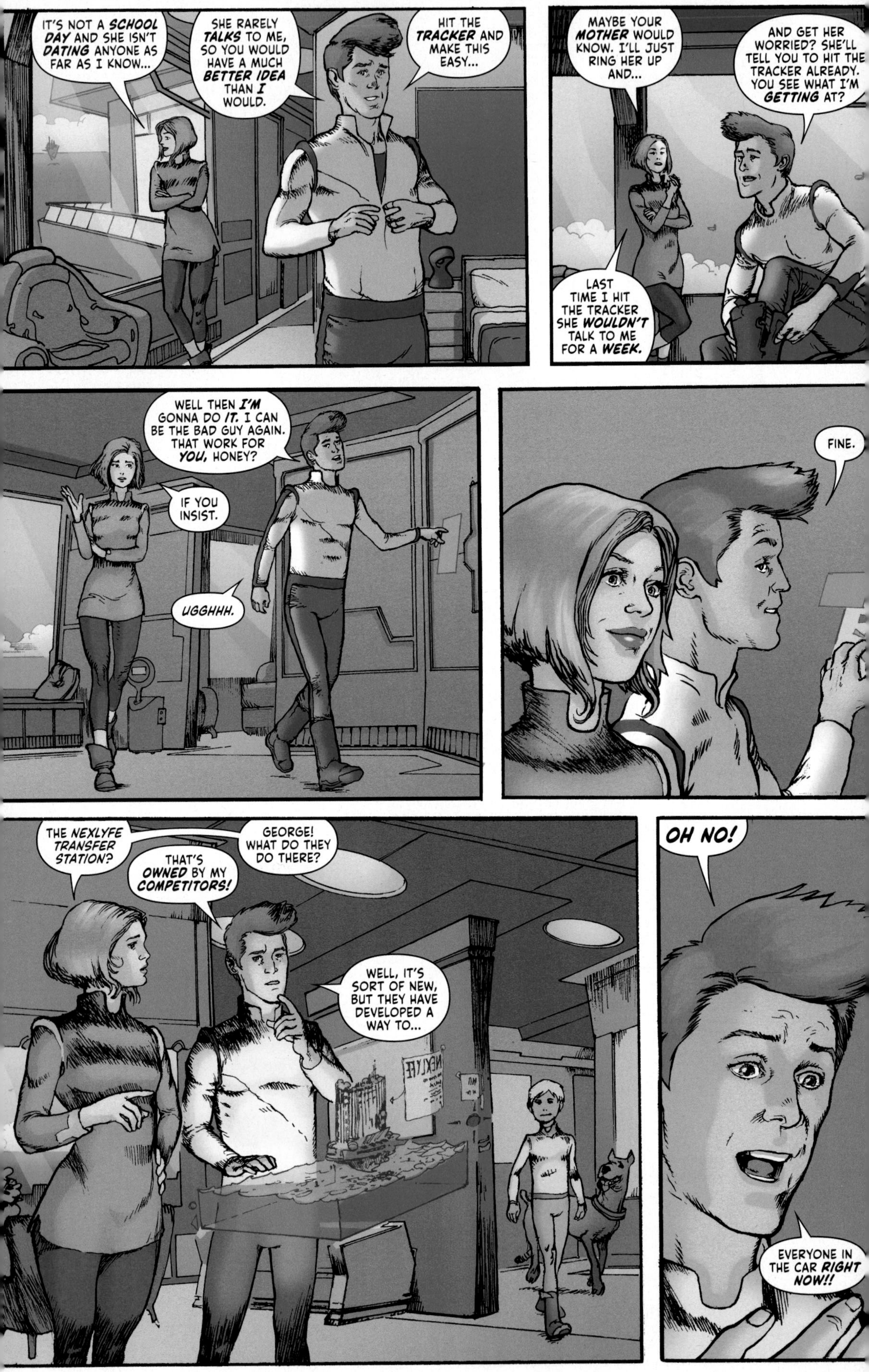
IT'S NOT A SCHOOL DAY AND SHE ISN'T DATING ANYONE AS FAR AS I KNOW...
SHE RARELY TALKS TO ME, SO YOU WOULD HAVE A MUCH BETTER IDEA THAN I WOULD.
HIT THE TRACKER AND MAKE THIS EASY...
MAYBE YOUR MOTHER WOULD KNOW. I'LL JUST RING HER UP AND...
AND GET HER WORRIED? SHE'LL TELL YOU TO HIT THE TRACKER ALREADY. YOU SEE WHAT I'M GETTING AT?
LAST TIME I HIT THE TRACKER SHE WOULDN'T TALK TO ME FOR A WEEK.
WELL THEN I'M GONNA DO IT. I CAN BE THE BAD GUY AGAIN. THAT WORK FOR YOU, HONEY?
IF YOU INSIST.
UGGHHH.
FINE.
THE NEXLYFE TRANSFER STATION?
THAT'S OWNED BY MY COMPETITORS!
GEORGE! WHAT DO THEY DO THERE?
WELL, IT'S SORT OF NEW, BUT THEY HAVE DEVELOPED A WAY TO...
OH NO!
EVERYONE IN THE CAR RIGHT NOW!!

JUDY, ROSEMARY, IT IS TIME TO PART.

I LOVE YOU, GRANDMA.

I LOVE YOU, TOO, SWEETIE. SEE YOU IN A FEW.

ARE YOU GONNA TELL ME WHAT'S *HAPPENING?*

YES, JUST *GET IN*, WE'RE RUNNING OUT OF *TIME.*

THIS IS THE *REFLECTION ROOM.* ONCE IT IS DONE, JENNIFER WILL TAKE YOU TO THE *GENESYS HALL.*

HOW *LONG* IS THIS GOING TO *TAKE?*

EVERYONE IS DIFFERENT BASED ON THEIR AGE, BUT THE AVERAGE IS ABOUT SIX MINUTES.

RELAX, ALL WILL BE *FINE.*

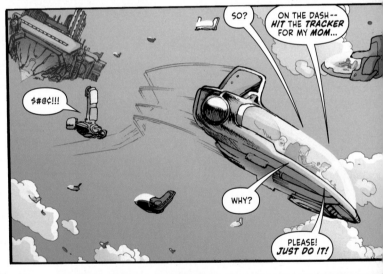

SO?

ON THE DASH-- *HIT* THE *TRACKER* FOR MY *MOM...*

$#@¢!!!

WHY?

PLEASE! *JUST DO IT!*

SHE'S AT THE [SA]ME BUILDING [A]S *JANE.* WHAT A *RELIEF!* SO, [W]HAT DO THEY DO THERE AGAIN?

IT'S A PLACE WHERE YOU...*HOW* DO I EXPLAIN THIS...

NEXLYFE IS AN *END-OF-LIFE OPTION CENTER!*

OH MY!

COOL!

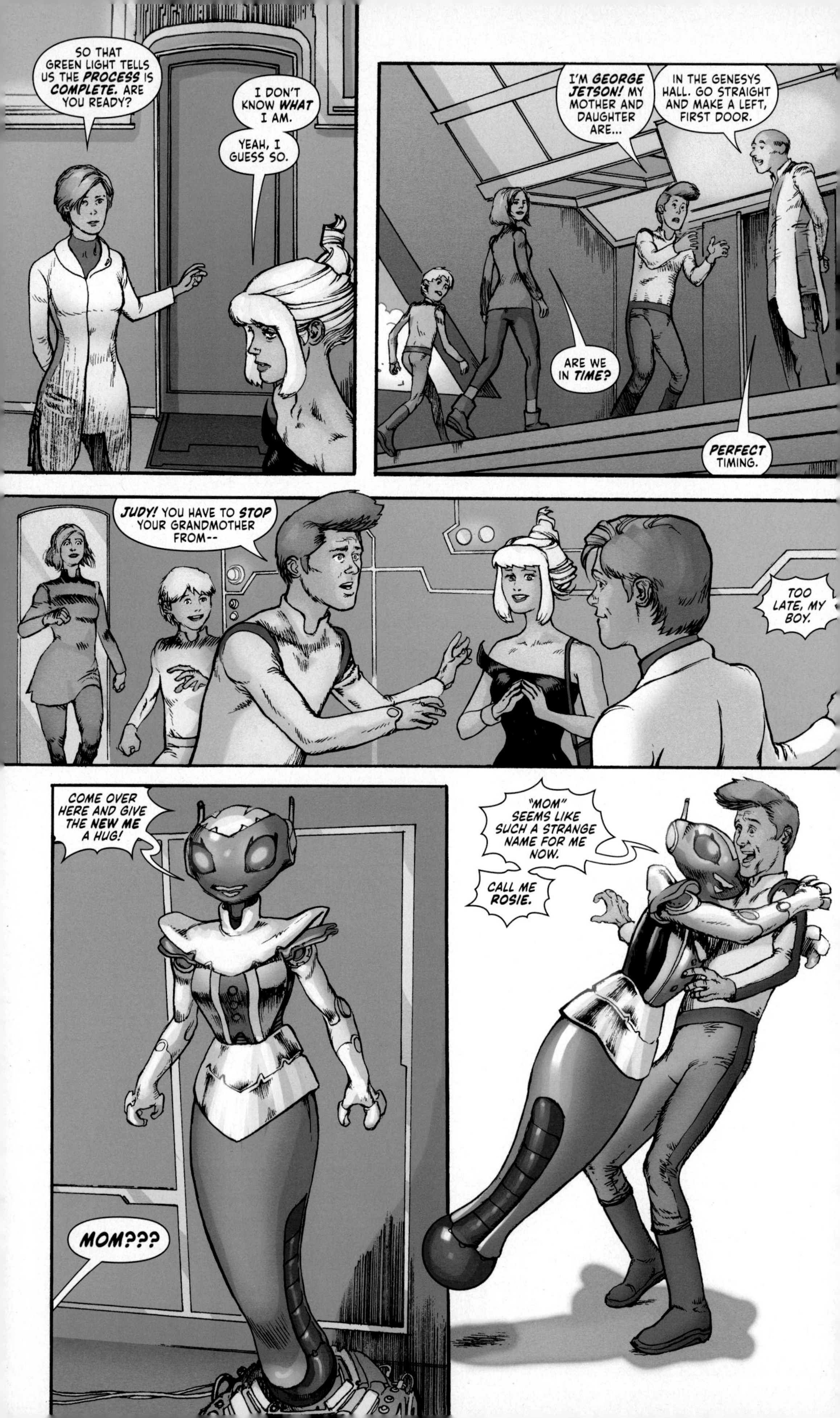
SO THAT GREEN LIGHT TELLS US THE PROCESS IS COMPLETE. ARE YOU READY?
I DON'T KNOW WHAT I AM.
YEAH, I GUESS SO.
I'M GEORGE JETSON! MY MOTHER AND DAUGHTER ARE...
IN THE GENESYS HALL. GO STRAIGHT AND MAKE A LEFT, FIRST DOOR.
ARE WE IN TIME?
PERFECT TIMING.
JUDY! YOU HAVE TO STOP YOUR GRANDMOTHER FROM--
TOO LATE, MY BOY.
COME OVER HERE AND GIVE THE NEW ME A HUG!
MOM???
"MOM" SEEMS LIKE SUCH A STRANGE NAME FOR ME NOW.
CALL ME ROSIE.

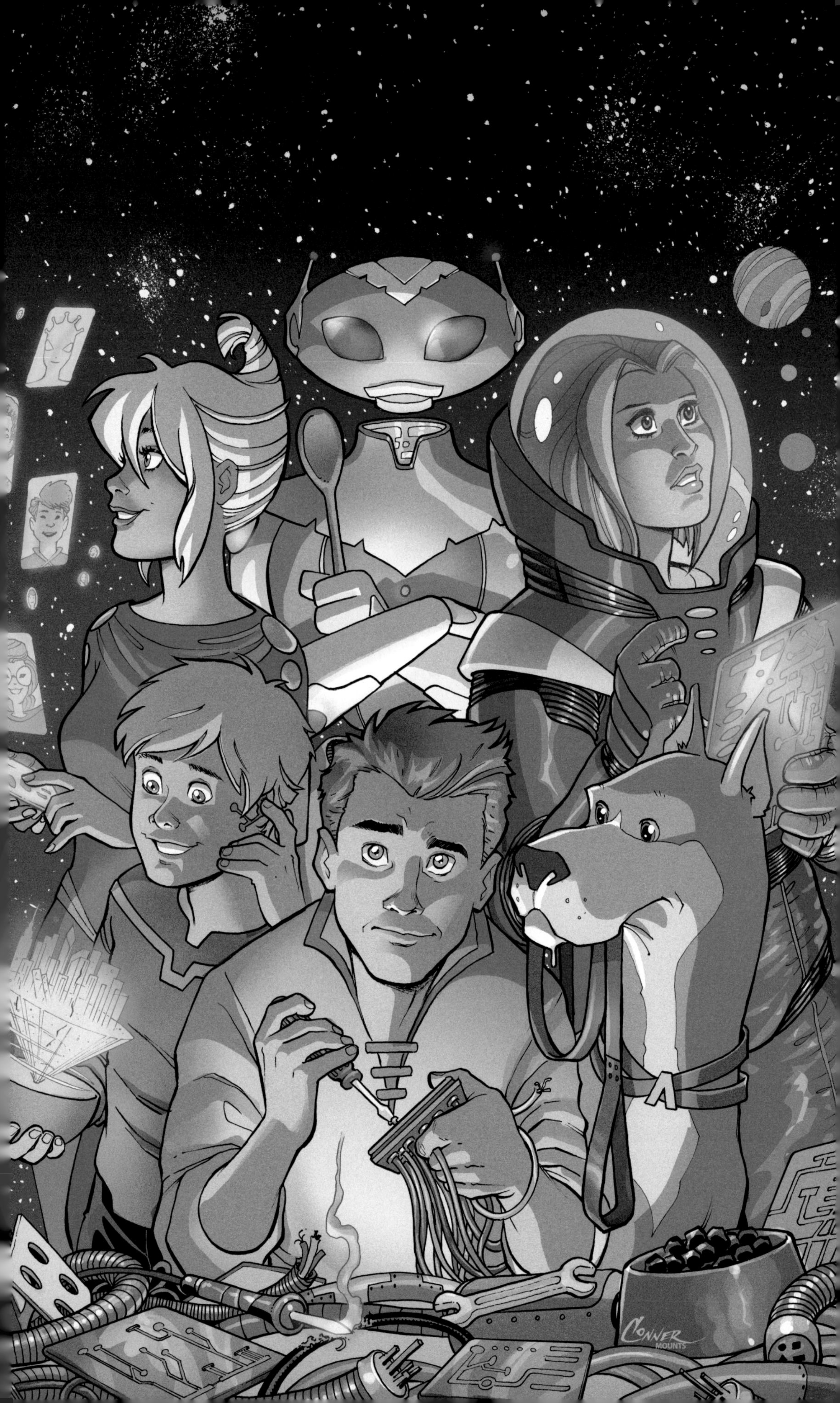
CONNER
MOUNTS

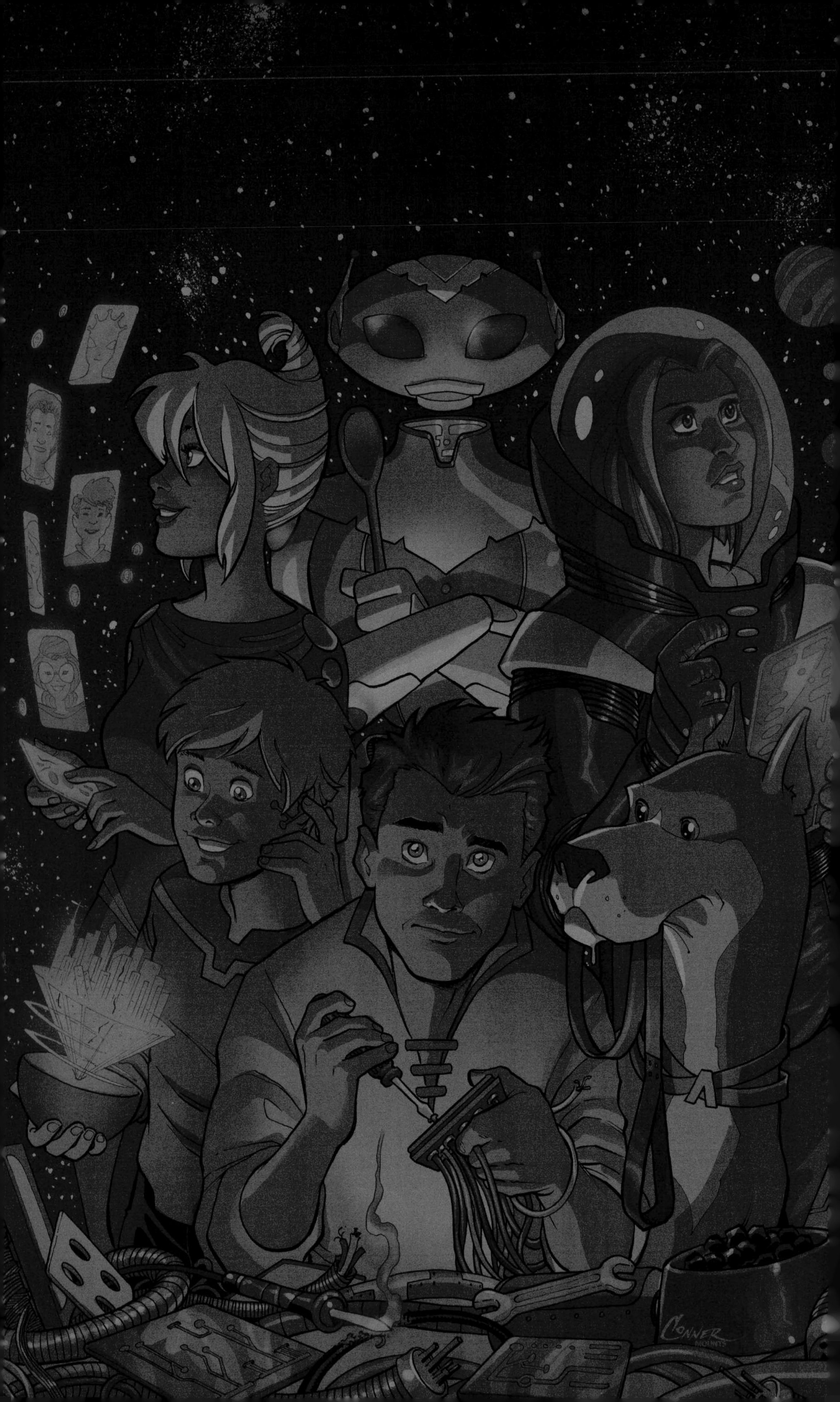

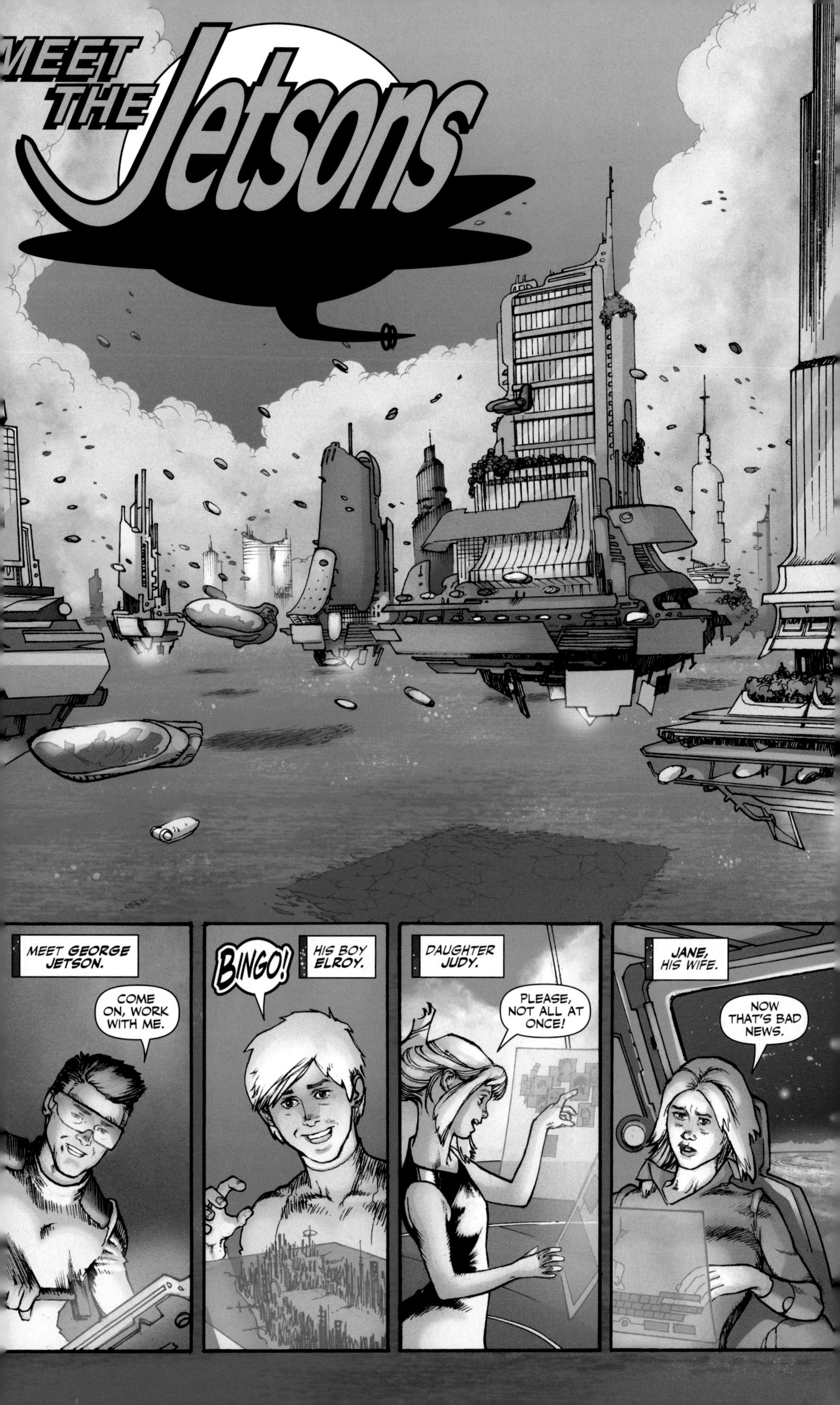
MEET THE Jetsons
MEET GEORGE JETSON.
COME ON, WORK WITH ME.
BINGO!
HIS BOY ELROY.
DAUGHTER JUDY.
PLEASE, NOT ALL AT ONCE!
JANE, HIS WIFE.
NOW THAT'S BAD NEWS.

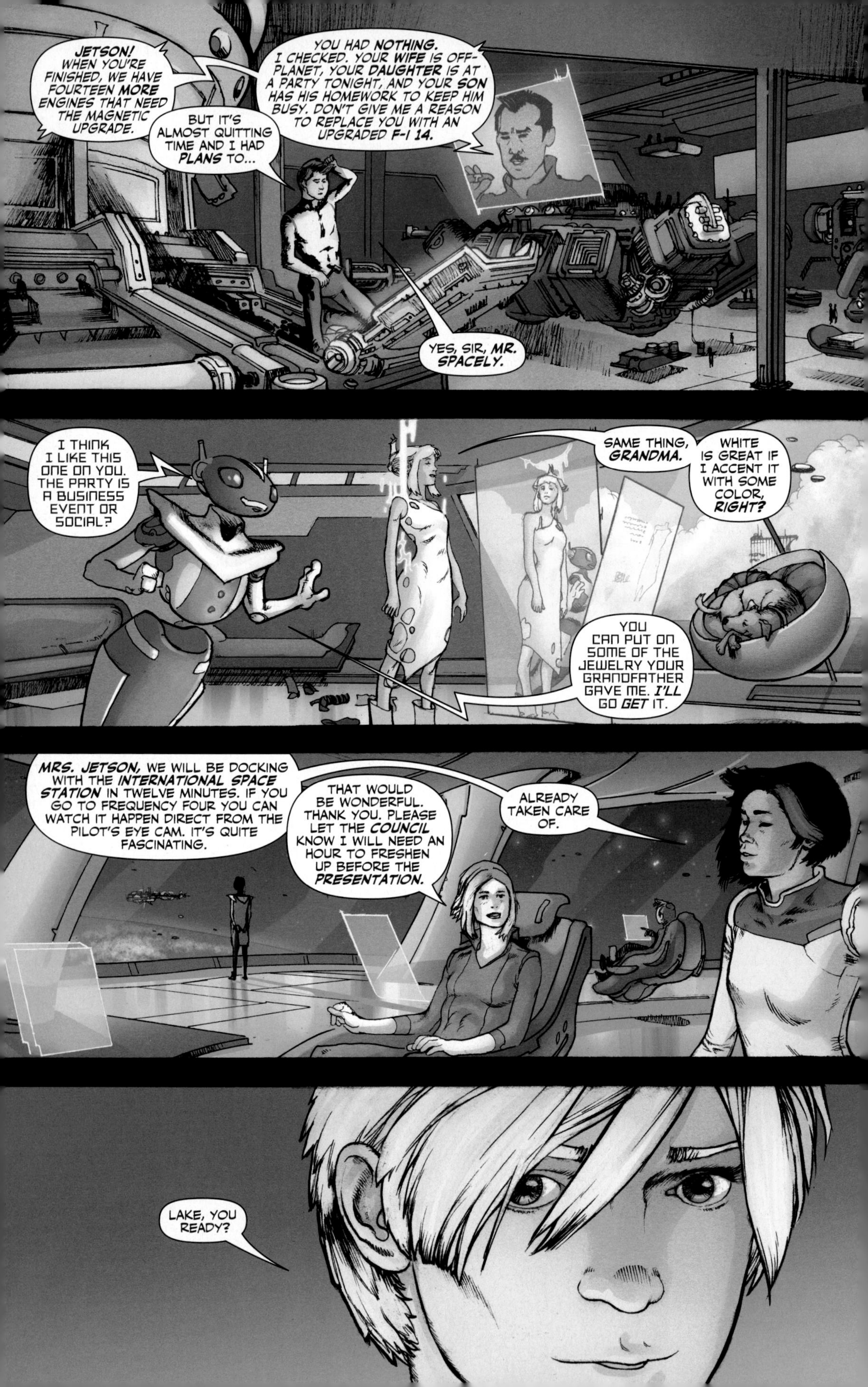
JETSON! WHEN YOU'RE FINISHED, WE HAVE FOURTEEN MORE ENGINES THAT NEED THE MAGNETIC UPGRADE.
BUT IT'S ALMOST QUITTING TIME AND I HAD PLANS TO...
YOU HAD NOTHING. I CHECKED. YOUR WIFE IS OFF-PLANET, YOUR DAUGHTER IS AT A PARTY TONIGHT, AND YOUR SON HAS HIS HOMEWORK TO KEEP HIM BUSY. DON'T GIVE ME A REASON TO REPLACE YOU WITH AN UPGRADED F-I 14.
YES, SIR, MR. SPACELY.
I THINK I LIKE THIS ONE ON YOU. THE PARTY IS A BUSINESS EVENT OR SOCIAL?
SAME THING, GRANDMA.
WHITE IS GREAT IF I ACCENT IT WITH SOME COLOR, RIGHT?
YOU CAN PUT ON SOME OF THE JEWELRY YOUR GRANDFATHER GAVE ME. I'LL GO GET IT.
MRS. JETSON, WE WILL BE DOCKING WITH THE INTERNATIONAL SPACE STATION IN TWELVE MINUTES. IF YOU GO TO FREQUENCY FOUR YOU CAN WATCH IT HAPPEN DIRECT FROM THE PILOT'S EYE CAM. IT'S QUITE FASCINATING.
THAT WOULD BE WONDERFUL. THANK YOU. PLEASE LET THE COUNCIL KNOW I WILL NEED AN HOUR TO FRESHEN UP BEFORE THE PRESENTATION.
ALREADY TAKEN CARE OF.
LAKE, YOU READY?

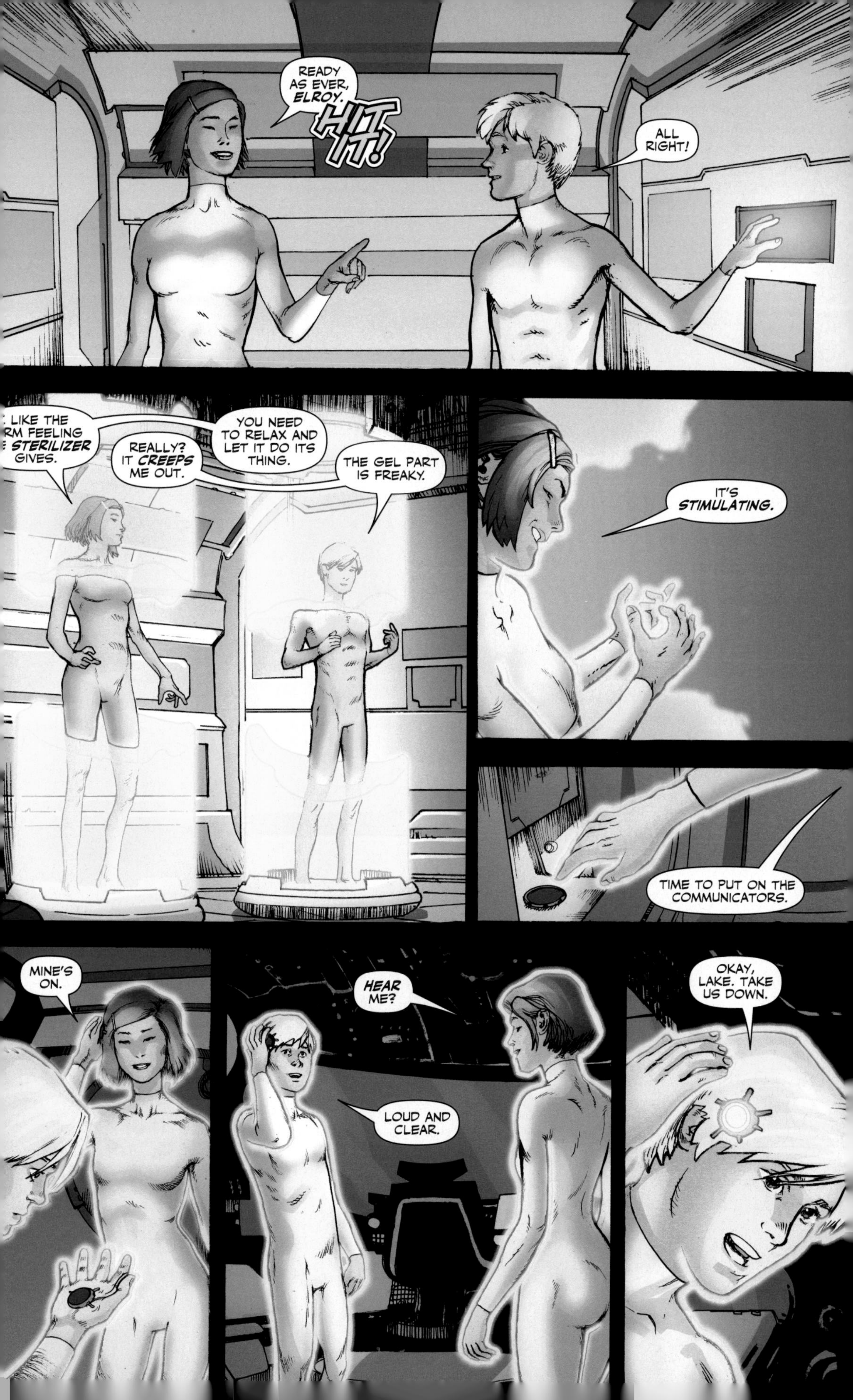

READY AS EVER, ELROY.
HIT IT!
ALL RIGHT!
LIKE THE RM FEELING E STERILIZER GIVES.
REALLY? IT CREEPS ME OUT.
YOU NEED TO RELAX AND LET IT DO ITS THING.
THE GEL PART IS FREAKY.
IT'S STIMULATING.
TIME TO PUT ON THE COMMUNICATORS.
MINE'S ON.
HEAR ME?
LOUD AND CLEAR.
OKAY, LAKE. TAKE US DOWN.

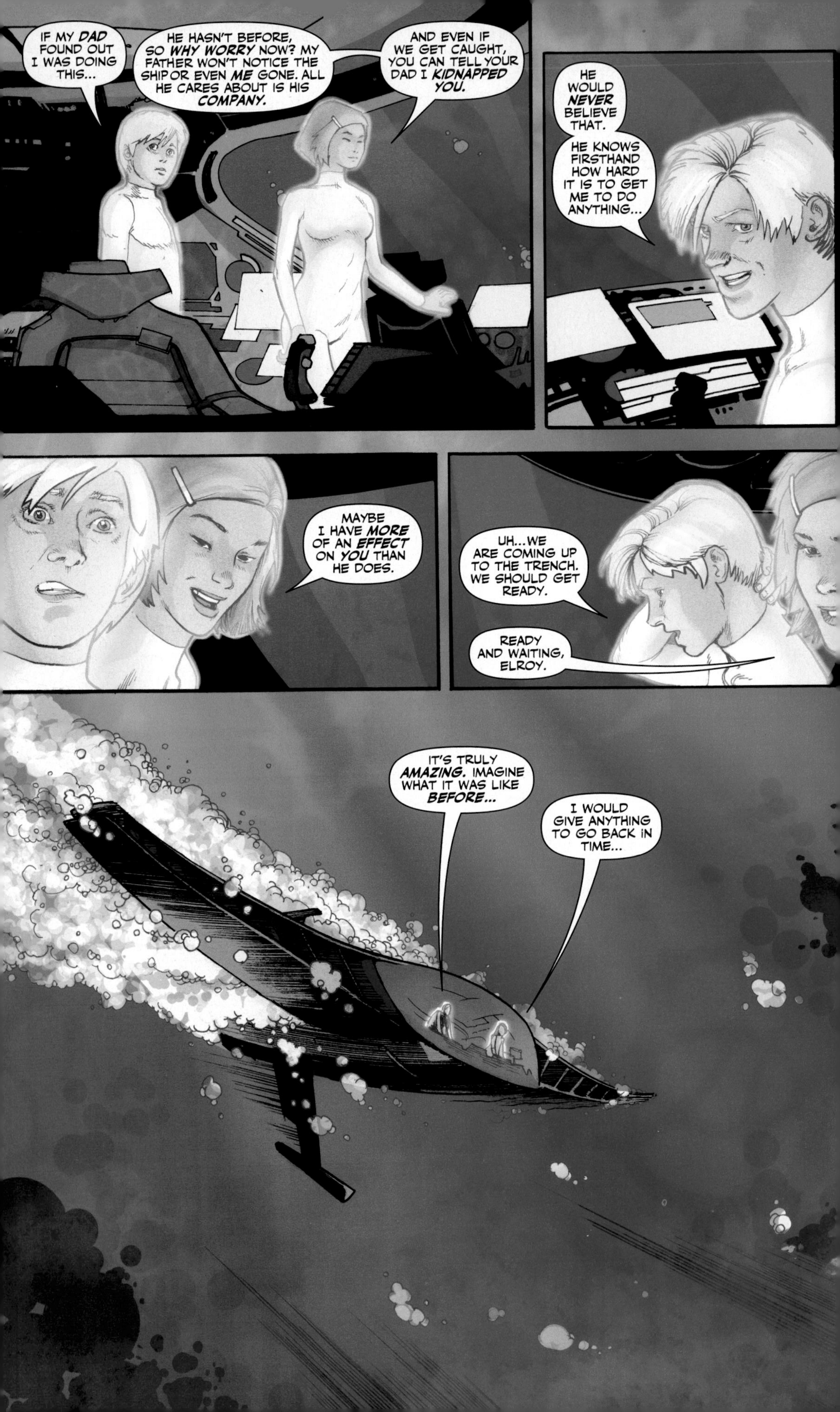
IF MY DAD FOUND OUT I WAS DOING THIS...
HE HASN'T BEFORE, SO WHY WORRY NOW? MY FATHER WON'T NOTICE THE SHIP OR EVEN ME GONE. ALL HE CARES ABOUT IS HIS COMPANY.
AND EVEN IF WE GET CAUGHT, YOU CAN TELL YOUR DAD I KIDNAPPED YOU.
HE WOULD NEVER BELIEVE THAT.
HE KNOWS FIRSTHAND HOW HARD IT IS TO GET ME TO DO ANYTHING...
MAYBE I HAVE MORE OF AN EFFECT ON YOU THAN HE DOES.
UH...WE ARE COMING UP TO THE TRENCH. WE SHOULD GET READY.
READY AND WAITING, ELROY.
IT'S TRULY AMAZING. IMAGINE WHAT IT WAS LIKE BEFORE...
I WOULD GIVE ANYTHING TO GO BACK IN TIME...

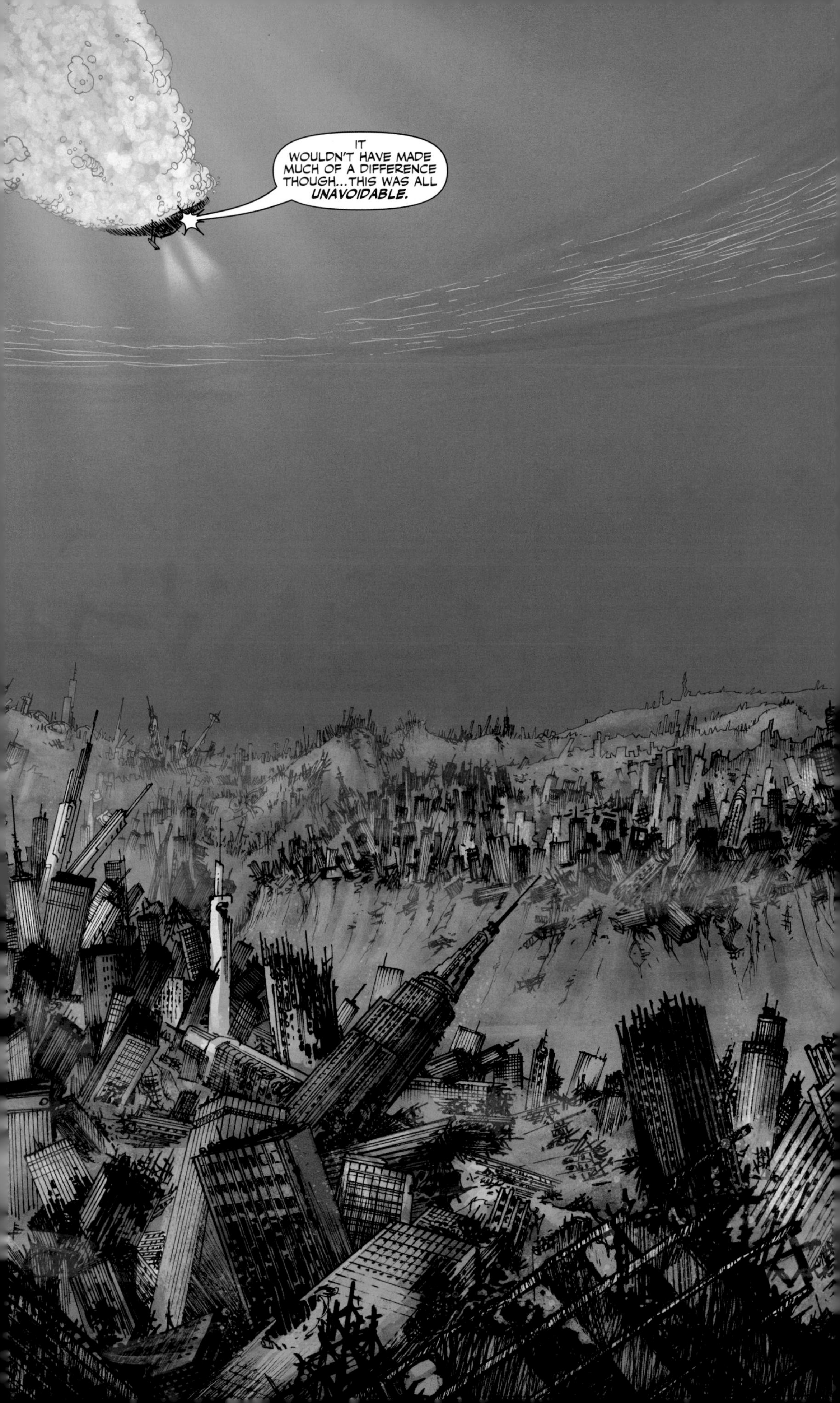
IT WOULDN'T HAVE MADE MUCH OF A DIFFERENCE THOUGH...THIS WAS ALL *UNAVOIDABLE.*

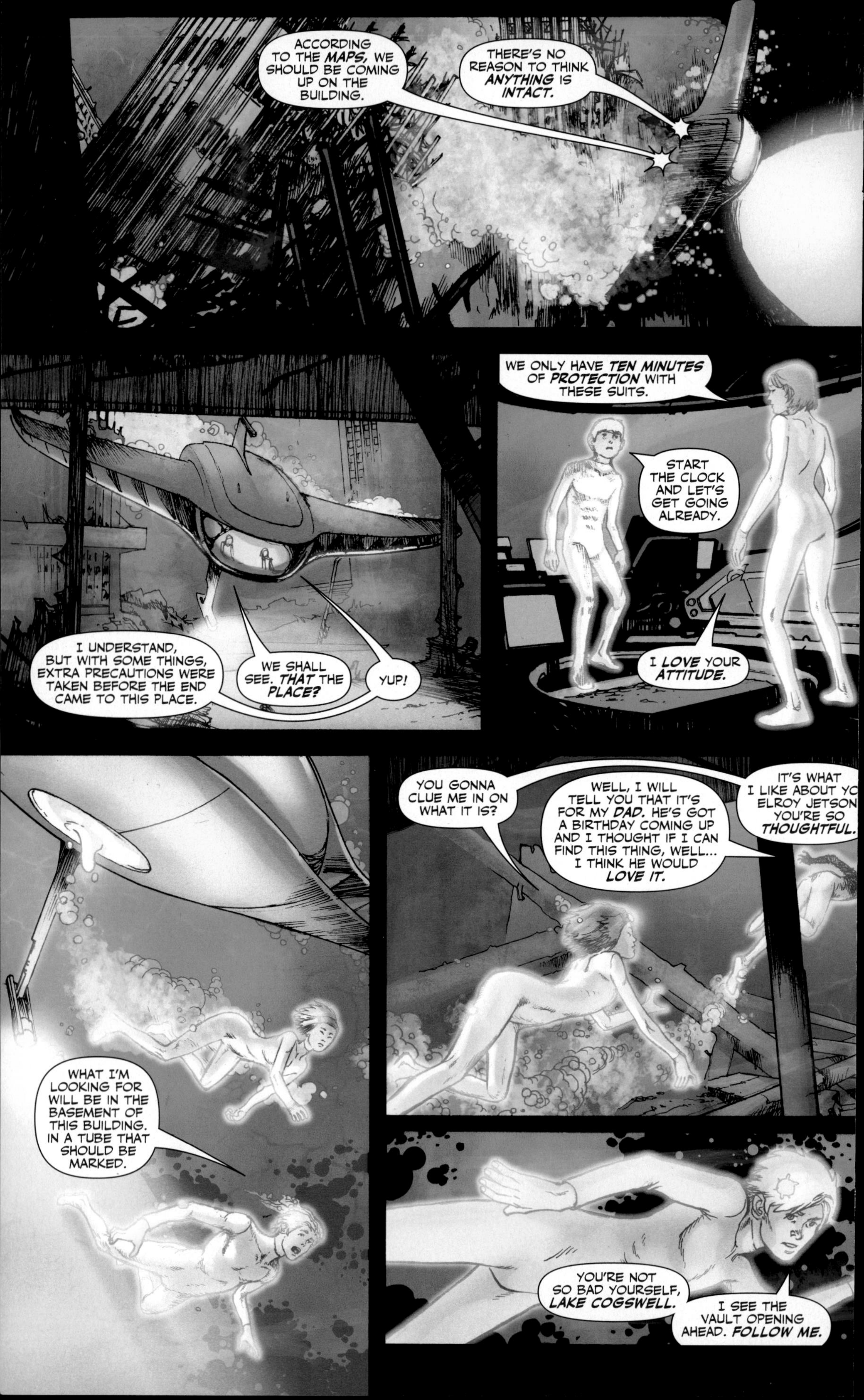

ACCORDING TO THE MAPS, WE SHOULD BE COMING UP ON THE BUILDING.
THERE'S NO REASON TO THINK ANYTHING IS INTACT.
I UNDERSTAND, BUT WITH SOME THINGS, EXTRA PRECAUTIONS WERE TAKEN BEFORE THE END CAME TO THIS PLACE.
WE SHALL SEE. THAT THE PLACE?
YUP!
WE ONLY HAVE TEN MINUTES OF PROTECTION WITH THESE SUITS.
START THE CLOCK AND LET'S GET GOING ALREADY.
I LOVE YOUR ATTITUDE.
WHAT I'M LOOKING FOR WILL BE IN THE BASEMENT OF THIS BUILDING. IN A TUBE THAT SHOULD BE MARKED.
YOU GONNA CLUE ME IN ON WHAT IT IS?
WELL, I WILL TELL YOU THAT IT'S FOR MY DAD. HE'S GOT A BIRTHDAY COMING UP AND I THOUGHT IF I CAN FIND THIS THING, WELL... I THINK HE WOULD LOVE IT.
IT'S WHAT I LIKE ABOUT YO ELROY JETSON YOU'RE SO THOUGHTFUL.
YOU'RE NOT SO BAD YOURSELF, LAKE COGSWELL.
I SEE THE VAULT OPENING AHEAD. FOLLOW ME.

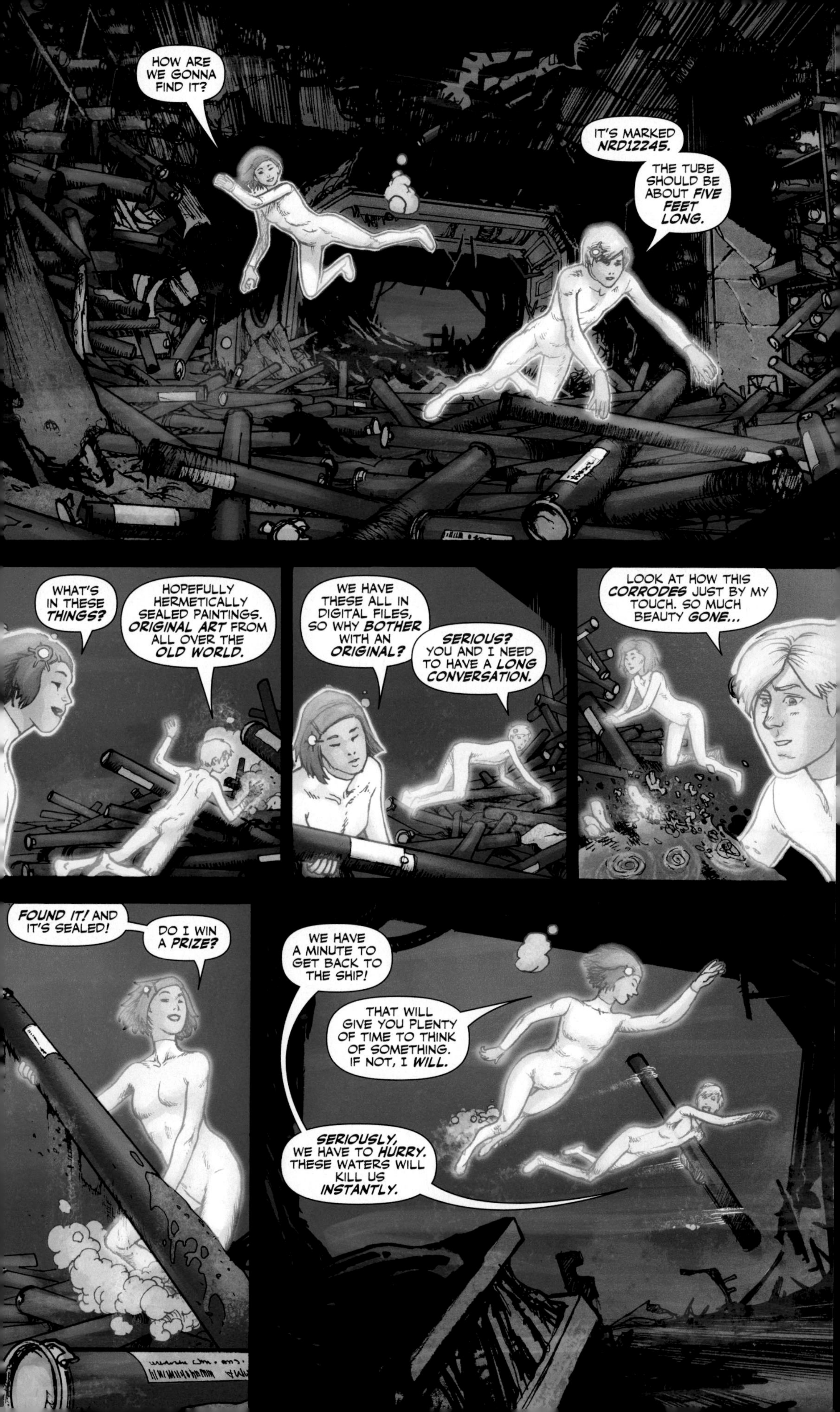
HOW ARE WE GONNA FIND IT?
IT'S MARKED NRD12245.
THE TUBE SHOULD BE ABOUT FIVE FEET LONG.
WHAT'S IN THESE THINGS?
HOPEFULLY HERMETICALLY SEALED PAINTINGS. ORIGINAL ART FROM ALL OVER THE OLD WORLD.
WE HAVE THESE ALL IN DIGITAL FILES, SO WHY BOTHER WITH AN ORIGINAL?
SERIOUS? YOU AND I NEED TO HAVE A LONG CONVERSATION.
LOOK AT HOW THIS CORRODES JUST BY MY TOUCH. SO MUCH BEAUTY GONE...
FOUND IT! AND IT'S SEALED!
DO I WIN A PRIZE?
WE HAVE A MINUTE TO GET BACK TO THE SHIP!
THAT WILL GIVE YOU PLENTY OF TIME TO THINK OF SOMETHING. IF NOT, I WILL.
SERIOUSLY, WE HAVE TO HURRY. THESE WATERS WILL KILL US INSTANTLY.

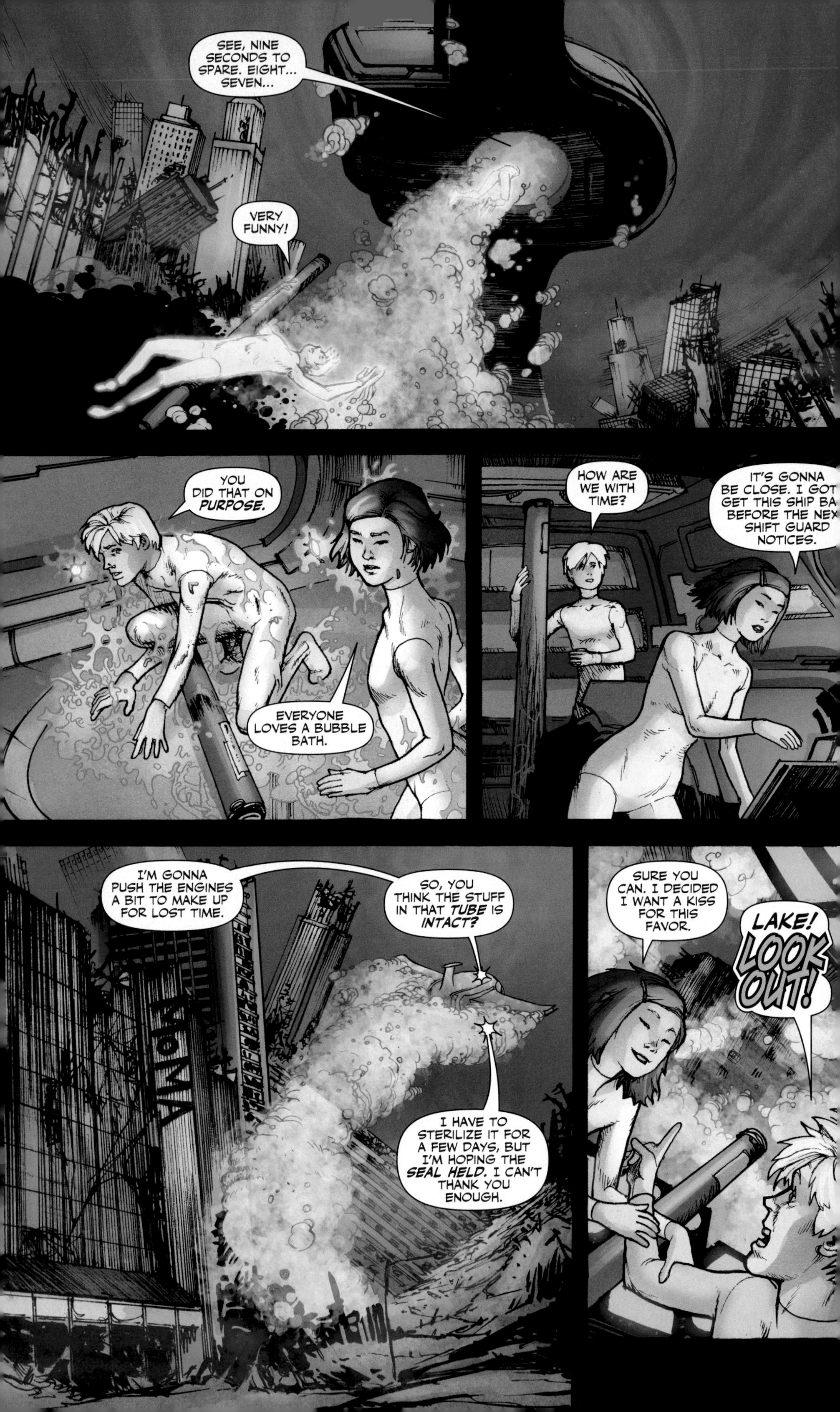
SEE, NINE SECONDS TO SPARE. EIGHT... SEVEN...
VERY FUNNY!
YOU DID THAT ON PURPOSE.
EVERYONE LOVES A BUBBLE BATH.
HOW ARE WE WITH TIME?
IT'S GONNA BE CLOSE. I GOT GET THIS SHIP BA BEFORE THE NEX SHIFT GUARD NOTICES.
I'M GONNA PUSH THE ENGINES A BIT TO MAKE UP FOR LOST TIME.
SO, YOU THINK THE STUFF IN THAT TUBE IS INTACT?
I HAVE TO STERILIZE IT FOR A FEW DAYS, BUT I'M HOPING THE SEAL HELD. I CAN'T THANK YOU ENOUGH.
MoMA
SURE YOU CAN. I DECIDED I WANT A KISS FOR THIS FAVOR.
LAKE! LOOK OUT!

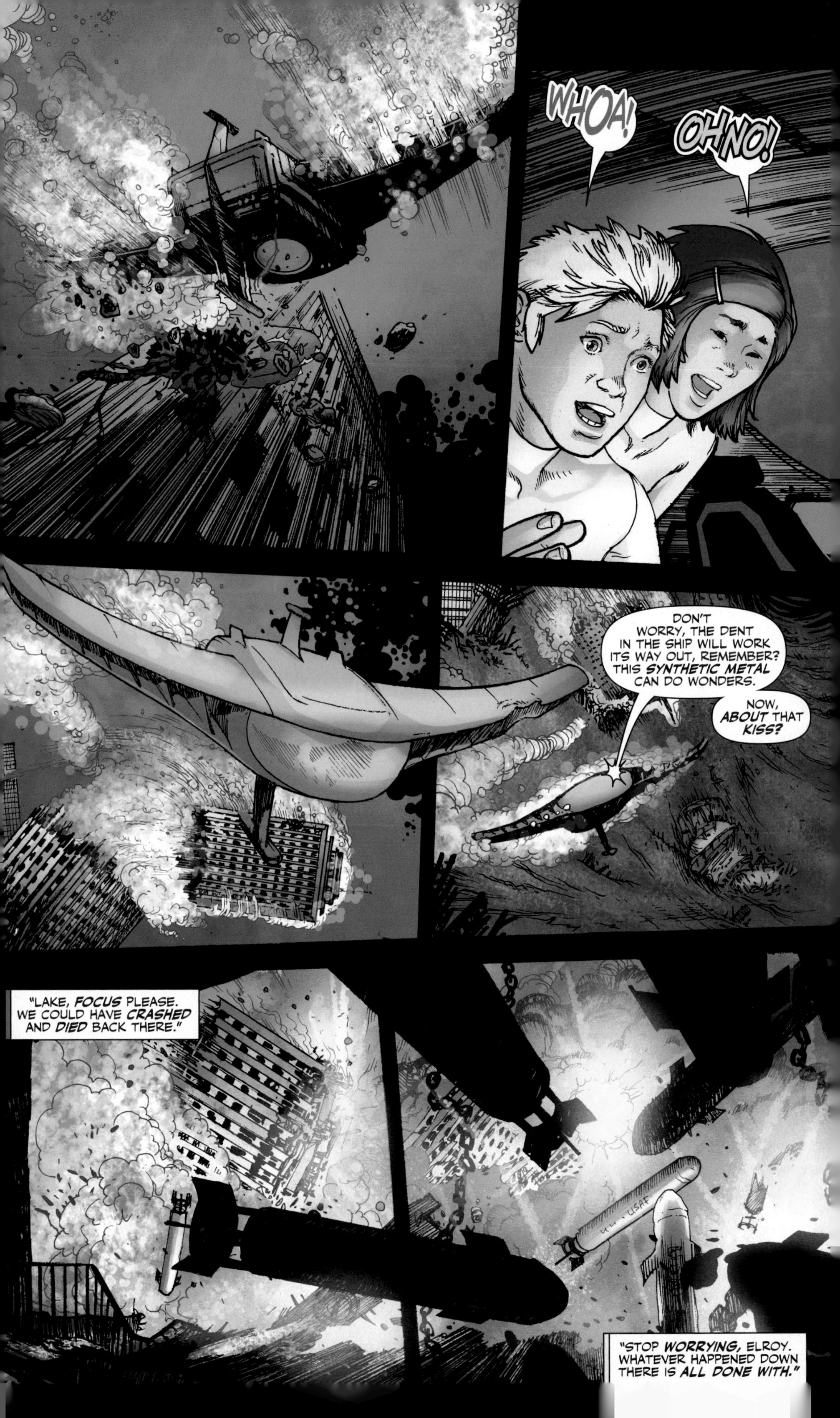
WHOA!
OH NO!
DON'T WORRY, THE DENT IN THE SHIP WILL WORK ITS WAY OUT, REMEMBER? THIS SYNTHETIC METAL CAN DO WONDERS.
NOW, ABOUT THAT KISS?
"LAKE, FOCUS PLEASE. WE COULD HAVE CRASHED AND DIED BACK THERE."
"STOP WORRYING, ELROY. WHATEVER HAPPENED DOWN THERE IS ALL DONE WITH."

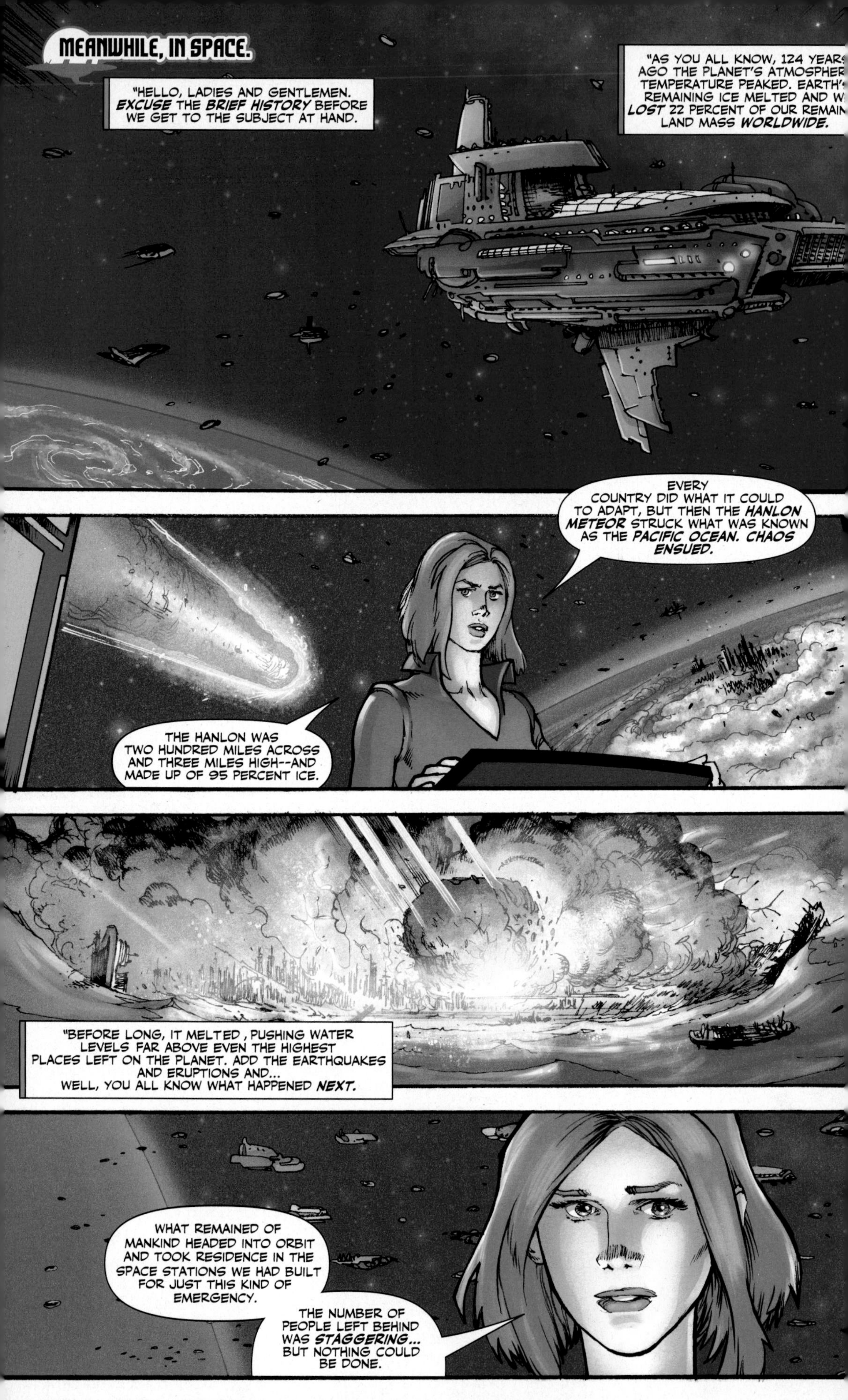
MEANWHILE, IN SPACE.
"HELLO, LADIES AND GENTLEMEN. *EXCUSE* THE *BRIEF HISTORY* BEFORE WE GET TO THE SUBJECT AT HAND.
"AS YOU ALL KNOW, 124 YEAR AGO THE PLANET'S ATMOSPHER TEMPERATURE PEAKED. EARTH' REMAINING ICE MELTED AND W *LOST* 22 PERCENT OF OUR REMAIN LAND MASS *WORLDWIDE.*
EVERY COUNTRY DID WHAT IT COULD TO ADAPT, BUT THEN THE *HANLON METEOR* STRUCK WHAT WAS KNOWN AS THE *PACIFIC OCEAN. CHAOS ENSUED.*
THE HANLON WAS TWO HUNDRED MILES ACROSS AND THREE MILES HIGH--AND MADE UP OF 95 PERCENT ICE.
"BEFORE LONG, IT MELTED, PUSHING WATER LEVELS FAR ABOVE EVEN THE HIGHEST PLACES LEFT ON THE PLANET. ADD THE EARTHQUAKES AND ERUPTIONS AND... WELL, YOU ALL KNOW WHAT HAPPENED *NEXT.*
WHAT REMAINED OF MANKIND HEADED INTO ORBIT AND TOOK RESIDENCE IN THE SPACE STATIONS WE HAD BUILT FOR JUST THIS KIND OF EMERGENCY.
THE NUMBER OF PEOPLE LEFT BEHIND WAS *STAGGERING...* BUT NOTHING COULD BE DONE.

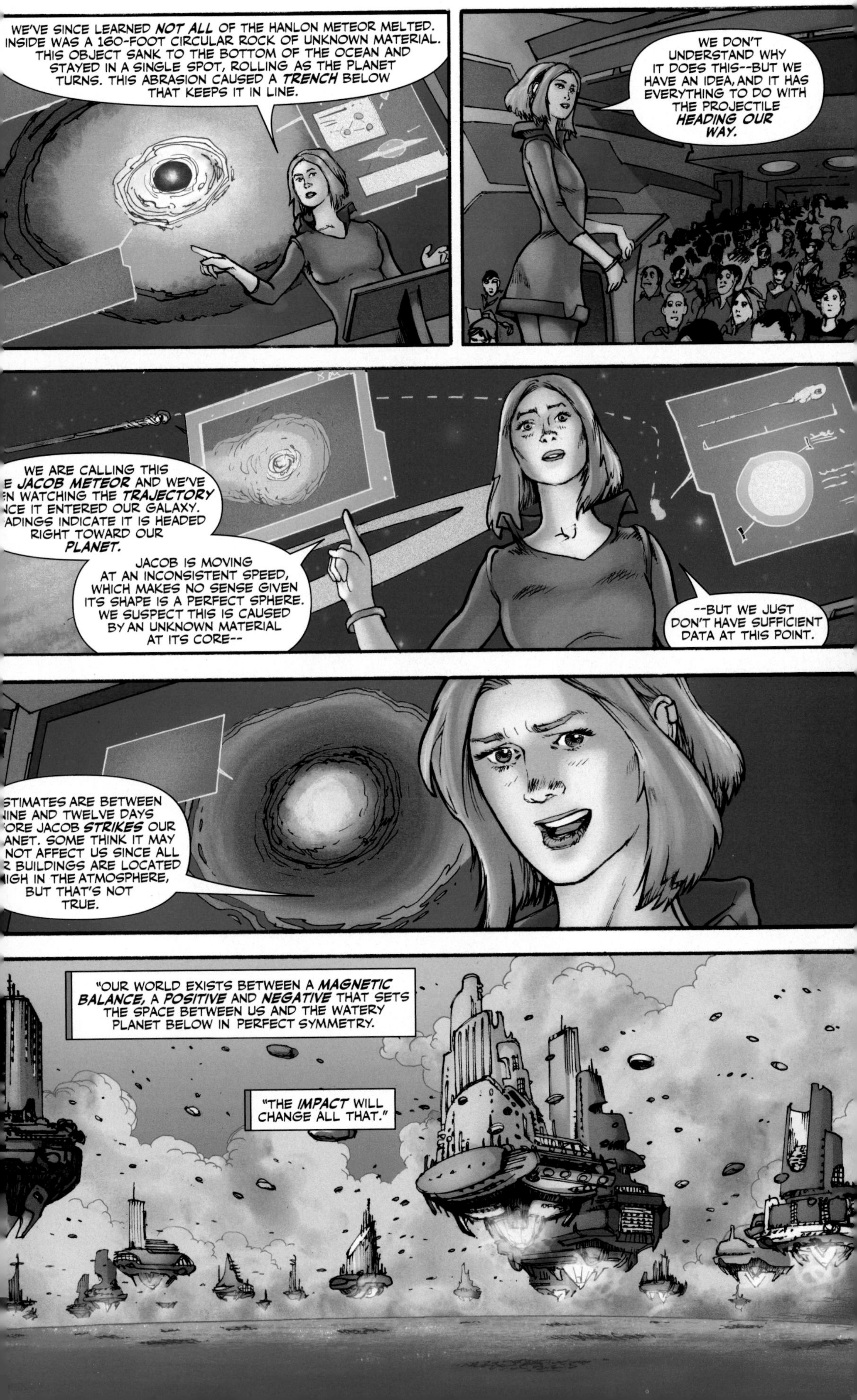
WE'VE SINCE LEARNED NOT ALL OF THE HANLON METEOR MELTED. INSIDE WAS A 160-FOOT CIRCULAR ROCK OF UNKNOWN MATERIAL. THIS OBJECT SANK TO THE BOTTOM OF THE OCEAN AND STAYED IN A SINGLE SPOT, ROLLING AS THE PLANET TURNS. THIS ABRASION CAUSED A TRENCH BELOW THAT KEEPS IT IN LINE.
WE DON'T UNDERSTAND WHY IT DOES THIS--BUT WE HAVE AN IDEA, AND IT HAS EVERYTHING TO DO WITH THE PROJECTILE HEADING OUR WAY.
WE ARE CALLING THIS E JACOB METEOR AND WE'VE EN WATCHING THE TRAJECTORY NCE IT ENTERED OUR GALAXY. ADINGS INDICATE IT IS HEADED RIGHT TOWARD OUR PLANET.
JACOB IS MOVING AT AN INCONSISTENT SPEED, WHICH MAKES NO SENSE GIVEN ITS SHAPE IS A PERFECT SPHERE. WE SUSPECT THIS IS CAUSED BY AN UNKNOWN MATERIAL AT ITS CORE--
--BUT WE JUST DON'T HAVE SUFFICIENT DATA AT THIS POINT.
STIMATES ARE BETWEEN NINE AND TWELVE DAYS ORE JACOB STRIKES OUR ANET. SOME THINK IT MAY NOT AFFECT US SINCE ALL R BUILDINGS ARE LOCATED IGH IN THE ATMOSPHERE, BUT THAT'S NOT TRUE.
"OUR WORLD EXISTS BETWEEN A MAGNETIC BALANCE, A POSITIVE AND NEGATIVE THAT SETS THE SPACE BETWEEN US AND THE WATERY PLANET BELOW IN PERFECT SYMMETRY.
"THE IMPACT WILL CHANGE ALL THAT."

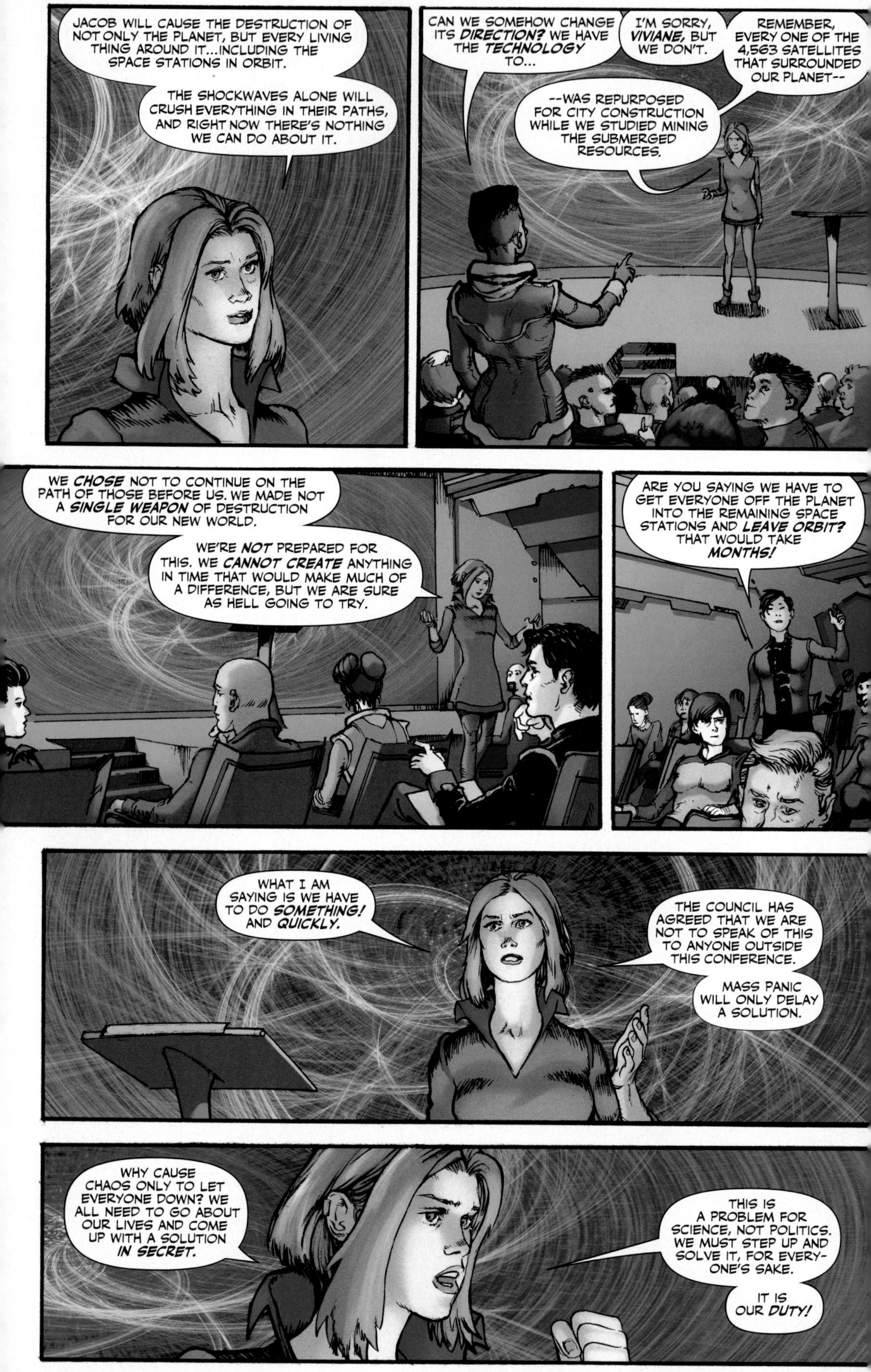
JACOB WILL CAUSE THE DESTRUCTION OF NOT ONLY THE PLANET, BUT EVERY LIVING THING AROUND IT...INCLUDING THE SPACE STATIONS IN ORBIT.
THE SHOCKWAVES ALONE WILL CRUSH EVERYTHING IN THEIR PATHS, AND RIGHT NOW THERE'S NOTHING WE CAN DO ABOUT IT.
CAN WE SOMEHOW CHANGE ITS *DIRECTION?* WE HAVE THE *TECHNOLOGY* TO...
I'M SORRY, *VIVIANE,* BUT WE DON'T.
REMEMBER, EVERY ONE OF THE 4,563 SATELLITES THAT SURROUNDED OUR PLANET--
--WAS REPURPOSED FOR CITY CONSTRUCTION WHILE WE STUDIED MINING THE SUBMERGED RESOURCES.
WE *CHOSE* NOT TO CONTINUE ON THE PATH OF THOSE BEFORE US. WE MADE NOT A *SINGLE WEAPON* OF DESTRUCTION FOR OUR NEW WORLD.
WE'RE *NOT* PREPARED FOR THIS. WE *CANNOT CREATE* ANYTHING IN TIME THAT WOULD MAKE MUCH OF A DIFFERENCE, BUT WE ARE SURE AS HELL GOING TO TRY.
ARE YOU SAYING WE HAVE TO GET EVERYONE OFF THE PLANET INTO THE REMAINING SPACE STATIONS AND *LEAVE ORBIT?* THAT WOULD TAKE *MONTHS!*
WHAT I AM SAYING IS WE HAVE TO DO *SOMETHING!* AND *QUICKLY.*
THE COUNCIL HAS AGREED THAT WE ARE NOT TO SPEAK OF THIS TO ANYONE OUTSIDE THIS CONFERENCE.
MASS PANIC WILL ONLY DELAY A SOLUTION.
WHY CAUSE CHAOS ONLY TO LET EVERYONE DOWN? WE ALL NEED TO GO ABOUT OUR LIVES AND COME UP WITH A SOLUTION *IN SECRET.*
THIS IS A PROBLEM FOR SCIENCE, NOT POLITICS. WE MUST STEP UP AND SOLVE IT, FOR EVERY-ONE'S SAKE.
IT IS OUR *DUTY!*

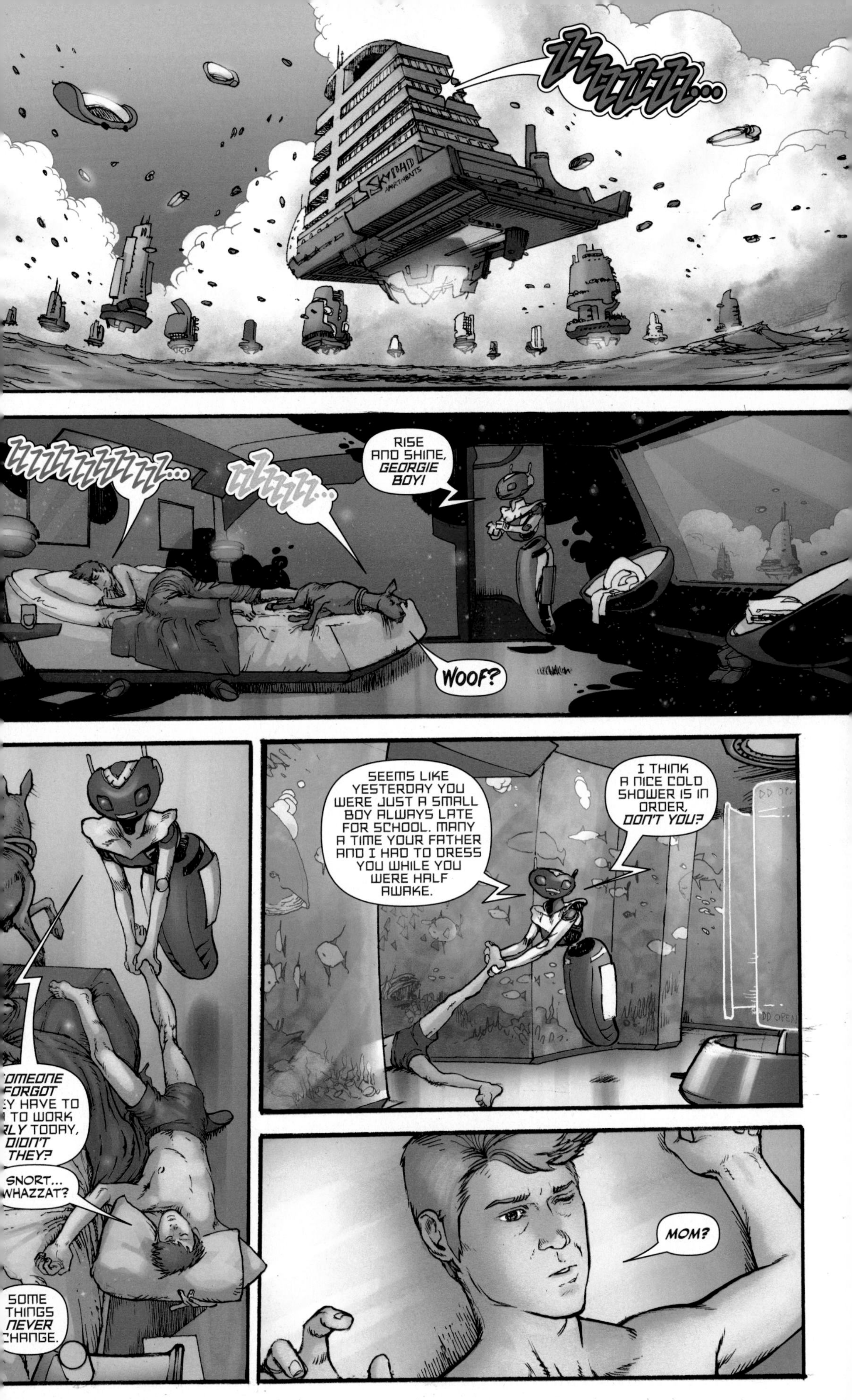
ZZZZZZZZ...
ZZZZZZZZZZZZZZZ...
ZZZZZZZZ...
RISE AND SHINE, GEORGIE BOY!
WOOF?
OMEONE FORGOT EY HAVE TO N TO WORK RLY TODAY, DIDN'T THEY?
SNORT... WHAZZAT?
SOME THINGS NEVER CHANGE.
SEEMS LIKE YESTERDAY YOU WERE JUST A SMALL BOY ALWAYS LATE FOR SCHOOL. MANY A TIME YOUR FATHER AND I HAD TO DRESS YOU WHILE YOU WERE HALF AWAKE.
I THINK A NICE COLD SHOWER IS IN ORDER, DON'T YOU?
MOM?

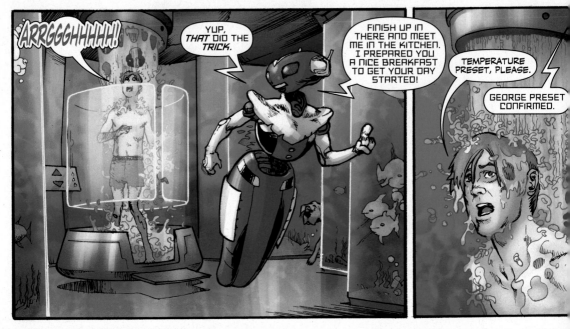

ARRGGGHHHHH!

YUP, *THAT* DID THE *TRICK*.

FINISH UP IN THERE AND MEET ME IN THE KITCHEN. I PREPARED YOU A NICE BREAKFAST TO GET YOUR DAY STARTED!

TEMPERATURE PRESET, PLEASE.

GEORGE PRESET CONFIRMED.

WHERE IS EVERYONE?

JANE IS STILL UP AT THE INTERNATIONAL SPACE STATION TILL TOMORROW EVENING. *ELROY AND JUDY* ARE STILL IN BED. THEY HAVE ANOTHER HOUR OF SLEEP AHEAD OF THEM, SO I DIDN'T WAKE THEM.

MOM, SINCE WE HAVE ALONE TIME TOGETHER, WHY DON'T YOU AND I HAVE A *TALK*...

WHAT'S THE SUBJECT?

YOU.

SINCE YOU MADE THE...TRANSFER... UH, SINCE YOU DECIDED TO END YOUR...WELL, GET A NEW...

SINCE I *WILLINGLY* ENDED MY LIFE IN MY OLD BODY AND NOW LIVE ON IN THIS *ROBOT FORM.* JUST SAY IT ALREADY.

YEAH, SINCE THAT HAPPENED... HOW ARE YOU... *FEELING?*

FEELING IS AN INTERESTING WORD NOW.
NO MORE ACHES AND PAINS, AND I DON'T FEEL LIKE I'M ABOUT TO SNAP IN HALF AT ANY MOMENT. IT'S FREEING TO NOT HAVE THE FEAR OF BEING FRAGILE.
THE METALS THEY USE ON ME SELF-REPAIR, SO EVEN IF I GET A DENT, THE SYNTHETIC CARBON REPRODUCES ITSELF TO THE ORIGINAL FRAME AND CONTOURS. PRETTY NIFTY.
I MEAN, ARE YOU ALL RIGHT? HOW ARE YOU DEALING WITH THE CHANGES?
YOU MEAN HOW AM I DEALING WITH THE POSSIBILITY OF BEING AROUND FOREVER?
NO... I MEAN YES, AND NO.
GEORGE, I HAVE TO BE HONEST. IT'S SURREAL.
THIS NEW BODY IS AMAZING, AND YET I MISS MANY THINGS. WATCHING THE WATER IN THE SHOWER A FEW MINUTES AGO, FOR INSTANCE. I HAVE SENSORS TELLING ME THAT THE OVERSPRAY OF WATER IS HITTING ME, BUT I CANNOT SENSE THE SENSATION OF IT, OR HOW IT FEELS TO BE CLEAN. OR THE SMELL OF THE WATER.
INTERNAL HARD DRIVE TELLS ME IT IS WATER, AT IT HAS A SCENT, BUT I CANNOT "SMELL" IT. MEMORY OF WHAT IT FEELS LIKE AND ITS SCENT GETS PROCESSED AND I ALMOST FEEL IT, BUT NOT QUITE.
LIKE THE BACON I'M EATING. WE BOTH KNOW IT'S NOT REAL BACON, BUT IT'S FORMED AND PROGRAMMED TO TASTE LIKE THE REAL THING...
YES, BUT UNLIKE YOU, I HAVE TASTED THE REAL THING, SO I CAN COMPARE AND MAKE A DISTINCTION. THAT BACON YOU EAT HAS ALWAYS BEEN PROCESSED AND NOT MADE FROM AN ANIMAL.
A PETAL OF A FLOWER, SKIN ON SKIN, GIVING AND RECEIVING A HUG OR KISS... SO MANY THINGS I'M MISSING AND YET MY SYSTEM TRIES TO WORK WITH MY BRAIN TO GIVE ME THE SENSATIONS ON SOME LEVEL, BUT IT'S NOT QUITE RIGHT.
IT DOESN'T LINE UP LIKE IT DID, BUT MY BRAIN IS QUICKLY TRYING TO FILL IN WHAT I CAN'T FEEL AND INTEGRATE WITH THE EXISTING PROCESSOR TO LEARN.
I SEE.

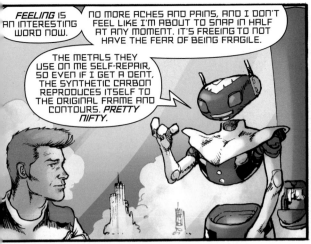

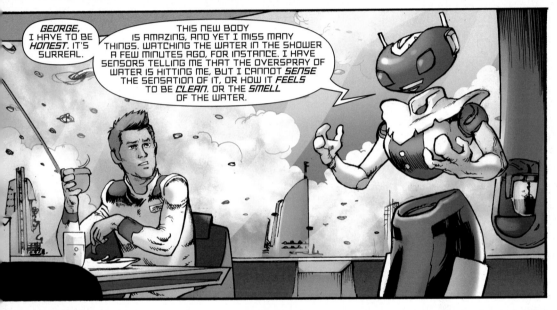

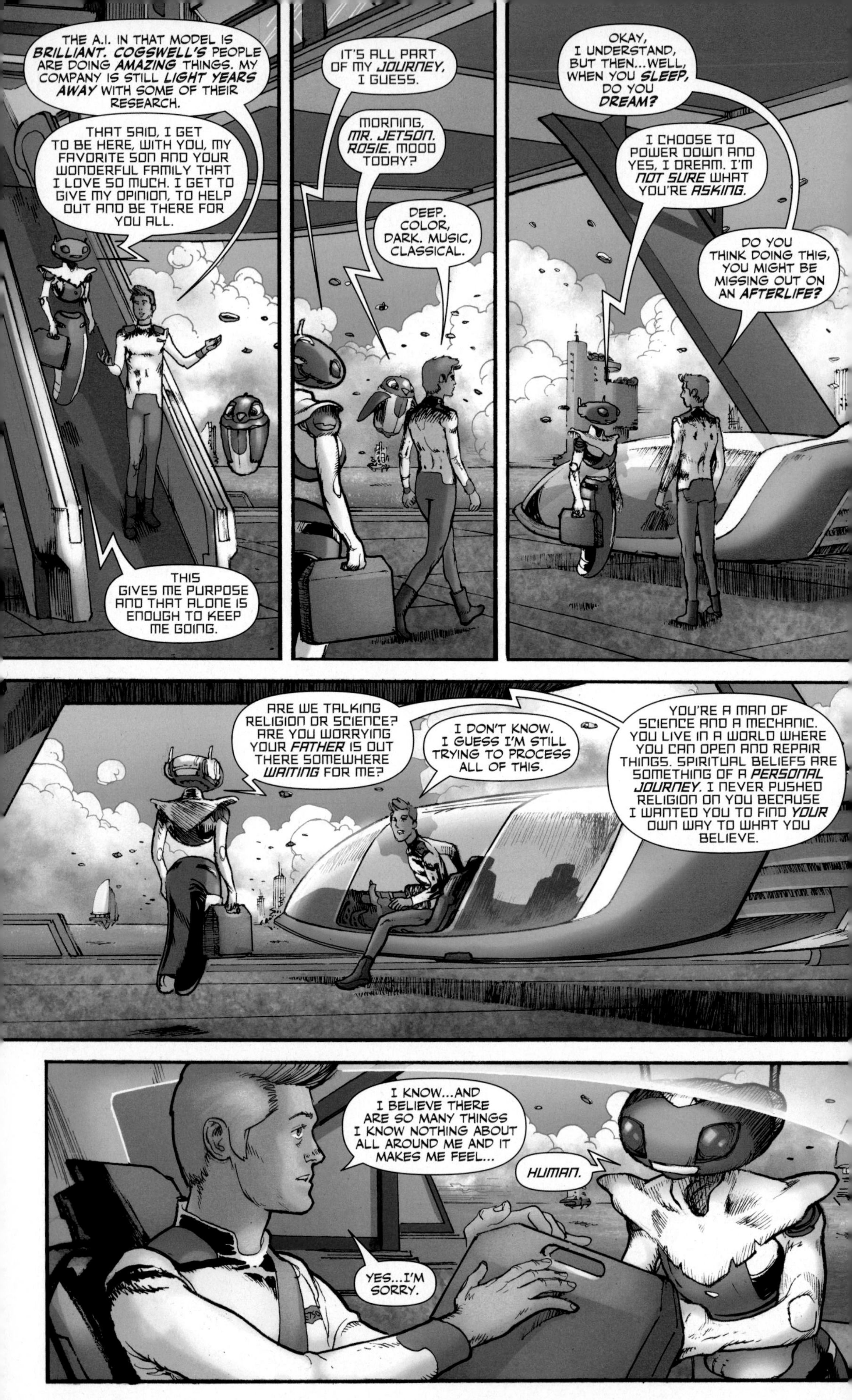
THE A.I. IN THAT MODEL IS BRILLIANT. COGSWELL'S PEOPLE ARE DOING AMAZING THINGS. MY COMPANY IS STILL LIGHT YEARS AWAY WITH SOME OF THEIR RESEARCH.
THAT SAID, I GET TO BE HERE, WITH YOU, MY FAVORITE SON AND YOUR WONDERFUL FAMILY THAT I LOVE SO MUCH. I GET TO GIVE MY OPINION, TO HELP OUT AND BE THERE FOR YOU ALL.
THIS GIVES ME PURPOSE AND THAT ALONE IS ENOUGH TO KEEP ME GOING.
IT'S ALL PART OF MY JOURNEY, I GUESS.
MORNING, MR. JETSON. ROSIE. MOOD TODAY?
DEEP. COLOR, DARK. MUSIC, CLASSICAL.
OKAY, I UNDERSTAND, BUT THEN...WELL, WHEN YOU SLEEP, DO YOU DREAM?
I CHOOSE TO POWER DOWN AND YES, I DREAM. I'M NOT SURE WHAT YOU'RE ASKING.
DO YOU THINK DOING THIS, YOU MIGHT BE MISSING OUT ON AN AFTERLIFE?
ARE WE TALKING RELIGION OR SCIENCE? ARE YOU WORRYING YOUR FATHER IS OUT THERE SOMEWHERE WAITING FOR ME?
I DON'T KNOW. I GUESS I'M STILL TRYING TO PROCESS ALL OF THIS.
YOU'RE A MAN OF SCIENCE AND A MECHANIC. YOU LIVE IN A WORLD WHERE YOU CAN OPEN AND REPAIR THINGS. SPIRITUAL BELIEFS ARE SOMETHING OF A PERSONAL JOURNEY. I NEVER PUSHED RELIGION ON YOU BECAUSE I WANTED YOU TO FIND YOUR OWN WAY TO WHAT YOU BELIEVE.
I KNOW...AND I BELIEVE THERE ARE SO MANY THINGS I KNOW NOTHING ABOUT ALL AROUND ME AND IT MAKES ME FEEL...
HUMAN.
YES...I'M SORRY.

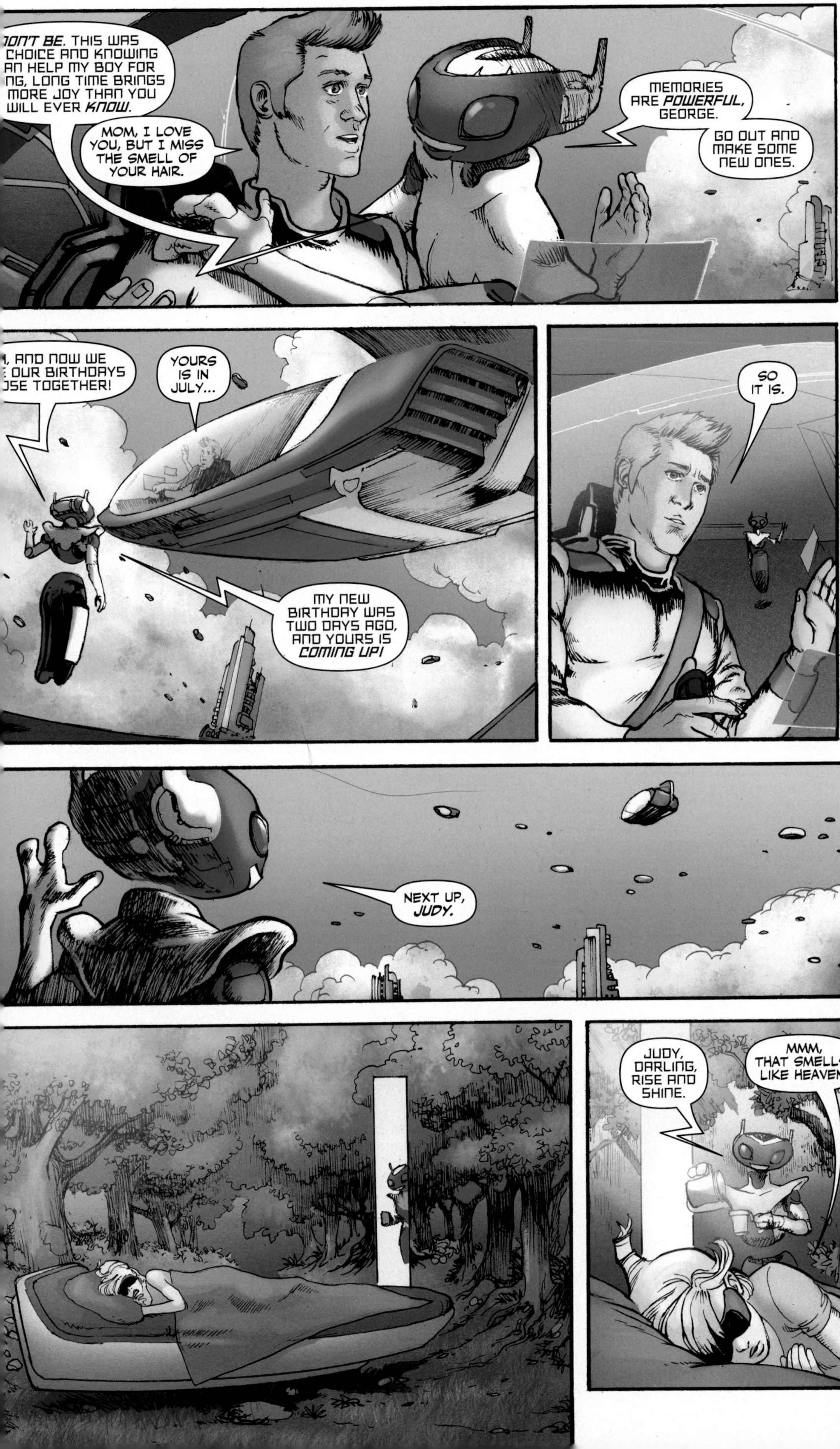

ON'T BE. THIS WAS CHOICE AND KNOWING AN HELP MY BOY FOR NG, LONG TIME BRINGS MORE JOY THAN YOU WILL EVER KNOW.
MOM, I LOVE YOU, BUT I MISS THE SMELL OF YOUR HAIR.
MEMORIES ARE POWERFUL, GEORGE.
GO OUT AND MAKE SOME NEW ONES.
, AND NOW WE OUR BIRTHDAYS OSE TOGETHER!
YOURS IS IN JULY...
MY NEW BIRTHDAY WAS TWO DAYS AGO, AND YOURS IS COMING UP!
SO IT IS.
NEXT UP, JUDY.
JUDY, DARLING, RISE AND SHINE.
MMM, THAT SMELLS LIKE HEAVEN.

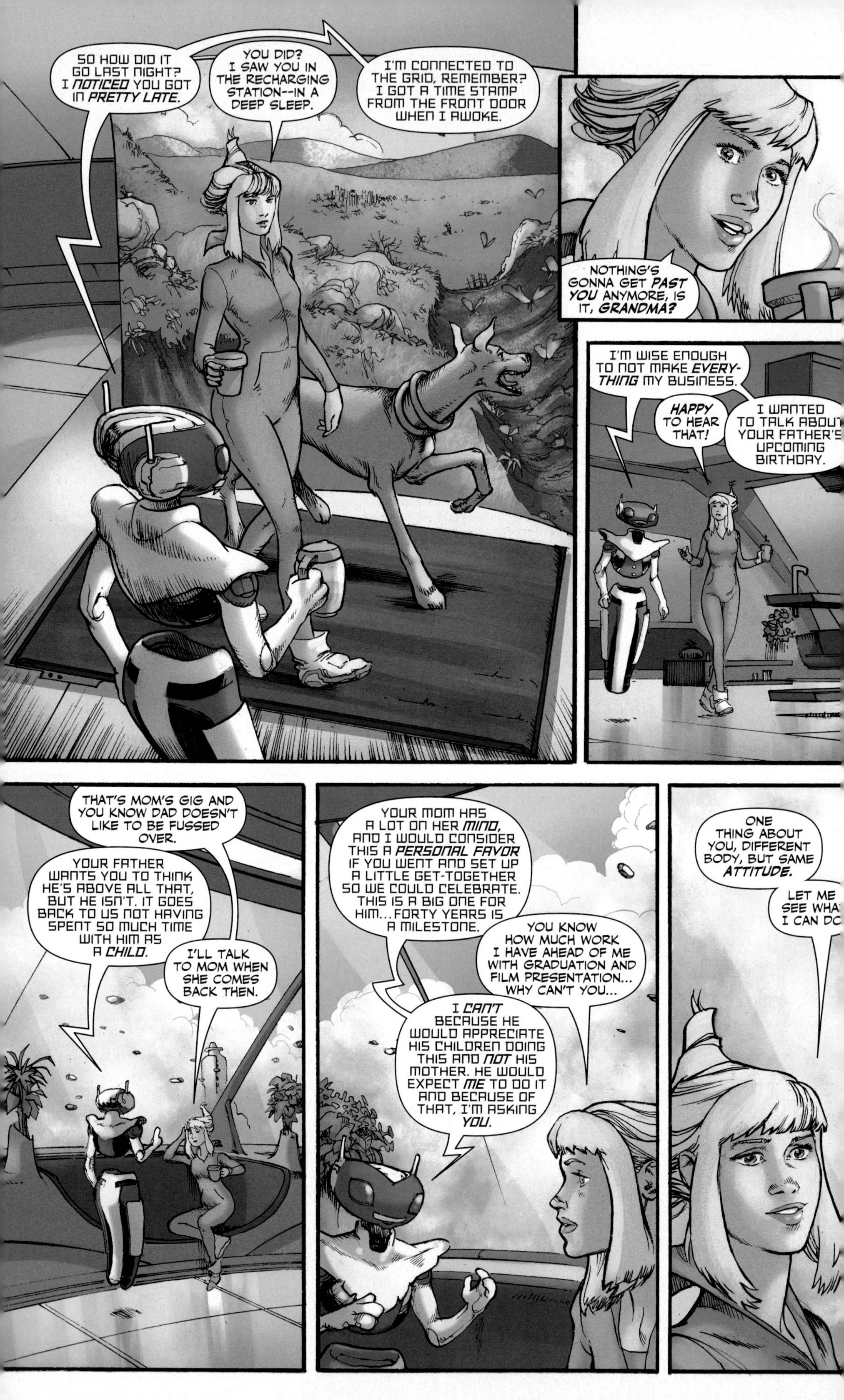

SO HOW DID IT GO LAST NIGHT? I *NOTICED* YOU GOT IN *PRETTY LATE*.
YOU DID? I SAW YOU IN THE RECHARGING STATION--IN A DEEP SLEEP.
I'M CONNECTED TO THE GRID, REMEMBER? I GOT A TIME STAMP FROM THE FRONT DOOR WHEN I AWOKE.
NOTHING'S GONNA GET *PAST YOU* ANYMORE, IS IT, *GRANDMA?*
I'M WISE ENOUGH TO NOT MAKE *EVERYTHING* MY BUSINESS.
HAPPY TO HEAR THAT!
I WANTED TO TALK ABOUT YOUR FATHER'S UPCOMING BIRTHDAY.
THAT'S MOM'S GIG AND YOU KNOW DAD DOESN'T LIKE TO BE FUSSED OVER.
YOUR FATHER WANTS YOU TO THINK HE'S ABOVE ALL THAT, BUT HE ISN'T. IT GOES BACK TO US NOT HAVING SPENT SO MUCH TIME WITH HIM AS A *CHILD*.
I'LL TALK TO MOM WHEN SHE COMES BACK THEN.
YOUR MOM HAS A LOT ON HER *MIND*, AND I WOULD CONSIDER THIS A *PERSONAL FAVOR* IF YOU WENT AND SET UP A LITTLE GET-TOGETHER SO WE COULD CELEBRATE. THIS IS A BIG ONE FOR HIM... FORTY YEARS IS A MILESTONE.
YOU KNOW HOW MUCH WORK I HAVE AHEAD OF ME WITH GRADUATION AND FILM PRESENTATION... WHY CAN'T YOU...
I *CAN'T* BECAUSE HE WOULD APPRECIATE HIS CHILDREN DOING THIS AND *NOT* HIS MOTHER. HE WOULD EXPECT *ME* TO DO IT AND BECAUSE OF THAT, I'M ASKING *YOU*.
ONE THING ABOUT YOU, DIFFERENT BODY, BUT SAME *ATTITUDE*.
LET ME SEE WHAT I CAN DO

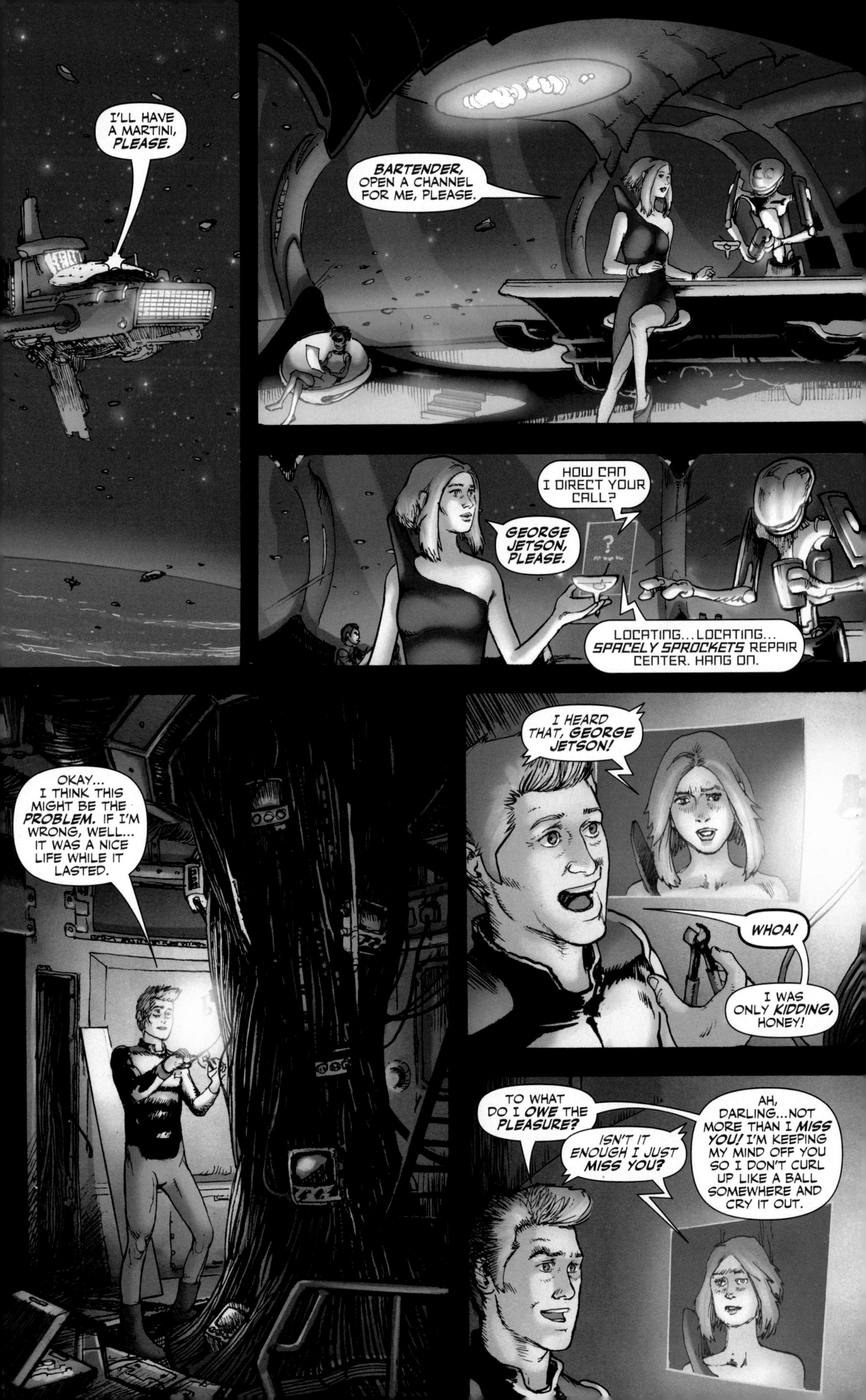
I'LL HAVE A MARTINI, PLEASE.
BARTENDER, OPEN A CHANNEL FOR ME, PLEASE.
HOW CAN I DIRECT YOUR CALL?
GEORGE JETSON, PLEASE.
LOCATING...LOCATING... SPACELY SPROCKETS REPAIR CENTER. HANG ON.
OKAY... I THINK THIS MIGHT BE THE PROBLEM. IF I'M WRONG, WELL... IT WAS A NICE LIFE WHILE IT LASTED.
I HEARD THAT, GEORGE JETSON!
WHOA!
I WAS ONLY KIDDING, HONEY!
TO WHAT DO I OWE THE PLEASURE?
ISN'T IT ENOUGH I JUST MISS YOU?
AH, DARLING...NOT MORE THAN I MISS YOU! I'M KEEPING MY MIND OFF YOU SO I DON'T CURL UP LIKE A BALL SOMEWHERE AND CRY IT OUT.

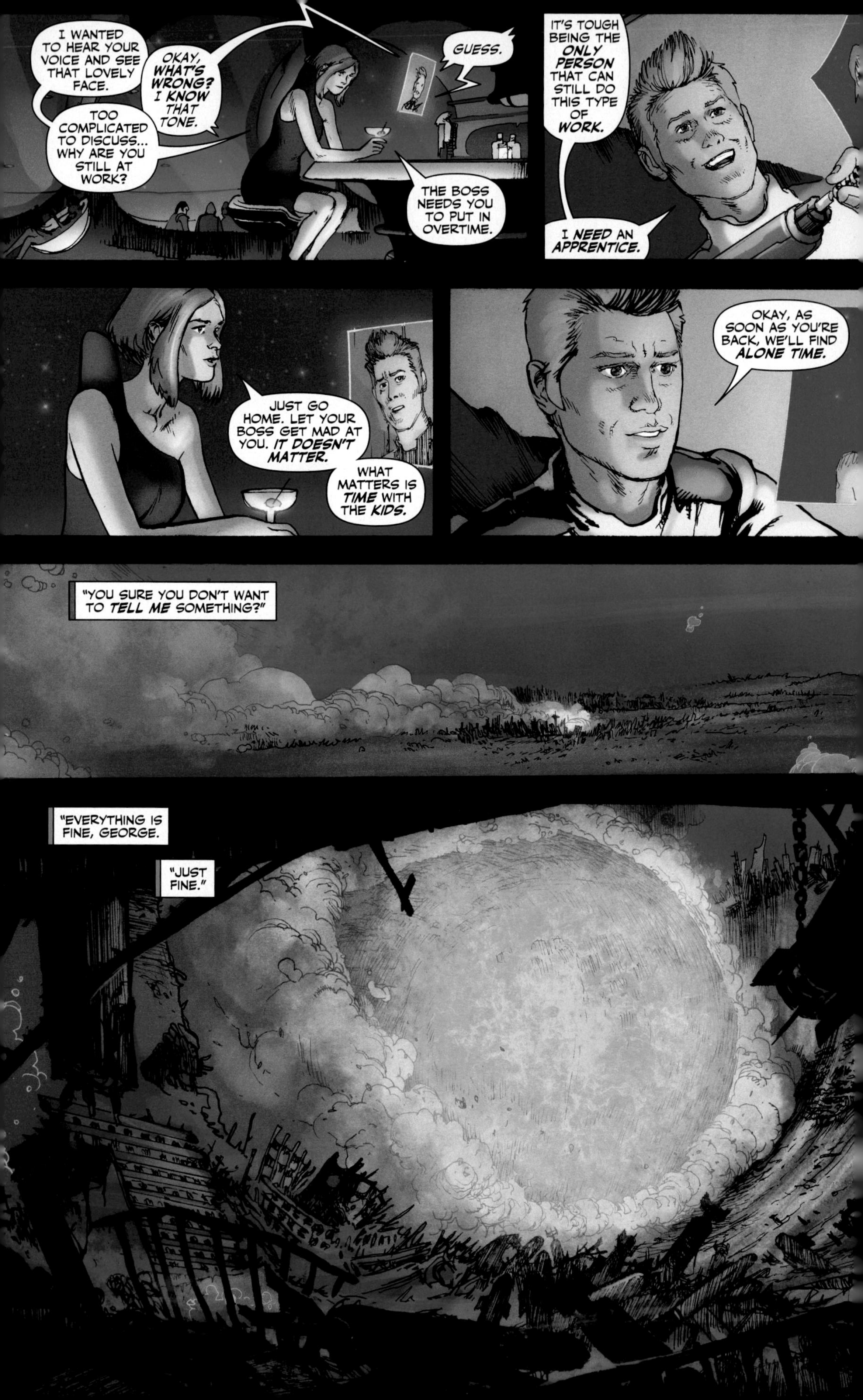

I WANTED TO HEAR YOUR VOICE AND SEE THAT LOVELY FACE.
OKAY, WHAT'S WRONG? I KNOW THAT TONE.
TOO COMPLICATED TO DISCUSS... WHY ARE YOU STILL AT WORK?
GUESS.
THE BOSS NEEDS YOU TO PUT IN OVERTIME.
IT'S TOUGH BEING THE ONLY PERSON THAT CAN STILL DO THIS TYPE OF WORK.
I NEED AN APPRENTICE.
JUST GO HOME. LET YOUR BOSS GET MAD AT YOU. IT DOESN'T MATTER.
WHAT MATTERS IS TIME WITH THE KIDS.
OKAY, AS SOON AS YOU'RE BACK, WE'LL FIND ALONE TIME.
"YOU SURE YOU DON'T WANT TO TELL ME SOMETHING?"
"EVERYTHING IS FINE, GEORGE.
"JUST FINE."

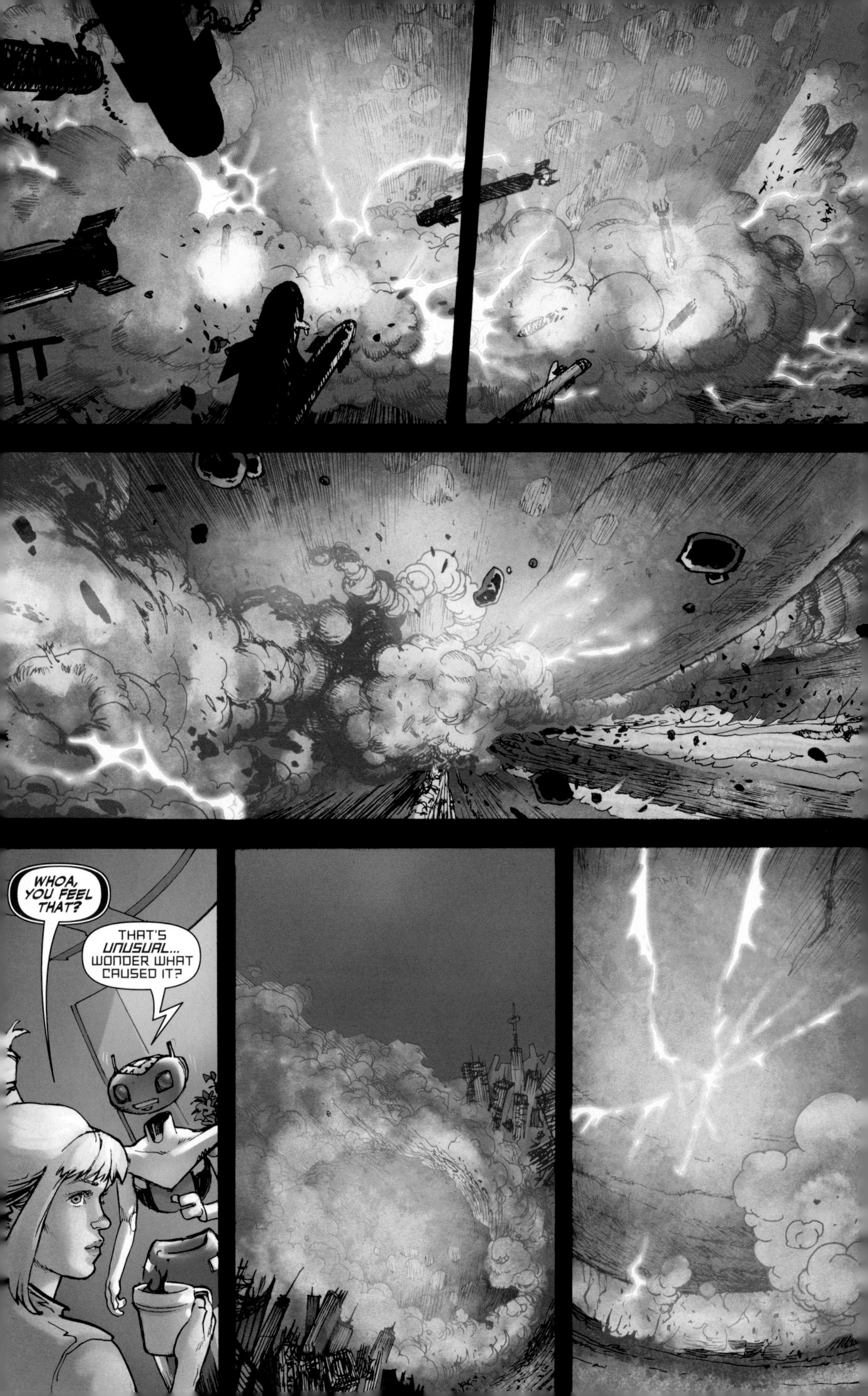
WHOA, YOU FEEL THAT?
THAT'S UNUSUAL... WONDER WHAT CAUSED IT?

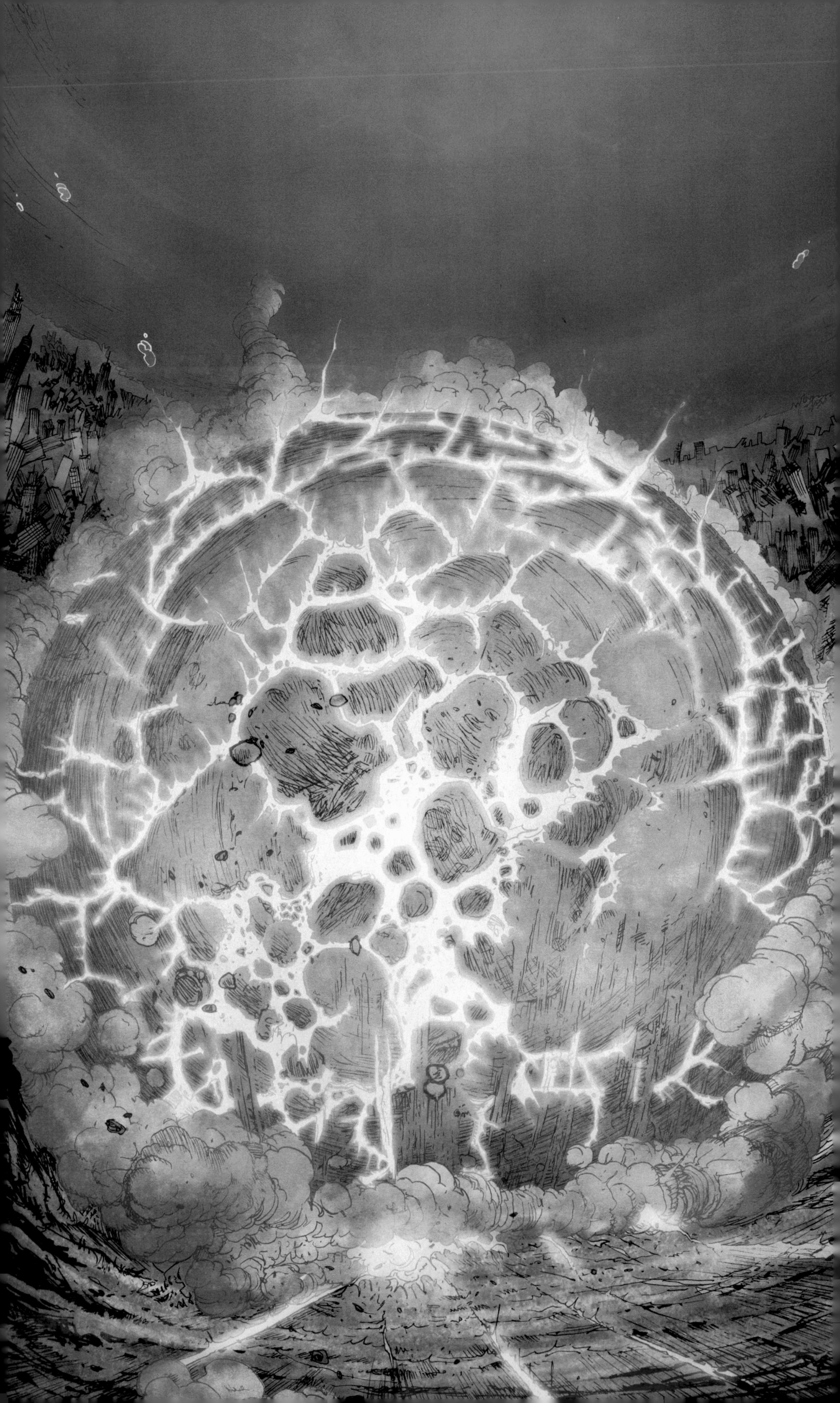

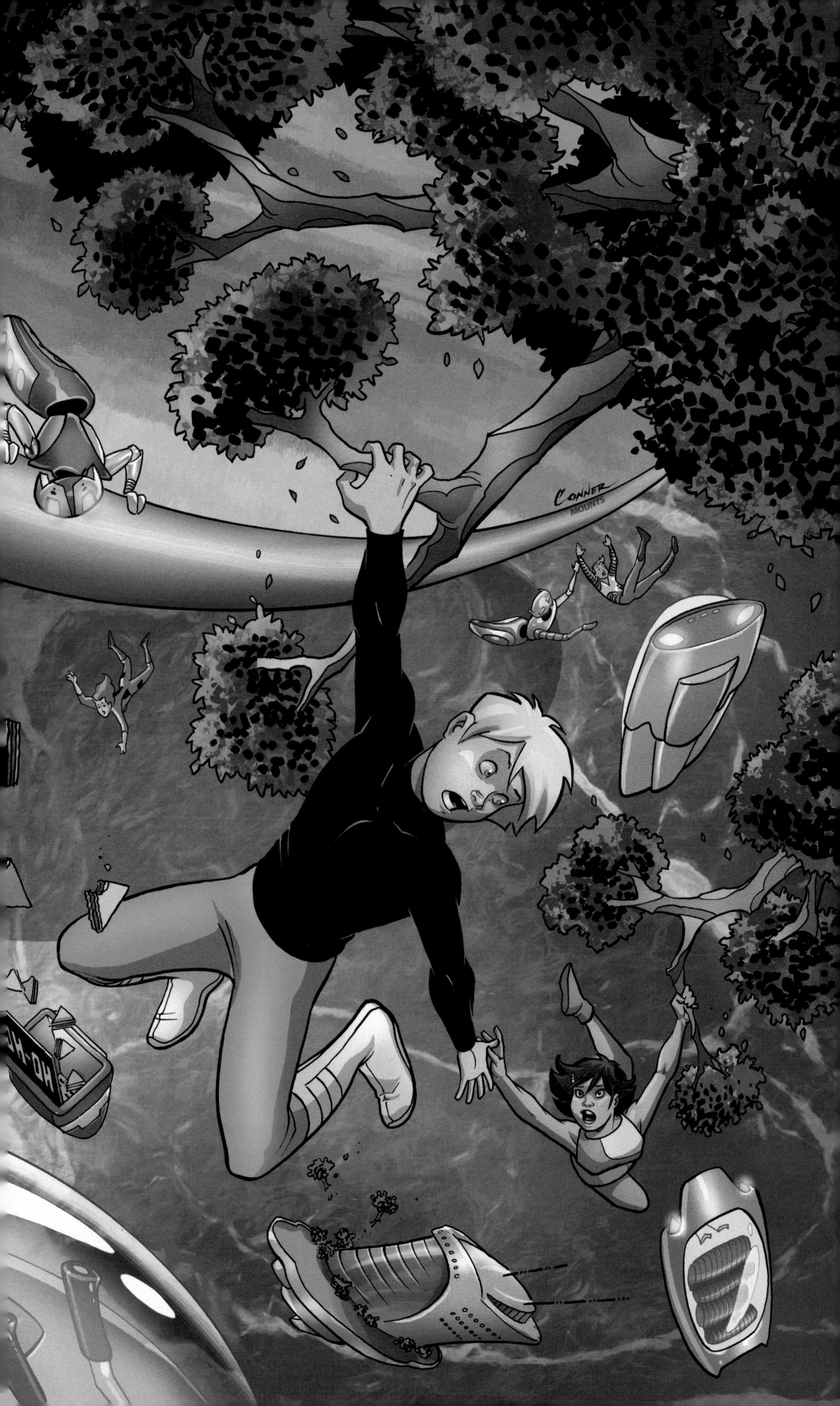
CONNER
MOUNTS

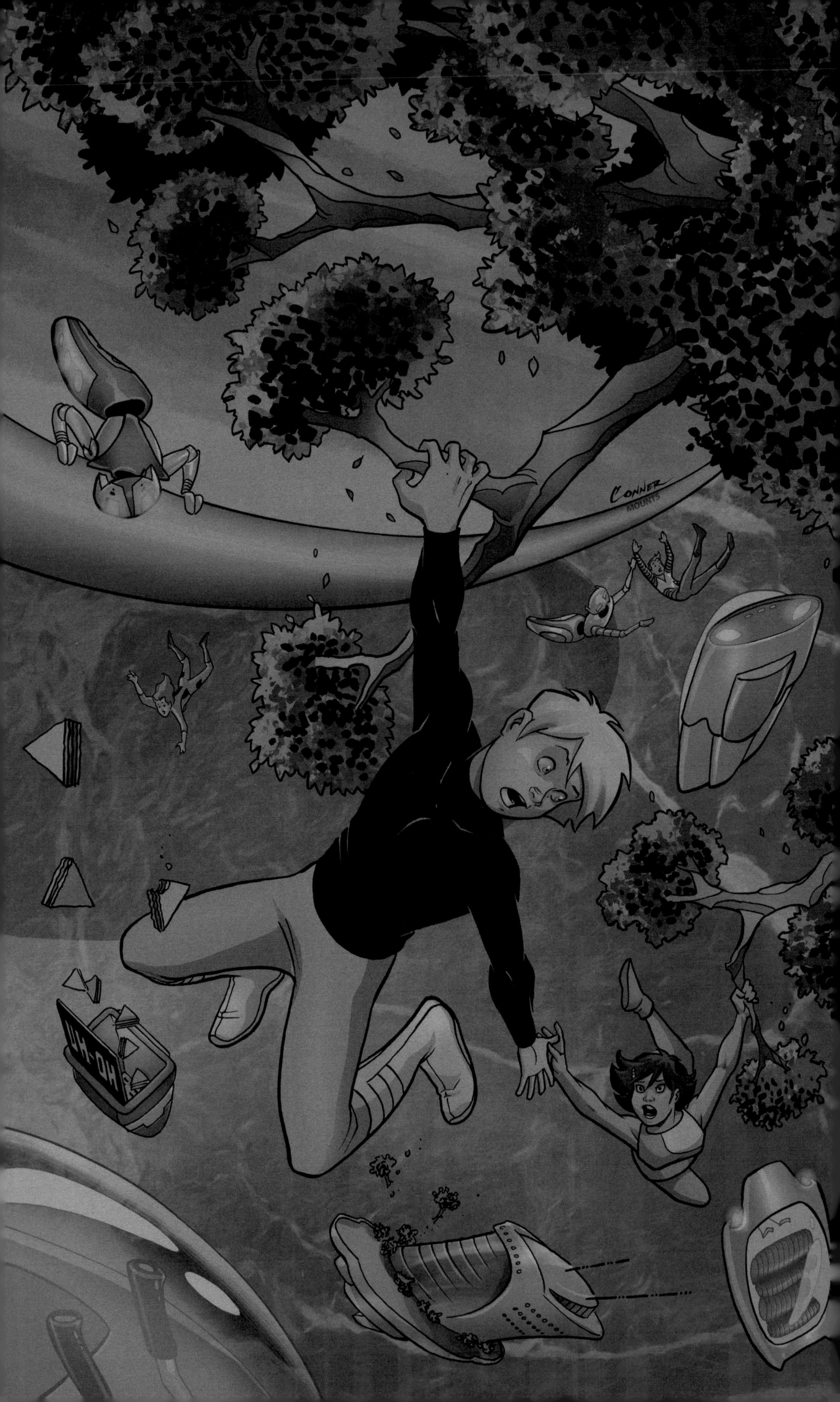
CONNER
MOUNTS

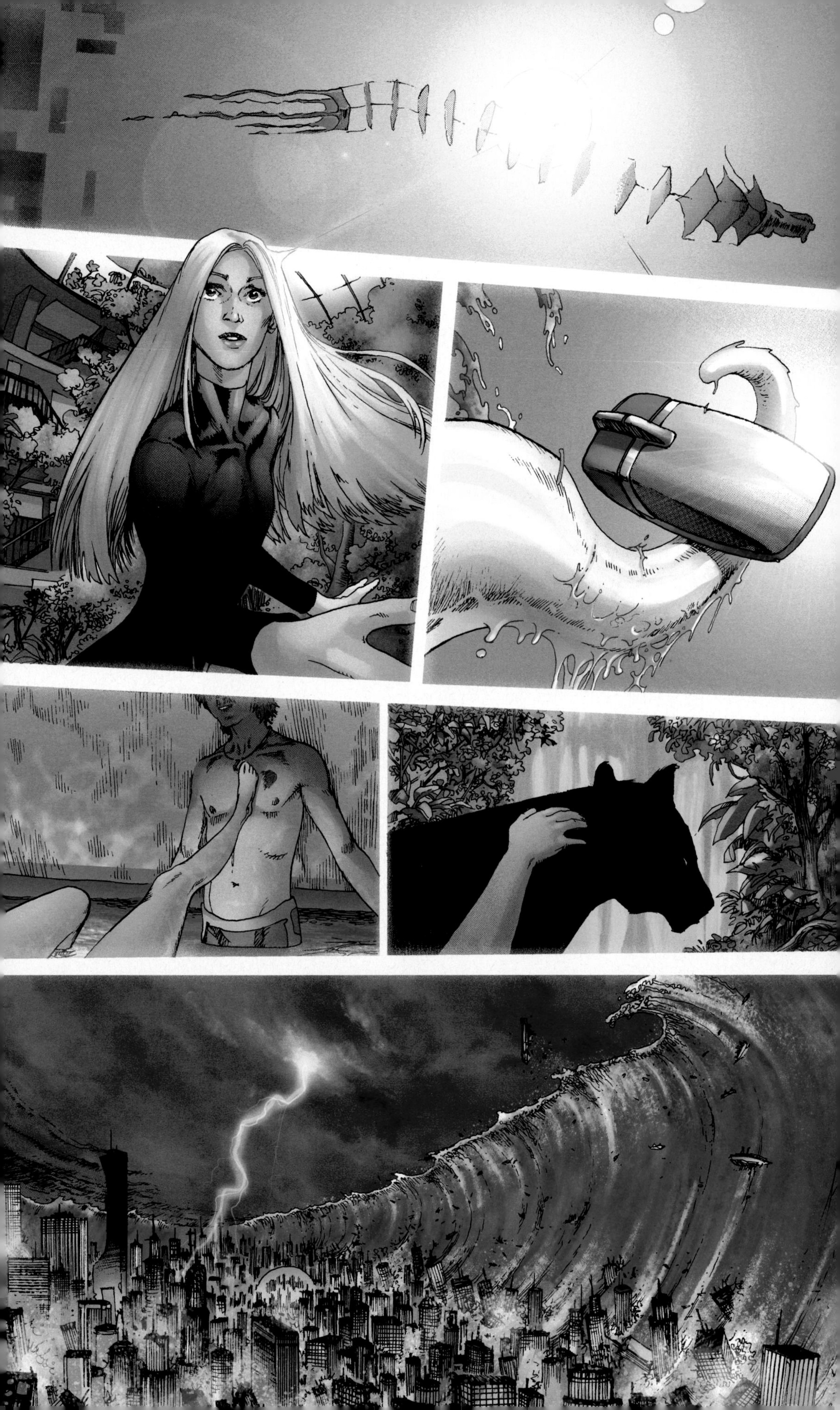

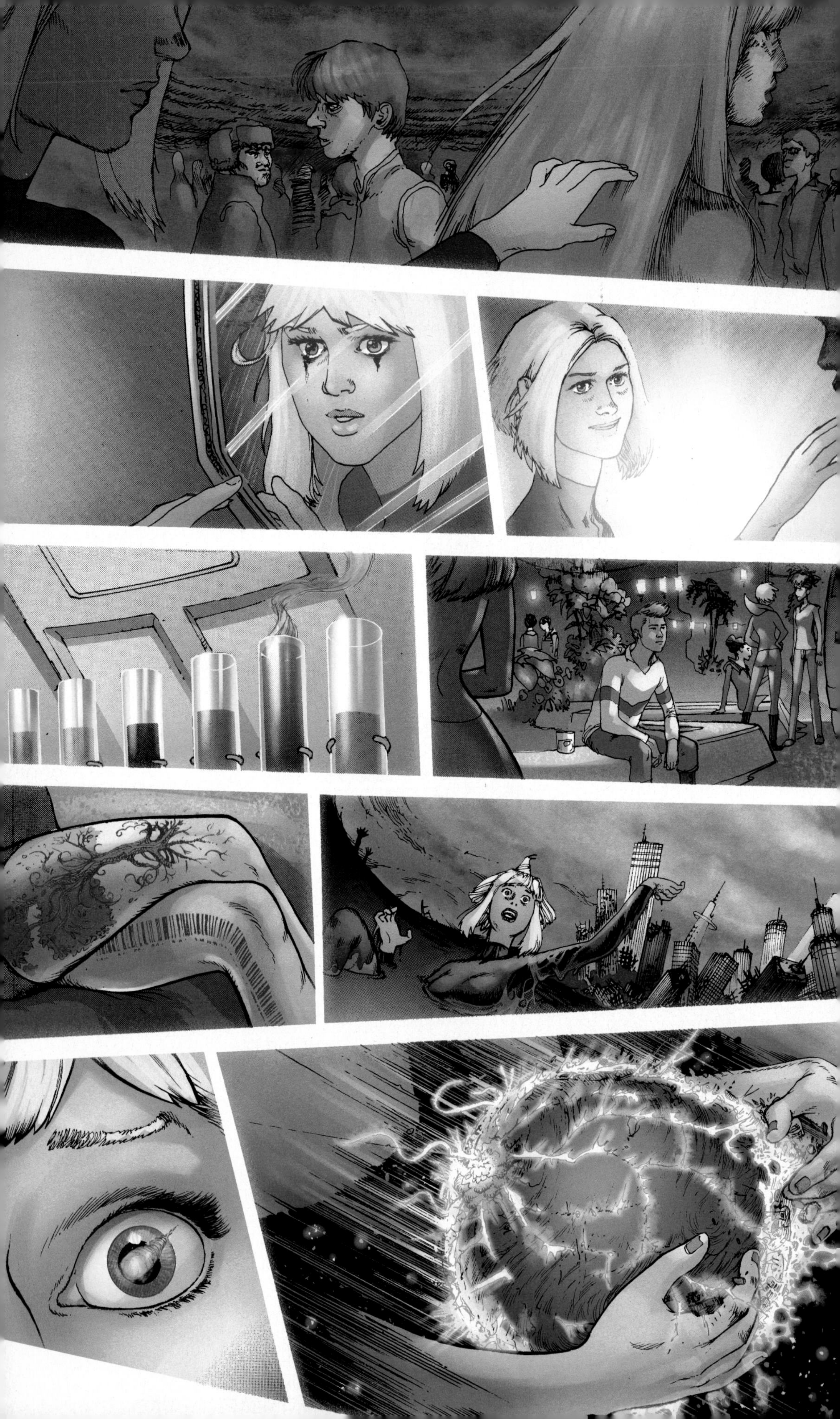

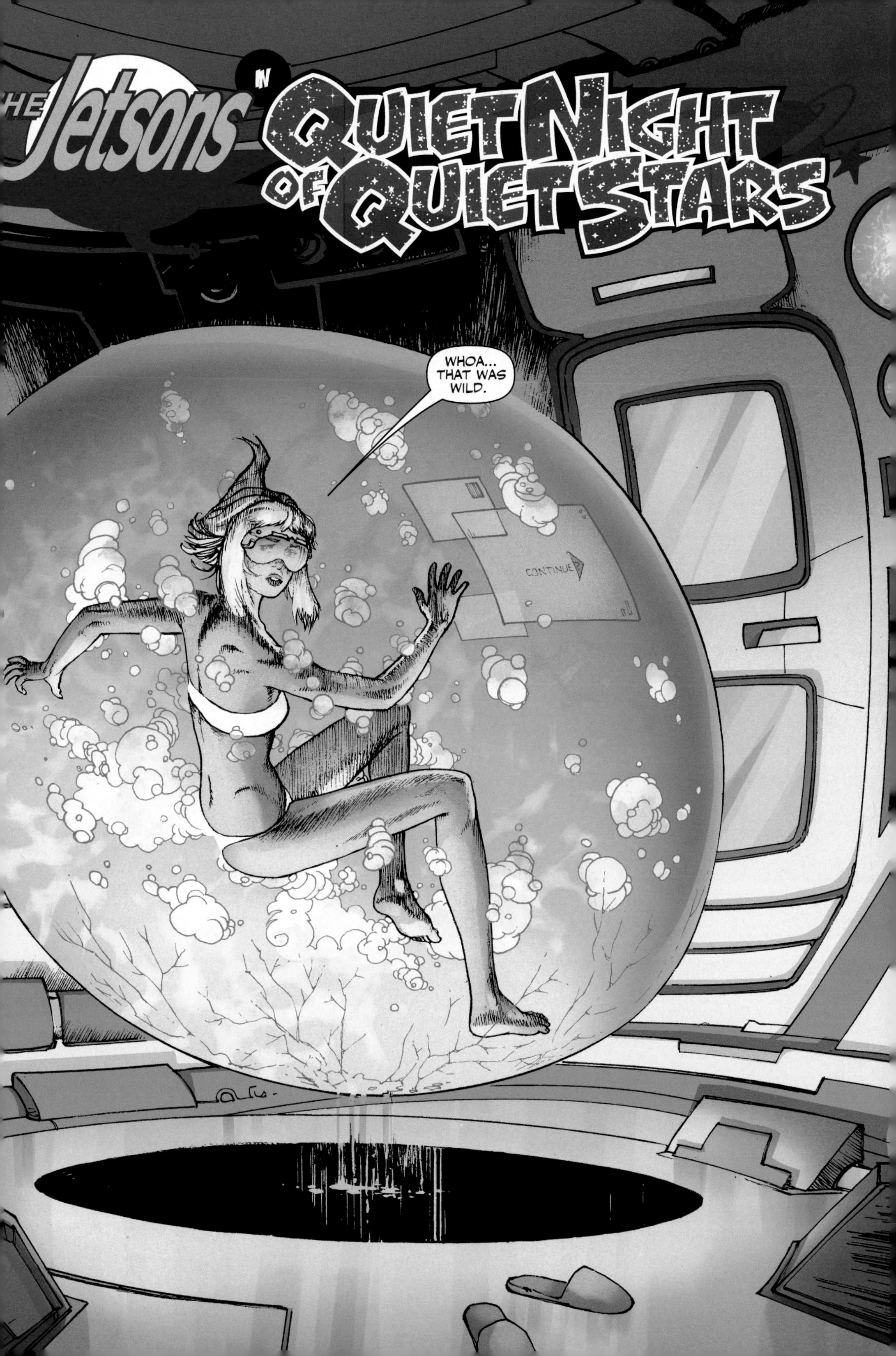
THE Jetsons IN
QUIET NIGHT OF QUIET STARS
WHOA... THAT WAS WILD.
CONTINUE

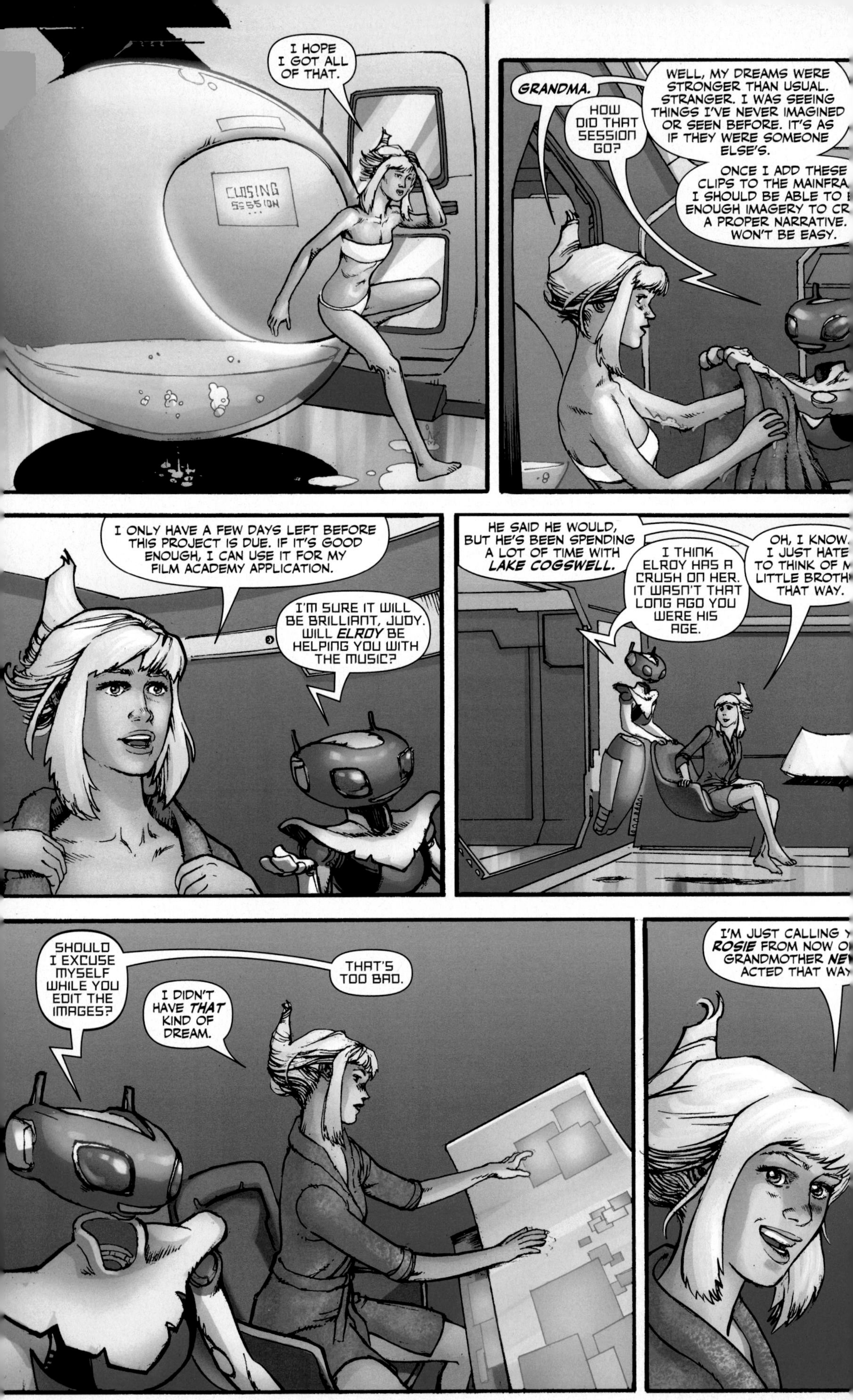
CLOSING SESSION ...
I HOPE I GOT ALL OF THAT.
GRANDMA.
HOW DID THAT SESSION GO?
WELL, MY DREAMS WERE STRONGER THAN USUAL. STRANGER. I WAS SEEING THINGS I'VE NEVER IMAGINED OR SEEN BEFORE. IT'S AS IF THEY WERE SOMEONE ELSE'S.
ONCE I ADD THESE CLIPS TO THE MAINFRA I SHOULD BE ABLE TO ENOUGH IMAGERY TO CR A PROPER NARRATIVE. WON'T BE EASY.
I ONLY HAVE A FEW DAYS LEFT BEFORE THIS PROJECT IS DUE. IF IT'S GOOD ENOUGH, I CAN USE IT FOR MY FILM ACADEMY APPLICATION.
I'M SURE IT WILL BE BRILLIANT, JUDY. WILL ELROY BE HELPING YOU WITH THE MUSIC?
HE SAID HE WOULD, BUT HE'S BEEN SPENDING A LOT OF TIME WITH LAKE COGSWELL.
I THINK ELROY HAS A CRUSH ON HER. IT WASN'T THAT LONG AGO YOU WERE HIS AGE.
OH, I KNOW. I JUST HATE TO THINK OF LITTLE BROTH THAT WAY.
SHOULD I EXCUSE MYSELF WHILE YOU EDIT THE IMAGES?
I DIDN'T HAVE THAT KIND OF DREAM.
THAT'S TOO BAD.
I'M JUST CALLING ROSIE FROM NOW O GRANDMOTHER NE ACTED THAT WAY

MEANWHILE...

SO, WHAT'S THE VERDICT, *JETSON?* HAVING THIS DOWN FOR MORE THAN A FEW HOURS IS ALREADY UPSETTING THE WEATHER PATTERNS AROUND US.

I KNOW MY CONTRACT WITH YOUR COMPANY *SPACELY SPACE SPROCKETS* IS STILL UNDER WARRANTY.

YES, I SAW WHAT'S GOING ON OUTSIDE, MR. SINGLETON. SOME SEISMIC ACTIVITY BELOW IS HAVING A WEIRD EFFECT ON A LOT OF THINGS.

ON MY WAY TO THE PROBLEM.

SOMETHING EXTERNAL DISLODGED A CONNECTION.

FOREIGN BODY. PLEASE IDENTIFY YOURSELF.

JETSON, GEORGE. SPACELY REPAIR. #1962-3CBS.

PROCESSING.

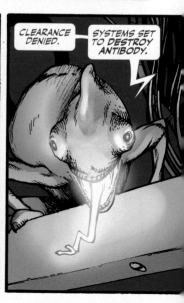

CLEARANCE DENIED.

SYSTEMS SET TO DESTROY ANTIBODY.

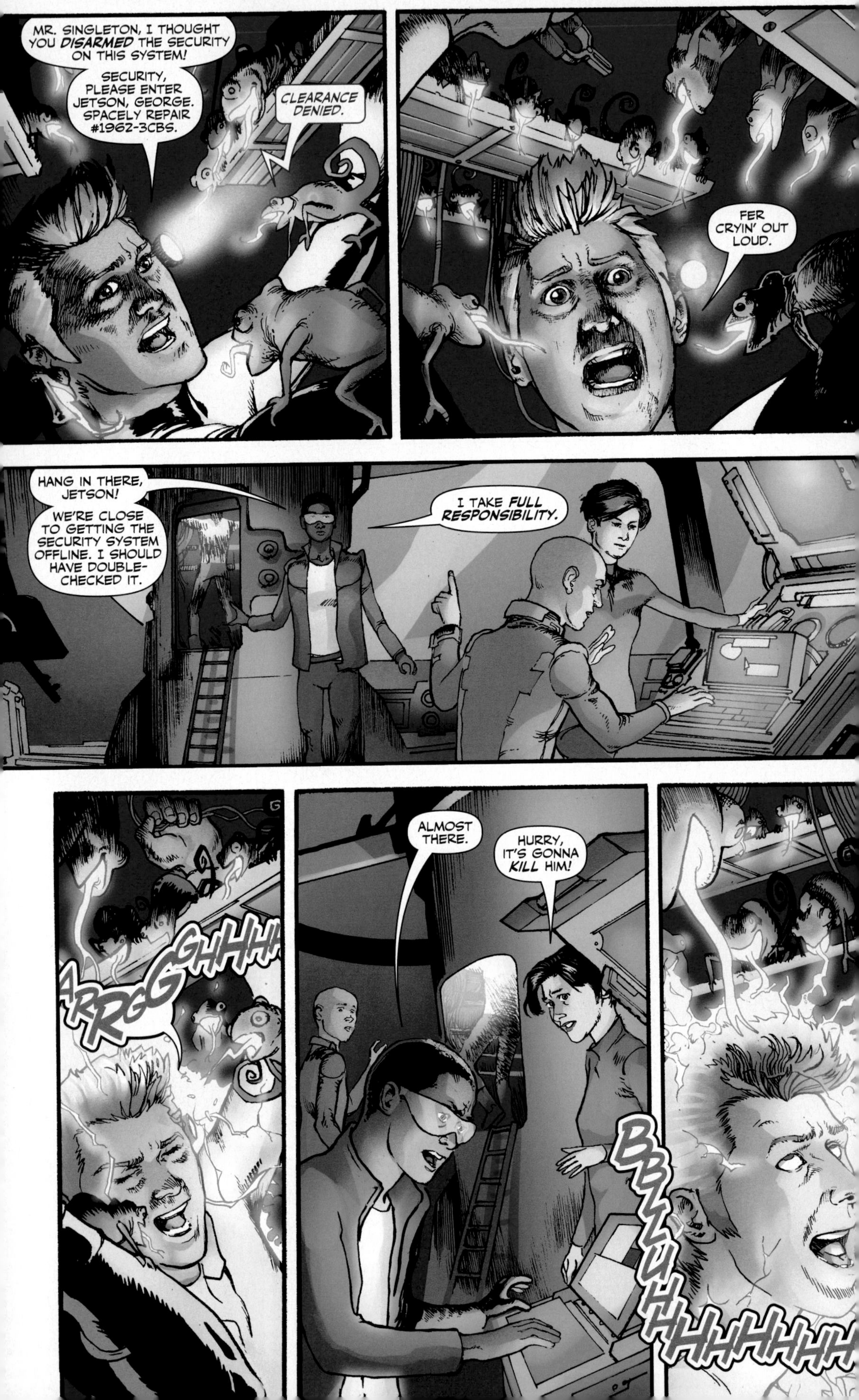
MR. SINGLETON, I THOUGHT YOU DISARMED THE SECURITY ON THIS SYSTEM!
SECURITY, PLEASE ENTER JETSON, GEORGE. SPACELY REPAIR #1962-3CBS.
CLEARANCE DENIED.
FER CRYIN' OUT LOUD.
HANG IN THERE, JETSON!
WE'RE CLOSE TO GETTING THE SECURITY SYSTEM OFFLINE. I SHOULD HAVE DOUBLE-CHECKED IT.
I TAKE FULL RESPONSIBILITY.
ARRGGGHHHH
ALMOST THERE.
HURRY, IT'S GONNA KILL HIM!
BBBLLUHHHHHHHHH

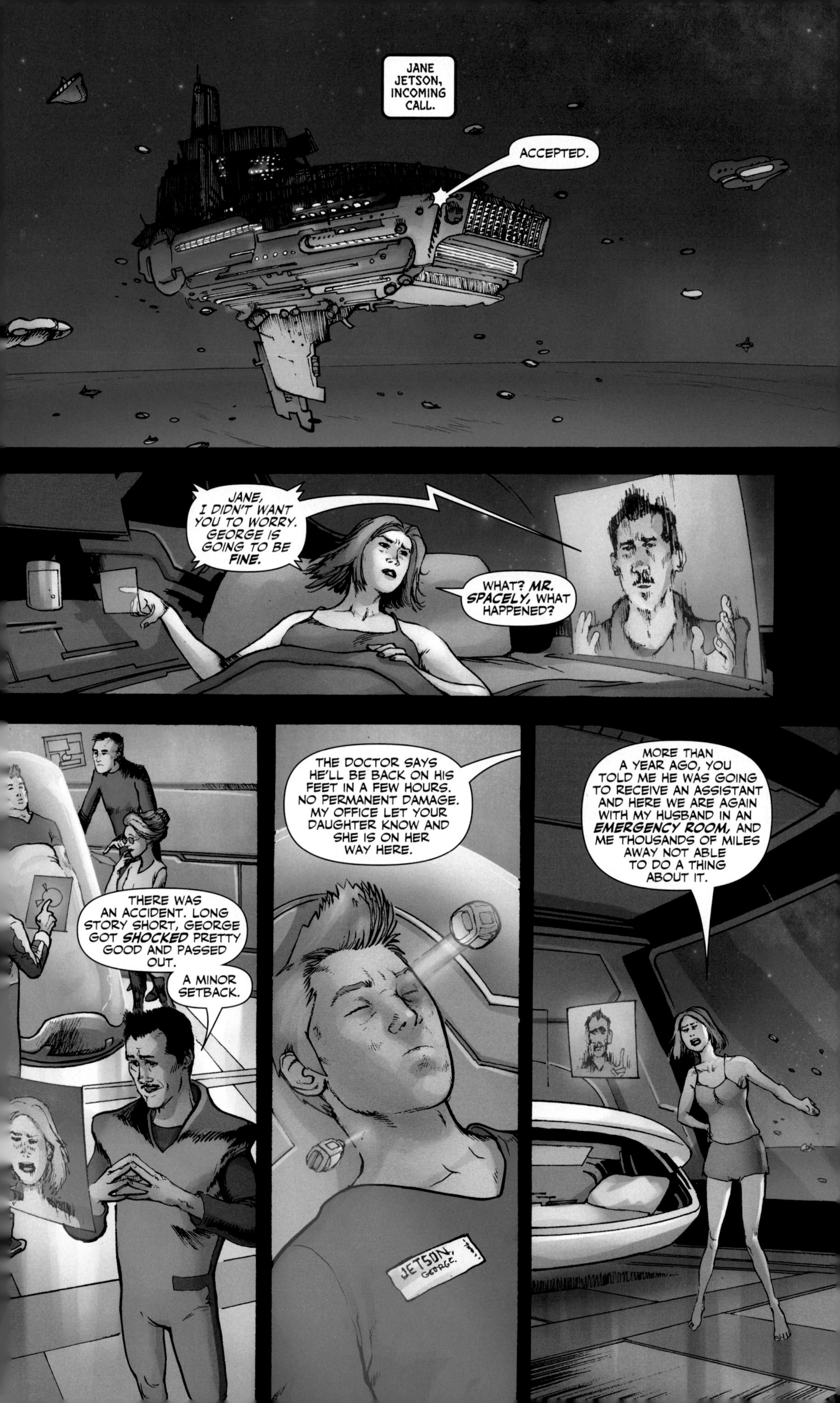
JANE JETSON, INCOMING CALL.
ACCEPTED.
JANE, I DIDN'T WANT YOU TO WORRY. GEORGE IS GOING TO BE FINE.
WHAT? MR. SPACELY, WHAT HAPPENED?
THERE WAS AN ACCIDENT. LONG STORY SHORT, GEORGE GOT SHOCKED PRETTY GOOD AND PASSED OUT.
A MINOR SETBACK.
THE DOCTOR SAYS HE'LL BE BACK ON HIS FEET IN A FEW HOURS. NO PERMANENT DAMAGE. MY OFFICE LET YOUR DAUGHTER KNOW AND SHE IS ON HER WAY HERE.
JETSON, GEORGE.
MORE THAN A YEAR AGO, YOU TOLD ME HE WAS GOING TO RECEIVE AN ASSISTANT AND HERE WE ARE AGAIN WITH MY HUSBAND IN AN EMERGENCY ROOM, AND ME THOUSANDS OF MILES AWAY NOT ABLE TO DO A THING ABOUT IT.

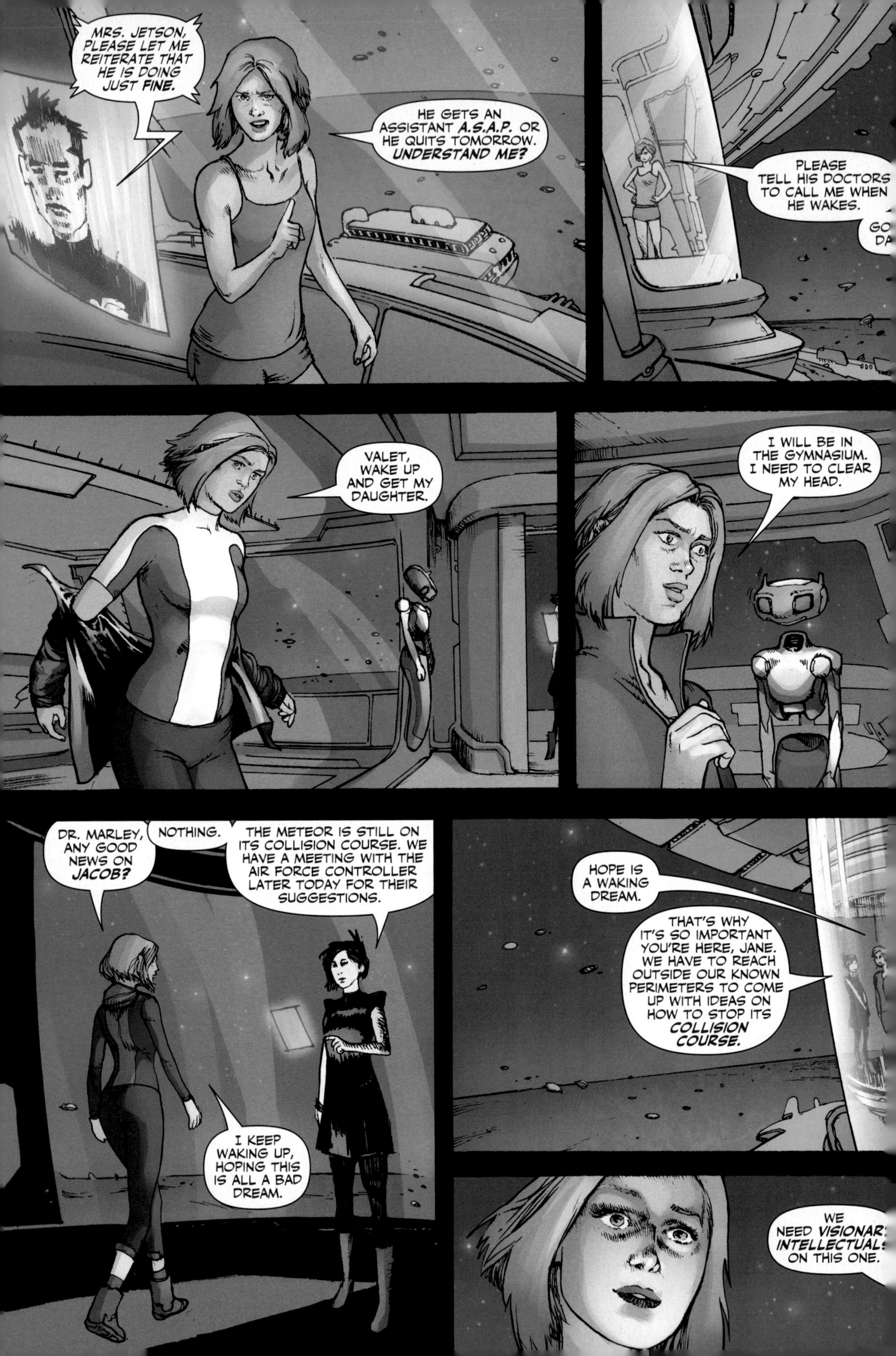
MRS. JETSON, PLEASE LET ME REITERATE THAT HE IS DOING JUST FINE.
HE GETS AN ASSISTANT A.S.A.P. OR HE QUITS TOMORROW. UNDERSTAND ME?
PLEASE TELL HIS DOCTORS TO CALL ME WHEN HE WAKES.
VALET, WAKE UP AND GET MY DAUGHTER.
I WILL BE IN THE GYMNASIUM. I NEED TO CLEAR MY HEAD.
DR. MARLEY, ANY GOOD NEWS ON JACOB?
NOTHING.
THE METEOR IS STILL ON ITS COLLISION COURSE. WE HAVE A MEETING WITH THE AIR FORCE CONTROLLER LATER TODAY FOR THEIR SUGGESTIONS.
I KEEP WAKING UP, HOPING THIS IS ALL A BAD DREAM.
HOPE IS A WAKING DREAM.
THAT'S WHY IT'S SO IMPORTANT YOU'RE HERE, JANE. WE HAVE TO REACH OUTSIDE OUR KNOWN PERIMETERS TO COME UP WITH IDEAS ON HOW TO STOP ITS COLLISION COURSE.
WE NEED VISIONAR INTELLECTUAL ON THIS ONE.

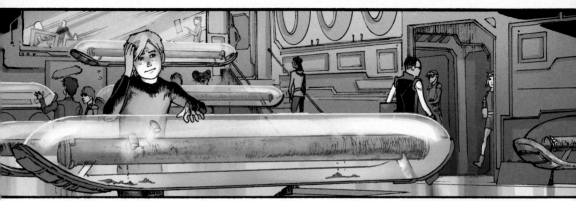

HOW'S IT GOING, ELROY?

LAKE.

TWO MORE DAYS AND IT'LL BE SAFE TO OPEN THIS UP AND SEE WHAT'S INSIDE. PLENTY OF TIME BEFORE MY DAD'S BIRTHDAY.

I KNOW IT'S A PAINTING OR SOMETHING. WHY NOT TELL ME WHICH ONE?

WELL, I CAN SEE HOW A SPOILED RICH GIRL NOT GETTING HER WAY WOULD DRIVE HER A BIT INSANE. SO, YOU HAVE TO WAIT.

GREAT OBSERVATION, JETSON. ANYTHING ELSE YOU SEE?

I CAN *HEAR* YOUR STOMACH GROWLING. YOU WANT LUNCH?

THERE'S HOPE FOR YOU YET. LET'S GET OUT OF HERE AND EAT ON THE GREAT LAWN.

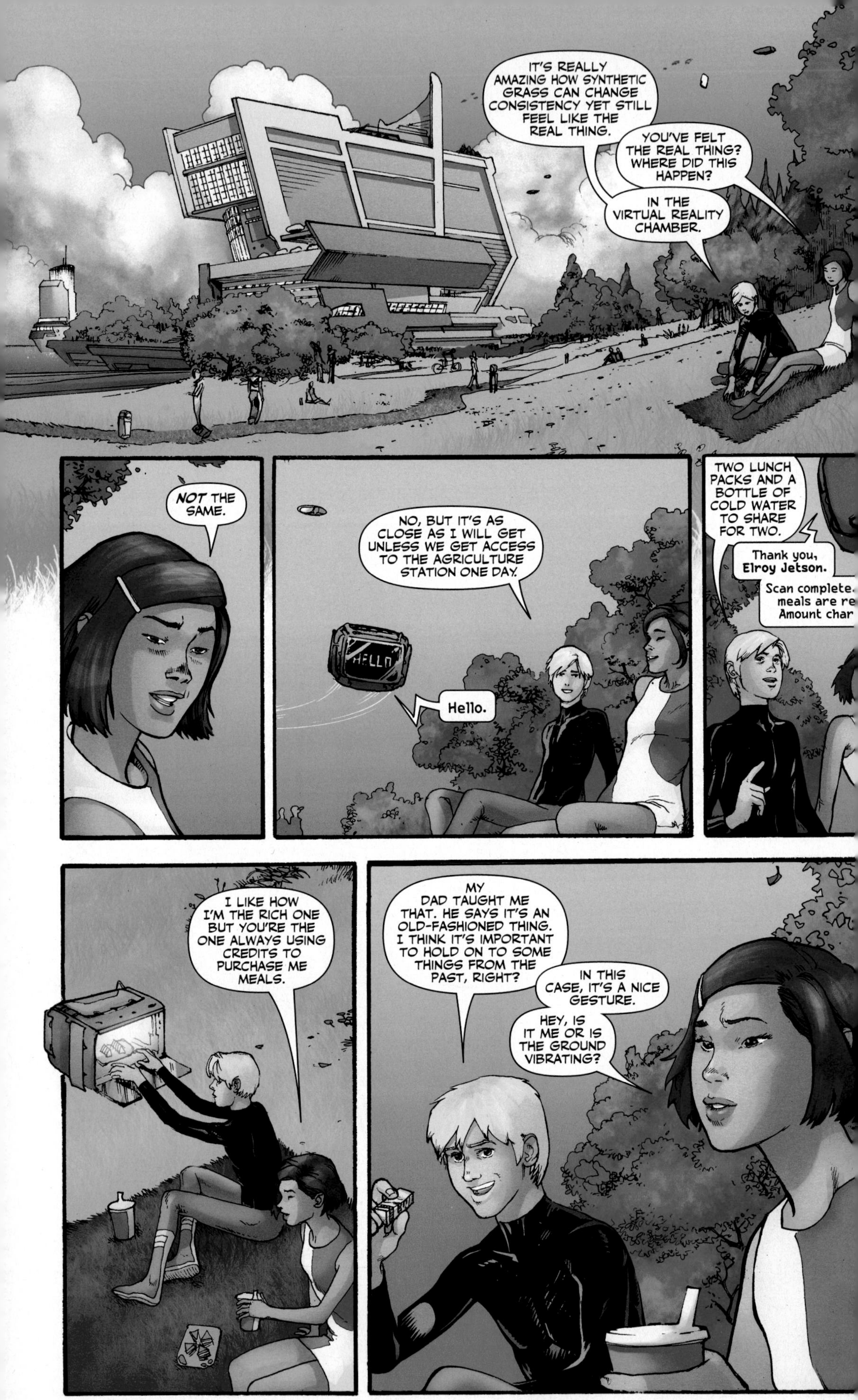
IT'S REALLY AMAZING HOW SYNTHETIC GRASS CAN CHANGE CONSISTENCY YET STILL FEEL LIKE THE REAL THING.
YOU'VE FELT THE REAL THING? WHERE DID THIS HAPPEN?
IN THE VIRTUAL REALITY CHAMBER.
NOT THE SAME.
NO, BUT IT'S AS CLOSE AS I WILL GET UNLESS WE GET ACCESS TO THE AGRICULTURE STATION ONE DAY.
HELLO
Hello.
TWO LUNCH PACKS AND A BOTTLE OF COLD WATER TO SHARE FOR TWO.
Thank you, **Elroy Jetson.**
Scan complete.
meals are re
Amount char
I LIKE HOW I'M THE RICH ONE BUT YOU'RE THE ONE ALWAYS USING CREDITS TO PURCHASE ME MEALS.
MY DAD TAUGHT ME THAT. HE SAYS IT'S AN OLD-FASHIONED THING. I THINK IT'S IMPORTANT TO HOLD ON TO SOME THINGS FROM THE PAST, RIGHT?
IN THIS CASE, IT'S A NICE GESTURE.
HEY, IS IT ME OR IS THE GROUND VIBRATING?

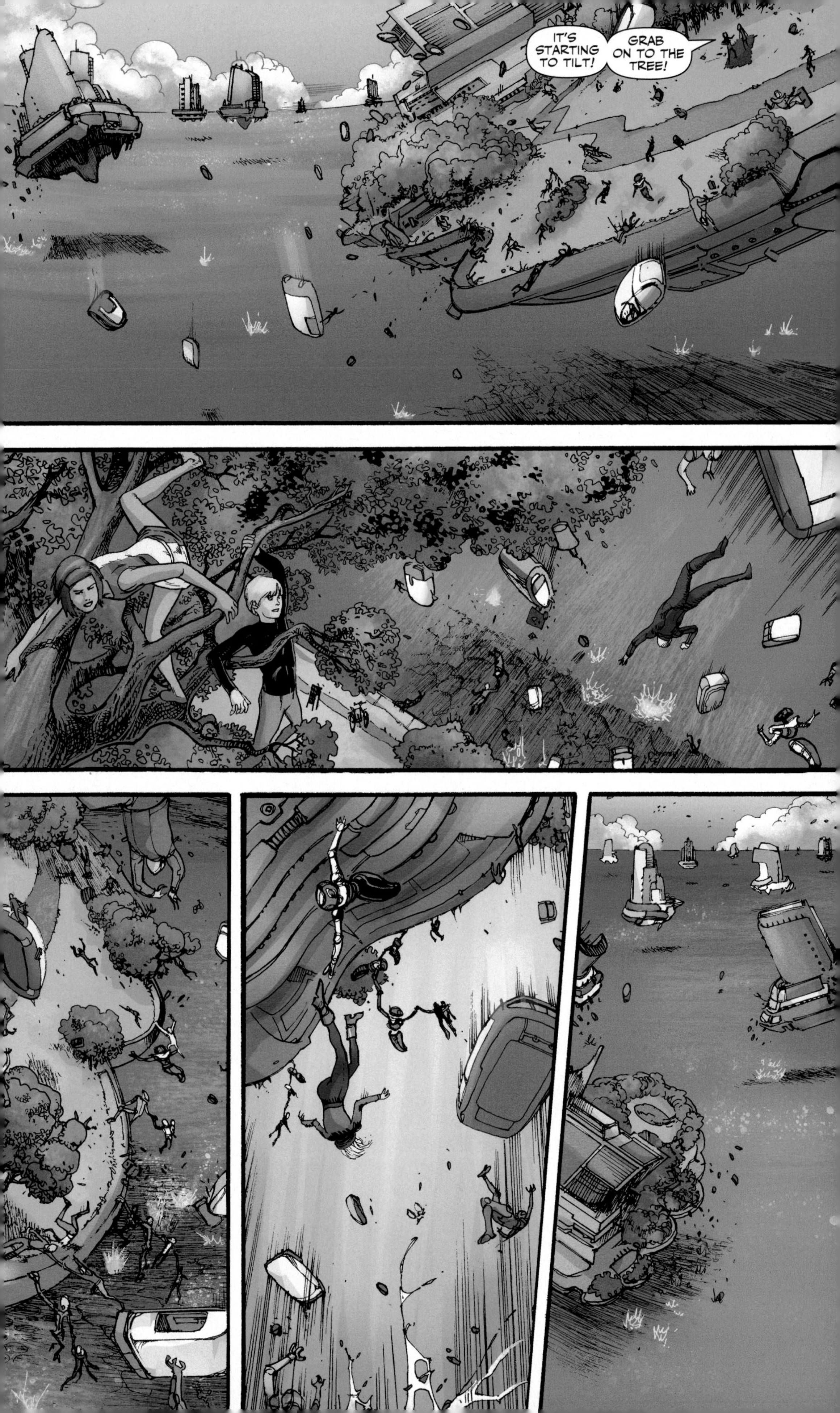
IT'S STARTING TO TILT!
GRAB ON TO THE TREE!

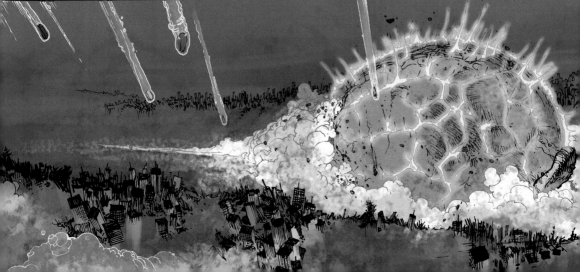

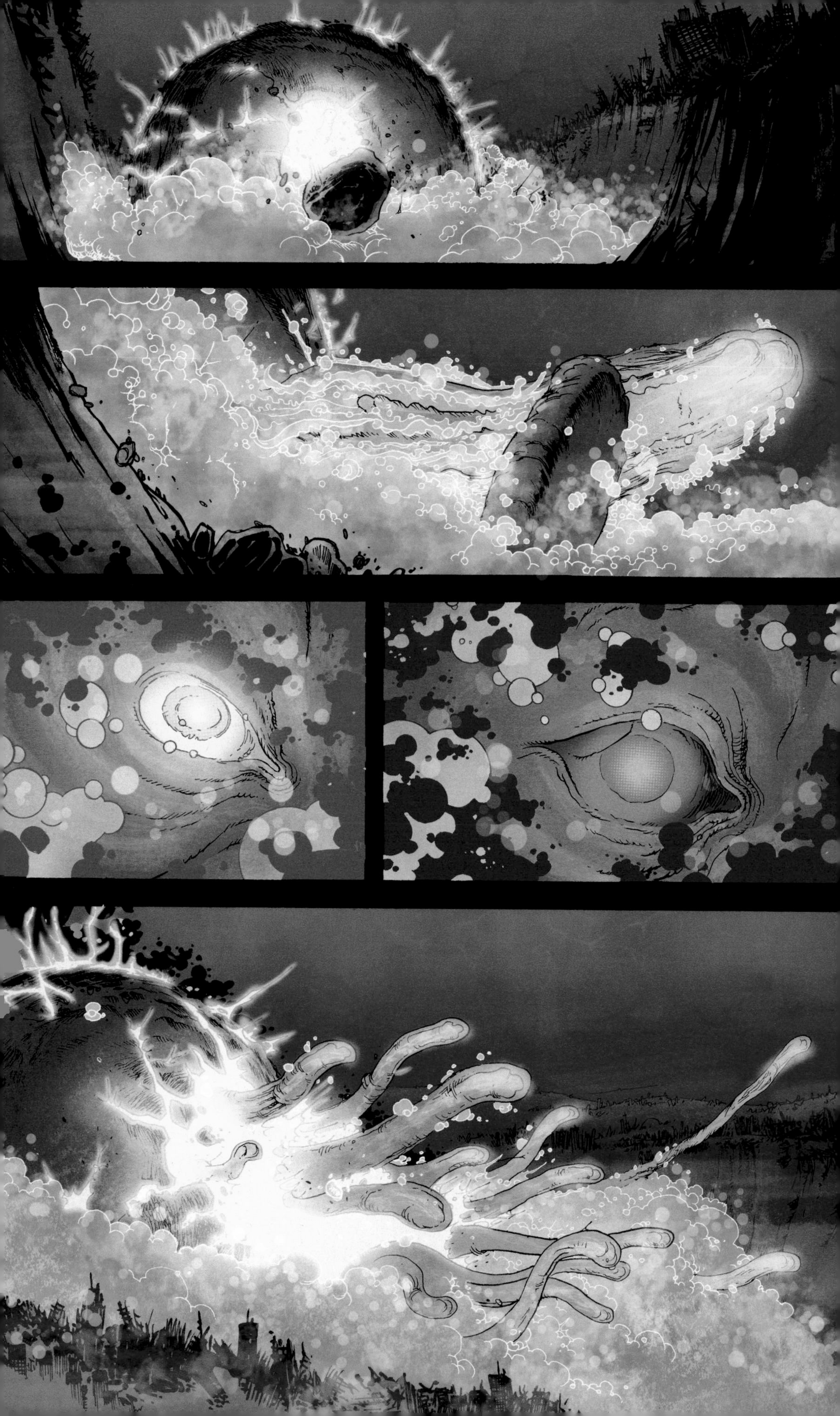

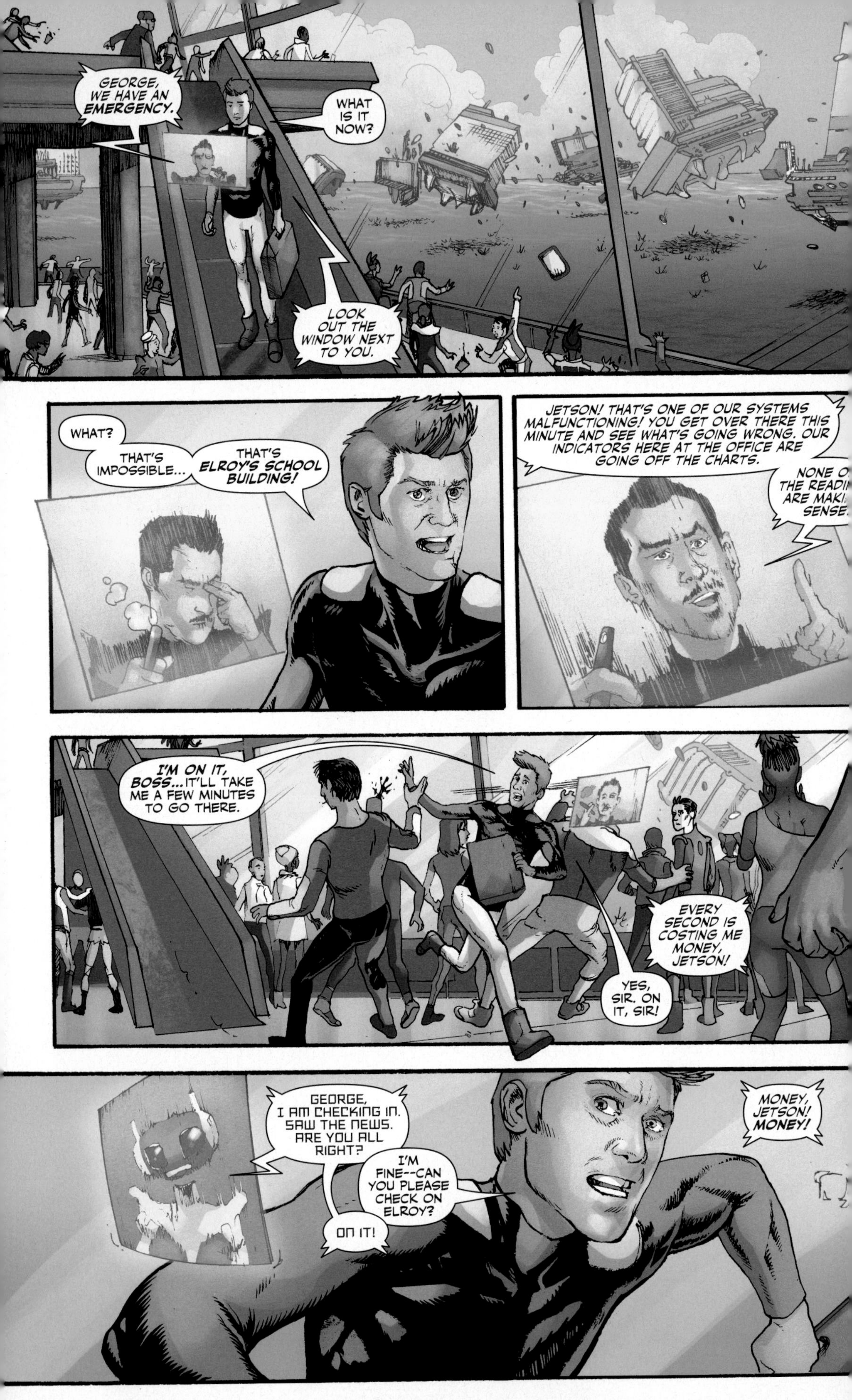
GEORGE, WE HAVE AN EMERGENCY.
WHAT IS IT NOW?
LOOK OUT THE WINDOW NEXT TO YOU.
WHAT?
THAT'S IMPOSSIBLE...
THAT'S ELROY'S SCHOOL BUILDING!
JETSON! THAT'S ONE OF OUR SYSTEMS MALFUNCTIONING! YOU GET OVER THERE THIS MINUTE AND SEE WHAT'S GOING WRONG. OUR INDICATORS HERE AT THE OFFICE ARE GOING OFF THE CHARTS.
I'M ON IT, BOSS...IT'LL TAKE ME A FEW MINUTES TO GO THERE.
EVERY SECOND IS COSTING ME MONEY, JETSON!
YES, SIR. ON IT, SIR!
GEORGE, I AM CHECKING IN. SAW THE NEWS. ARE YOU ALL RIGHT?
I'M FINE--CAN YOU PLEASE CHECK ON ELROY?
ON IT!
MONEY, JETSON! MONEY!

IT STOPPED. YOU CAN GET OFF NOW.

YOU WOULD LIKE THAT, WOULDN'T YOU?

STOP FOOLING AROUND. I'M GETTING A CALL FROM HOME.

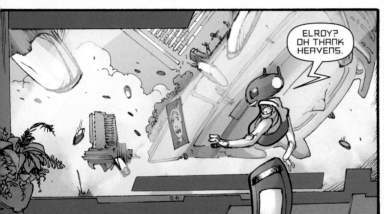

ELROY? OH THANK HEAVENS.

I JUST CHECKED IN ON YOUR FATHER AND IT SEEMS THE DISTURBANCE WAS LOCATED ONLY IN YOUR AREA. I'M WATCHING THE NEWS FOR ANY UPDATES.

MRS. JETSON, I WAS ASKED TO RETRIEVE YOU FOR AN EMERGENCY SESSION.

HUH?

WHO ARE YOU?

MY NAME IS COMMANDER KEITH CROSS. THEY CALLED ME IN AS WELL AND ASKED ME TO RELAY THE ORDER TO YOU.

HERE, LET ME HELP YOU OUT OF THAT.

THANK YOU.

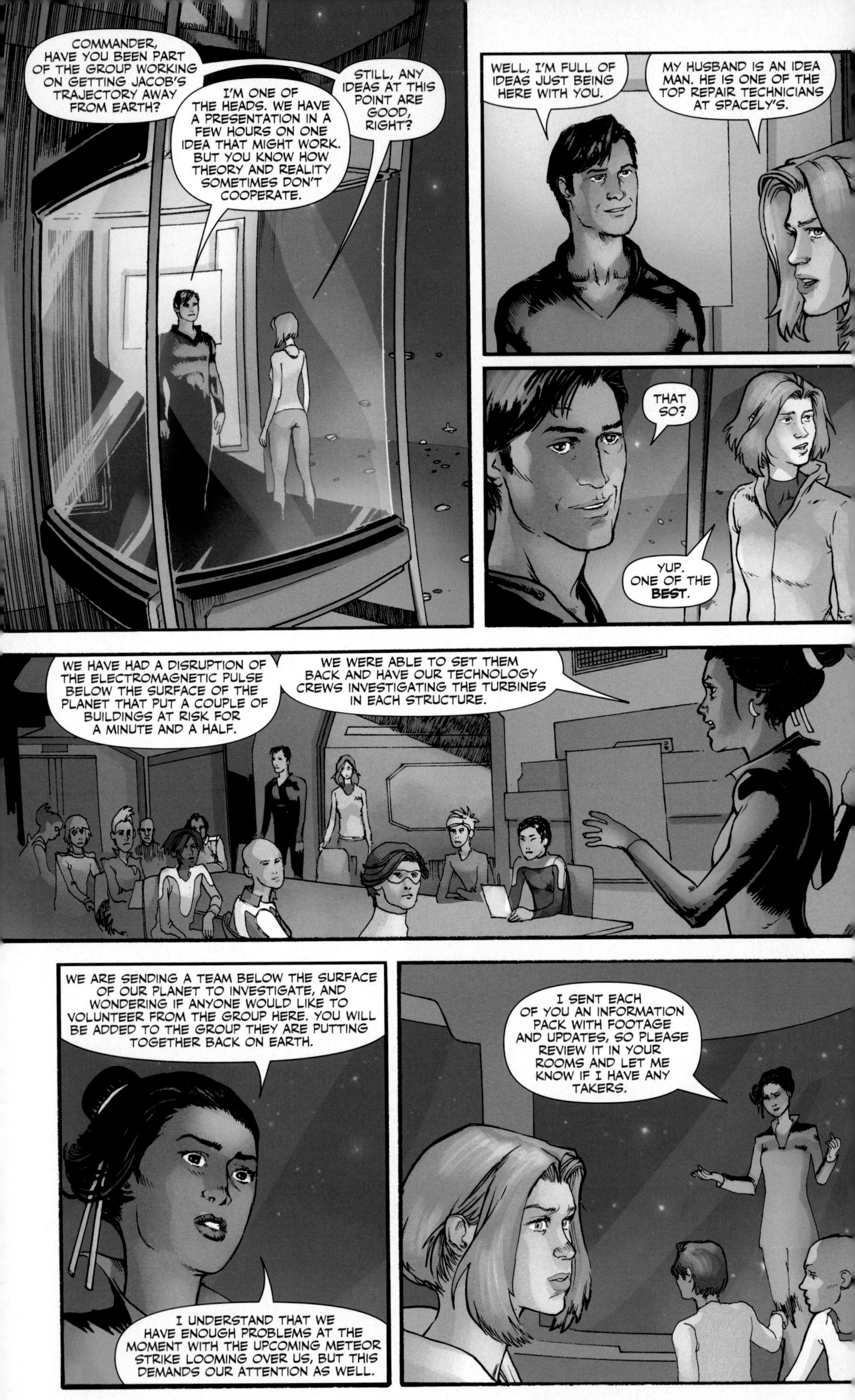

COMMANDER, HAVE YOU BEEN PART OF THE GROUP WORKING ON GETTING JACOB'S TRAJECTORY AWAY FROM EARTH?
I'M ONE OF THE HEADS. WE HAVE A PRESENTATION IN A FEW HOURS ON ONE IDEA THAT MIGHT WORK. BUT YOU KNOW HOW THEORY AND REALITY SOMETIMES DON'T COOPERATE.
STILL, ANY IDEAS AT THIS POINT ARE GOOD, RIGHT?
WELL, I'M FULL OF IDEAS JUST BEING HERE WITH YOU.
MY HUSBAND IS AN IDEA MAN. HE IS ONE OF THE TOP REPAIR TECHNICIANS AT SPACELY'S.
THAT SO?
YUP. ONE OF THE **BEST**.
WE HAVE HAD A DISRUPTION OF THE ELECTROMAGNETIC PULSE BELOW THE SURFACE OF THE PLANET THAT PUT A COUPLE OF BUILDINGS AT RISK FOR A MINUTE AND A HALF.
WE WERE ABLE TO SET THEM BACK AND HAVE OUR TECHNOLOGY CREWS INVESTIGATING THE TURBINES IN EACH STRUCTURE.
WE ARE SENDING A TEAM BELOW THE SURFACE OF OUR PLANET TO INVESTIGATE, AND WONDERING IF ANYONE WOULD LIKE TO VOLUNTEER FROM THE GROUP HERE. YOU WILL BE ADDED TO THE GROUP THEY ARE PUTTING TOGETHER BACK ON EARTH.
I UNDERSTAND THAT WE HAVE ENOUGH PROBLEMS AT THE MOMENT WITH THE UPCOMING METEOR STRIKE LOOMING OVER US, BUT THIS DEMANDS OUR ATTENTION AS WELL.
I SENT EACH OF YOU AN INFORMATION PACK WITH FOOTAGE AND UPDATES, SO PLEASE REVIEW IT IN YOUR ROOMS AND LET ME KNOW IF I HAVE ANY TAKERS.

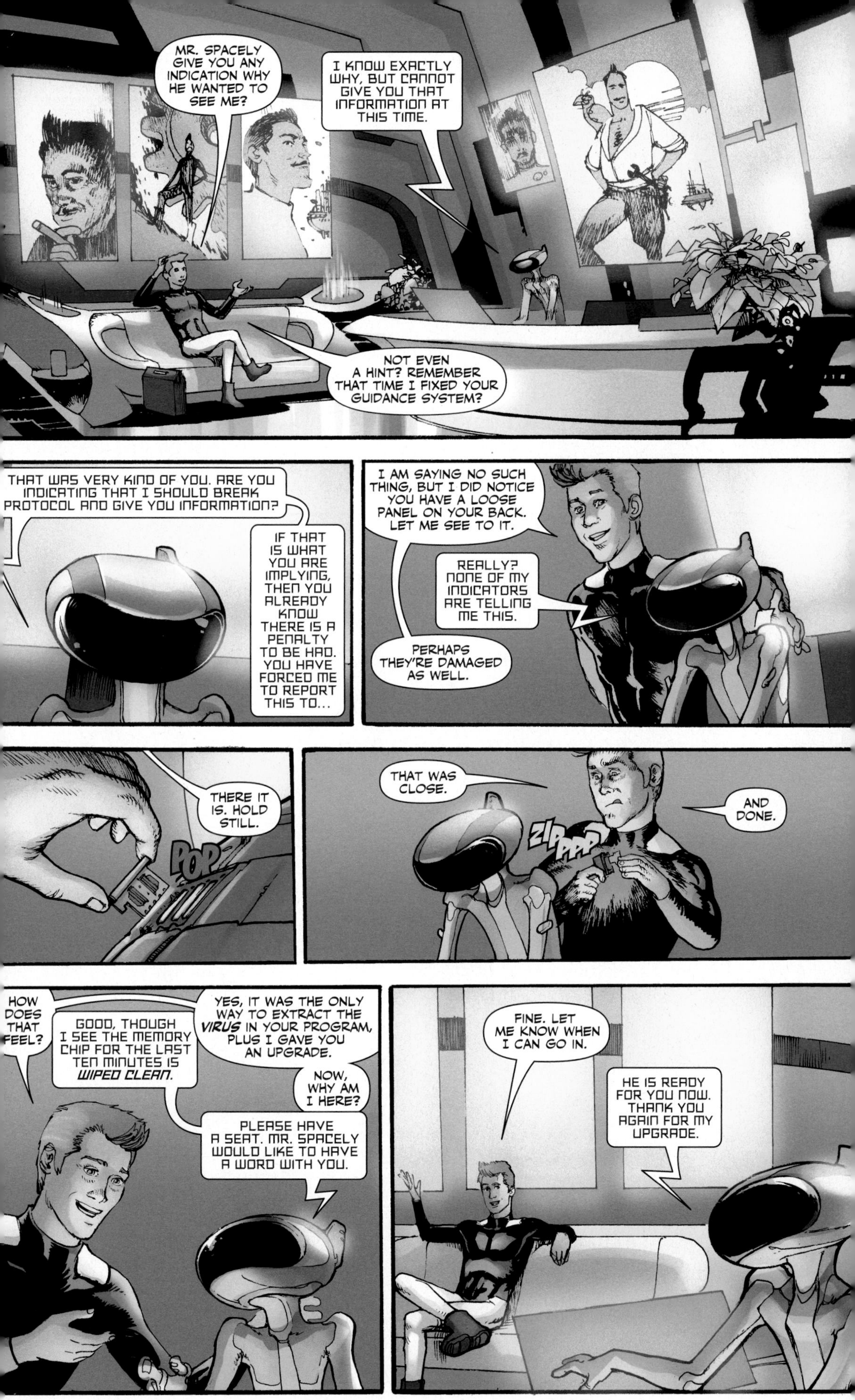
MR. SPACELY GIVE YOU ANY INDICATION WHY HE WANTED TO SEE ME?
I KNOW EXACTLY WHY, BUT CANNOT GIVE YOU THAT INFORMATION AT THIS TIME.
NOT EVEN A HINT? REMEMBER THAT TIME I FIXED YOUR GUIDANCE SYSTEM?
THAT WAS VERY KIND OF YOU. ARE YOU INDICATING THAT I SHOULD BREAK PROTOCOL AND GIVE YOU INFORMATION?
IF THAT IS WHAT YOU ARE IMPLYING, THEN YOU ALREADY KNOW THERE IS A PENALTY TO BE HAD. YOU HAVE FORCED ME TO REPORT THIS TO...
I AM SAYING NO SUCH THING, BUT I DID NOTICE YOU HAVE A LOOSE PANEL ON YOUR BACK. LET ME SEE TO IT.
REALLY? NONE OF MY INDICATORS ARE TELLING ME THIS.
PERHAPS THEY'RE DAMAGED AS WELL.
THERE IT IS. HOLD STILL.
POP
THAT WAS CLOSE.
ZIPPPP
AND DONE.
HOW DOES THAT FEEL?
GOOD, THOUGH I SEE THE MEMORY CHIP FOR THE LAST TEN MINUTES IS WIPED CLEAN.
YES, IT WAS THE ONLY WAY TO EXTRACT THE VIRUS IN YOUR PROGRAM, PLUS I GAVE YOU AN UPGRADE.
NOW, WHY AM I HERE?
PLEASE HAVE A SEAT. MR. SPACELY WOULD LIKE TO HAVE A WORD WITH YOU.
FINE. LET ME KNOW WHEN I CAN GO IN.
HE IS READY FOR YOU NOW. THANK YOU AGAIN FOR MY UPGRADE.

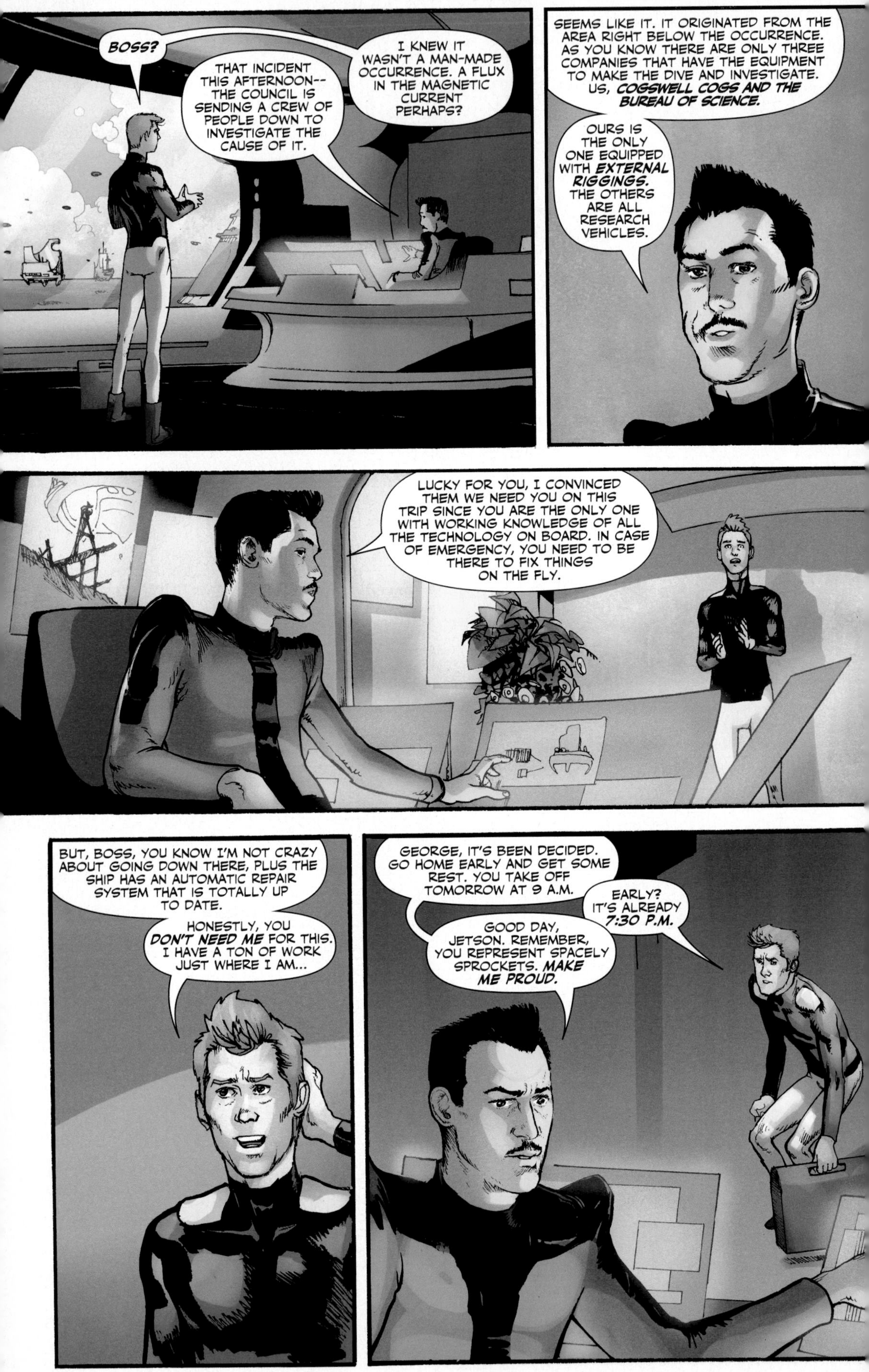
BOSS?
THAT INCIDENT THIS AFTERNOON-- THE COUNCIL IS SENDING A CREW OF PEOPLE DOWN TO INVESTIGATE THE CAUSE OF IT.
I KNEW IT WASN'T A MAN-MADE OCCURRENCE. A FLUX IN THE MAGNETIC CURRENT PERHAPS?
SEEMS LIKE IT. IT ORIGINATED FROM THE AREA RIGHT BELOW THE OCCURRENCE. AS YOU KNOW THERE ARE ONLY THREE COMPANIES THAT HAVE THE EQUIPMENT TO MAKE THE DIVE AND INVESTIGATE. US, COGSWELL COGS AND THE BUREAU OF SCIENCE.
OURS IS THE ONLY ONE EQUIPPED WITH EXTERNAL RIGGINGS. THE OTHERS ARE ALL RESEARCH VEHICLES.
LUCKY FOR YOU, I CONVINCED THEM WE NEED YOU ON THIS TRIP SINCE YOU ARE THE ONLY ONE WITH WORKING KNOWLEDGE OF ALL THE TECHNOLOGY ON BOARD. IN CASE OF EMERGENCY, YOU NEED TO BE THERE TO FIX THINGS ON THE FLY.
BUT, BOSS, YOU KNOW I'M NOT CRAZY ABOUT GOING DOWN THERE, PLUS THE SHIP HAS AN AUTOMATIC REPAIR SYSTEM THAT IS TOTALLY UP TO DATE.
HONESTLY, YOU DON'T NEED ME FOR THIS. I HAVE A TON OF WORK JUST WHERE I AM...
GEORGE, IT'S BEEN DECIDED. GO HOME EARLY AND GET SOME REST. YOU TAKE OFF TOMORROW AT 9 A.M.
EARLY? IT'S ALREADY 7:30 P.M.
GOOD DAY, JETSON. REMEMBER, YOU REPRESENT SPACELY SPROCKETS. MAKE ME PROUD.

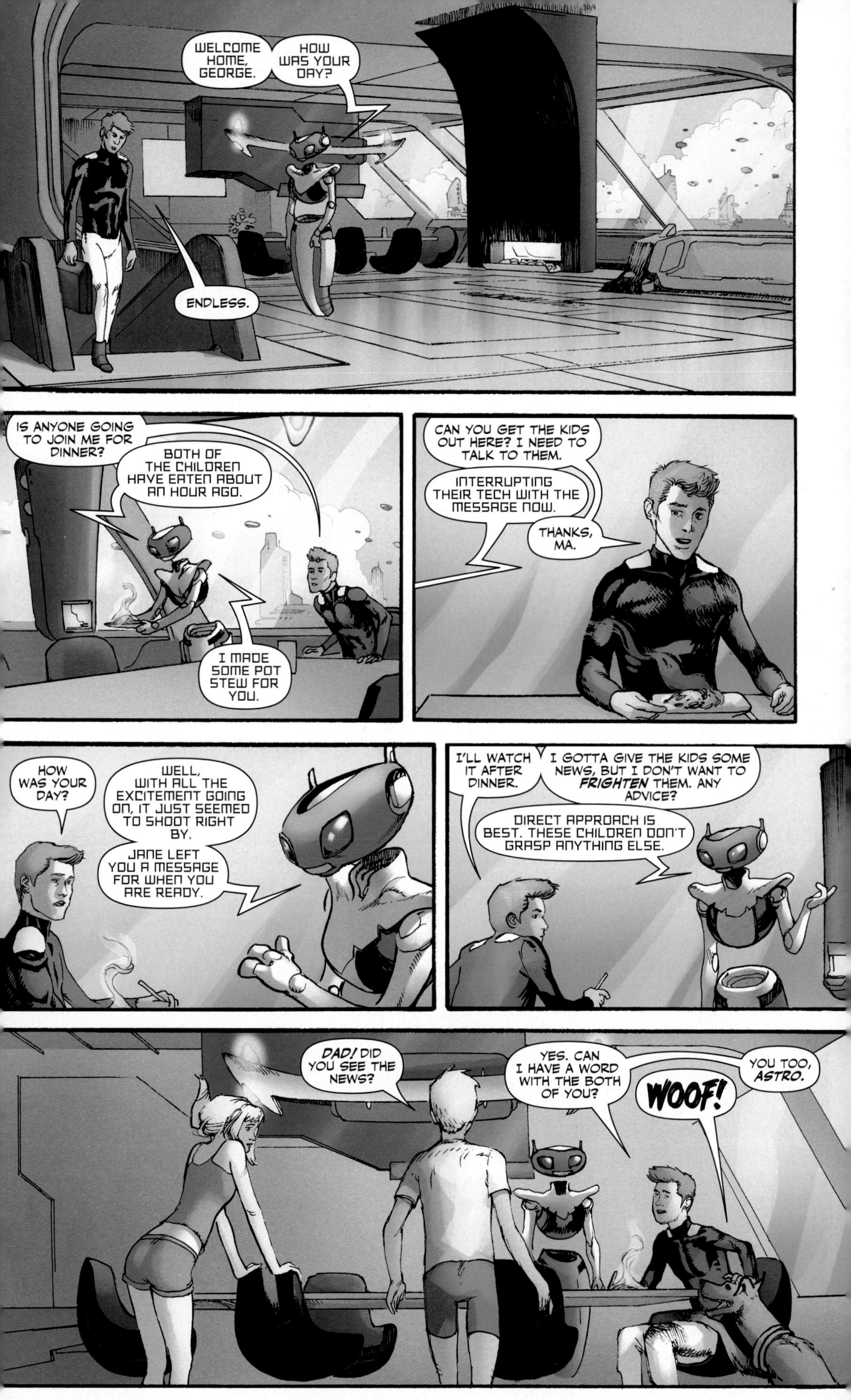

WELCOME HOME, GEORGE.
HOW WAS YOUR DAY?
ENDLESS.
IS ANYONE GOING TO JOIN ME FOR DINNER?
BOTH OF THE CHILDREN HAVE EATEN ABOUT AN HOUR AGO.
I MADE SOME POT STEW FOR YOU.
CAN YOU GET THE KIDS OUT HERE? I NEED TO TALK TO THEM.
INTERRUPTING THEIR TECH WITH THE MESSAGE NOW.
THANKS, MA.
HOW WAS YOUR DAY?
WELL, WITH ALL THE EXCITEMENT GOING ON, IT JUST SEEMED TO SHOOT RIGHT BY.
JANE LEFT YOU A MESSAGE FOR WHEN YOU ARE READY.
I'LL WATCH IT AFTER DINNER.
I GOTTA GIVE THE KIDS SOME NEWS, BUT I DON'T WANT TO *FRIGHTEN* THEM. ANY ADVICE?
DIRECT APPROACH IS BEST. THESE CHILDREN DON'T GRASP ANYTHING ELSE.
DAD! DID YOU SEE THE NEWS?
YES. CAN I HAVE A WORD WITH THE BOTH OF YOU?
WOOF!
YOU TOO, *ASTRO.*

YOUR DEAR FATHER HAS BEEN CHOSEN TO BE PART OF A DANGEROUS MISSION TO INVESTIGATE THE CAUSE OF TODAY'S DISTURBANCE.
I WILL BE GOING DOWN BELOW THE SURFACE OF THE WATER TOMORROW MORNING.
WHAT TIME DOES THIS HAPPEN? I HOPE BEFORE MY FIRST PERIOD TOMORROW. I WOULD LIKE TO BE THERE--
THE STRUCTURES BELOW ARE DECOMPOSING AT SUCH AN ALARMING RATE THAT THEY ARE MUCH MORE FRAGILE THAN ANYONE EXPECTED.
YOU THINK IT'S SOME KIND OF ANCIENT SENTIENT TECHNOLOGY COMING BACK TO EXISTENCE?
WHAT YOUR FATHER IS TRYING TO SAY IS, THIS IS A DANGEROUS OPERATION, ESPECIALLY IF WHAT DID THIS TODAY SOMEHOW AFFECTS THE SHIP THEY ARE TAKING DOWN THERE.
I--I DIDN'T EVEN THINK OF THAT.
GRANDMA IS RIGHT. IF SOMETHING HAPPENS TO THE SHIELDS, YOU, THE SHIP AND EVERY-ONE INSIDE WILL BE DISINTEGRATED.
DAD, YOUR BIRTHDAY IS IN A FEW DAYS. MAYBE YOU SHOULD WAIT? OR SEE IF THEY CAN GET SOMEONE ELSE TO DO IT?

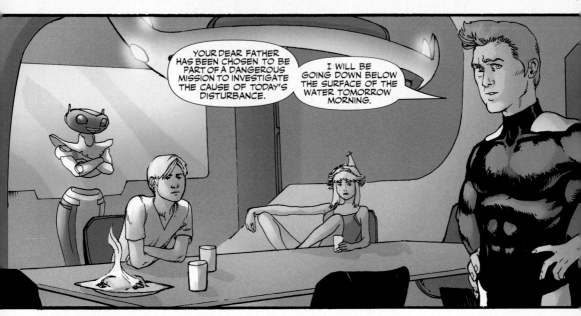

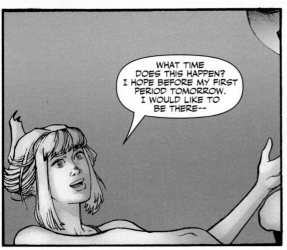

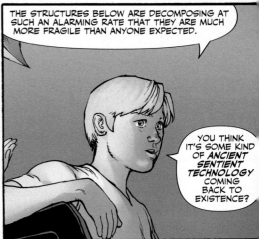

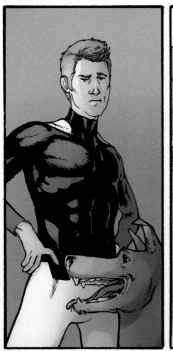

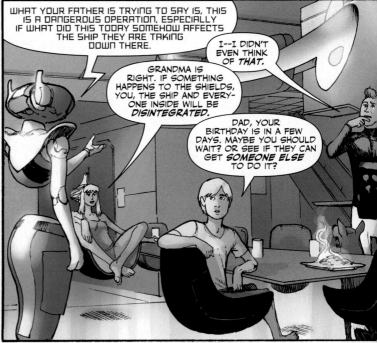

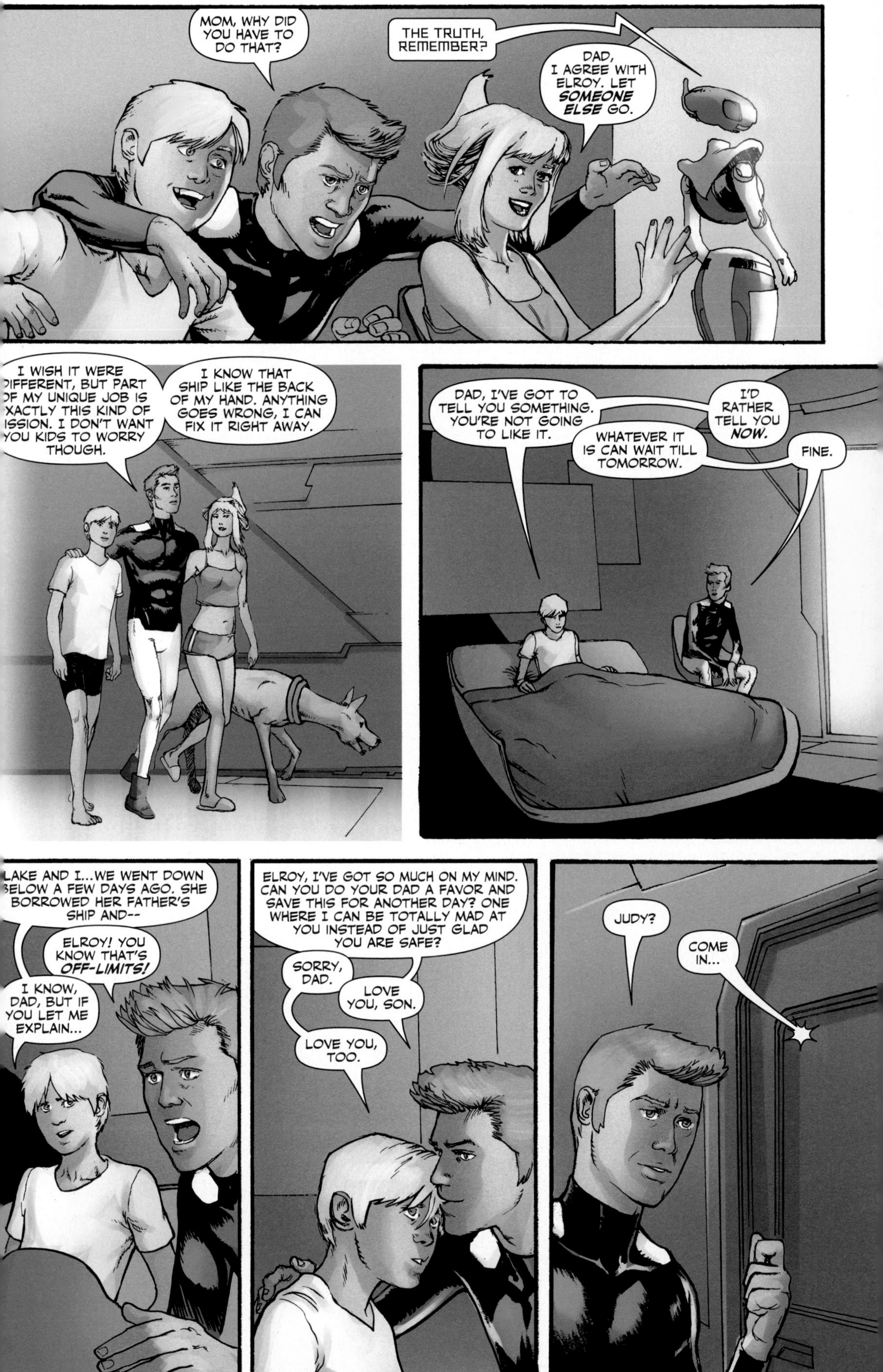
MOM, WHY DID YOU HAVE TO DO THAT?
THE TRUTH, REMEMBER?
DAD, I AGREE WITH ELROY. LET SOMEONE ELSE GO.
I WISH IT WERE DIFFERENT, BUT PART OF MY UNIQUE JOB IS EXACTLY THIS KIND OF MISSION. I DON'T WANT YOU KIDS TO WORRY THOUGH.
I KNOW THAT SHIP LIKE THE BACK OF MY HAND. ANYTHING GOES WRONG, I CAN FIX IT RIGHT AWAY.
DAD, I'VE GOT TO TELL YOU SOMETHING. YOU'RE NOT GOING TO LIKE IT.
WHATEVER IT IS CAN WAIT TILL TOMORROW.
I'D RATHER TELL YOU NOW.
FINE.
LAKE AND I...WE WENT DOWN BELOW A FEW DAYS AGO. SHE BORROWED HER FATHER'S SHIP AND--
ELROY! YOU KNOW THAT'S OFF-LIMITS!
I KNOW, DAD, BUT IF YOU LET ME EXPLAIN...
ELROY, I'VE GOT SO MUCH ON MY MIND. CAN YOU DO YOUR DAD A FAVOR AND SAVE THIS FOR ANOTHER DAY? ONE WHERE I CAN BE TOTALLY MAD AT YOU INSTEAD OF JUST GLAD YOU ARE SAFE?
SORRY, DAD.
LOVE YOU, SON.
LOVE YOU, TOO.
JUDY?
COME IN...

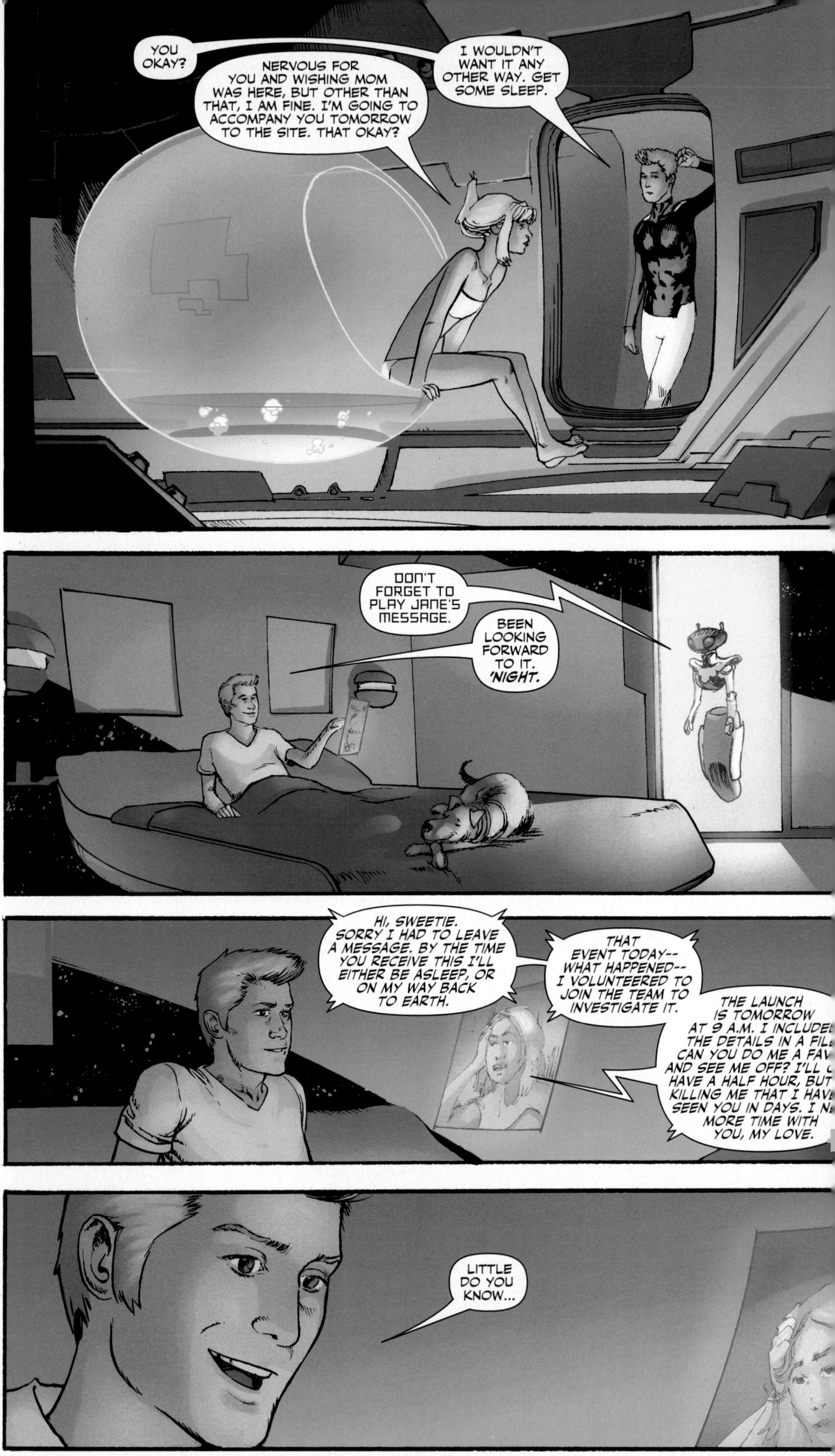
YOU OKAY?
NERVOUS FOR YOU AND WISHING MOM WAS HERE, BUT OTHER THAN THAT, I AM FINE. I'M GOING TO ACCOMPANY YOU TOMORROW TO THE SITE. THAT OKAY?
I WOULDN'T WANT IT ANY OTHER WAY. GET SOME SLEEP.
DON'T FORGET TO PLAY JANE'S MESSAGE.
BEEN LOOKING FORWARD TO IT. 'NIGHT.
HI, SWEETIE. SORRY I HAD TO LEAVE A MESSAGE. BY THE TIME YOU RECEIVE THIS I'LL EITHER BE ASLEEP, OR ON MY WAY BACK TO EARTH.
THAT EVENT TODAY-- WHAT HAPPENED-- I VOLUNTEERED TO JOIN THE TEAM TO INVESTIGATE IT.
THE LAUNCH IS TOMORROW AT 9 A.M. I THE DETAILS IN A CAN YOU DO ME A AND SEE ME OFF? HAVE A HALF HOUR, KILLING ME THAT I SEEN YOU IN DAYS. MORE TIME WITH YOU, MY LOVE.
LITTLE DO YOU KNOW...

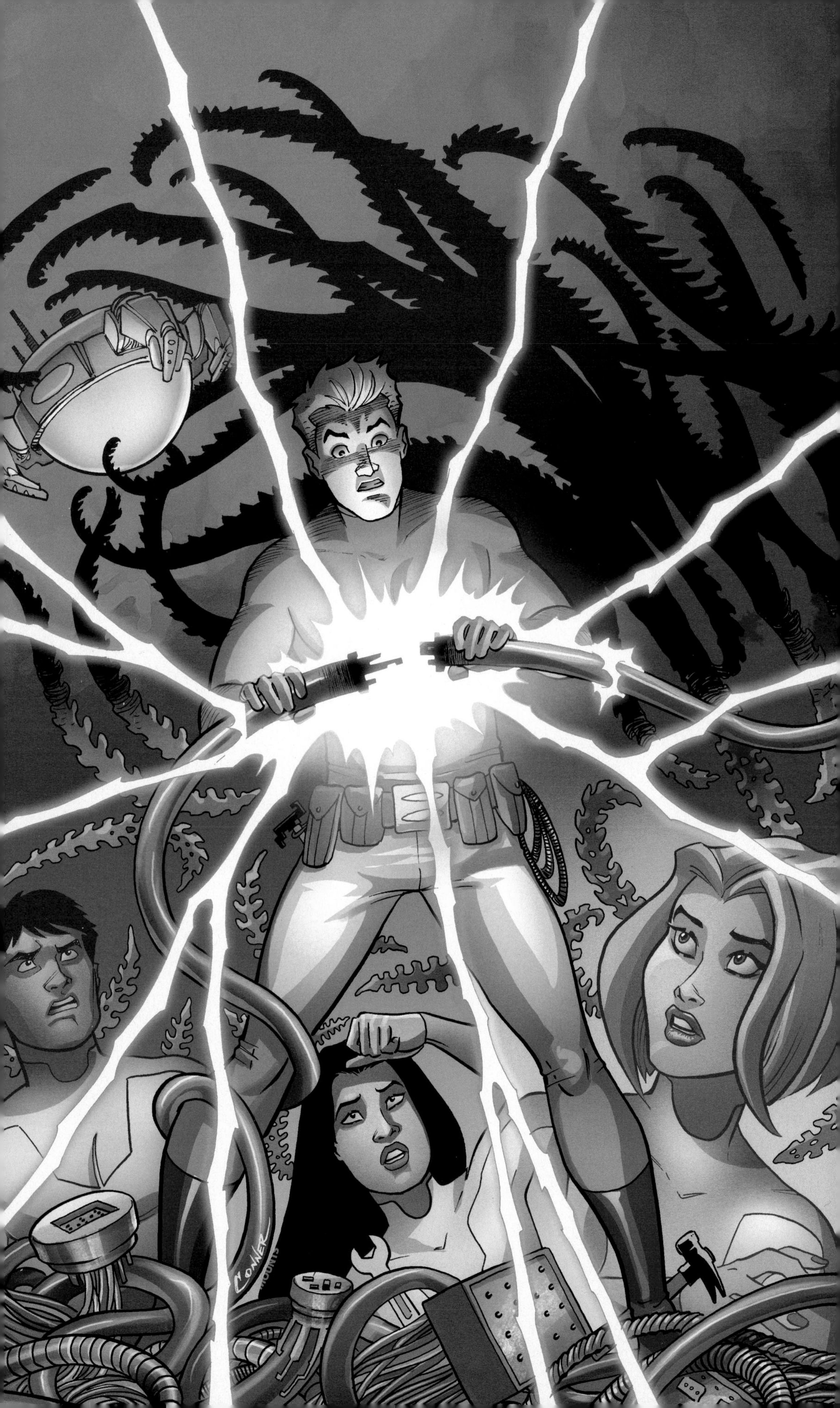
CONNER

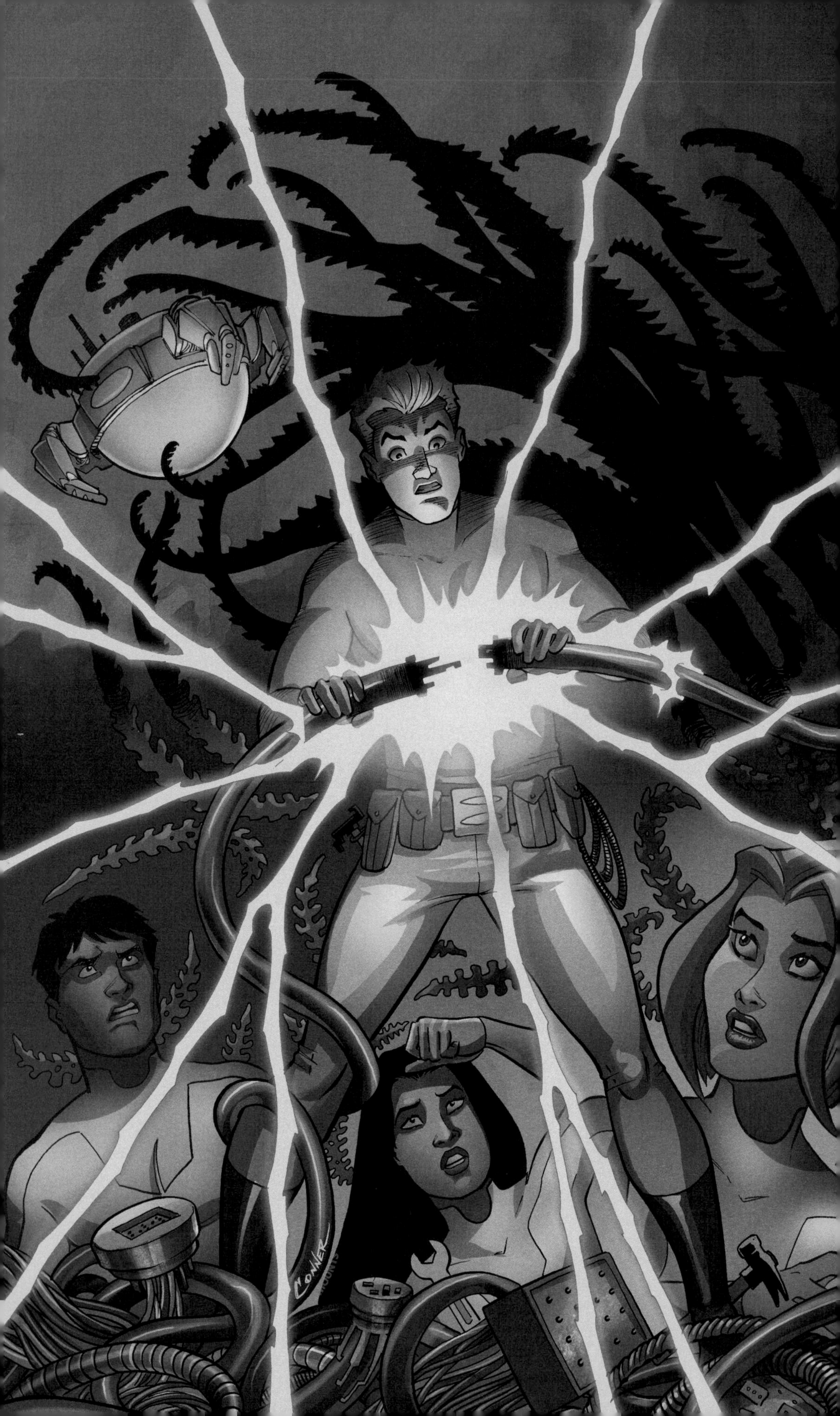
CONNER
MOUNTS

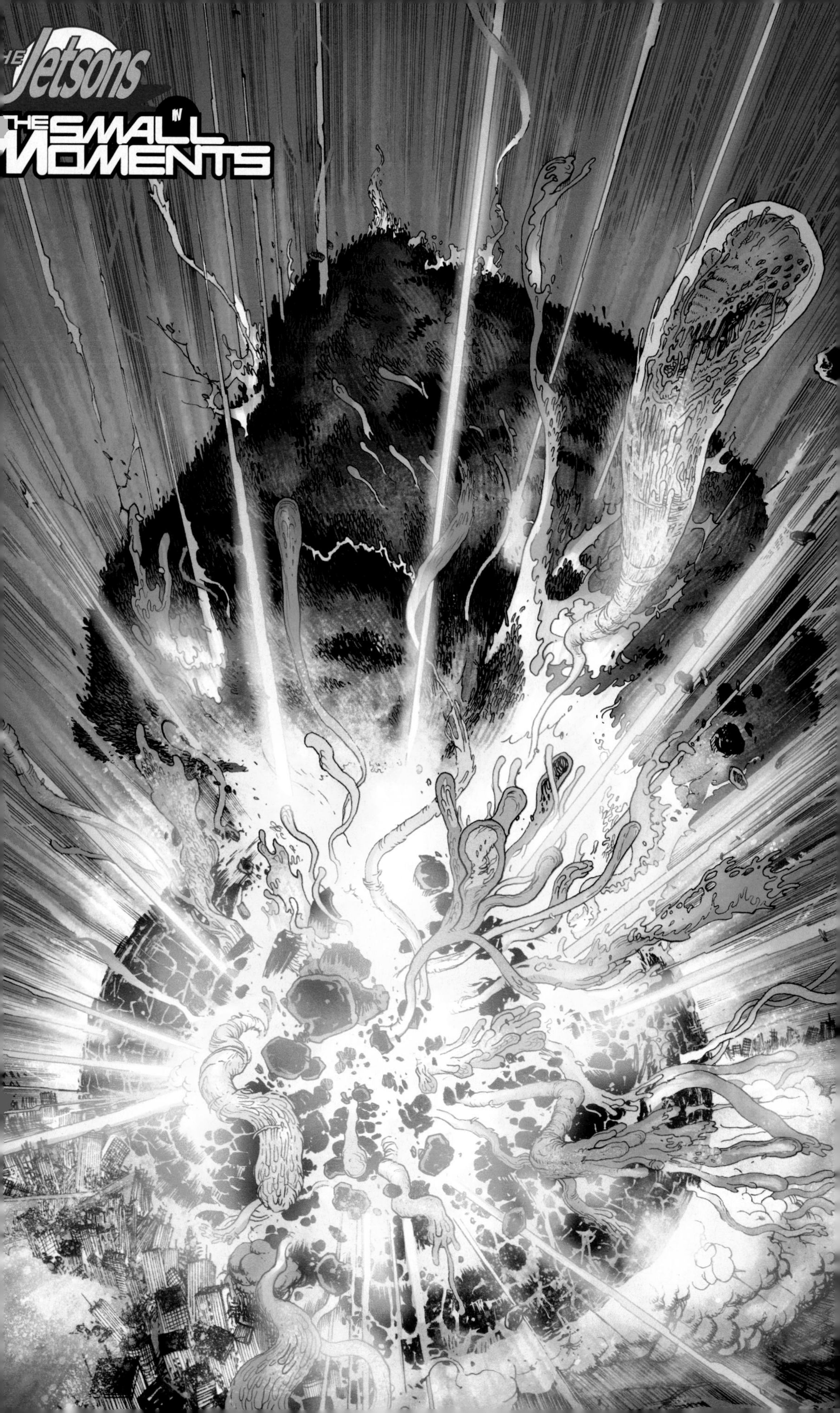
The Jetsons
IN
THE SMALL MOMENTS

HUH?

I SEE YOU. I'M COMING UP.

LAKE COGSWELL! IS THAT ONE OF MY BOOKS?

DAD, YOU ALREADY KNOW THE ANSWER TO THAT QUESTION, SO WHY BOTHER ASKING?

YOU DO KNOW THAT BOOK IS PRICELESS, CORRECT?

ANOTHER QUESTION YOU KNOW THE ANSWER TO. YOUR POINT?

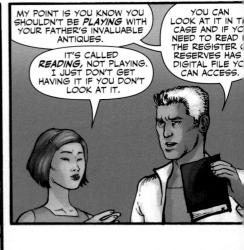

MY POINT IS YOU KNOW YOU SHOULDN'T BE PLAYING WITH YOUR FATHER'S INVALUABLE ANTIQUES.

IT'S CALLED READING, NOT PLAYING. I JUST DON'T GET HAVING IT IF YOU DON'T LOOK AT IT.

YOU CAN LOOK AT IT IN T CASE AND IF YO NEED TO READ THE REGISTER C RESERVES HAS DIGITAL FILE YO CAN ACCESS.

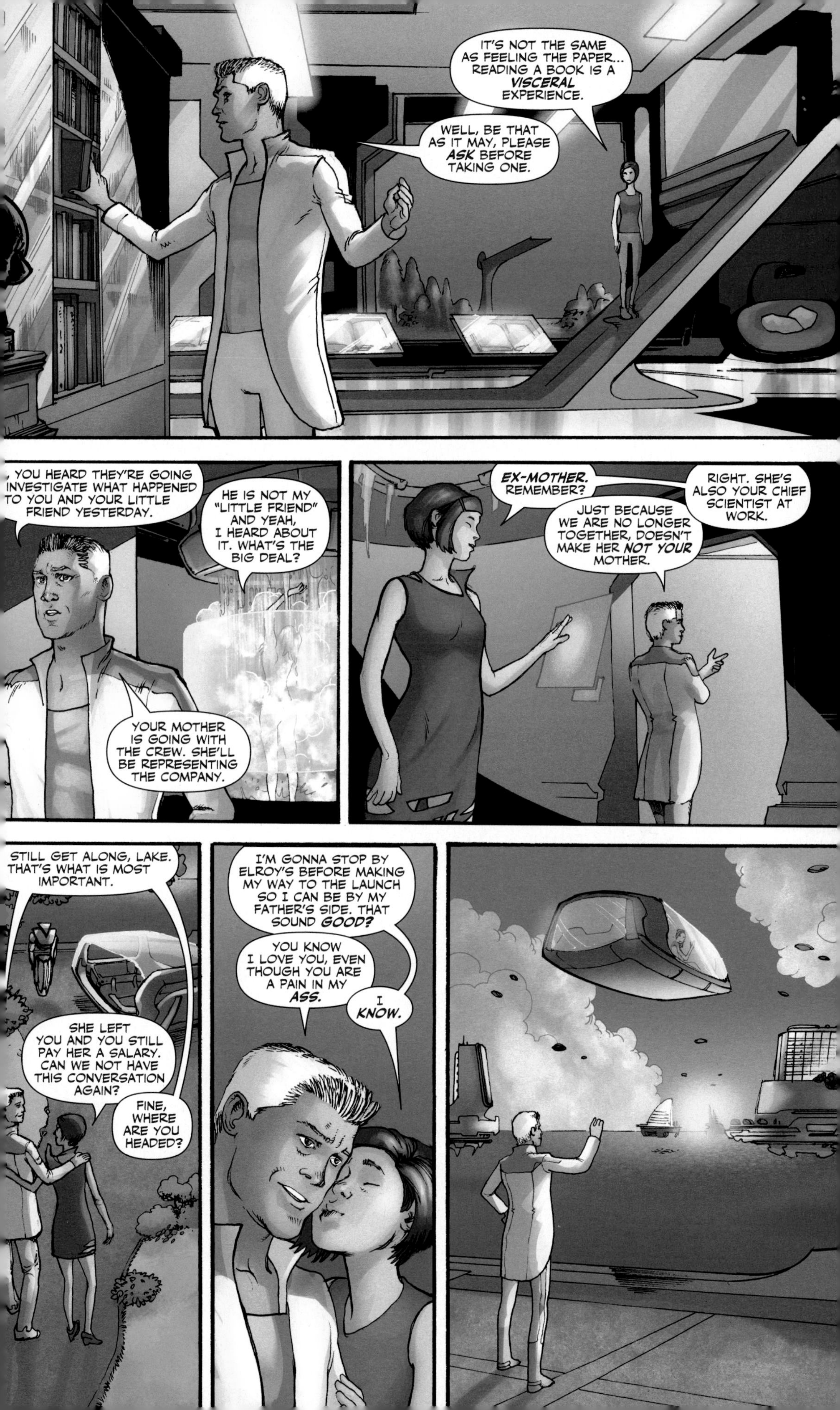
IT'S NOT THE SAME AS FEELING THE PAPER... READING A BOOK IS A VISCERAL EXPERIENCE.
WELL, BE THAT AS IT MAY, PLEASE ASK BEFORE TAKING ONE.
, YOU HEARD THEY'RE GOING INVESTIGATE WHAT HAPPENED TO YOU AND YOUR LITTLE FRIEND YESTERDAY.
HE IS NOT MY "LITTLE FRIEND" AND YEAH, I HEARD ABOUT IT. WHAT'S THE BIG DEAL?
YOUR MOTHER IS GOING WITH THE CREW. SHE'LL BE REPRESENTING THE COMPANY.
EX-MOTHER. REMEMBER?
RIGHT. SHE'S ALSO YOUR CHIEF SCIENTIST AT WORK.
JUST BECAUSE WE ARE NO LONGER TOGETHER, DOESN'T MAKE HER NOT YOUR MOTHER.
STILL GET ALONG, LAKE. THAT'S WHAT IS MOST IMPORTANT.
SHE LEFT YOU AND YOU STILL PAY HER A SALARY. CAN WE NOT HAVE THIS CONVERSATION AGAIN?
FINE, WHERE ARE YOU HEADED?
I'M GONNA STOP BY ELROY'S BEFORE MAKING MY WAY TO THE LAUNCH SO I CAN BE BY MY FATHER'S SIDE. THAT SOUND GOOD?
YOU KNOW I LOVE YOU, EVEN THOUGH YOU ARE A PAIN IN MY ASS.
I KNOW.

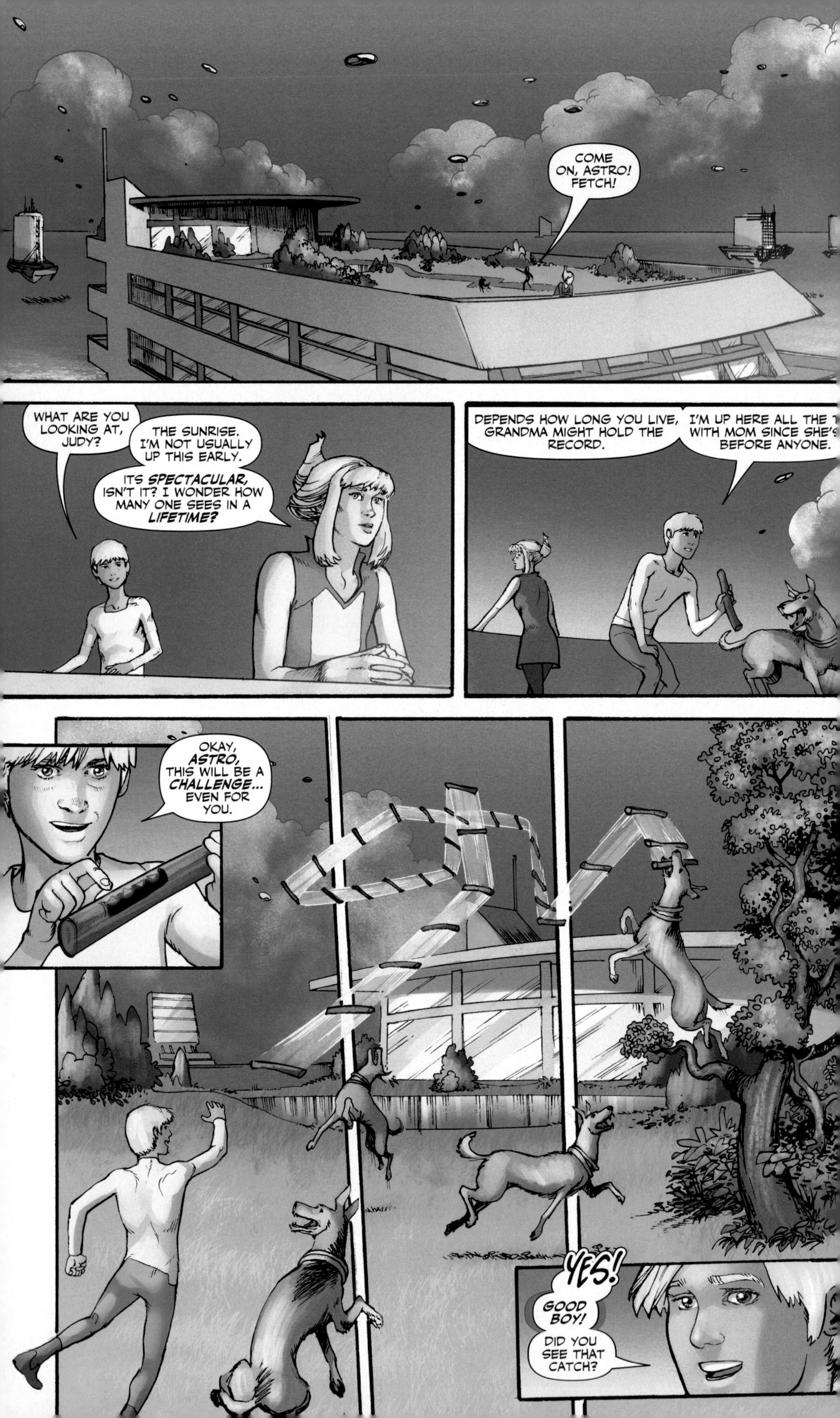
COME ON, ASTRO! FETCH!
WHAT ARE YOU LOOKING AT, JUDY?
THE SUNRISE. I'M NOT USUALLY UP THIS EARLY.
ITS SPECTACULAR, ISN'T IT? I WONDER HOW MANY ONE SEES IN A LIFETIME?
DEPENDS HOW LONG YOU LIVE, GRANDMA MIGHT HOLD THE RECORD.
I'M UP HERE ALL THE T WITH MOM SINCE SHE'S BEFORE ANYONE.
OKAY, ASTRO, THIS WILL BE A CHALLENGE... EVEN FOR YOU.
YES!
GOOD BOY!
DID YOU SEE THAT CATCH?

OH! YOUR *GIRLFRIEND'S* COMING IN. TO VISIT. DID YOU INVITE HER TO DAD'S BIRTHDAY FRIDAY?

WE'RE JUST FRIENDS, AND YEAH, I ALREADY DID.

ABOUT THAT... I TOLD DAD I WENT *BELOW* LAST NIGHT.

AND YOU'RE STILL *ALIVE?*

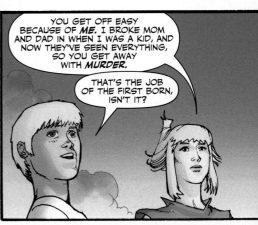

YOU GET OFF EASY BECAUSE OF *ME.* I BROKE MOM AND DAD IN WHEN I WAS A KID, AND NOW THEY'VE SEEN EVERYTHING, SO YOU GET AWAY WITH *MURDER.*

THAT'S THE JOB OF THE FIRST BORN, ISN'T IT?

I GUESS. SHE COMING WITH US THIS MORNING TO SEE DAD OFF?

HER DAD WILL BE THERE TOO, *REMEMBER?*

SHE'S *YOUR* GIRLFRIEND. JUST SAY IT.

IS NOT.

HI, LOVER. *MISS ME?*

WHA--

HA HA.

HAR-HAR. Y FUNNY. IT'S O EARLY FOR . I NEED MY REAKFAST.

OME ON, ON, I WAS DDING.

ELROY, DON'T BE SO *SENSITIVE!*

THAT'S ACTUALLY EXACTLY *WHY* I LIKE YOUR BROTHER.

YEAH. HE'S GOT A GOOD HEART FOR SURE. YOU GONNA COME WITH US TO THE LAUNCH OR MEET US THERE?

I THINK IT'S BEST I JUST MEET YOU.

I'LL LET ELROY KNOW.

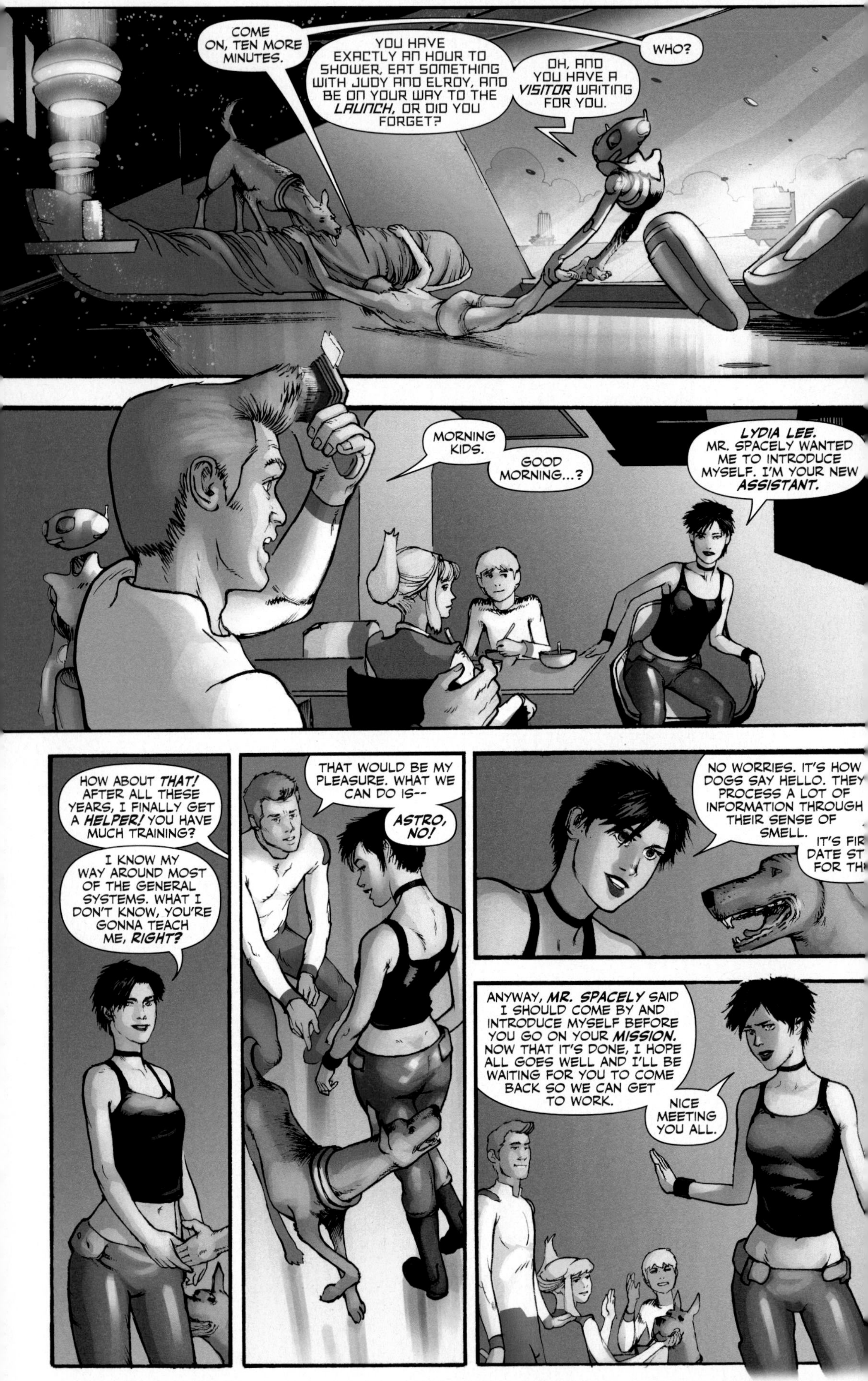
COME ON, TEN MORE MINUTES.
YOU HAVE EXACTLY AN HOUR TO SHOWER, EAT SOMETHING WITH JUDY AND ELROY, AND BE ON YOUR WAY TO THE LAUNCH, OR DID YOU FORGET?
OH, AND YOU HAVE A VISITOR WAITING FOR YOU.
WHO?
MORNING KIDS.
GOOD MORNING...?
LYDIA LEE. MR. SPACELY WANTED ME TO INTRODUCE MYSELF. I'M YOUR NEW ASSISTANT.
HOW ABOUT THAT! AFTER ALL THESE YEARS, I FINALLY GET A HELPER! YOU HAVE MUCH TRAINING?
I KNOW MY WAY AROUND MOST OF THE GENERAL SYSTEMS. WHAT I DON'T KNOW, YOU'RE GONNA TEACH ME, RIGHT?
THAT WOULD BE MY PLEASURE. WHAT WE CAN DO IS--
ASTRO, NO!
NO WORRIES. IT'S HOW DOGS SAY HELLO. THEY PROCESS A LOT OF INFORMATION THROUGH THEIR SENSE OF SMELL.
IT'S FIR
DATE ST
FOR TH
ANYWAY, MR. SPACELY SAID I SHOULD COME BY AND INTRODUCE MYSELF BEFORE YOU GO ON YOUR MISSION. NOW THAT IT'S DONE, I HOPE ALL GOES WELL AND I'LL BE WAITING FOR YOU TO COME BACK SO WE CAN GET TO WORK.
NICE MEETING YOU ALL.

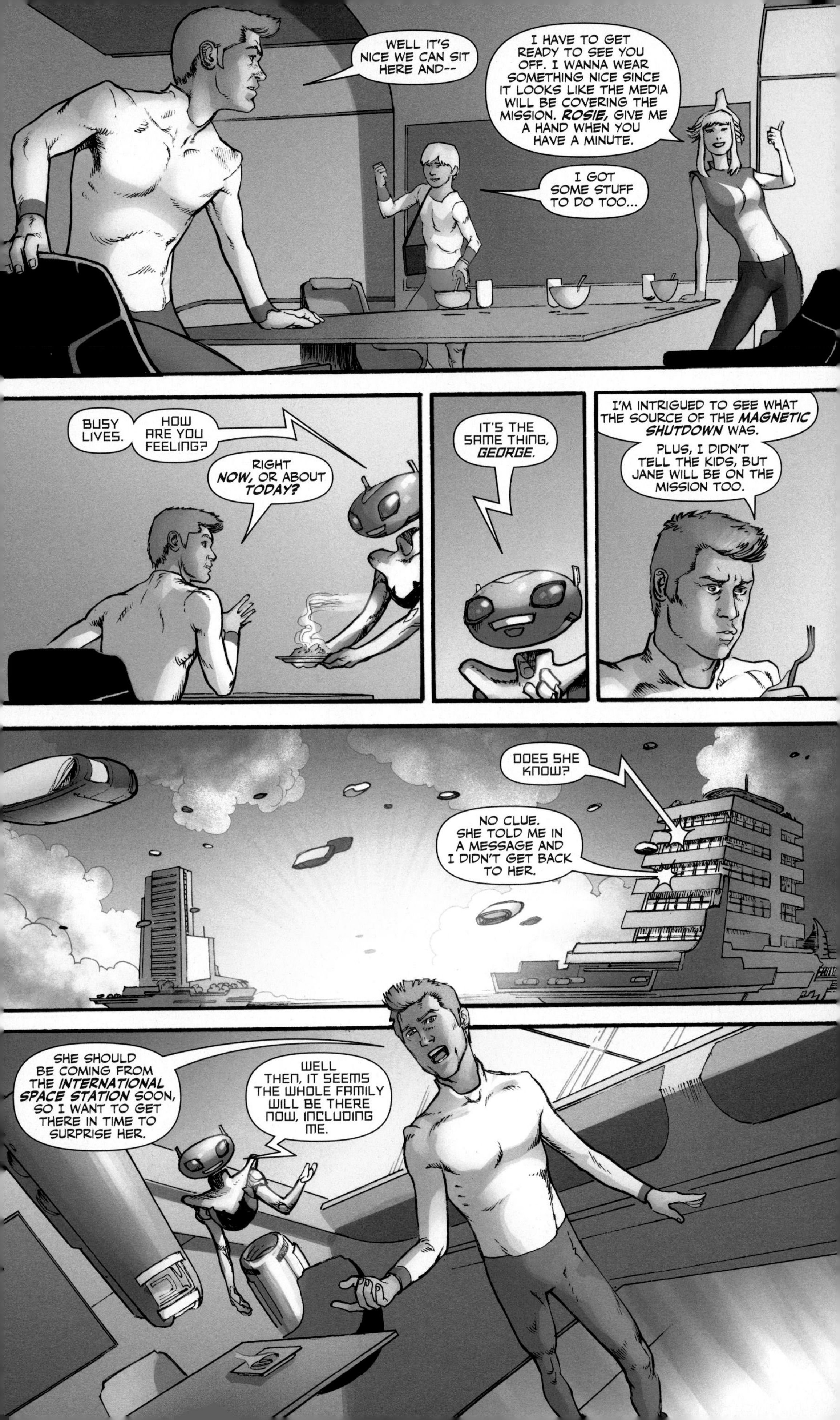
WELL IT'S NICE WE CAN SIT HERE AND--
I HAVE TO GET READY TO SEE YOU OFF. I WANNA WEAR SOMETHING NICE SINCE IT LOOKS LIKE THE MEDIA WILL BE COVERING THE MISSION. ROSIE, GIVE ME A HAND WHEN YOU HAVE A MINUTE.
I GOT SOME STUFF TO DO TOO...
BUSY LIVES.
HOW ARE YOU FEELING?
RIGHT NOW, OR ABOUT TODAY?
IT'S THE SAME THING, GEORGE.
I'M INTRIGUED TO SEE WHAT THE SOURCE OF THE MAGNETIC SHUTDOWN WAS.
PLUS, I DIDN'T TELL THE KIDS, BUT JANE WILL BE ON THE MISSION TOO.
DOES SHE KNOW?
NO CLUE. SHE TOLD ME IN A MESSAGE AND I DIDN'T GET BACK TO HER.
SHE SHOULD BE COMING FROM THE INTERNATIONAL SPACE STATION SOON, SO I WANT TO GET THERE IN TIME TO SURPRISE HER.
WELL THEN, IT SEEMS THE WHOLE FAMILY WILL BE THERE NOW, INCLUDING ME.

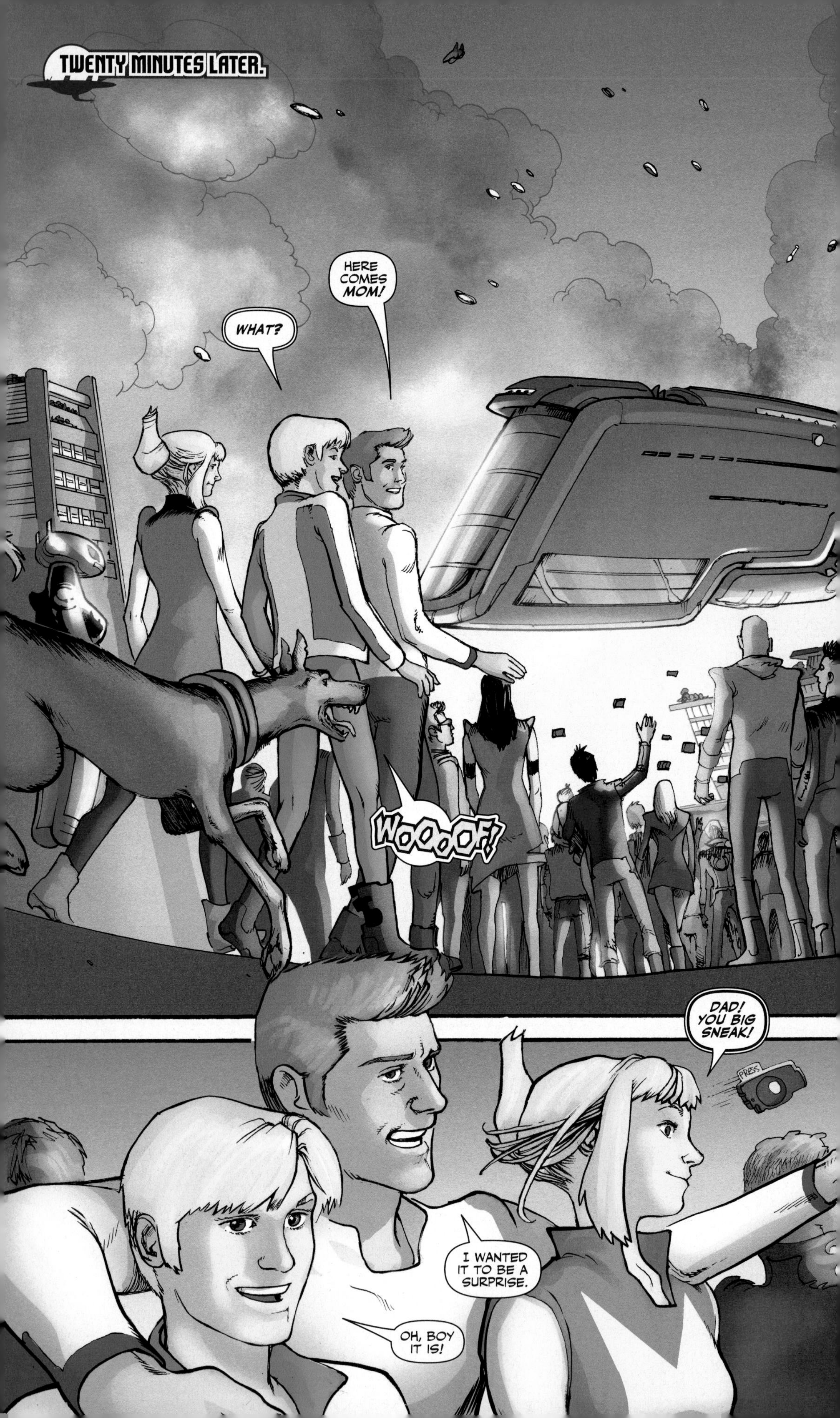
TWENTY MINUTES LATER.
WHAT?
HERE COMES MOM!
WOOOOF!
DAD! YOU BIG SNEAK!
PRESS
I WANTED IT TO BE A SURPRISE.
OH, BOY IT IS!

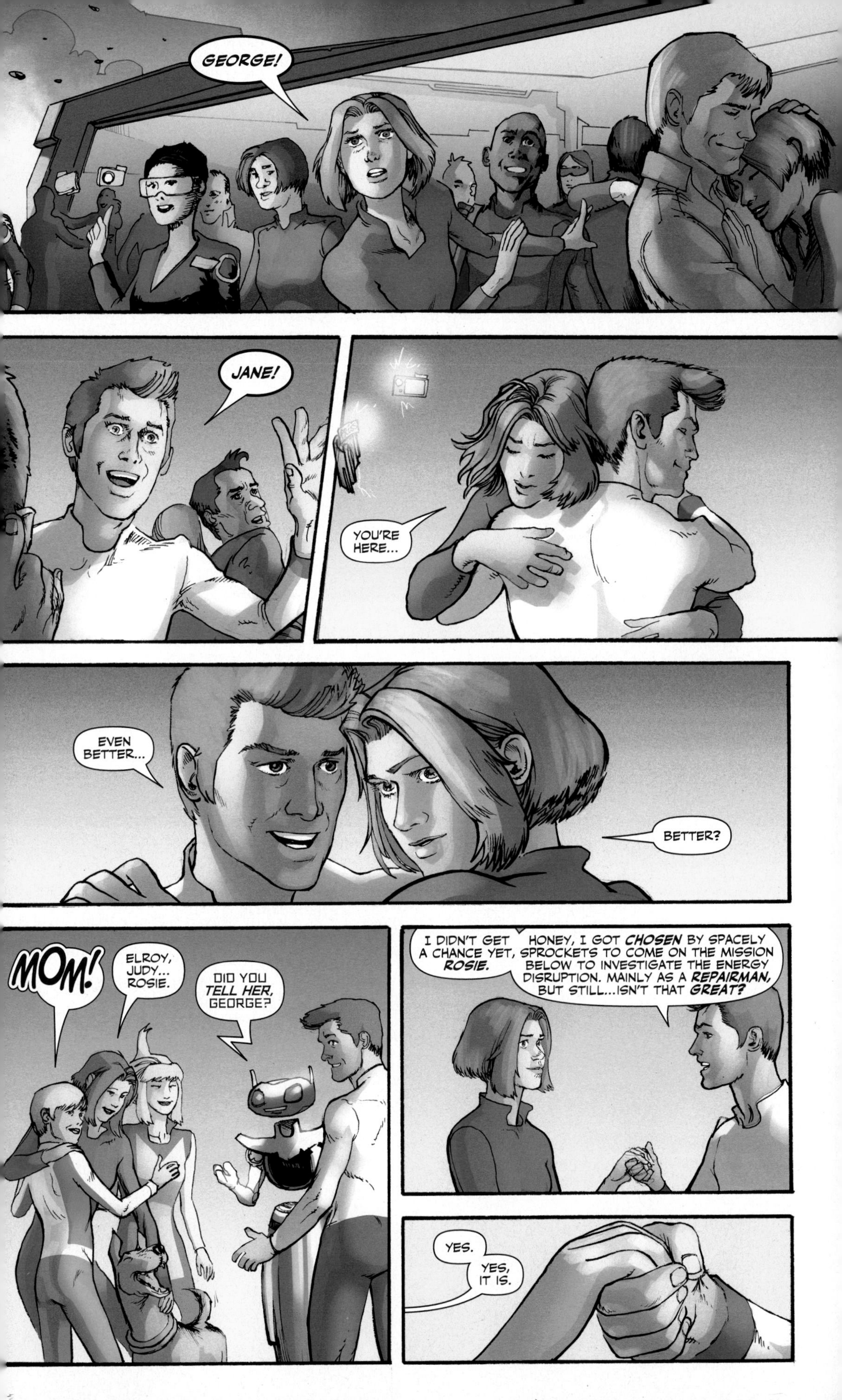
GEORGE!
JANE!
YOU'RE HERE...
EVEN BETTER...
BETTER?
MOM!
ELROY, JUDY... ROSIE.
DID YOU TELL HER, GEORGE?
I DIDN'T GET A CHANCE YET, ROSIE.
HONEY, I GOT CHOSEN BY SPACELY SPROCKETS TO COME ON THE MISSION BELOW TO INVESTIGATE THE ENERGY DISRUPTION. MAINLY AS A REPAIRMAN, BUT STILL...ISN'T THAT GREAT?
YES.
YES, IT IS.

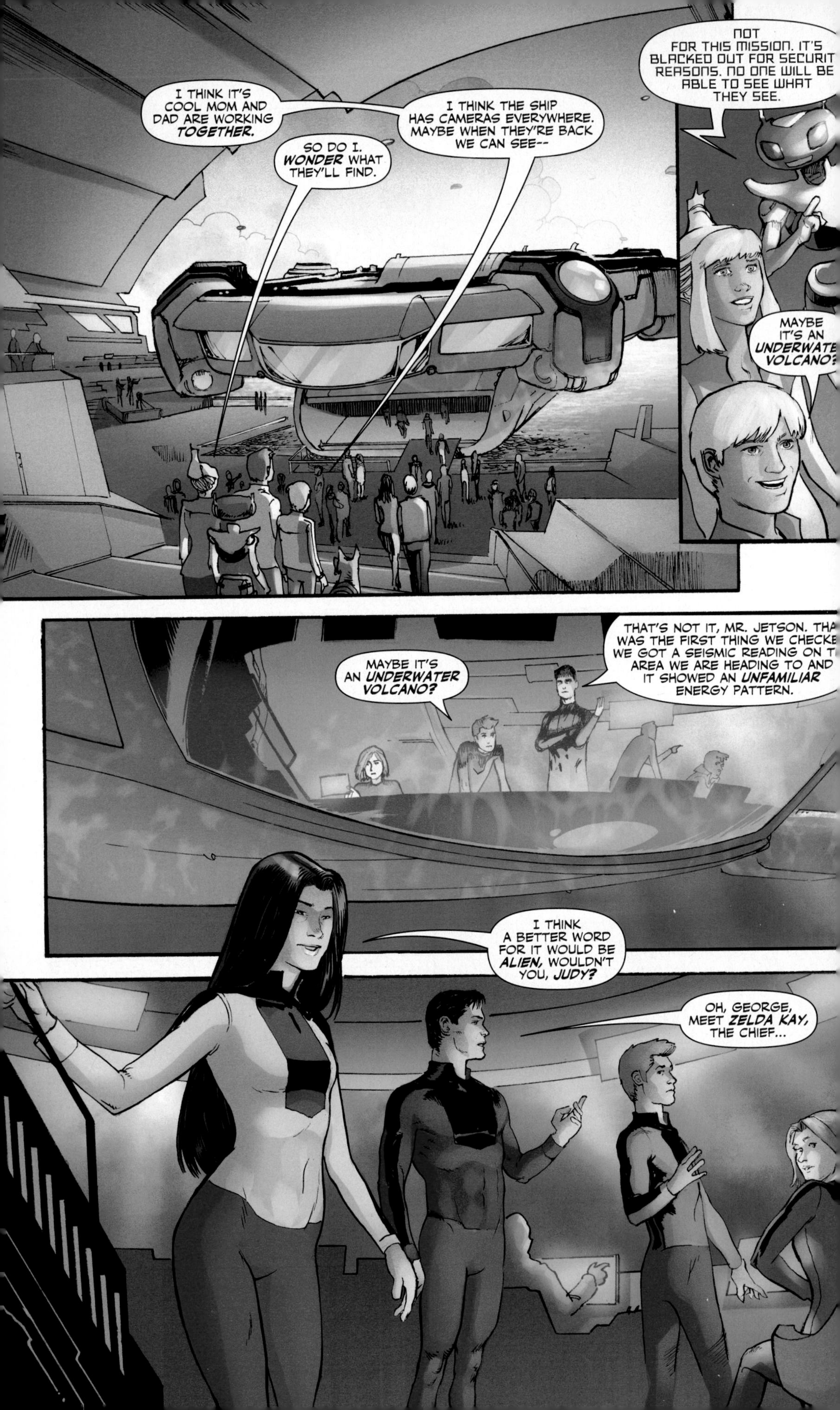
I THINK IT'S COOL MOM AND DAD ARE WORKING *TOGETHER.*
SO DO I. *WONDER* WHAT THEY'LL FIND.
I THINK THE SHIP HAS CAMERAS EVERYWHERE. MAYBE WHEN THEY'RE BACK WE CAN SEE--
NOT FOR THIS MISSION. IT'S BLACKED OUT FOR SECURIT REASONS. NO ONE WILL BE ABLE TO SEE WHAT THEY SEE.
MAYBE IT'S AN *UNDERWATE VOLCANO?*
MAYBE IT'S AN *UNDERWATER VOLCANO?*
THAT'S NOT IT, MR. JETSON. THA WAS THE FIRST THING WE CHECKE WE GOT A SEISMIC READING ON T AREA WE ARE HEADING TO AND IT SHOWED AN *UNFAMILIAR* ENERGY PATTERN.
I THINK A BETTER WORD FOR IT WOULD BE *ALIEN,* WOULDN'T YOU, *JUDY?*
OH, GEORGE, MEET *ZELDA KAY,* THE CHIEF...

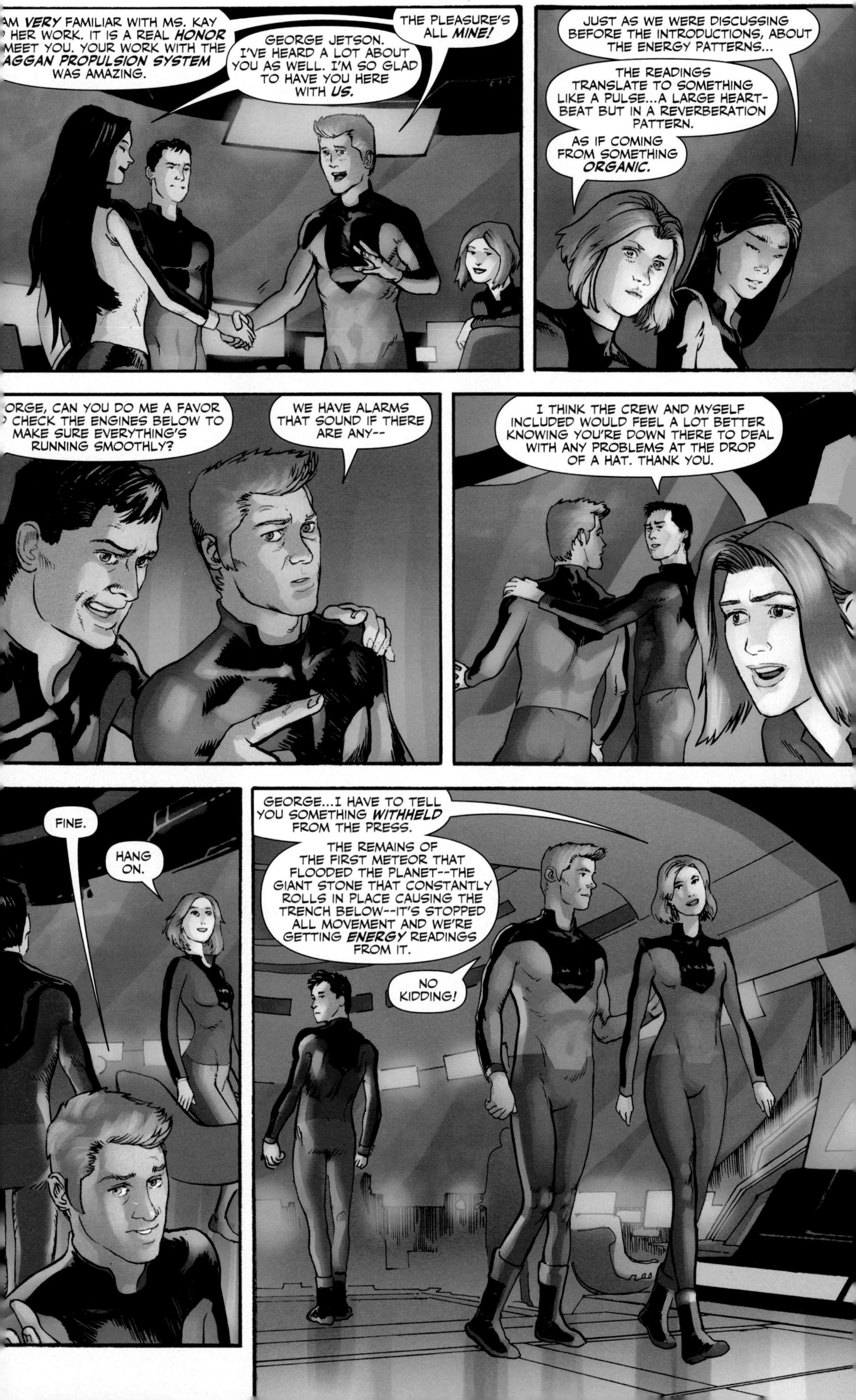
AM VERY FAMILIAR WITH MS. KAY
HER WORK. IT IS A REAL HONOR
MEET YOU. YOUR WORK WITH THE
AGGAN PROPULSION SYSTEM
WAS AMAZING.
GEORGE JETSON. I'VE HEARD A LOT ABOUT YOU AS WELL. I'M SO GLAD TO HAVE YOU HERE WITH US.
THE PLEASURE'S ALL MINE!
JUST AS WE WERE DISCUSSING BEFORE THE INTRODUCTIONS, ABOUT THE ENERGY PATTERNS...
THE READINGS TRANSLATE TO SOMETHING LIKE A PULSE...A LARGE HEART-BEAT BUT IN A REVERBERATION PATTERN.
AS IF COMING FROM SOMETHING ORGANIC.
ORGE, CAN YOU DO ME A FAVOR
CHECK THE ENGINES BELOW TO
MAKE SURE EVERYTHING'S
RUNNING SMOOTHLY?
WE HAVE ALARMS THAT SOUND IF THERE ARE ANY--
I THINK THE CREW AND MYSELF INCLUDED WOULD FEEL A LOT BETTER KNOWING YOU'RE DOWN THERE TO DEAL WITH ANY PROBLEMS AT THE DROP OF A HAT. THANK YOU.
FINE.
HANG ON.
GEORGE...I HAVE TO TELL YOU SOMETHING WITHHELD FROM THE PRESS.
THE REMAINS OF THE FIRST METEOR THAT FLOODED THE PLANET--THE GIANT STONE THAT CONSTANTLY ROLLS IN PLACE CAUSING THE TRENCH BELOW--IT'S STOPPED ALL MOVEMENT AND WE'RE GETTING ENERGY READINGS FROM IT.
NO KIDDING!

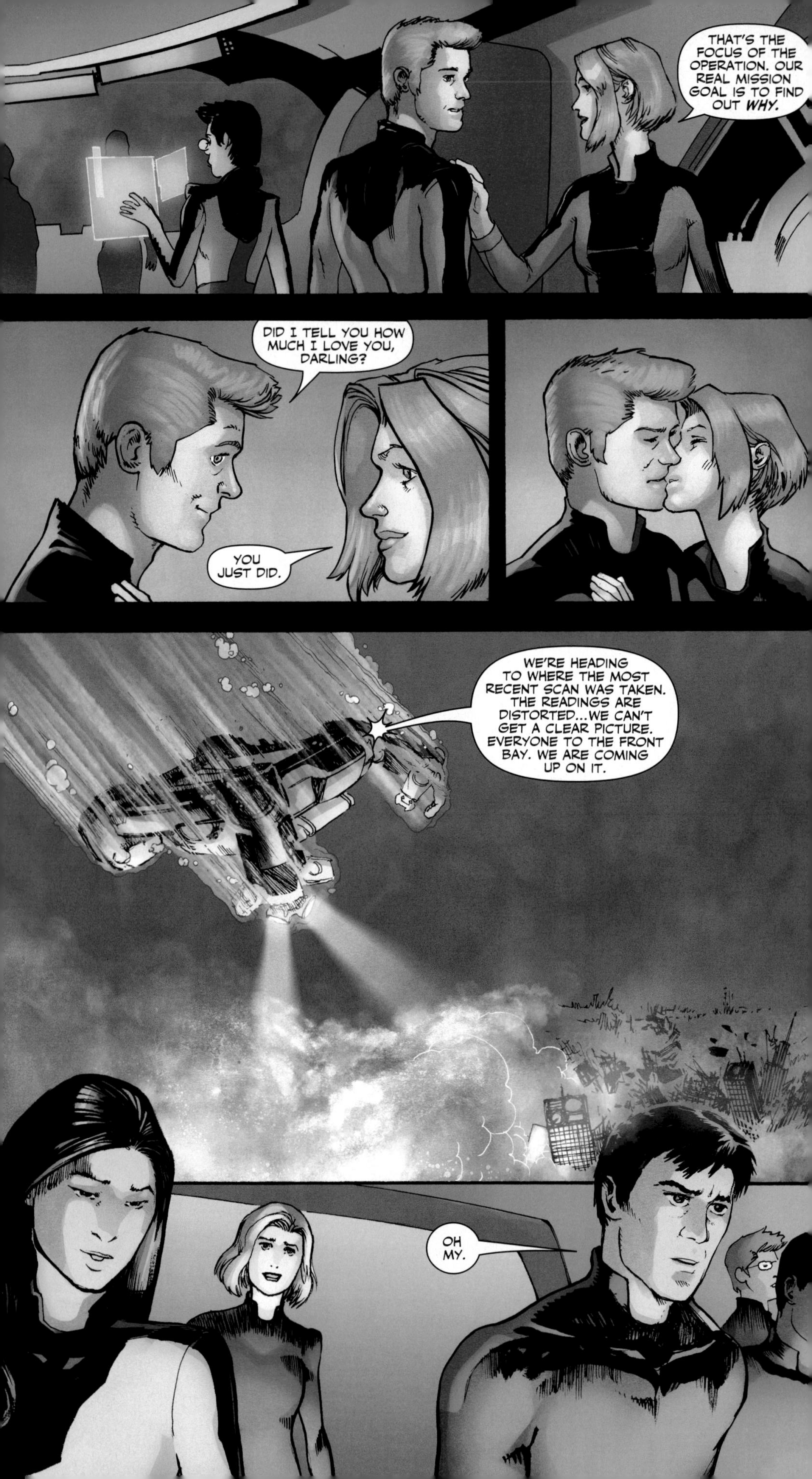
THAT'S THE FOCUS OF THE OPERATION. OUR REAL MISSION GOAL IS TO FIND OUT WHY.
DID I TELL YOU HOW MUCH I LOVE YOU, DARLING?
YOU JUST DID.
WE'RE HEADING TO WHERE THE MOST RECENT SCAN WAS TAKEN. THE READINGS ARE DISTORTED...WE CAN'T GET A CLEAR PICTURE. EVERYONE TO THE FRONT BAY. WE ARE COMING UP ON IT.
OH MY.

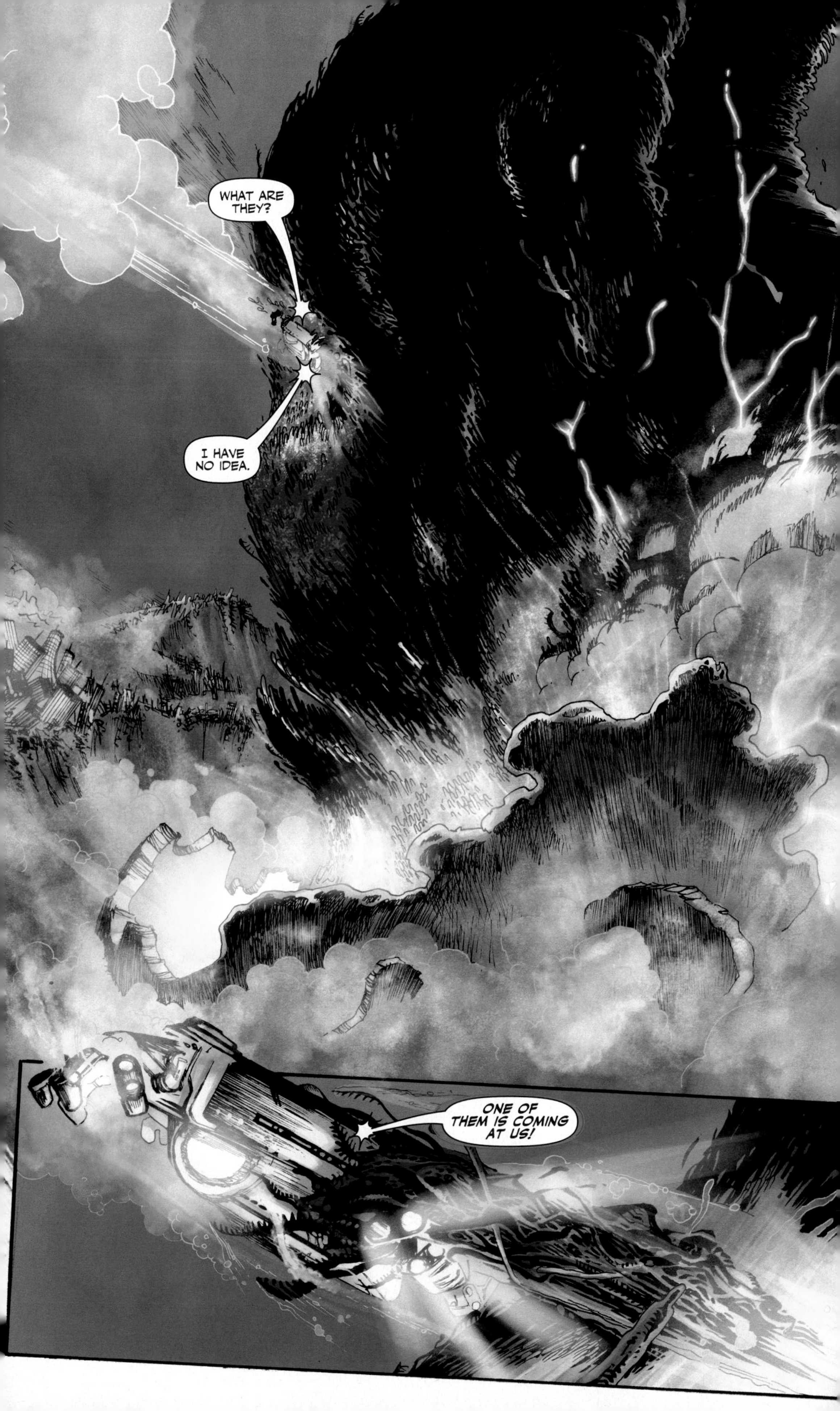
WHAT ARE THEY?
I HAVE NO IDEA.
ONE OF THEM IS COMING AT US!

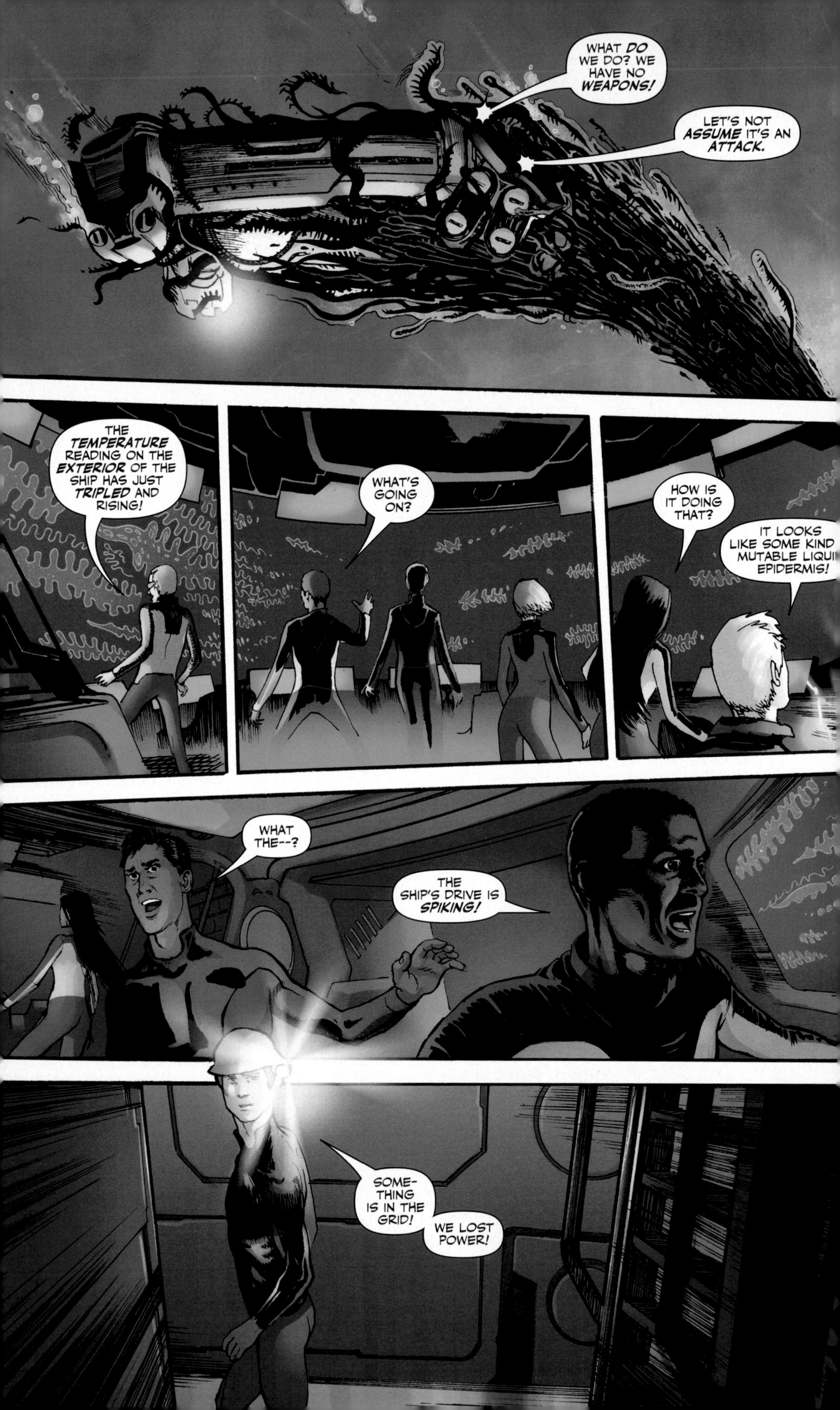

WHAT DO WE DO? WE HAVE NO WEAPONS!
LET'S NOT ASSUME IT'S AN ATTACK.
THE TEMPERATURE READING ON THE EXTERIOR OF THE SHIP HAS JUST TRIPLED AND RISING!
WHAT'S GOING ON?
HOW IS IT DOING THAT?
IT LOOKS LIKE SOME KIND MUTABLE LIQUI EPIDERMIS!
WHAT THE--?
THE SHIP'S DRIVE IS SPIKING!
SOME-THING IS IN THE GRID!
WE LOST POWER!

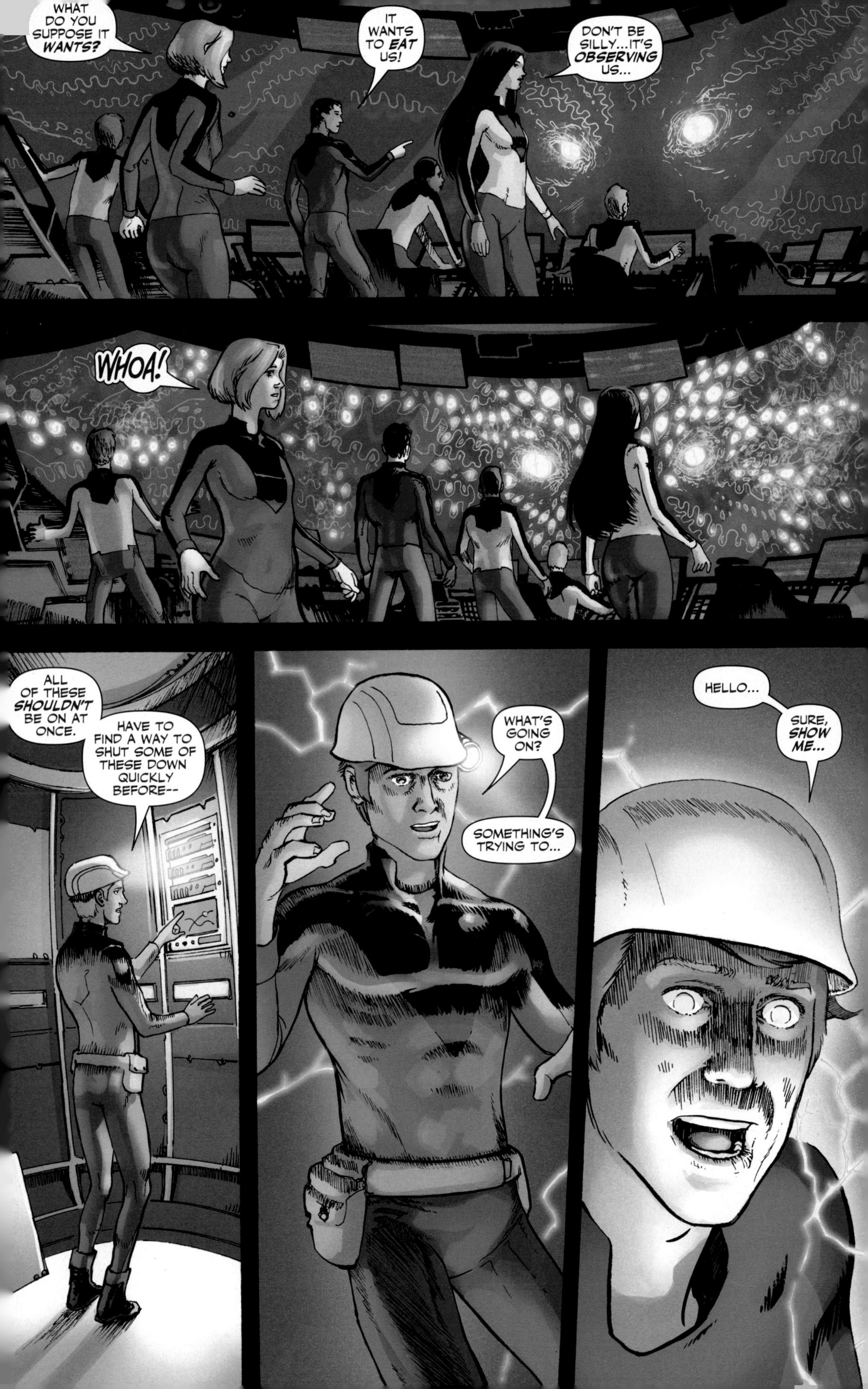
WHAT DO YOU SUPPOSE IT WANTS?
IT WANTS TO EAT US!
DON'T BE SILLY...IT'S OBSERVING US...
WHOA!
ALL OF THESE SHOULDN'T BE ON AT ONCE.
HAVE TO FIND A WAY TO SHUT SOME OF THESE DOWN QUICKLY BEFORE--
WHAT'S GOING ON?
SOMETHING'S TRYING TO...
HELLO...
SURE, SHOW ME...

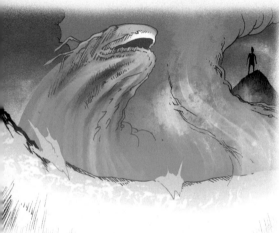

GEORGE, ARE YOU ALL RIGHT?

UGGH...

I THINK SO...WHAT *HAPPENED?*

WE TRIED GETTING IN CONTACT WITH YOU AND WHEN WE HEARD NOTHING, CAME DOWN HERE. I WAS SO *WORRIED!*

HOW LONG WAS I *OUT?*

A FEW MINUTES, *MAYBE?*

INCOM MESSA FROM BRIDG

GO AHEAD...

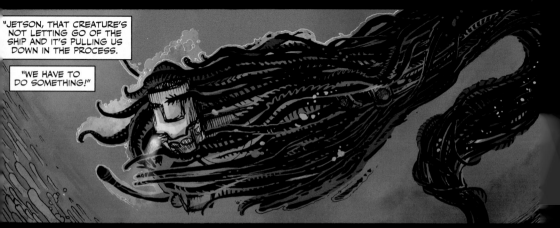

"JETSON, THAT CREATURE'S NOT LETTING GO OF THE SHIP AND IT'S PULLING US DOWN IN THE PROCESS.

"WE HAVE TO DO SOMETHING!"

WE HAVE A SEPARATE *RESERVE* POWER SOURCE THAT I CAN DIRECT TOWARD THE ENGINES TO TRY TO PUSH BACK AGAINST ITS FORCE. BUT I DON'T KNOW IF THAT'S GOING TO BE *ENOUGH.*

JANE, I'M GOING TO NEED YOUR HELP. I CAN'T FOCUS... WHATEVER GOT INTO MY HEAD HASN'T FULLY LEFT.

WE FOUND YOU PASSED OUT AND HAVING A CONVERSATION WITH *YOURSELF.* SOME-THING ABOUT HYPER GENESIS CONCEPTION FRAGMENTS AND A TRAVELER... THAT MEAN *ANYTHING?*

TO BE HONEST, I CAN'T REMEMBER. BUT IT'S NOT IMPORTANT AT THIS MOMENT.

WARNING! WARNING!

WHAT NOW?

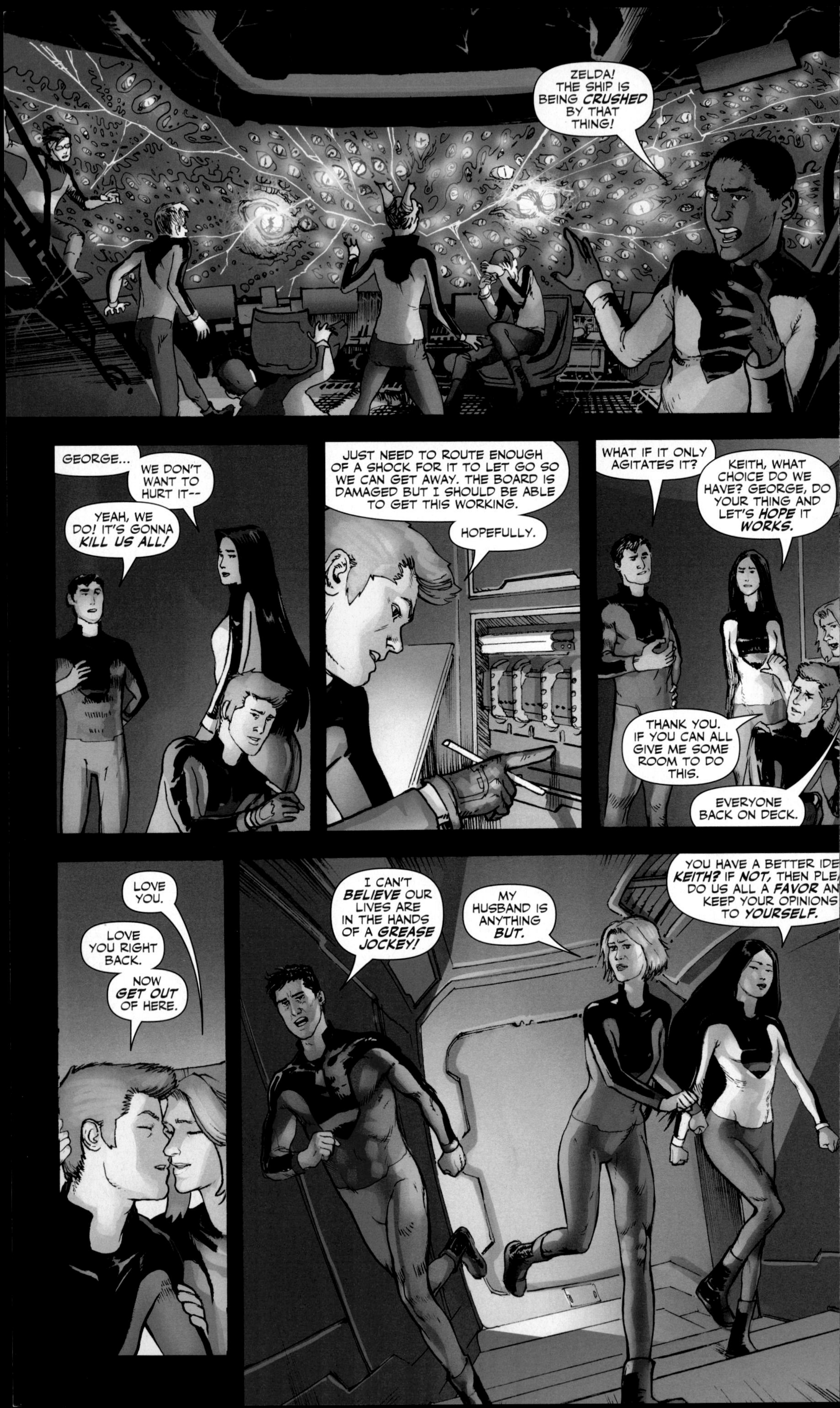
ZELDA! THE SHIP IS BEING CRUSHED BY THAT THING!
GEORGE...
WE DON'T WANT TO HURT IT--
YEAH, WE DO! IT'S GONNA KILL US ALL!
JUST NEED TO ROUTE ENOUGH OF A SHOCK FOR IT TO LET GO SO WE CAN GET AWAY. THE BOARD IS DAMAGED BUT I SHOULD BE ABLE TO GET THIS WORKING.
HOPEFULLY.
WHAT IF IT ONLY AGITATES IT?
KEITH, WHAT CHOICE DO WE HAVE? GEORGE, DO YOUR THING AND LET'S HOPE IT WORKS.
THANK YOU. IF YOU CAN ALL GIVE ME SOME ROOM TO DO THIS.
EVERYONE BACK ON DECK.
LOVE YOU.
LOVE YOU RIGHT BACK.
NOW GET OUT OF HERE.
I CAN'T BELIEVE OUR LIVES ARE IN THE HANDS OF A GREASE JOCKEY!
MY HUSBAND IS ANYTHING BUT.
YOU HAVE A BETTER IDE KEITH? IF NOT, THEN PLE DO US ALL A FAVOR AN KEEP YOUR OPINIONS TO YOURSELF.

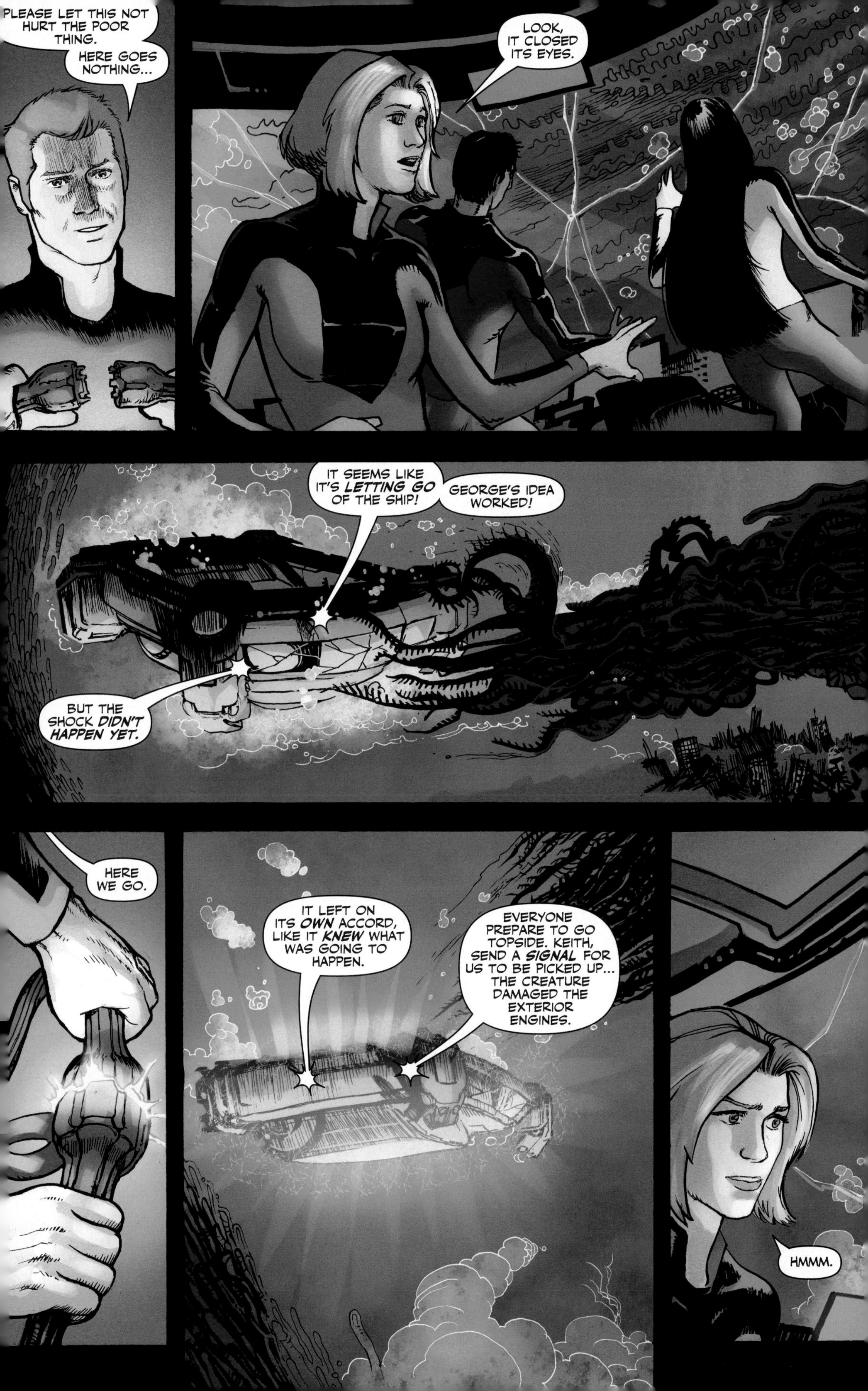
PLEASE LET THIS NOT HURT THE POOR THING.
HERE GOES NOTHING...
LOOK, IT CLOSED ITS EYES.
IT SEEMS LIKE IT'S LETTING GO OF THE SHIP!
GEORGE'S IDEA WORKED!
BUT THE SHOCK DIDN'T HAPPEN YET.
HERE WE GO.
IT LEFT ON ITS OWN ACCORD, LIKE IT KNEW WHAT WAS GOING TO HAPPEN.
EVERYONE PREPARE TO GO TOPSIDE. KEITH, SEND A SIGNAL FOR US TO BE PICKED UP... THE CREATURE DAMAGED THE EXTERIOR ENGINES.
HMMM.

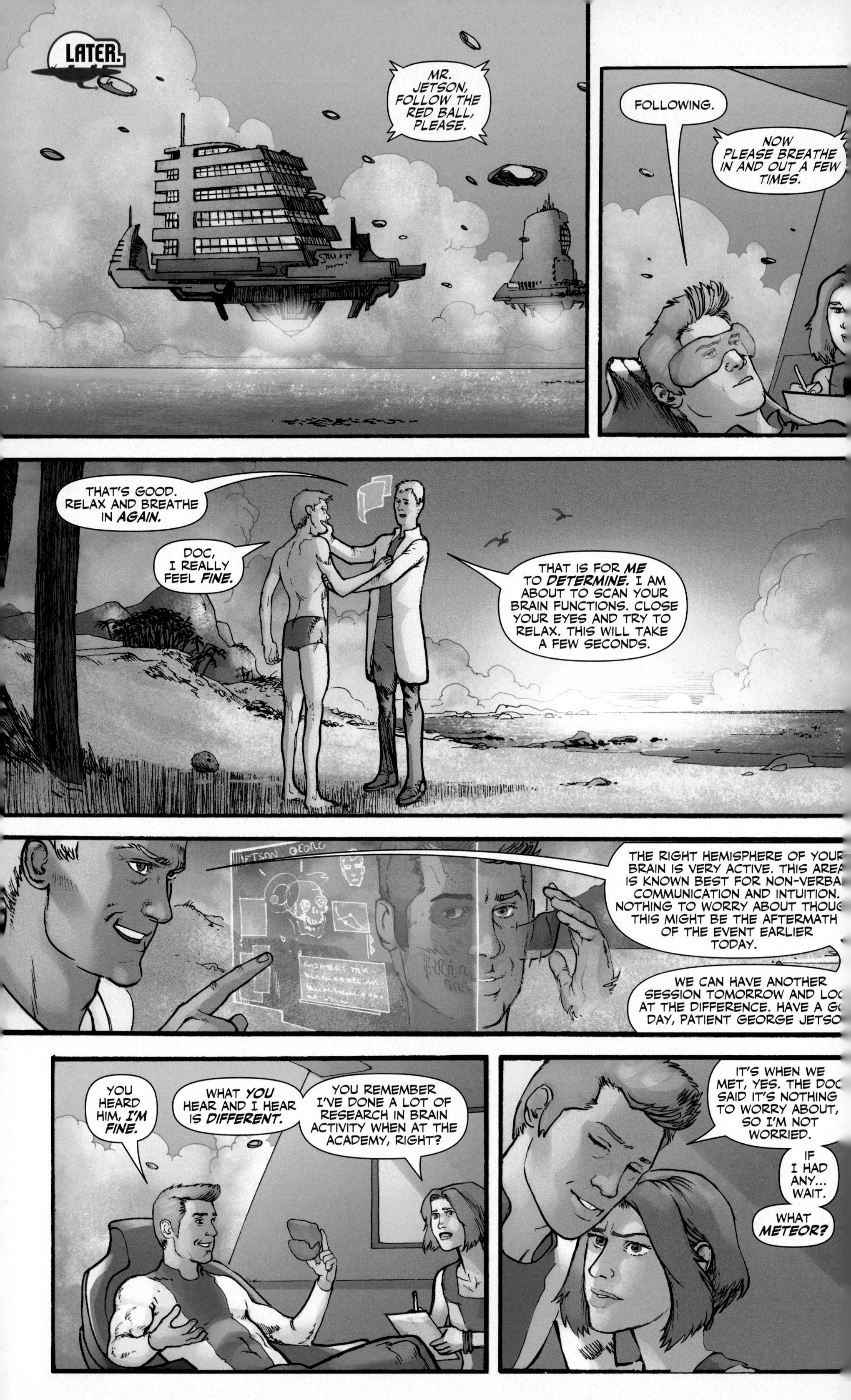
LATER.
MR. JETSON, FOLLOW THE RED BALL, PLEASE.
FOLLOWING.
NOW PLEASE BREATHE IN AND OUT A FEW TIMES.
THAT'S GOOD. RELAX AND BREATHE IN AGAIN.
DOC, I REALLY FEEL FINE.
THAT IS FOR ME TO DETERMINE. I AM ABOUT TO SCAN YOUR BRAIN FUNCTIONS. CLOSE YOUR EYES AND TRY TO RELAX. THIS WILL TAKE A FEW SECONDS.
THE RIGHT HEMISPHERE OF YOUR BRAIN IS VERY ACTIVE. THIS AREA IS KNOWN BEST FOR NON-VERBAL COMMUNICATION AND INTUITION. NOTHING TO WORRY ABOUT THOUG THIS MIGHT BE THE AFTERMATH OF THE EVENT EARLIER TODAY.
WE CAN HAVE ANOTHER SESSION TOMORROW AND LOO AT THE DIFFERENCE. HAVE A G DAY, PATIENT GEORGE JETSO
YOU HEARD HIM, I'M FINE.
WHAT YOU HEAR AND I HEAR IS DIFFERENT.
YOU REMEMBER I'VE DONE A LOT OF RESEARCH IN BRAIN ACTIVITY WHEN AT THE ACADEMY, RIGHT?
IT'S WHEN WE MET, YES. THE DOC SAID IT'S NOTHING TO WORRY ABOUT, SO I'M NOT WORRIED.
IF I HAD ANY... WAIT.
WHAT METEOR?

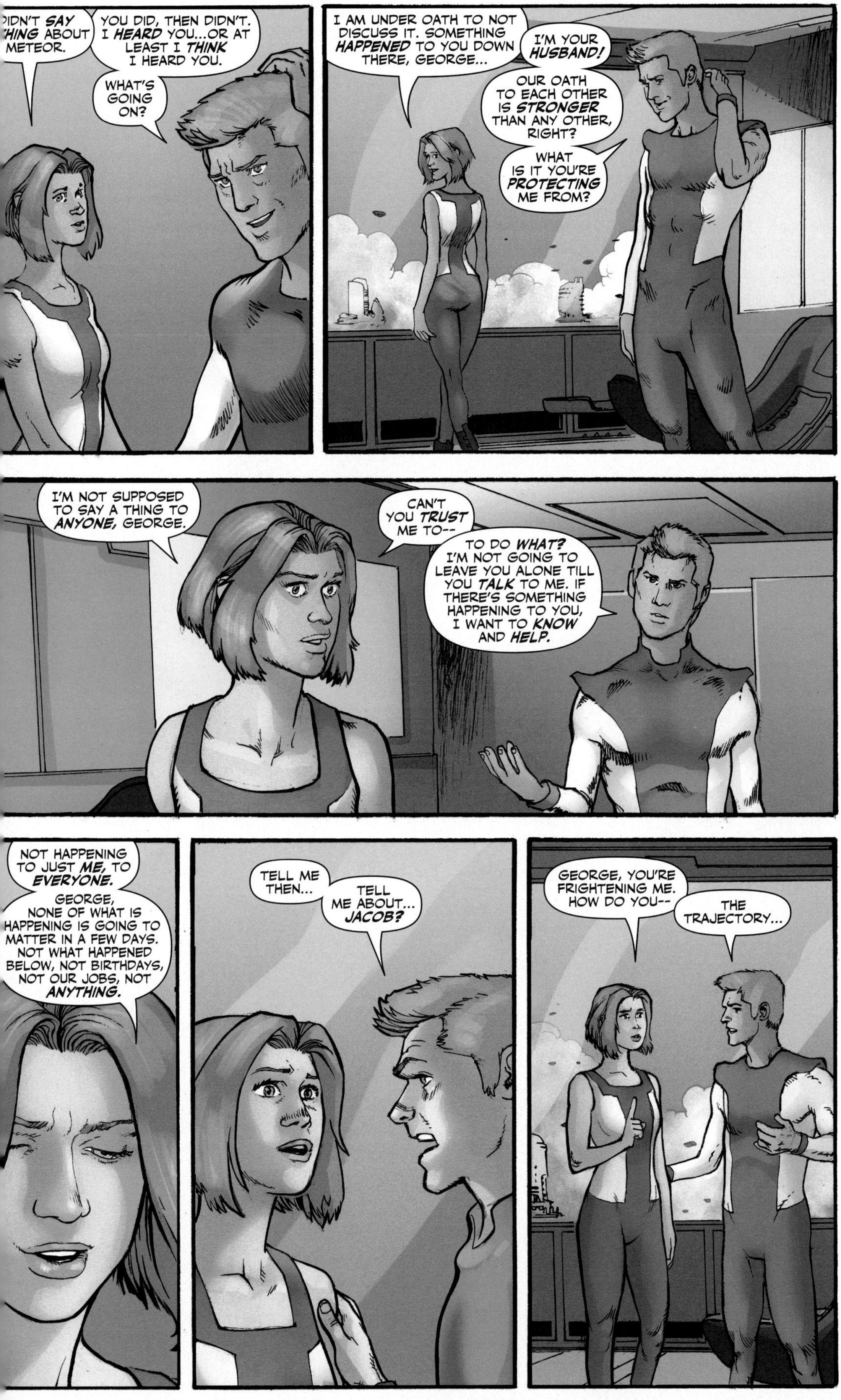

...IDN'T SAY ...THING ABOUT METEOR.
YOU DID, THEN DIDN'T. I HEARD YOU...OR AT LEAST I THINK I HEARD YOU.
WHAT'S GOING ON?
I AM UNDER OATH TO NOT DISCUSS IT. SOMETHING HAPPENED TO YOU DOWN THERE, GEORGE...
I'M YOUR HUSBAND!
OUR OATH TO EACH OTHER IS STRONGER THAN ANY OTHER, RIGHT?
WHAT IS IT YOU'RE PROTECTING ME FROM?
I'M NOT SUPPOSED TO SAY A THING TO ANYONE, GEORGE.
CAN'T YOU TRUST ME TO--
TO DO WHAT? I'M NOT GOING TO LEAVE YOU ALONE TILL YOU TALK TO ME. IF THERE'S SOMETHING HAPPENING TO YOU, I WANT TO KNOW AND HELP.
NOT HAPPENING TO JUST ME, TO EVERYONE.
GEORGE, NONE OF WHAT IS HAPPENING IS GOING TO MATTER IN A FEW DAYS. NOT WHAT HAPPENED BELOW, NOT BIRTHDAYS, NOT OUR JOBS, NOT ANYTHING.
TELL ME THEN...
TELL ME ABOUT... JACOB?
GEORGE, YOU'RE FRIGHTENING ME. HOW DO YOU--
THE TRAJECTORY...

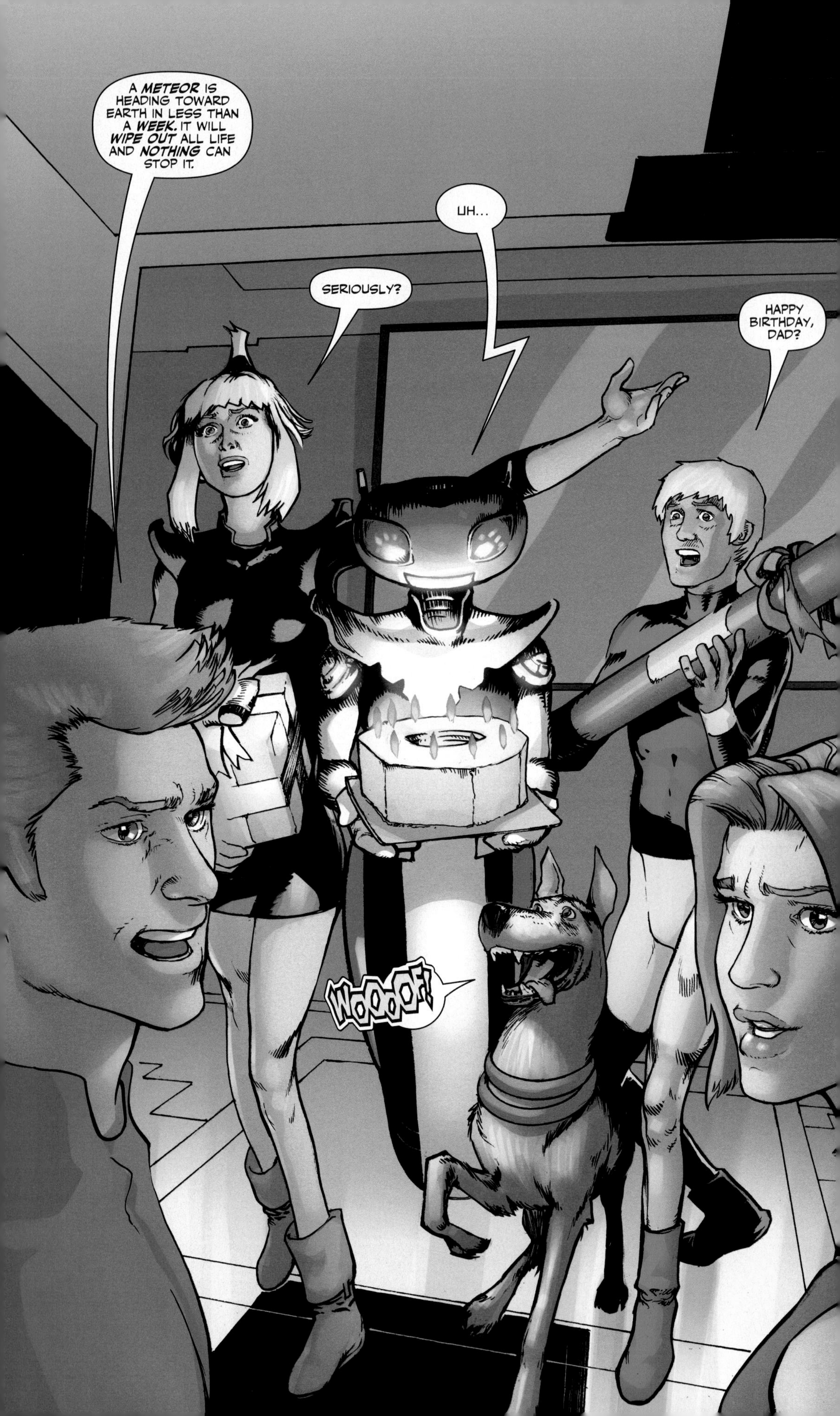
A METEOR IS HEADING TOWARD EARTH IN LESS THAN A WEEK. IT WILL WIPE OUT ALL LIFE AND NOTHING CAN STOP IT.
SERIOUSLY?
UH...
HAPPY BIRTHDAY, DAD?
WOOOOF!

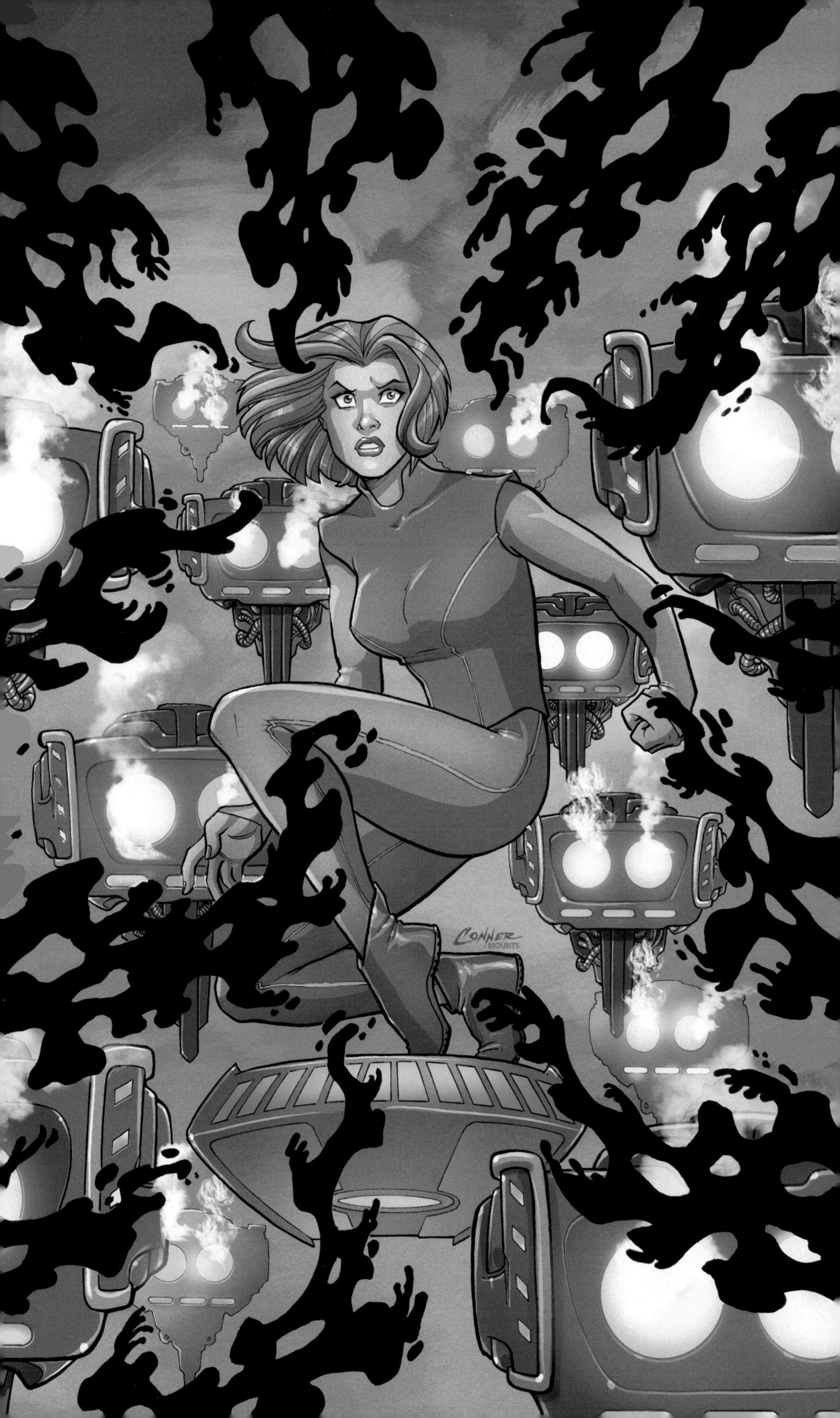
CONNER
MOUNTS

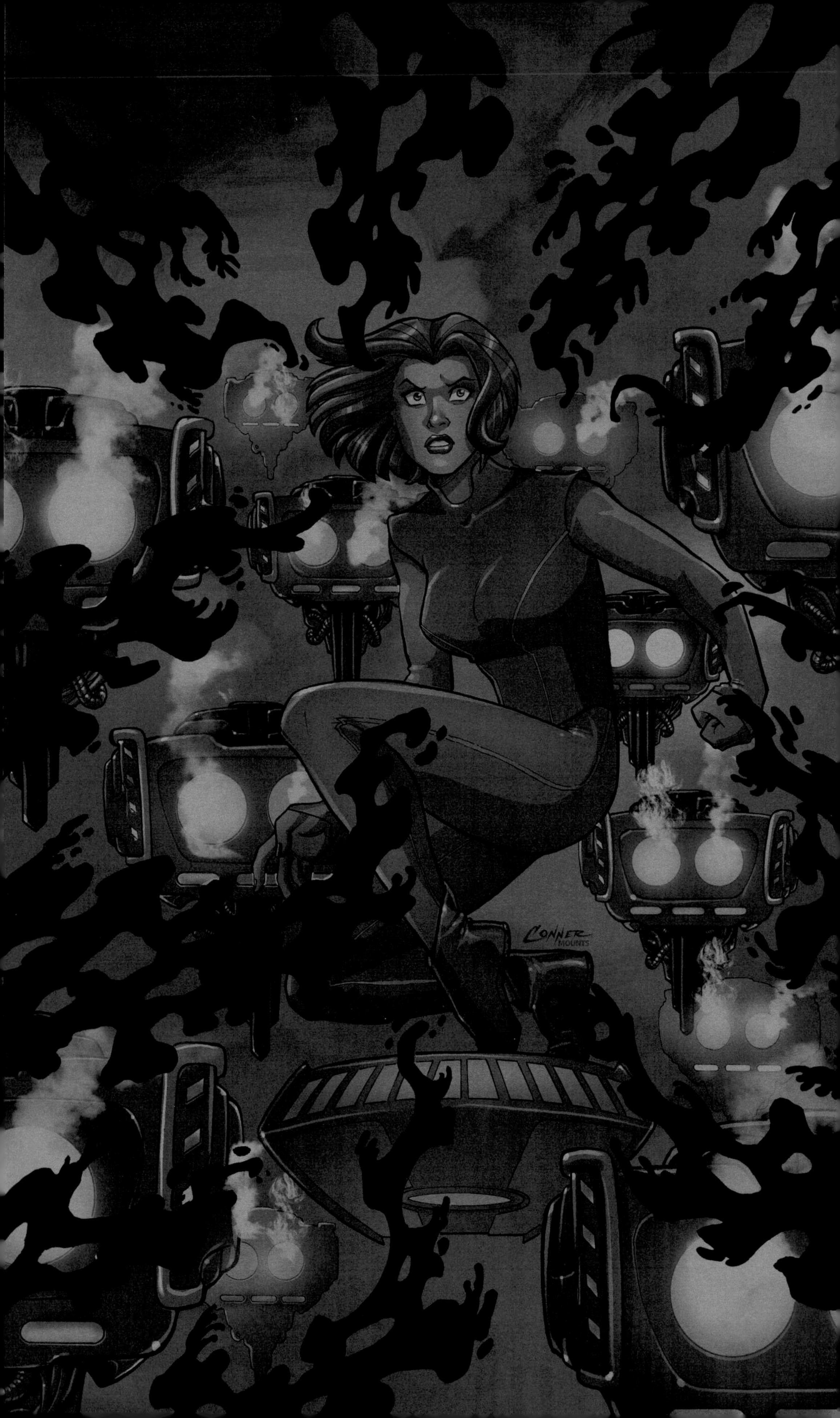
CONNER
MOUNTS

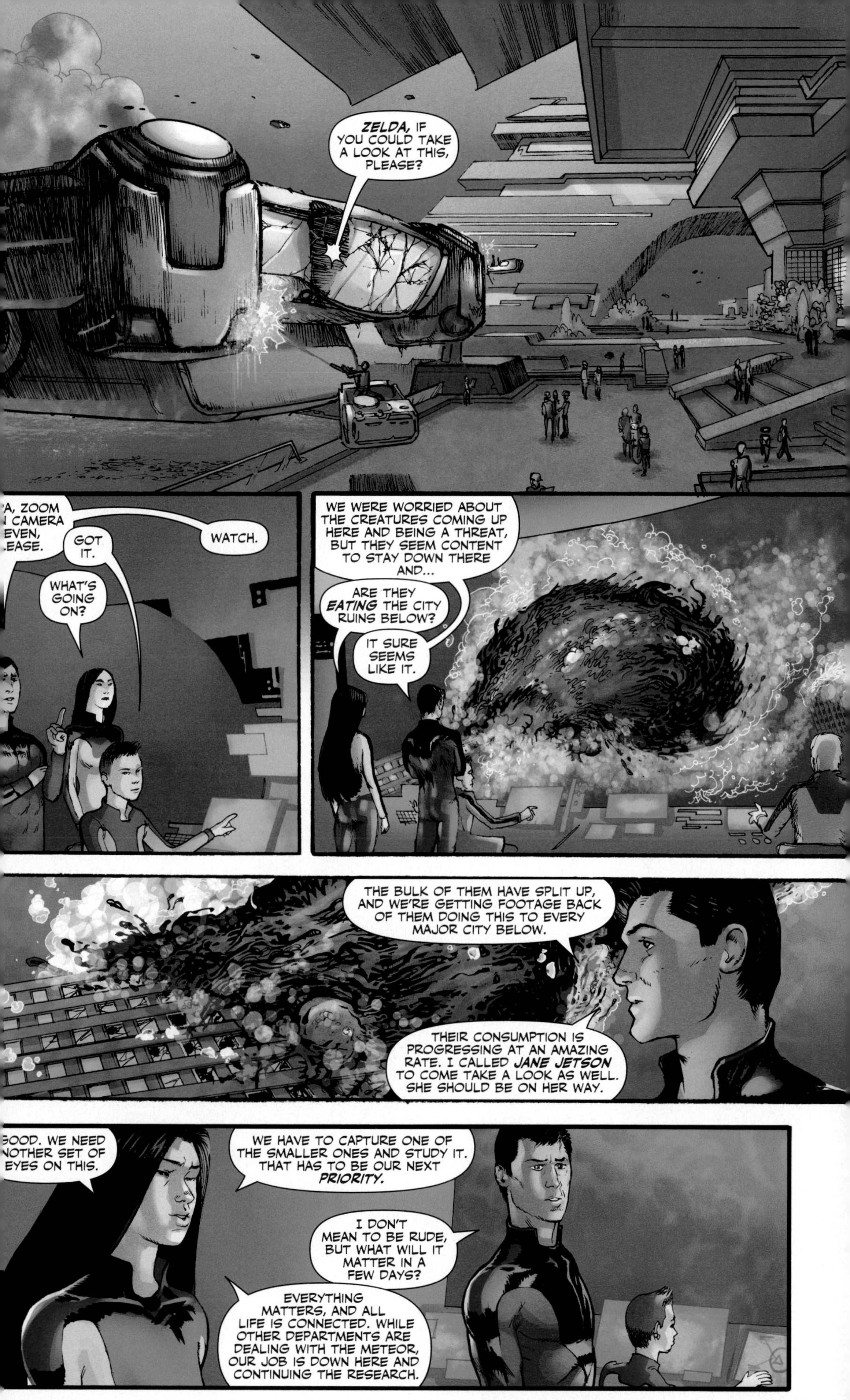
ZELDA, IF YOU COULD TAKE A LOOK AT THIS, PLEASE?
A, ZOOM
N CAMERA
EVEN,
EASE.
GOT IT.
WATCH.
WHAT'S GOING ON?
WE WERE WORRIED ABOUT THE CREATURES COMING UP HERE AND BEING A THREAT, BUT THEY SEEM CONTENT TO STAY DOWN THERE AND...
ARE THEY EATING THE CITY RUINS BELOW?
IT SURE SEEMS LIKE IT.
THE BULK OF THEM HAVE SPLIT UP, AND WE'RE GETTING FOOTAGE BACK OF THEM DOING THIS TO EVERY MAJOR CITY BELOW.
THEIR CONSUMPTION IS PROGRESSING AT AN AMAZING RATE. I CALLED JANE JETSON TO COME TAKE A LOOK AS WELL. SHE SHOULD BE ON HER WAY.
GOOD. WE NEED
NOTHER SET OF
EYES ON THIS.
WE HAVE TO CAPTURE ONE OF THE SMALLER ONES AND STUDY IT. THAT HAS TO BE OUR NEXT PRIORITY.
I DON'T MEAN TO BE RUDE, BUT WHAT WILL IT MATTER IN A FEW DAYS?
EVERYTHING MATTERS, AND ALL LIFE IS CONNECTED. WHILE OTHER DEPARTMENTS ARE DEALING WITH THE METEOR, OUR JOB IS DOWN HERE AND CONTINUING THE RESEARCH.

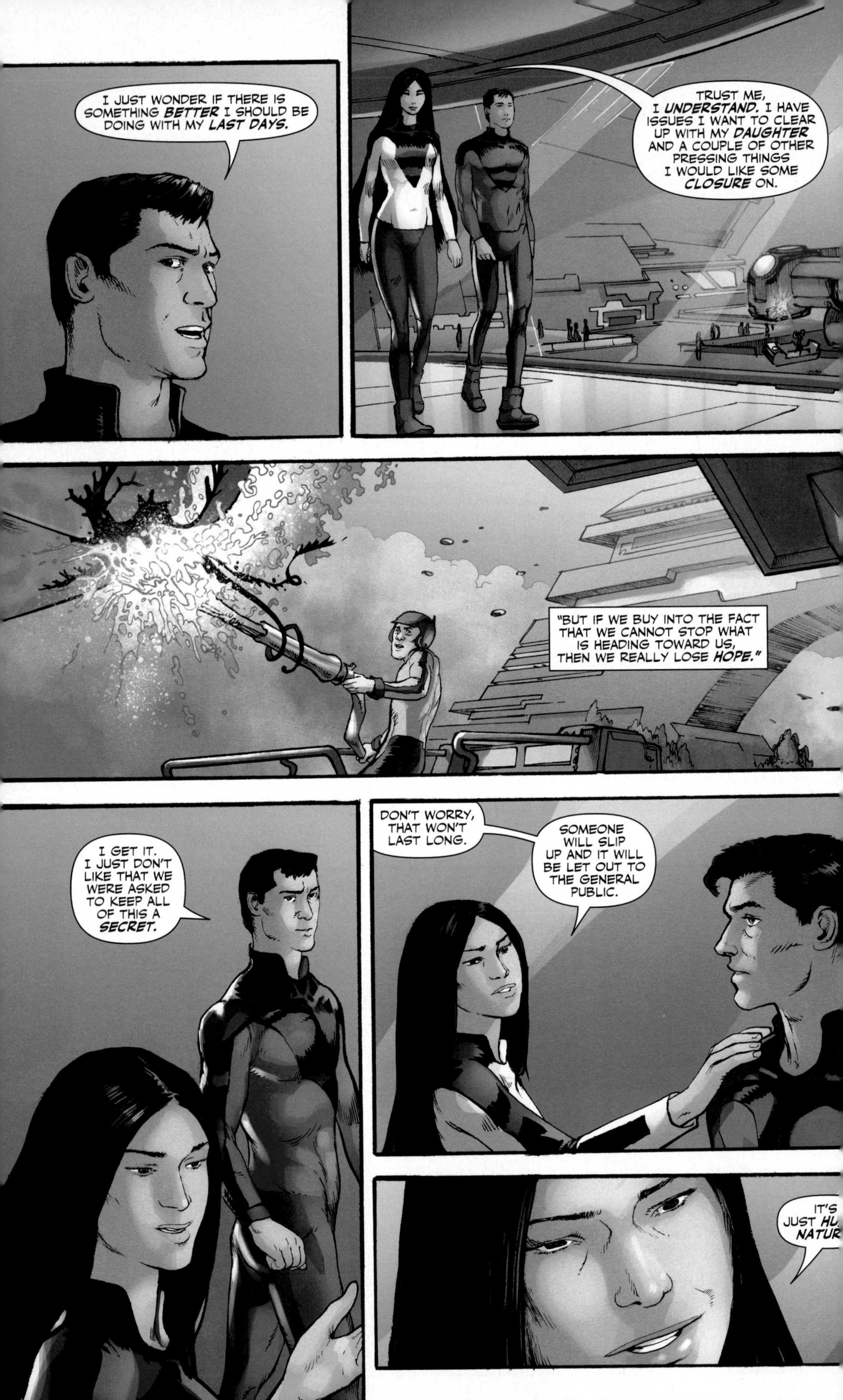
I JUST WONDER IF THERE IS SOMETHING BETTER I SHOULD BE DOING WITH MY LAST DAYS.
TRUST ME, I UNDERSTAND. I HAVE ISSUES I WANT TO CLEAR UP WITH MY DAUGHTER AND A COUPLE OF OTHER PRESSING THINGS I WOULD LIKE SOME CLOSURE ON.
"BUT IF WE BUY INTO THE FACT THAT WE CANNOT STOP WHAT IS HEADING TOWARD US, THEN WE REALLY LOSE HOPE."
I GET IT. I JUST DON'T LIKE THAT WE WERE ASKED TO KEEP ALL OF THIS A SECRET.
DON'T WORRY, THAT WON'T LAST LONG.
SOMEONE WILL SLIP UP AND IT WILL BE LET OUT TO THE GENERAL PUBLIC.

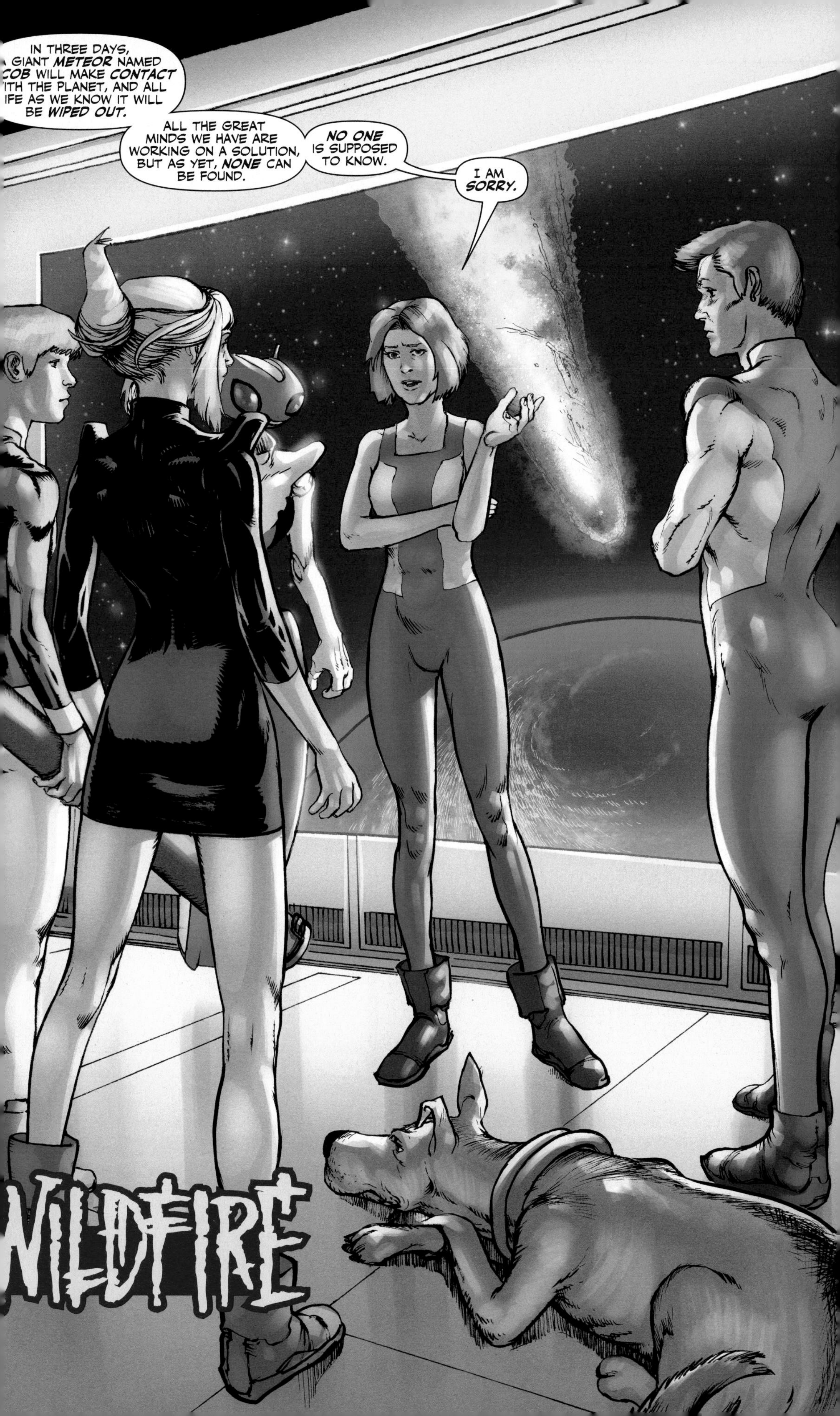

IN THREE DAYS, A GIANT *METEOR* NAMED COB WILL MAKE *CONTACT* WITH THE PLANET, AND ALL LIFE AS WE KNOW IT WILL BE *WIPED OUT.*
ALL THE GREAT MINDS WE HAVE ARE WORKING ON A SOLUTION, BUT AS YET, *NONE* CAN BE FOUND.
NO ONE IS SUPPOSED TO KNOW.
I AM *SORRY.*
WILDFIRE

ARE YOU *SERIOUS*, MRS. JETSON?

WHO?

UH-OH.

LAKE COGSWELL, YOU WERE *NOT* SUPPOSED TO HEAR THAT.

SORRY, BUT...

I CAN'T "UN-HEAR" IT.

WHO ELSE KNOWS ABOUT THIS?

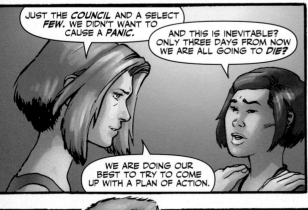

JUST THE *COUNCIL* AND A SELECT *FEW.* WE DIDN'T WANT TO CAUSE A *PANIC.*

AND THIS IS INEVITABLE? ONLY THREE DAYS FROM NOW WE ARE ALL GOING TO *DIE?*

WE ARE DOING OUR BEST TO TRY TO COME UP WITH A PLAN OF ACTION.

LAKE, *PLEASE,* IF IT GOT OUT THAT *I* LEAKED THIS INFORMATION...

I'M SORRY, BUT THIS IS TOO BIG, AND HONESTLY, WHAT CAN THEY DO TO YOU?

I AGREE WITH OUR LITTLE FRIEND HERE. THEY NEED TO LET EVERYONE KNOW! THERE MIGHT BE SOMEONE OUTSIDE YOUR GROUP WHO HAS AN IDEA NO ONE ELSE HAS THOUGHT OF.

PEOPLE WOULD WANT TO HAVE SOME CLOSURE AS WELL...

I AGREE, MOM. THINK OF ALL THE STUDENTS AND TEACHERS IN MY SCHOOL ALONE WHO COULD BE PUTTING THEIR MINDS TO WORK COMING UP WITH A SOLUTION!

THAT IS ALL TRUE.

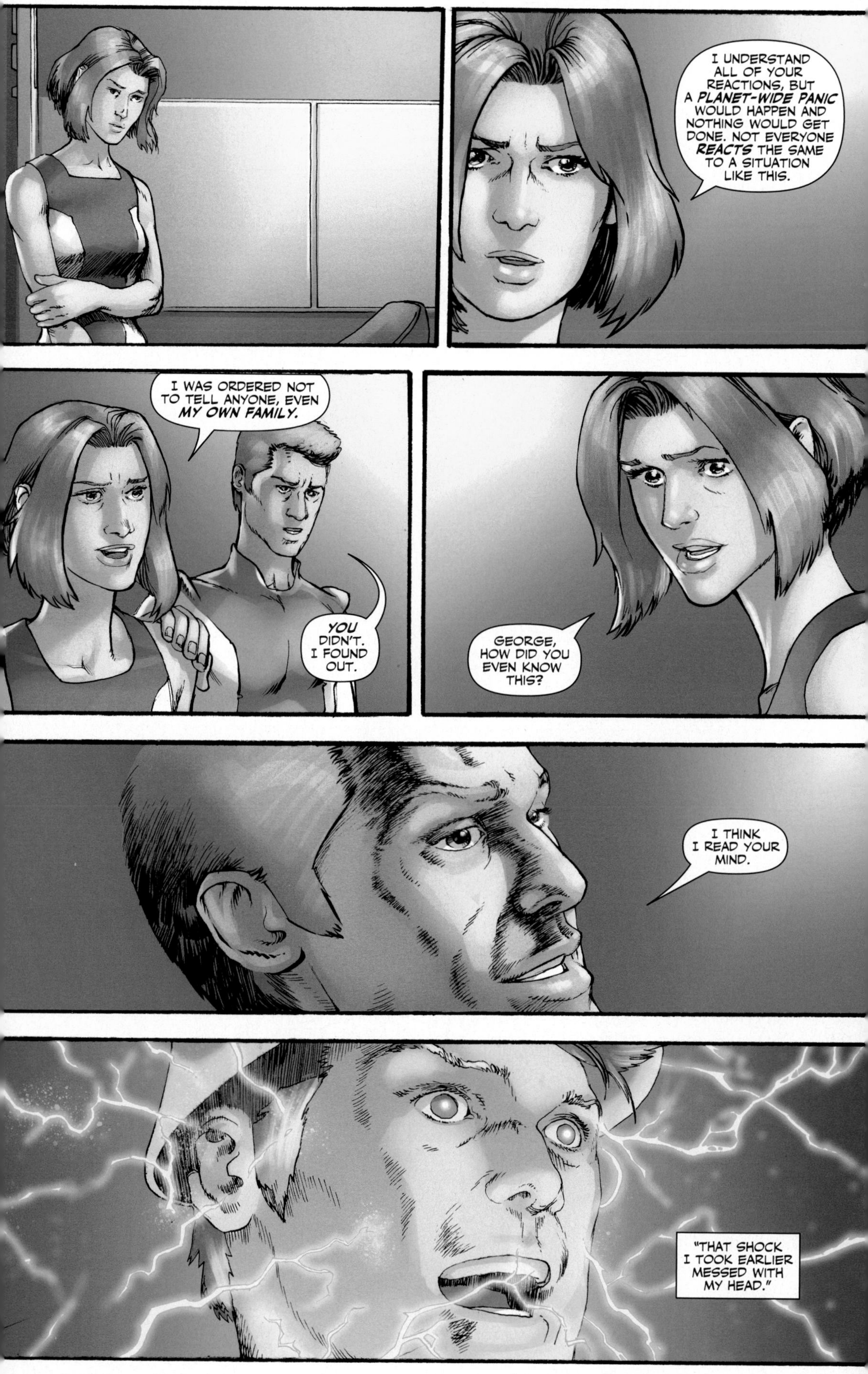
I UNDERSTAND ALL OF YOUR REACTIONS, BUT A *PLANET-WIDE PANIC* WOULD HAPPEN AND NOTHING WOULD GET DONE. NOT EVERYONE *REACTS* THE SAME TO A SITUATION LIKE THIS.
I WAS ORDERED NOT TO TELL ANYONE, EVEN *MY OWN FAMILY.*
YOU DIDN'T. I FOUND OUT.
GEORGE, HOW DID YOU EVEN KNOW THIS?
I THINK I READ YOUR MIND.
"THAT SHOCK I TOOK EARLIER MESSED WITH MY HEAD."

WE HAVE TO GET YOU *CHECKED OUT* AGAIN! WHAT IF...

WE HAVE THREE DAYS LEFT... *WHY BOTHER?* WE GOT *OTHER* THINGS TO WORRY ABOUT.

MRS. JETSON, YOU MADE A *PROMISE* NOT TO TELL, BUT I *DIDN'T.* I HAVE MY OWN FAMILY, AND TO BE HONEST, THERE IS NO WAY I *CAN'T* WARN THEM.

I HOPE YOU CAN FORGIVE ME.

LAKE...

SORRY, ELROY. I WILL TALK TO YOU LATER. *I HOPE.*

I UNDER-STAND.

KIDS, THIS PLANET HAS FACED CHALLENGES BEFORE, AND THERE IS A GOOD CHANCE WE CAN COME UP WITH A *SOLUTION* IF WE ALL STICK *TOGETHER.*

LET'S PUT THE PARTY O HOLD FOR A B AND GIVE YO MOM AND DA SOME TIME *ALONE.*

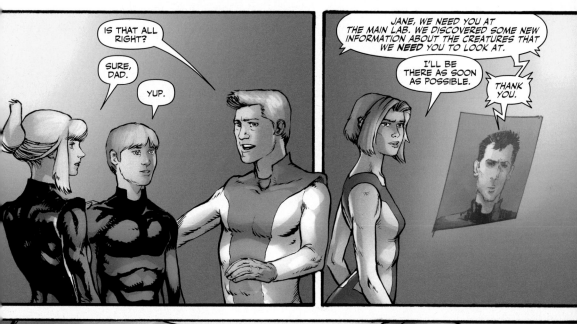

IS THAT ALL RIGHT?

SURE, DAD.

YUP.

JANE, WE NEED YOU AT THE MAIN LAB. WE DISCOVERED SOME NEW INFORMATION ABOUT THE CREATURES THAT WE **NEED** YOU TO LOOK AT.

I'LL BE THERE AS SOON AS POSSIBLE.

THANK YOU.

JANE, THE CAT'S OUT OF THE BAG. BEST THING TO DO IS LET YOUR PEOPLE KNOW WHAT'S HAPPENING. YOU KNOW WHO LAKE'S **FATHER** IS...THIS WILL BE ON THE NEWS IN **NO TIME.**

I KNOW AND I WILL.

I MESSED UP, GEORGE.

DON'T BEAT YOURSELF UP ABOUT IT.

I THINK WHAT HAPPENED IS FOR THE BEST. THAT IS, I SURE HOPE IT IS.

SEND ME ALL THE INFO YOU HAVE AND GET OVER TO THE LAB AND DO YOUR THING. I'LL CHECK ON THE KIDS. STOP WORRYING, PLEASE.

I WISH JUST WORDS HAD THAT POWER.

ME, TOO, BUT WE HAVE TO MOVE FORWARD AND STAY POSITIVE.

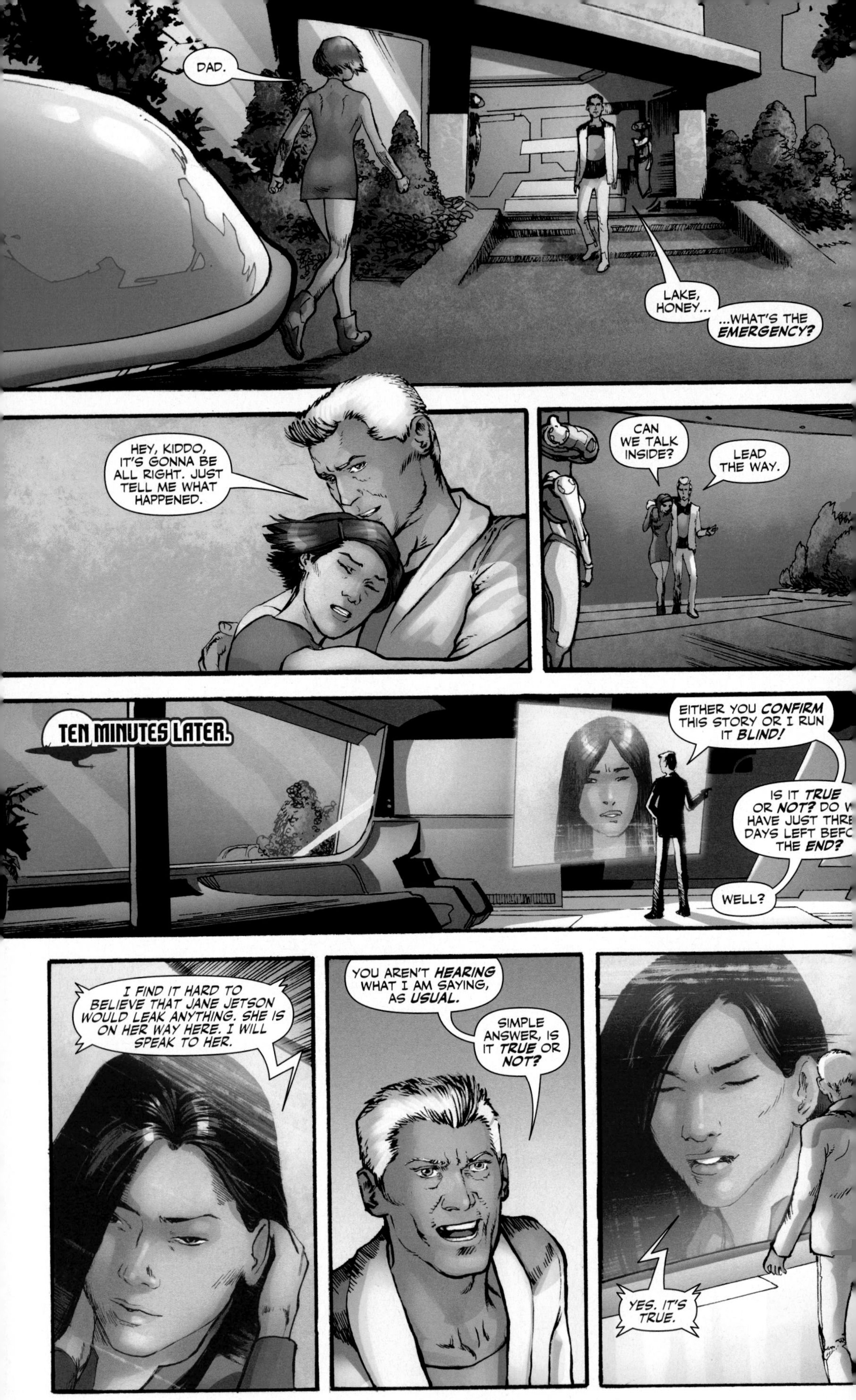
DAD.
LAKE, HONEY...
...WHAT'S THE EMERGENCY?
HEY, KIDDO, IT'S GONNA BE ALL RIGHT. JUST TELL ME WHAT HAPPENED.
CAN WE TALK INSIDE?
LEAD THE WAY.
TEN MINUTES LATER.
EITHER YOU CONFIRM THIS STORY OR I RUN IT BLIND!
IS IT TRUE OR NOT? DO W HAVE JUST THRE DAYS LEFT BEFO THE END?
WELL?
I FIND IT HARD TO BELIEVE THAT JANE JETSON WOULD LEAK ANYTHING. SHE IS ON HER WAY HERE. I WILL SPEAK TO HER.
YOU AREN'T HEARING WHAT I AM SAYING, AS USUAL.
SIMPLE ANSWER, IS IT TRUE OR NOT?
YES. IT'S TRUE.

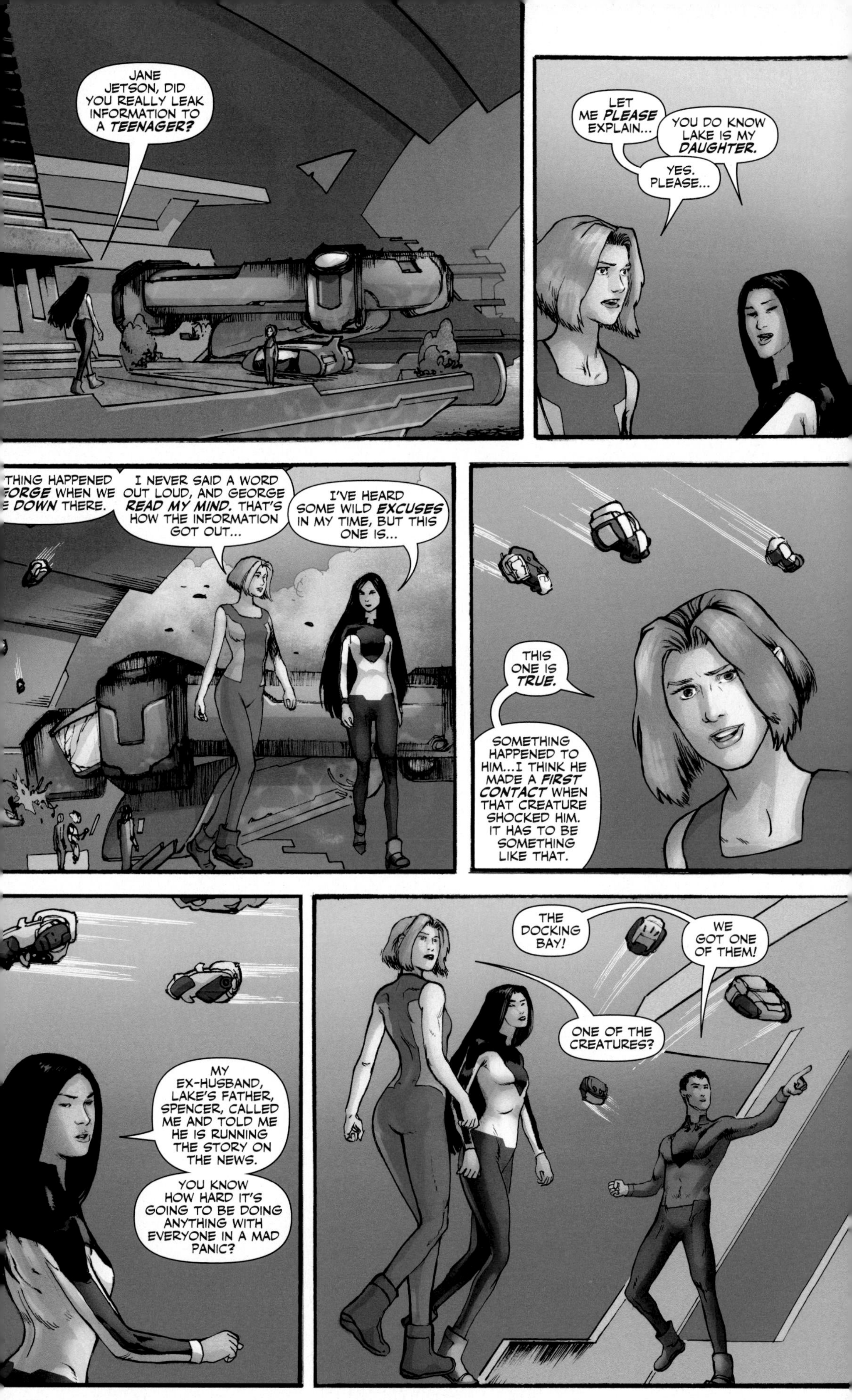

JANE JETSON, DID YOU REALLY LEAK INFORMATION TO A *TEENAGER?*
LET ME *PLEASE* EXPLAIN...
YOU DO KNOW LAKE IS MY *DAUGHTER.*
YES. PLEASE...
THING HAPPENED *ORGE* WHEN WE *E DOWN* THERE.
I NEVER SAID A WORD OUT LOUD, AND GEORGE *READ MY MIND.* THAT'S HOW THE INFORMATION GOT OUT...
I'VE HEARD SOME WILD *EXCUSES* IN MY TIME, BUT THIS ONE IS...
THIS ONE IS *TRUE.*
SOMETHING HAPPENED TO HIM...I THINK HE MADE A *FIRST CONTACT* WHEN THAT CREATURE SHOCKED HIM. IT HAS TO BE SOMETHING LIKE THAT.
MY EX-HUSBAND, LAKE'S FATHER, SPENCER, CALLED ME AND TOLD ME HE IS RUNNING THE STORY ON THE NEWS.
YOU KNOW HOW HARD IT'S GOING TO BE DOING ANYTHING WITH EVERYONE IN A MAD PANIC?
THE DOCKING BAY!
WE GOT ONE OF THEM!
ONE OF THE CREATURES?

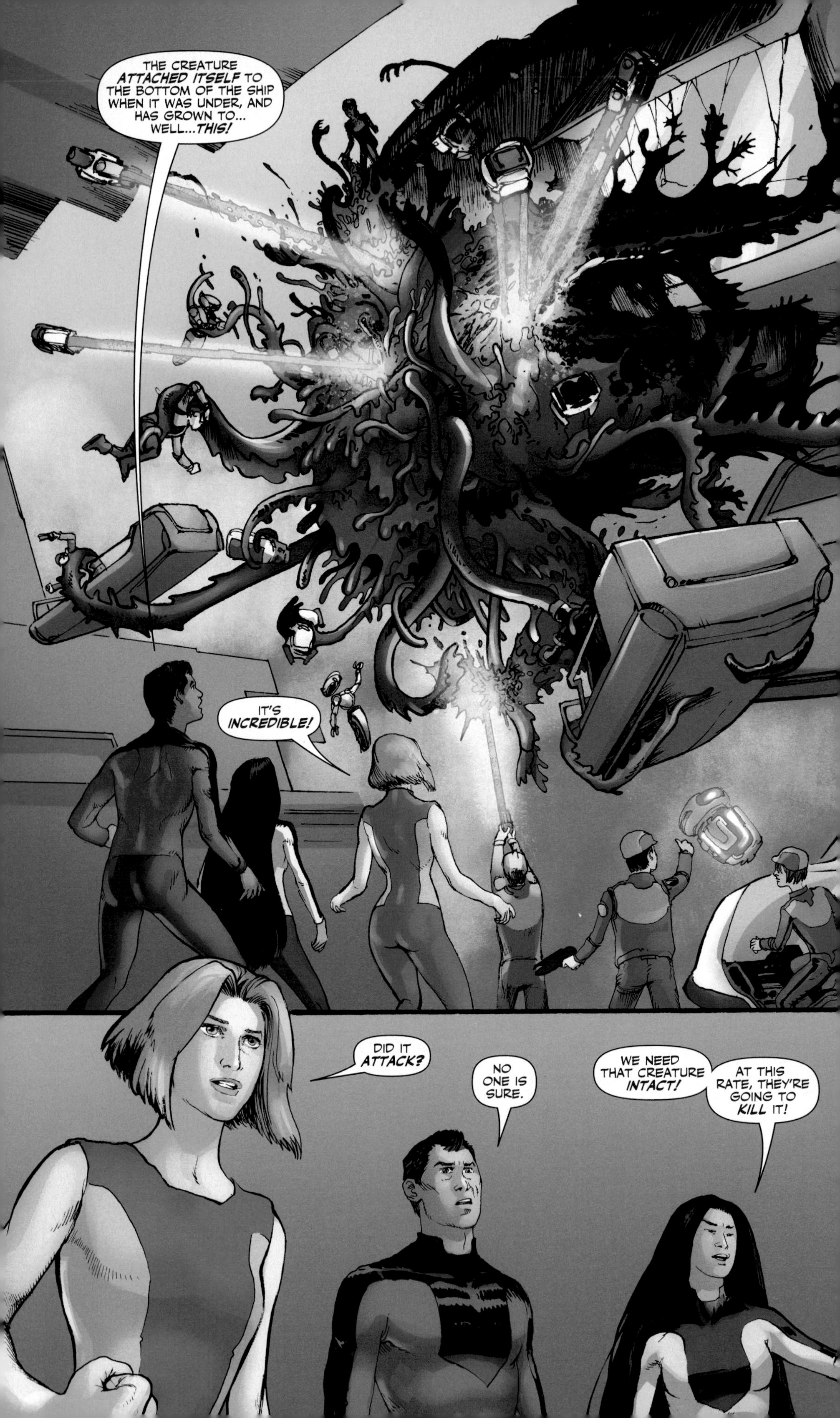
THE CREATURE ATTACHED ITSELF TO THE BOTTOM OF THE SHIP WHEN IT WAS UNDER, AND HAS GROWN TO... WELL...THIS!
IT'S INCREDIBLE!
DID IT ATTACK?
NO ONE IS SURE.
WE NEED THAT CREATURE INTACT!
AT THIS RATE, THEY'RE GOING TO KILL IT!

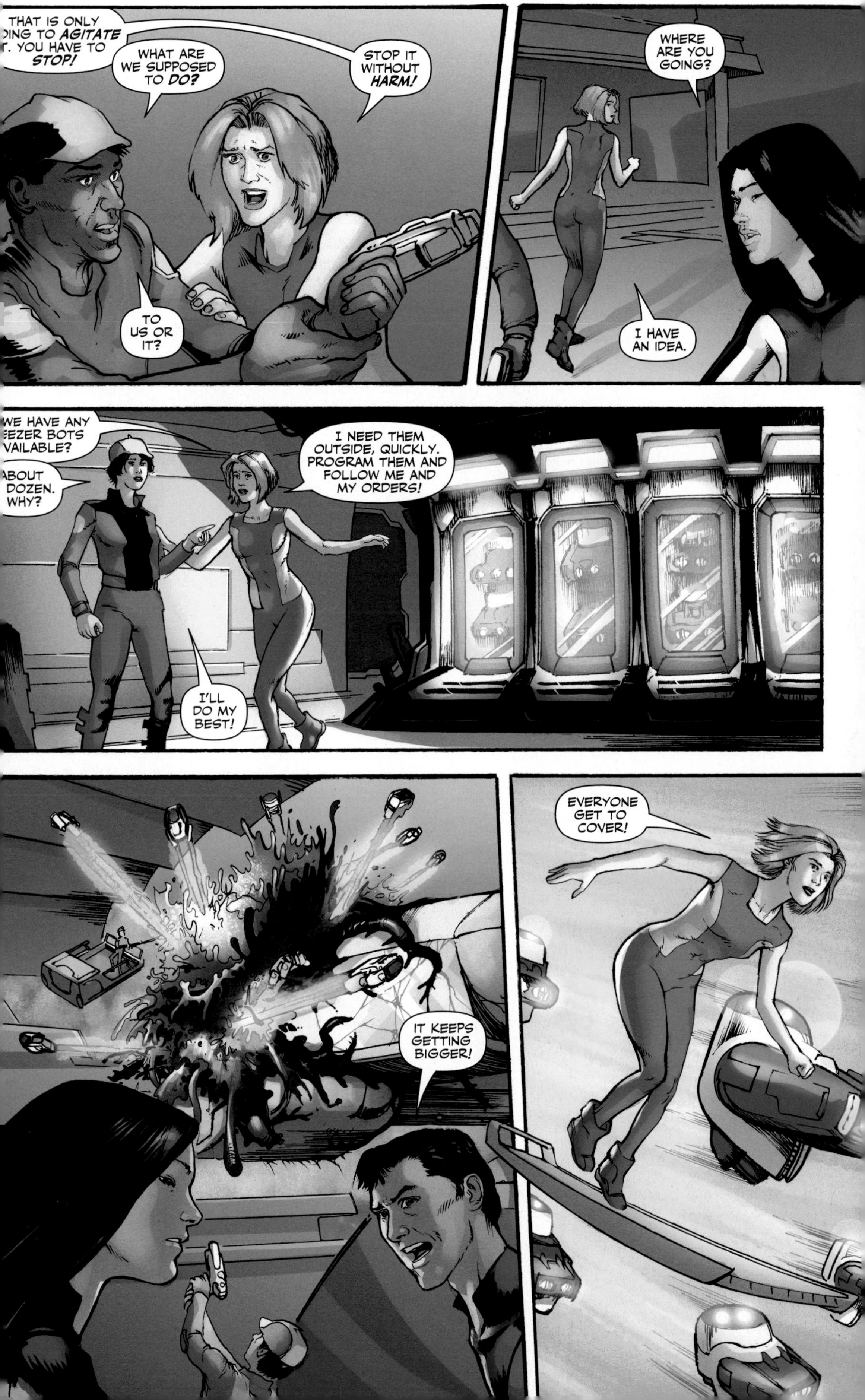
THAT IS ONLY
OING TO AGITATE
T. YOU HAVE TO
STOP!
WHAT ARE WE SUPPOSED TO DO?
STOP IT WITHOUT HARM!
TO US OR IT?
WHERE ARE YOU GOING?
I HAVE AN IDEA.
WE HAVE ANY
EEZER BOTS
VAILABLE?
ABOUT
DOZEN.
WHY?
I NEED THEM OUTSIDE, QUICKLY. PROGRAM THEM AND FOLLOW ME AND MY ORDERS!
I'LL DO MY BEST!
IT KEEPS GETTING BIGGER!
EVERYONE GET TO COVER!

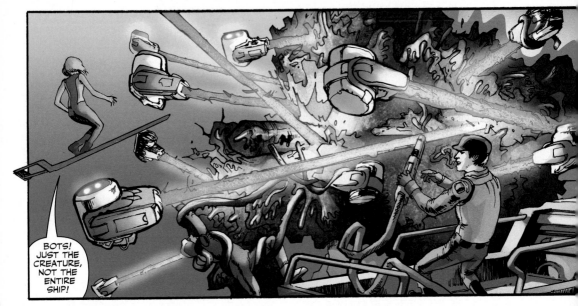

BOTS! JUST THE CREATURE, NOT THE ENTIRE SHIP!

OH, NO!

THEY AREN'T LISTENING!

CAN SOMEONE GET THEM LISTEN?

THE CREATURE IS *BLOCKING* THE FREQUENCY COMMAND!

THE SHIP AND DECK CANNOT TAKE THE *ADDITIONAL WEIGHT!*

EVERYONE CLEAR THE AREA!

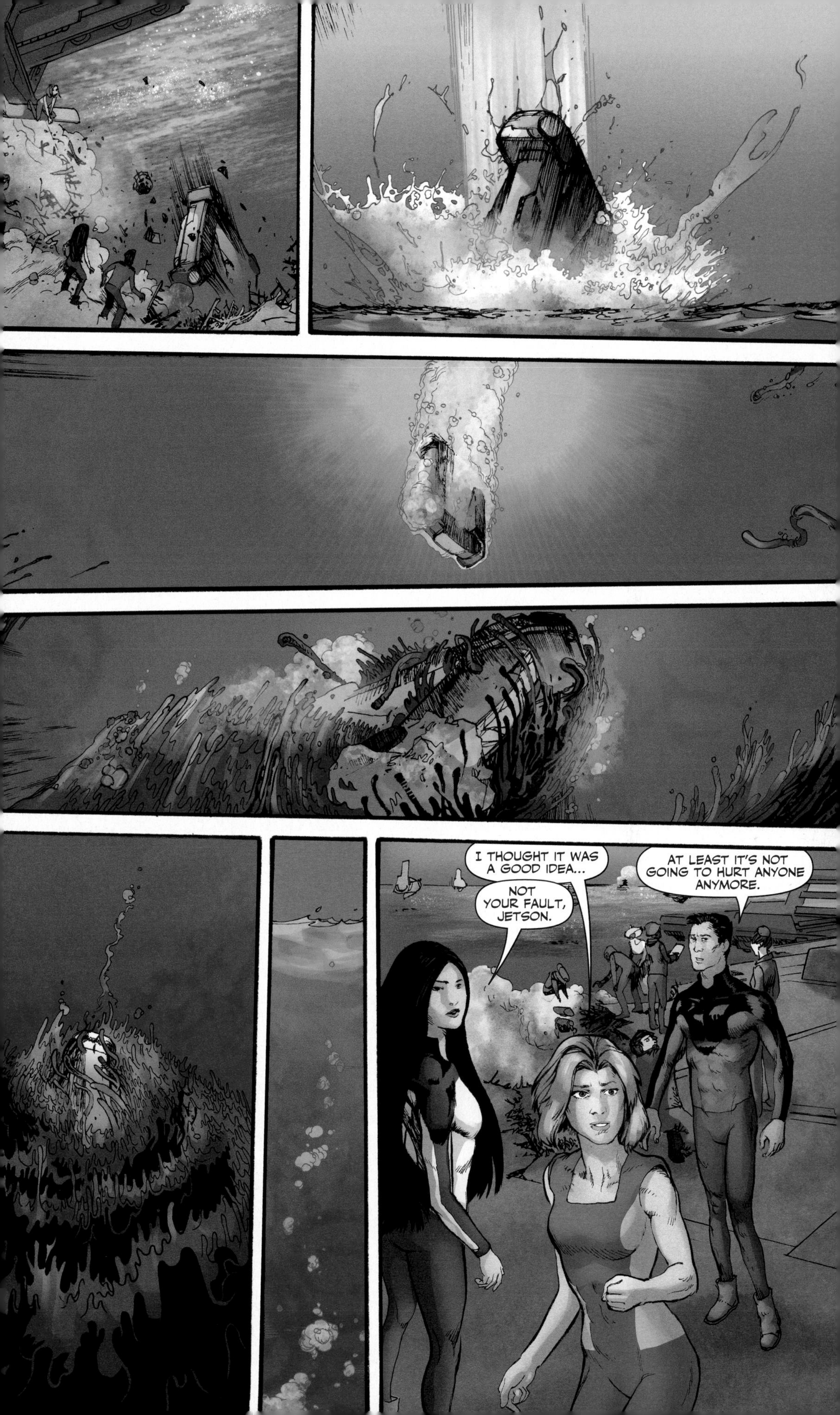
I THOUGHT IT WAS A GOOD IDEA...
NOT YOUR FAULT, JETSON.
AT LEAST IT'S NOT GOING TO HURT ANYONE ANYMORE.

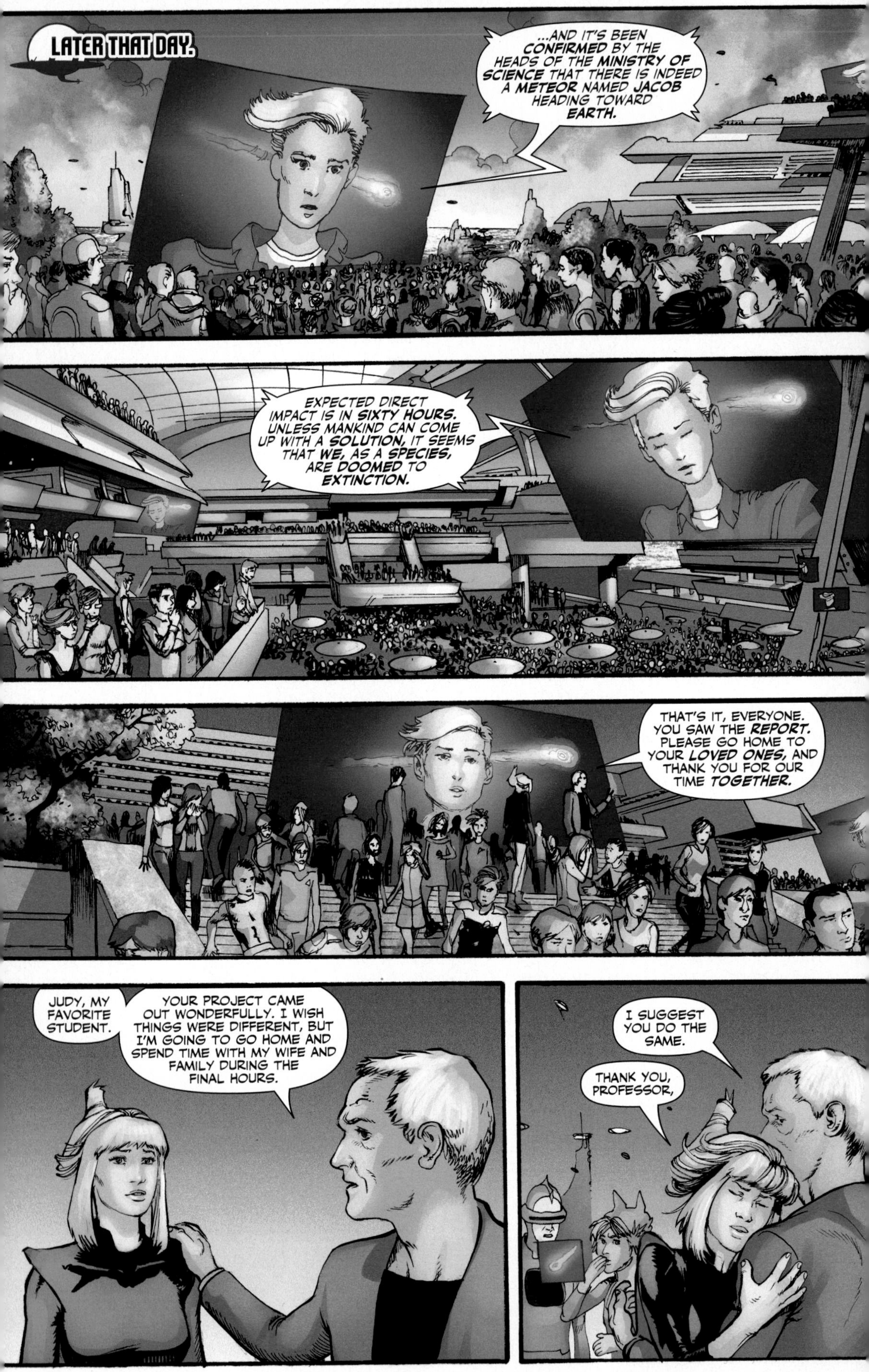
LATER THAT DAY.
...AND IT'S BEEN CONFIRMED BY THE HEADS OF THE MINISTRY OF SCIENCE THAT THERE IS INDEED A METEOR NAMED JACOB HEADING TOWARD EARTH.
EXPECTED DIRECT IMPACT IS IN SIXTY HOURS. UNLESS MANKIND CAN COME UP WITH A SOLUTION, IT SEEMS THAT WE, AS A SPECIES, ARE DOOMED TO EXTINCTION.
THAT'S IT, EVERYONE. YOU SAW THE REPORT. PLEASE GO HOME TO YOUR LOVED ONES, AND THANK YOU FOR OUR TIME TOGETHER.
JUDY, MY FAVORITE STUDENT.
YOUR PROJECT CAME OUT WONDERFULLY. I WISH THINGS WERE DIFFERENT, BUT I'M GOING TO GO HOME AND SPEND TIME WITH MY WIFE AND FAMILY DURING THE FINAL HOURS.
I SUGGEST YOU DO THE SAME.
THANK YOU, PROFESSOR,

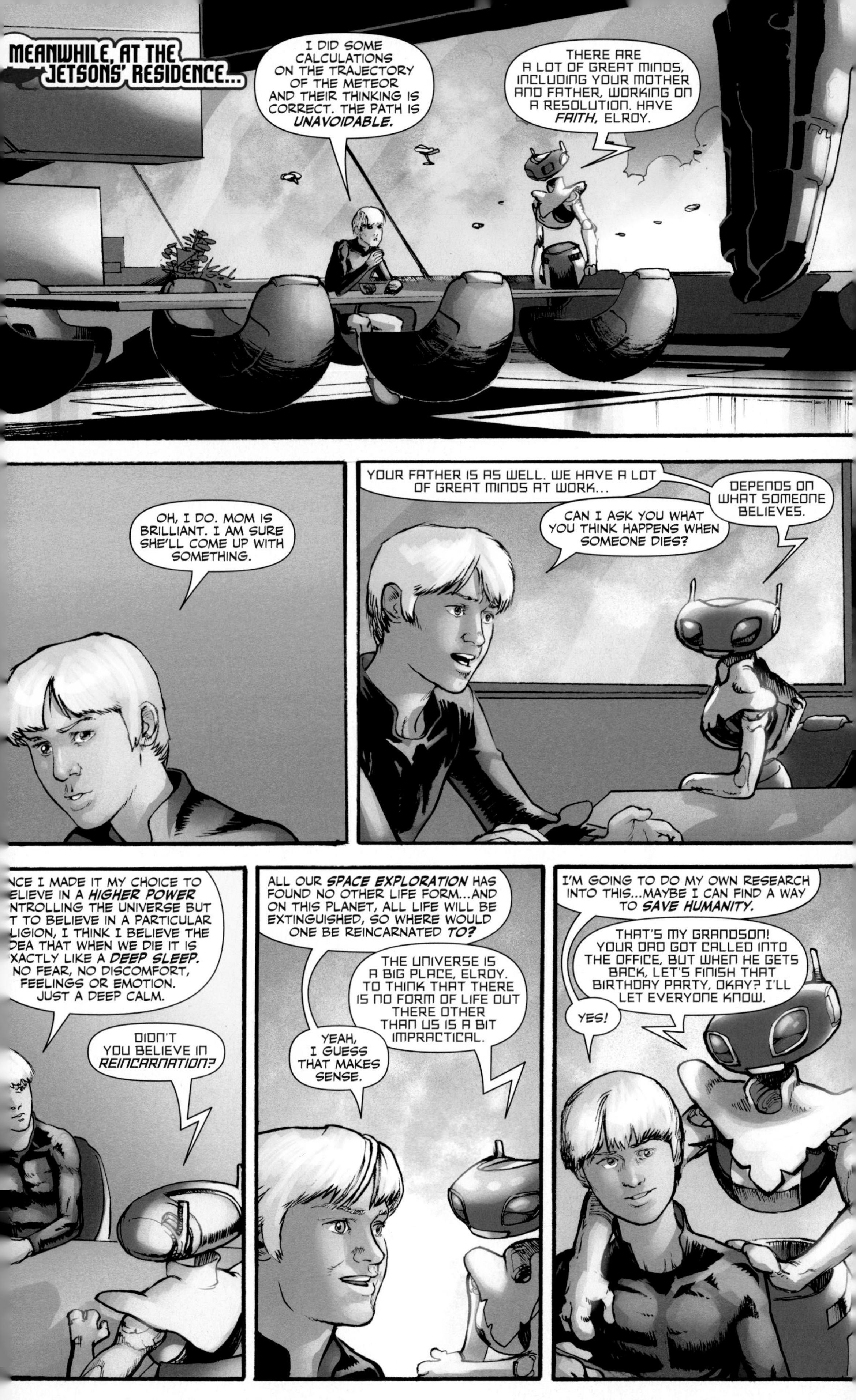
MEANWHILE, AT THE JETSONS' RESIDENCE...
I DID SOME CALCULATIONS ON THE TRAJECTORY OF THE METEOR AND THEIR THINKING IS CORRECT. THE PATH IS *UNAVOIDABLE.*
THERE ARE A LOT OF GREAT MINDS, INCLUDING YOUR MOTHER AND FATHER, WORKING ON A RESOLUTION. HAVE *FAITH,* ELROY.
OH, I DO. MOM IS BRILLIANT. I AM SURE SHE'LL COME UP WITH SOMETHING.
YOUR FATHER IS AS WELL. WE HAVE A LOT OF GREAT MINDS AT WORK...
CAN I ASK YOU WHAT YOU THINK HAPPENS WHEN SOMEONE DIES?
DEPENDS ON WHAT SOMEONE BELIEVES.
NCE I MADE IT MY CHOICE TO ELIEVE IN A *HIGHER POWER* NTROLLING THE UNIVERSE BUT T TO BELIEVE IN A PARTICULAR LIGION, I THINK I BELIEVE THE DEA THAT WHEN WE DIE IT IS XACTLY LIKE A *DEEP SLEEP.* NO FEAR, NO DISCOMFORT, FEELINGS OR EMOTION. JUST A DEEP CALM.
DIDN'T YOU BELIEVE IN *REINCARNATION?*
ALL OUR *SPACE EXPLORATION* HAS FOUND NO OTHER LIFE FORM...AND ON THIS PLANET, ALL LIFE WILL BE EXTINGUISHED, SO WHERE WOULD ONE BE REINCARNATED *TO?*
THE UNIVERSE IS A BIG PLACE, ELROY. TO THINK THAT THERE IS NO FORM OF LIFE OUT THERE OTHER THAN US IS A BIT IMPRACTICAL.
YEAH, I GUESS THAT MAKES SENSE.
I'M GOING TO DO MY OWN RESEARCH INTO THIS...MAYBE I CAN FIND A WAY TO *SAVE HUMANITY.*
THAT'S MY GRANDSON! YOUR DAD GOT CALLED INTO THE OFFICE, BUT WHEN HE GETS BACK, LET'S FINISH THAT BIRTHDAY PARTY, OKAY? I'LL LET EVERYONE KNOW.
YES!

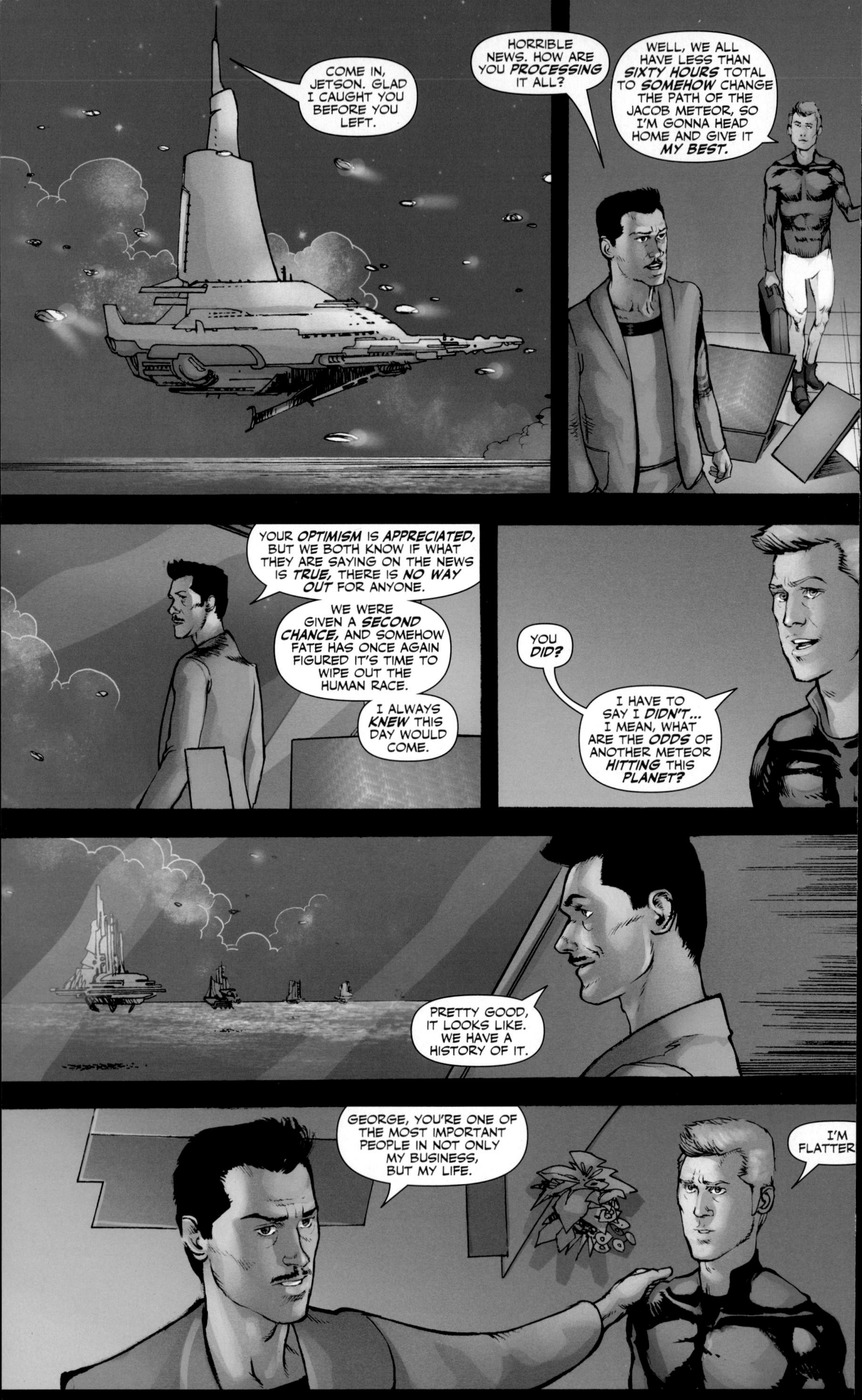
COME IN, JETSON. GLAD I CAUGHT YOU BEFORE YOU LEFT.
HORRIBLE NEWS. HOW ARE YOU PROCESSING IT ALL?
WELL, WE ALL HAVE LESS THAN SIXTY HOURS TOTAL TO SOMEHOW CHANGE THE PATH OF THE JACOB METEOR, SO I'M GONNA HEAD HOME AND GIVE IT MY BEST.
YOUR OPTIMISM IS APPRECIATED, BUT WE BOTH KNOW IF WHAT THEY ARE SAYING ON THE NEWS IS TRUE, THERE IS NO WAY OUT FOR ANYONE.
WE WERE GIVEN A SECOND CHANCE, AND SOMEHOW FATE HAS ONCE AGAIN FIGURED IT'S TIME TO WIPE OUT THE HUMAN RACE.
I ALWAYS KNEW THIS DAY WOULD COME.
YOU DID?
I HAVE TO SAY I DIDN'T... I MEAN, WHAT ARE THE ODDS OF ANOTHER METEOR HITTING THIS PLANET?
PRETTY GOOD, IT LOOKS LIKE. WE HAVE A HISTORY OF IT.
GEORGE, YOU'RE ONE OF THE MOST IMPORTANT PEOPLE IN NOT ONLY MY BUSINESS, BUT MY LIFE.
I'M FLATTER

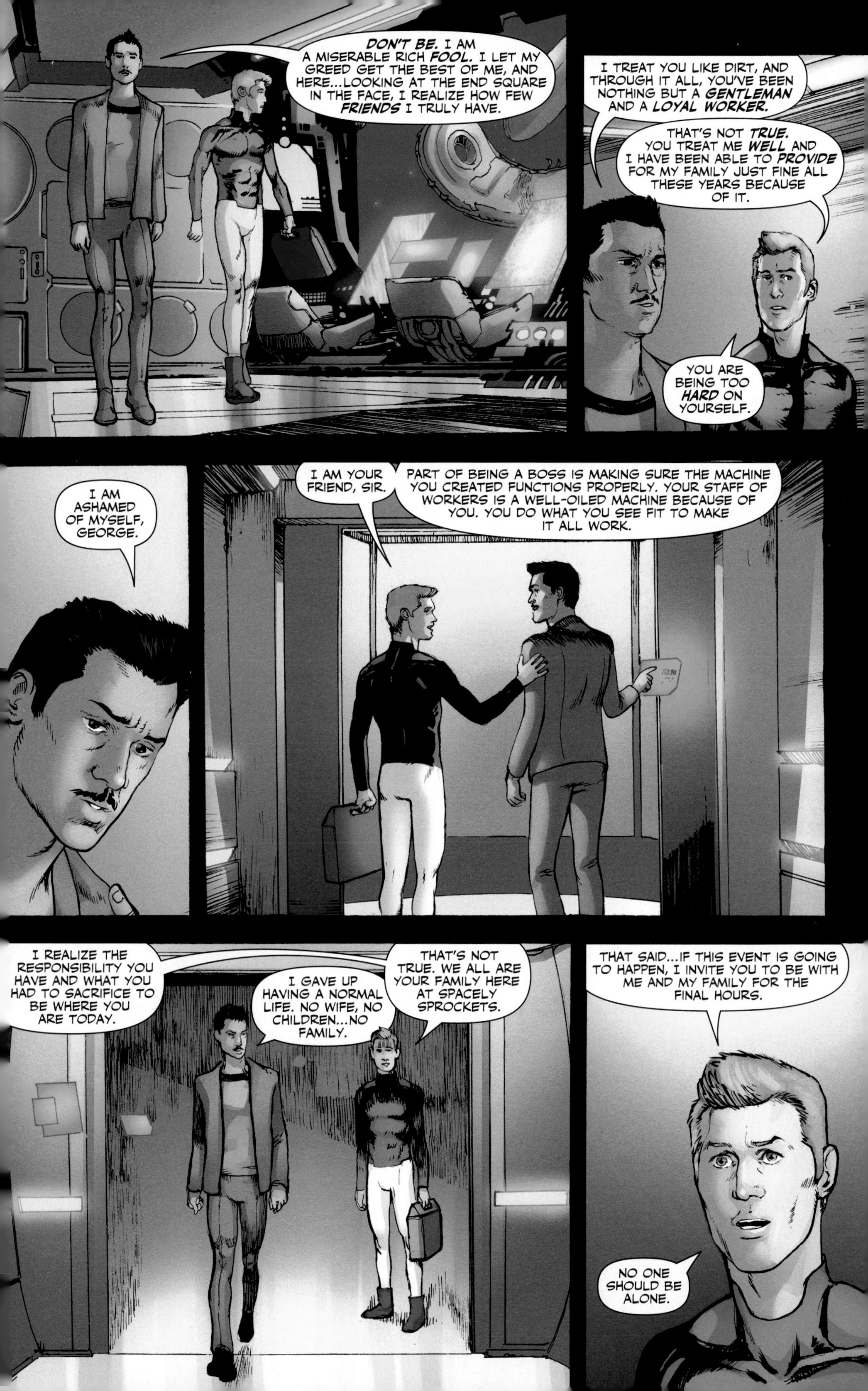
DON'T BE. I AM A MISERABLE RICH FOOL. I LET MY GREED GET THE BEST OF ME, AND HERE...LOOKING AT THE END SQUARE IN THE FACE, I REALIZE HOW FEW FRIENDS I TRULY HAVE.
I TREAT YOU LIKE DIRT, AND THROUGH IT ALL, YOU'VE BEEN NOTHING BUT A GENTLEMAN AND A LOYAL WORKER.
THAT'S NOT TRUE. YOU TREAT ME WELL AND I HAVE BEEN ABLE TO PROVIDE FOR MY FAMILY JUST FINE ALL THESE YEARS BECAUSE OF IT.
YOU ARE BEING TOO HARD ON YOURSELF.
I AM ASHAMED OF MYSELF, GEORGE.
I AM YOUR FRIEND, SIR.
PART OF BEING A BOSS IS MAKING SURE THE MACHINE YOU CREATED FUNCTIONS PROPERLY. YOUR STAFF OF WORKERS IS A WELL-OILED MACHINE BECAUSE OF YOU. YOU DO WHAT YOU SEE FIT TO MAKE IT ALL WORK.
I REALIZE THE RESPONSIBILITY YOU HAVE AND WHAT YOU HAD TO SACRIFICE TO BE WHERE YOU ARE TODAY.
I GAVE UP HAVING A NORMAL LIFE. NO WIFE, NO CHILDREN...NO FAMILY.
THAT'S NOT TRUE. WE ALL ARE YOUR FAMILY HERE AT SPACELY SPROCKETS.
THAT SAID...IF THIS EVENT IS GOING TO HAPPEN, I INVITE YOU TO BE WITH ME AND MY FAMILY FOR THE FINAL HOURS.
NO ONE SHOULD BE ALONE.

THANK YOU FOR THAT. IT MEANS THE *WORLD* TO ME. REALLY.

I MEAN IT. YOU'RE PART OF MY *FAMILY.*

WELL, AS YOU KNOW, I AM A BILLIONAIRE, ONE OF THE THREE *RICHEST MEN* ON THE *PLANET.*

EVERYONE KNOWS THAT, SIR.

HUMOR ME, GEORGE.

I DON'T KNOW THIS ELEVATOR. DID YOU JUST HAVE IT INSTALLED?

I HAVE BEEN KEEPING IT SECRET, AND WOULD LIKE IT TO REMAIN SO.

NO WORRIES. MY LIPS ARE SEALED. YOU WERE SAYING

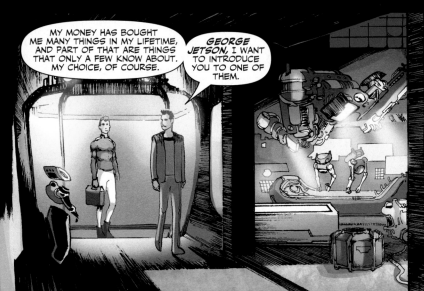

MY MONEY HAS BOUGHT ME MANY THINGS IN MY LIFETIME, AND PART OF THAT ARE THINGS THAT ONLY A FEW KNOW ABOUT. MY CHOICE, OF COURSE.

GEORGE JETSON, I WANT TO INTRODUCE YOU TO ONE OF THEM.

GEORGE, I WOULD LIKE YOU TO MEET THE *SS7.*

WO'

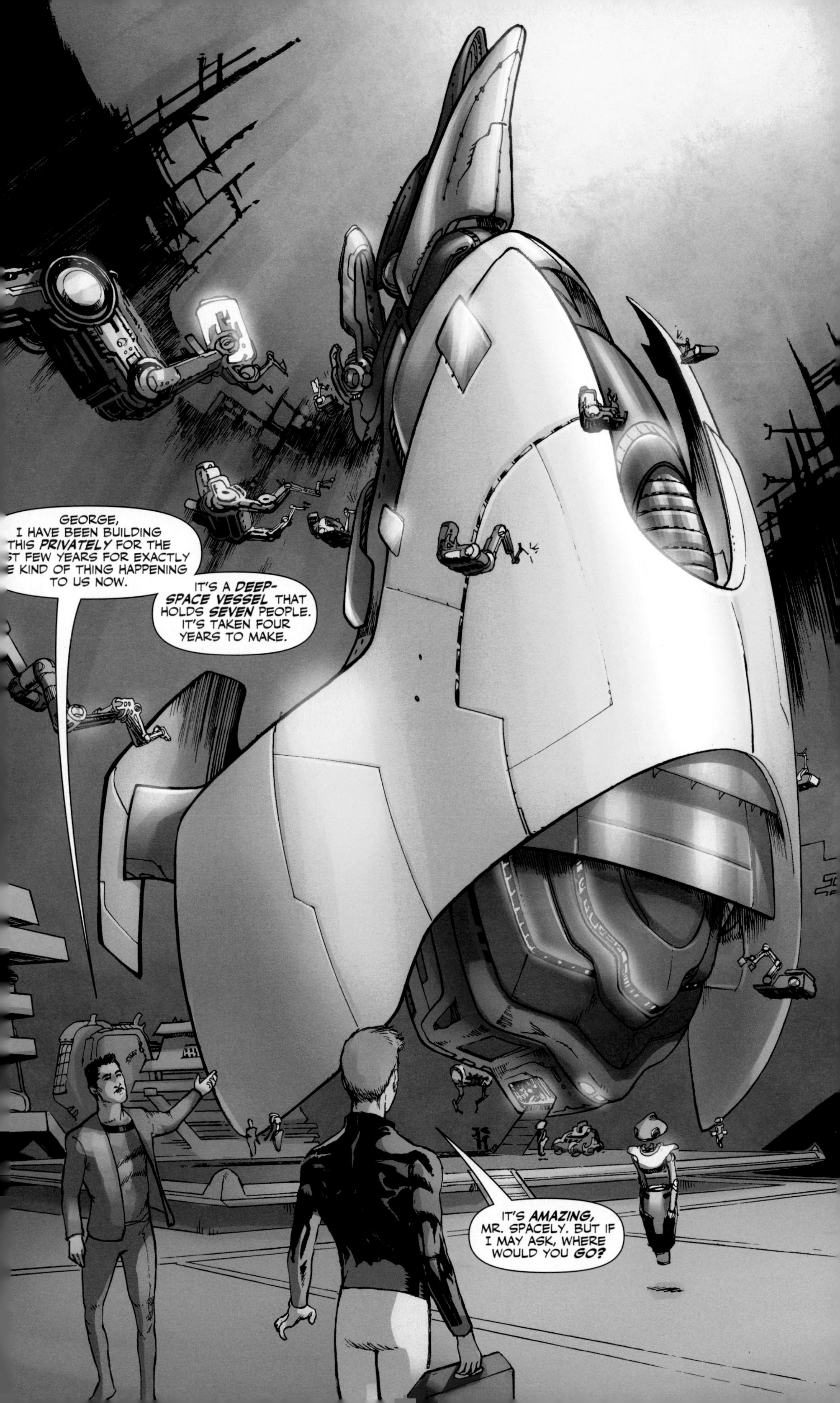
GEORGE, I HAVE BEEN BUILDING THIS *PRIVATELY* FOR THE ST FEW YEARS FOR EXACTLY E KIND OF THING HAPPENING TO US NOW.
IT'S A *DEEP-SPACE VESSEL* THAT HOLDS *SEVEN* PEOPLE. IT'S TAKEN FOUR YEARS TO MAKE.
IT'S *AMAZING,* MR. SPACELY. BUT IF I MAY ASK, WHERE WOULD YOU *GO?*

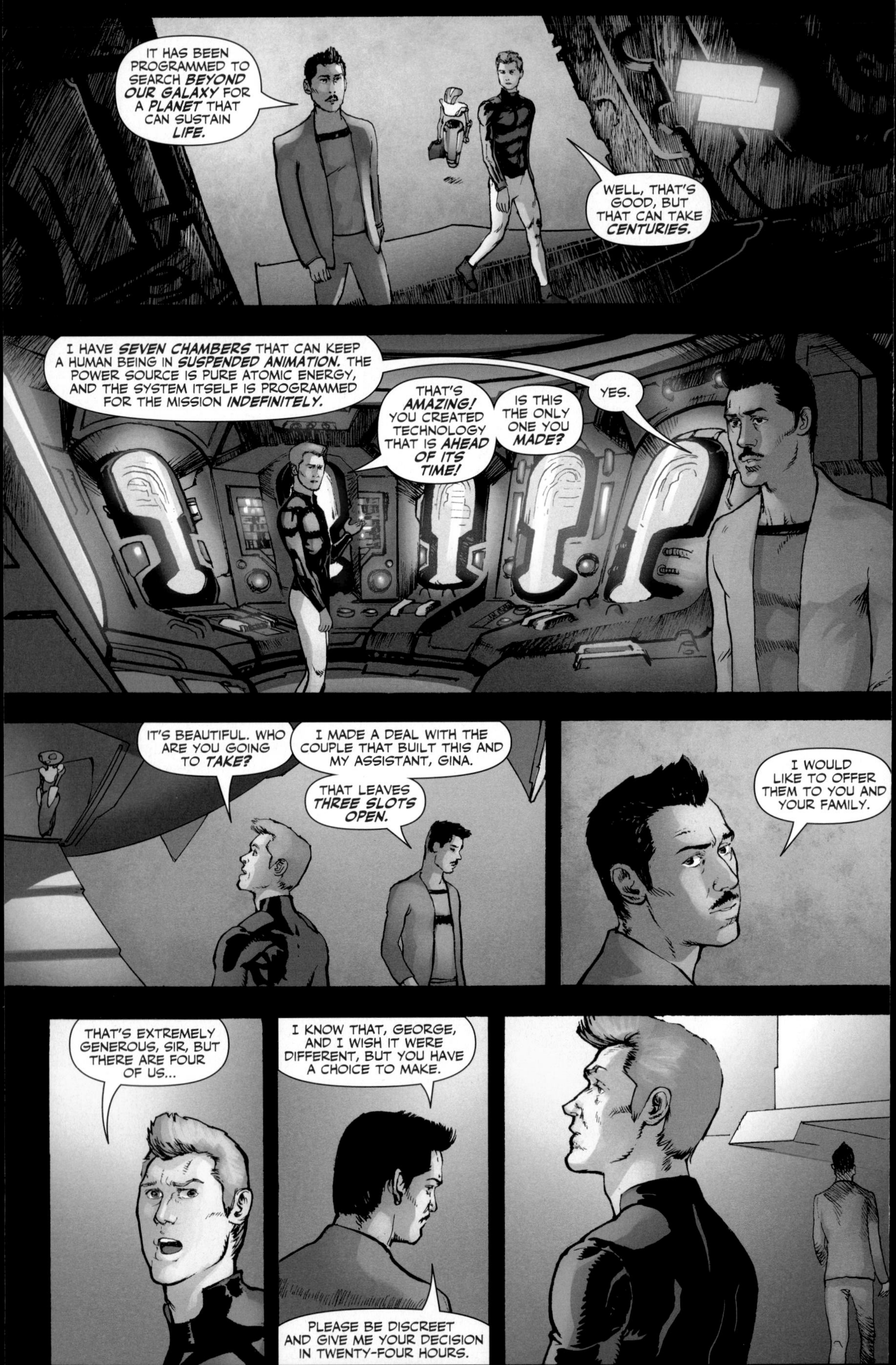

IT HAS BEEN PROGRAMMED TO SEARCH BEYOND OUR GALAXY FOR A PLANET THAT CAN SUSTAIN LIFE.
WELL, THAT'S GOOD, BUT THAT CAN TAKE CENTURIES.
I HAVE SEVEN CHAMBERS THAT CAN KEEP A HUMAN BEING IN SUSPENDED ANIMATION. THE POWER SOURCE IS PURE ATOMIC ENERGY, AND THE SYSTEM ITSELF IS PROGRAMMED FOR THE MISSION INDEFINITELY.
THAT'S AMAZING! YOU CREATED TECHNOLOGY THAT IS AHEAD OF ITS TIME!
IS THIS THE ONLY ONE YOU MADE?
YES.
IT'S BEAUTIFUL. WHO ARE YOU GOING TO TAKE?
I MADE A DEAL WITH THE COUPLE THAT BUILT THIS AND MY ASSISTANT, GINA.
THAT LEAVES THREE SLOTS OPEN.
I WOULD LIKE TO OFFER THEM TO YOU AND YOUR FAMILY.
THAT'S EXTREMELY GENEROUS, SIR, BUT THERE ARE FOUR OF US...
I KNOW THAT, GEORGE, AND I WISH IT WERE DIFFERENT, BUT YOU HAVE A CHOICE TO MAKE.
PLEASE BE DISCREET AND GIVE ME YOUR DECISION IN TWENTY-FOUR HOURS.

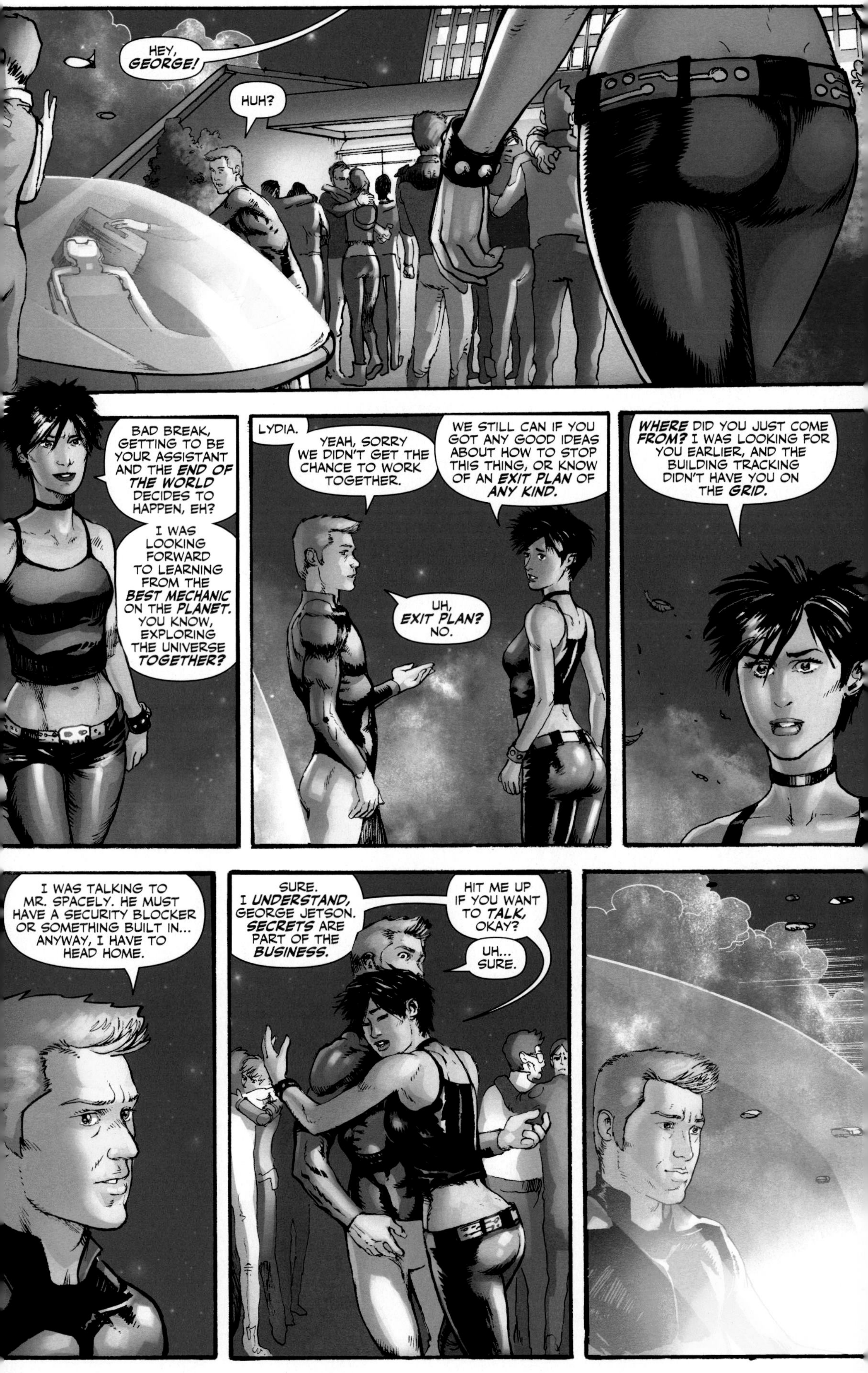
HEY, GEORGE!
HUH?
BAD BREAK, GETTING TO BE YOUR ASSISTANT AND THE END OF THE WORLD DECIDES TO HAPPEN, EH?
I WAS LOOKING FORWARD TO LEARNING FROM THE BEST MECHANIC ON THE PLANET. YOU KNOW, EXPLORING THE UNIVERSE TOGETHER?
LYDIA.
YEAH, SORRY WE DIDN'T GET THE CHANCE TO WORK TOGETHER.
WE STILL CAN IF YOU GOT ANY GOOD IDEAS ABOUT HOW TO STOP THIS THING, OR KNOW OF AN EXIT PLAN OF ANY KIND.
UH, EXIT PLAN? NO.
WHERE DID YOU JUST COME FROM? I WAS LOOKING FOR YOU EARLIER, AND THE BUILDING TRACKING DIDN'T HAVE YOU ON THE GRID.
I WAS TALKING TO MR. SPACELY. HE MUST HAVE A SECURITY BLOCKER OR SOMETHING BUILT IN... ANYWAY, I HAVE TO HEAD HOME.
SURE. I UNDERSTAND, GEORGE JETSON. SECRETS ARE PART OF THE BUSINESS.
HIT ME UP IF YOU WANT TO TALK, OKAY?
UH... SURE.

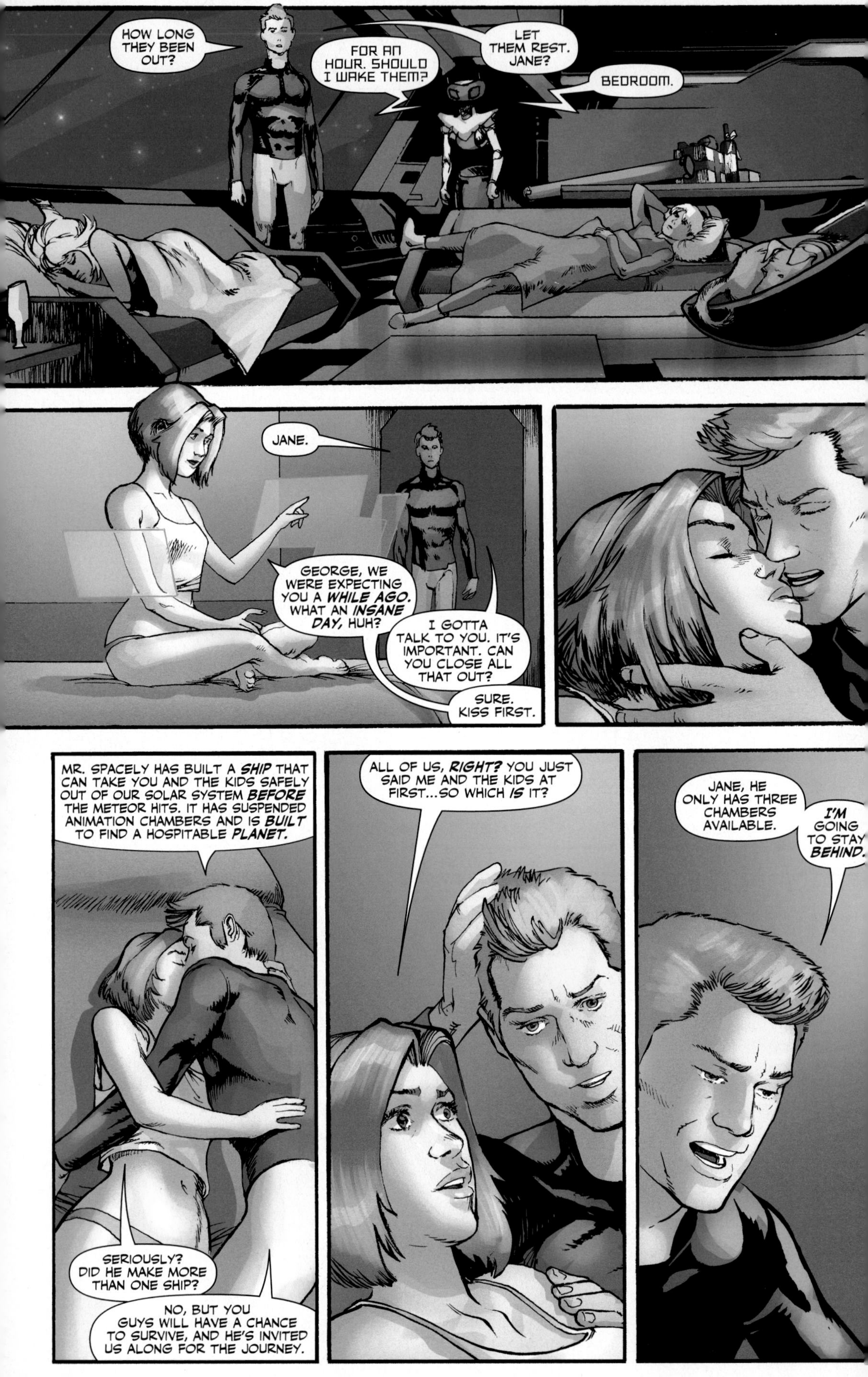
HOW LONG THEY BEEN OUT?
FOR AN HOUR. SHOULD I WAKE THEM?
LET THEM REST. JANE?
BEDROOM.
JANE.
GEORGE, WE WERE EXPECTING YOU A WHILE AGO. WHAT AN INSANE DAY, HUH?
I GOTTA TALK TO YOU. IT'S IMPORTANT. CAN YOU CLOSE ALL THAT OUT?
SURE. KISS FIRST.
MR. SPACELY HAS BUILT A SHIP THAT CAN TAKE YOU AND THE KIDS SAFELY OUT OF OUR SOLAR SYSTEM BEFORE THE METEOR HITS. IT HAS SUSPENDED ANIMATION CHAMBERS AND IS BUILT TO FIND A HOSPITABLE PLANET.
SERIOUSLY? DID HE MAKE MORE THAN ONE SHIP?
NO, BUT YOU GUYS WILL HAVE A CHANCE TO SURVIVE, AND HE'S INVITED US ALONG FOR THE JOURNEY.
ALL OF US, RIGHT? YOU JUST SAID ME AND THE KIDS AT FIRST...SO WHICH IS IT?
JANE, HE ONLY HAS THREE CHAMBERS AVAILABLE.
I'M GOING TO STAY BEHIND.

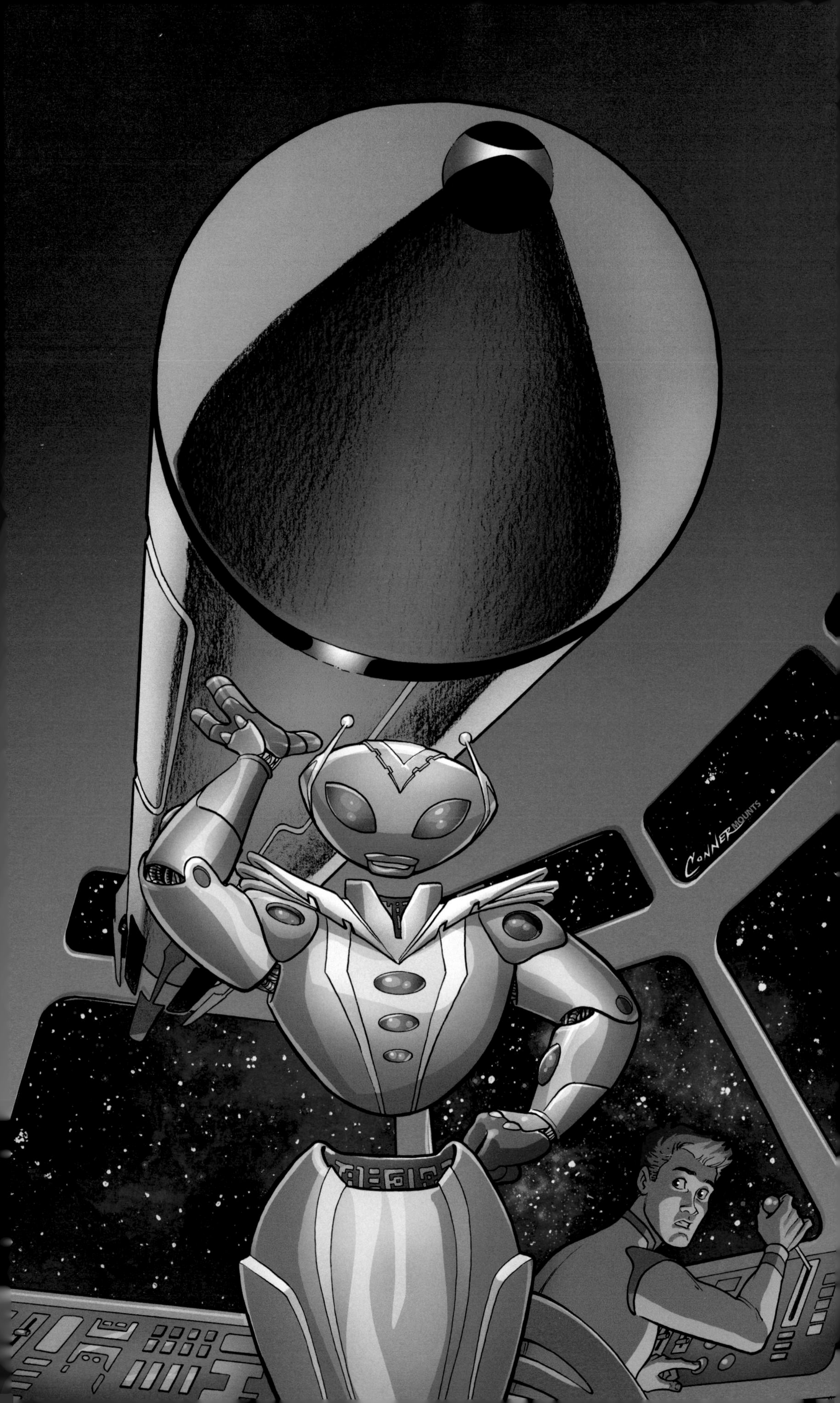
CONNER MOUNTS

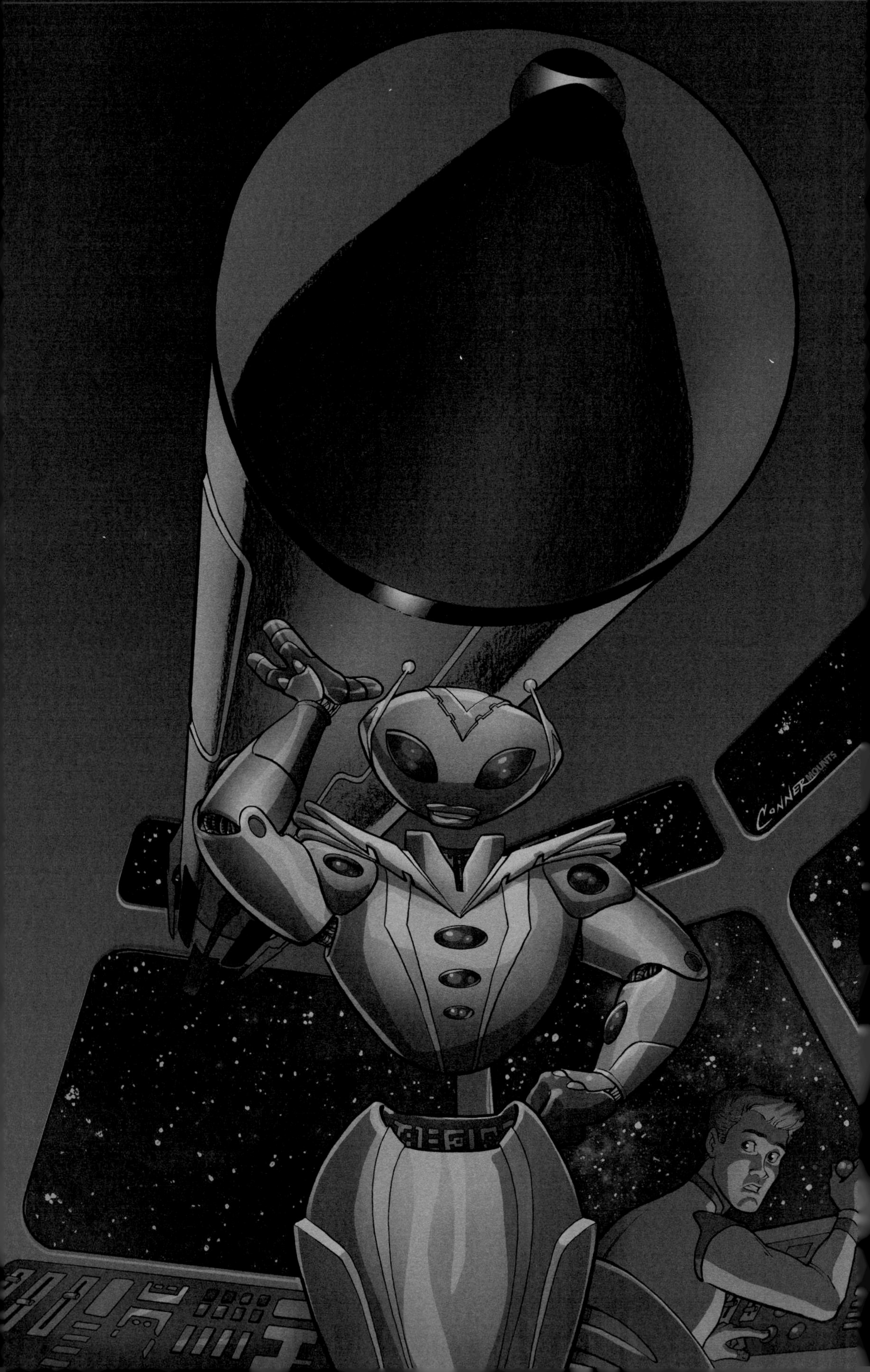
CONNER MOUNTS

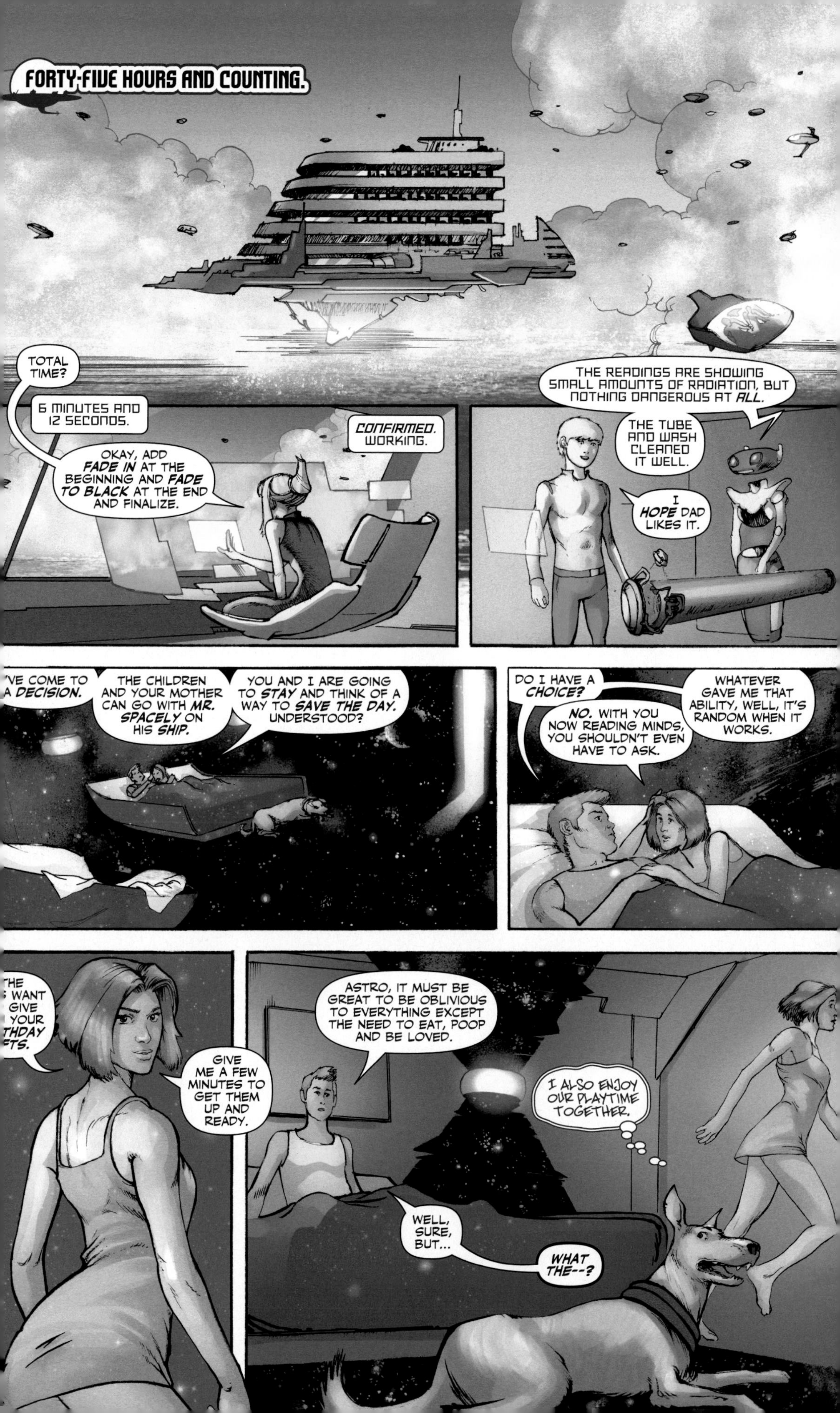
FORTY-FIVE HOURS AND COUNTING.
TOTAL TIME?
6 MINUTES AND 12 SECONDS.
OKAY, ADD FADE IN AT THE BEGINNING AND FADE TO BLACK AT THE END AND FINALIZE.
CONFIRMED. WORKING.
THE READINGS ARE SHOWING SMALL AMOUNTS OF RADIATION, BUT NOTHING DANGEROUS AT ALL.
THE TUBE AND WASH CLEANED IT WELL.
I HOPE DAD LIKES IT.
'VE COME TO A DECISION.
THE CHILDREN AND YOUR MOTHER CAN GO WITH MR. SPACELY ON HIS SHIP.
YOU AND I ARE GOING TO STAY AND THINK OF A WAY TO SAVE THE DAY. UNDERSTOOD?
DO I HAVE A CHOICE?
NO. WITH YOU NOW READING MINDS, YOU SHOULDN'T EVEN HAVE TO ASK.
WHATEVER GAVE ME THAT ABILITY, WELL, IT'S RANDOM WHEN IT WORKS.
THE WANT GIVE YOUR THDAY FTS.
GIVE ME A FEW MINUTES TO GET THEM UP AND READY.
ASTRO, IT MUST BE GREAT TO BE OBLIVIOUS TO EVERYTHING EXCEPT THE NEED TO EAT, POOP AND BE LOVED.
I ALSO ENJOY OUR PLAYTIME TOGETHER.
WELL, SURE, BUT...
WHAT THE--?

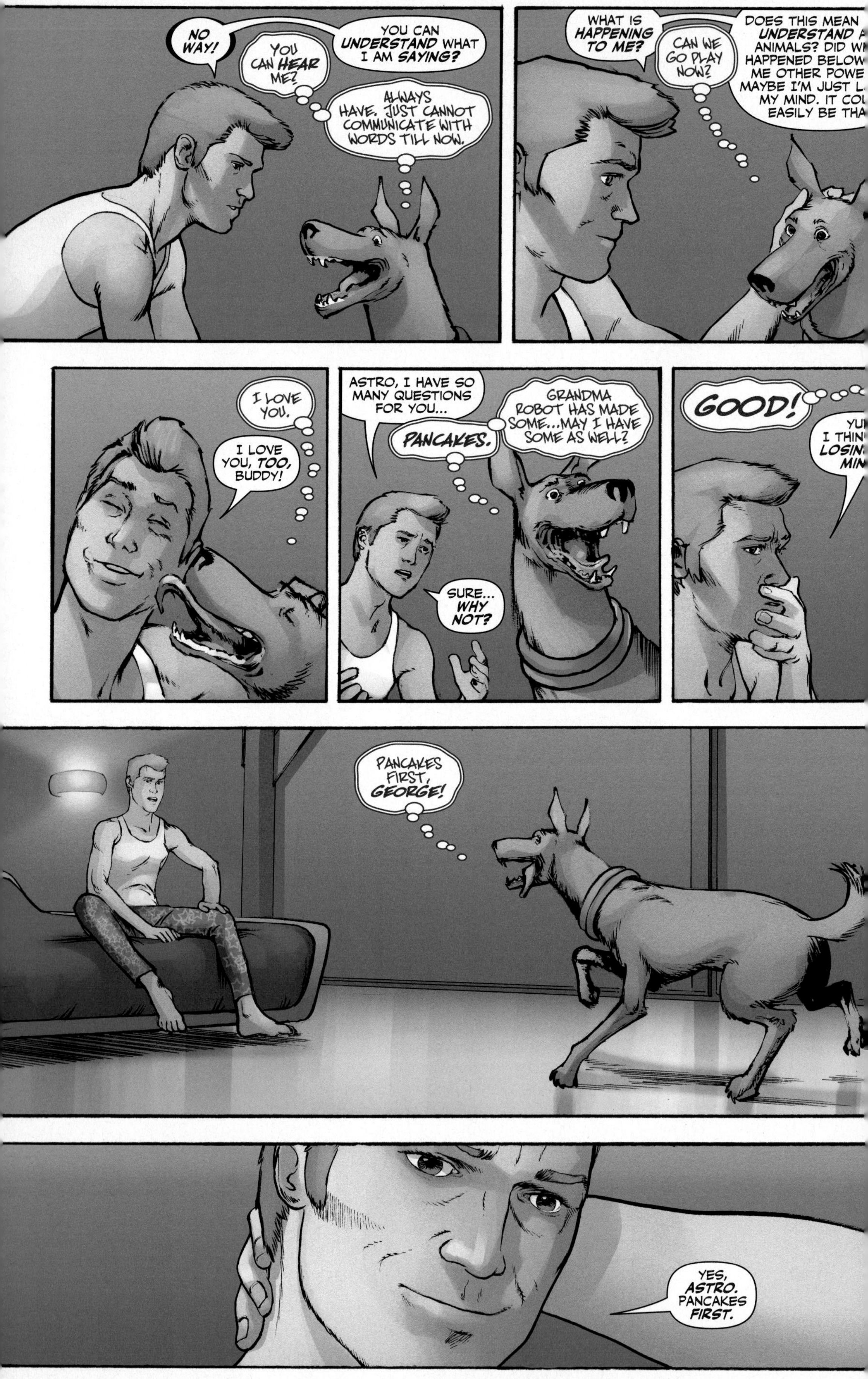
NO WAY!
YOU CAN HEAR ME?
YOU CAN UNDERSTAND WHAT I AM SAYING?
ALWAYS HAVE. JUST CANNOT COMMUNICATE WITH WORDS TILL NOW.
WHAT IS HAPPENING TO ME?
CAN WE GO PLAY NOW?
DOES THIS MEAN UNDERSTAND ANIMALS? DID HAPPENED BELOW ME OTHER MAYBE I'M JUST MY MIND. IT EASILY BE
I LOVE YOU.
I LOVE YOU, TOO, BUDDY!
ASTRO, I HAVE SO MANY QUESTIONS FOR YOU...
PANCAKES.
GRANDMA ROBOT HAS MADE SOME...MAY I HAVE SOME AS WELL?
SURE... WHY NOT?
GOOD!
PANCAKES FIRST, GEORGE!
YES, ASTRO. PANCAKES FIRST.

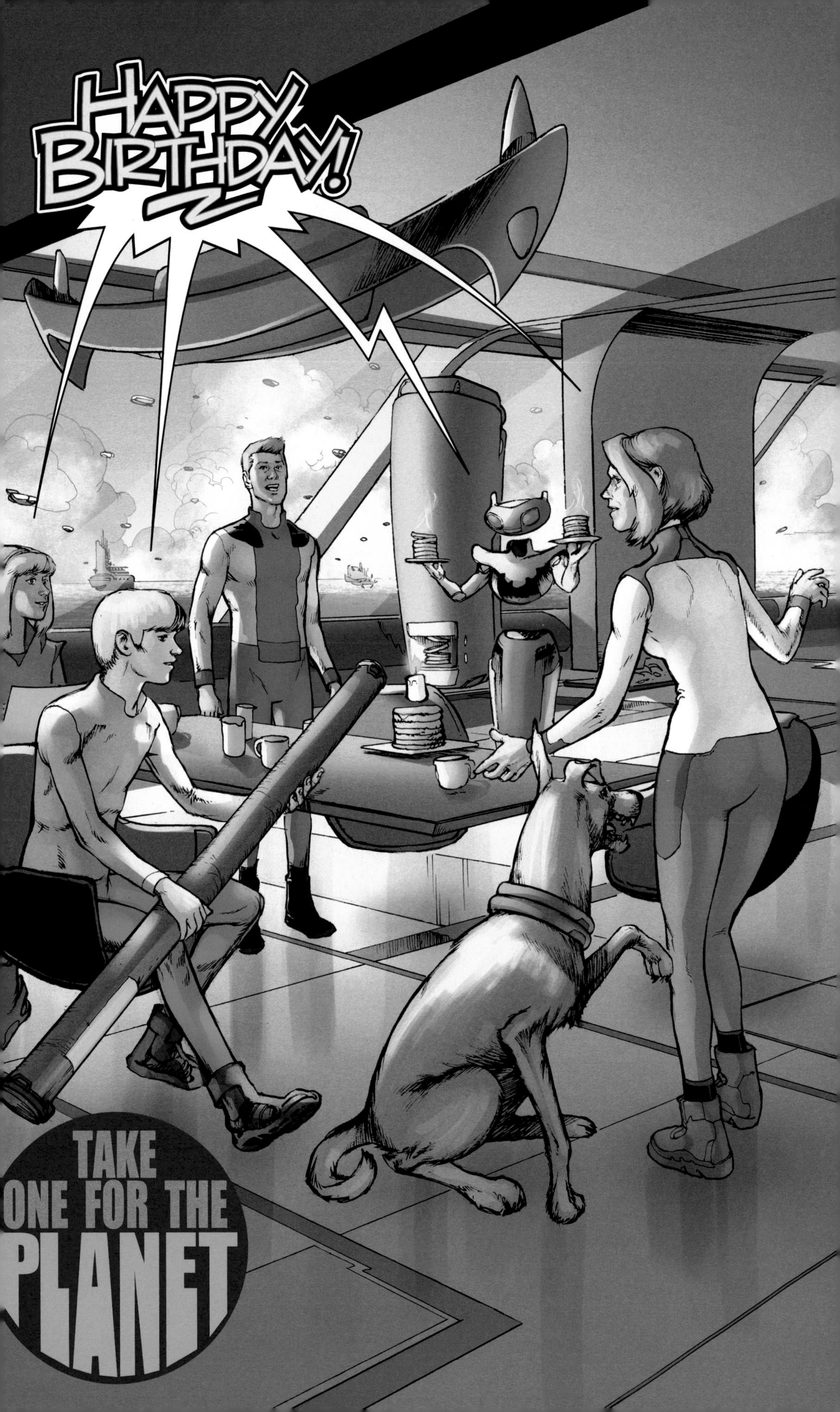

HAPPY BIRTHDAY!
TAKE ONE FOR THE PLANET

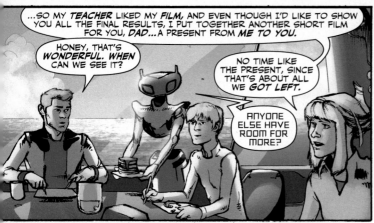

...SO MY *TEACHER* LIKED MY *FILM,* AND EVEN THOUGH I'D LIKE TO SHOW YOU ALL THE FINAL RESULTS, I PUT TOGETHER ANOTHER SHORT FILM FOR YOU, *DAD*...A PRESENT FROM *ME TO YOU.*

HONEY, THAT'S *WONDERFUL. WHEN* CAN WE SEE IT?

NO TIME LIKE THE PRESENT, SINCE THAT'S ABOUT ALL WE *GOT LEFT.*

ANYONE ELSE HAVE ROOM FOR MORE?

MOM, ASTRO SAID HE WOULD *LIKE* SOME PANCAKES, IF YOU DON'T MIND.

HE *TOLD* YOU THAT?

SURE, ALSO T US WHE NEEDS A WHEN T AN INTR AND A W LOT O OTHE STU

LIGHT LOW.

COMPUTER, PLEASE RUN *FILE 002.*

I *HOPE* YOU LIKE IT, *DAD.*

AH, THE BEST DAY OF MY *LIFE,* WHEN I *MARRIED* YOUR *BEAUTIFUL MOTHER.*

OH, *GEORG*

"THE NEXT BEST DAY, WHEN WE HAD YOU, *JUDY.* I CAN'T BELIEVE YOU FOUND THIS OLD FOOTAGE."

"THAT'S MY *BEAUTIFUL ELROY,* LOOK AT YOU! YOU BELIEVE YOU WE EVER THAT SMALL?"

LOOK, *GRANDMA,* IT'S *YOU* IN YOUR *OLD BODY.*

IT'S LIKE I AM LOOKING AT ANOTHER PERSON...

I FEEL THE SAME, BUT IN A DIFFERENT WAY, *RIGHT?*

YOU DEAR BOY.

LOOK AT *YOU KIDS!* I REMEMBER THAT *SPACELY PICNIC*...WE CAME IN SECOND PLACE IN THE FATHER-DAUGHTER COMPETITION

THAT'S ONLY BECAUSE YOU *TRIPPED* RIGHT BEFORE THE FINISH LINE.

GRAVITY IS MY *ENEMY.*

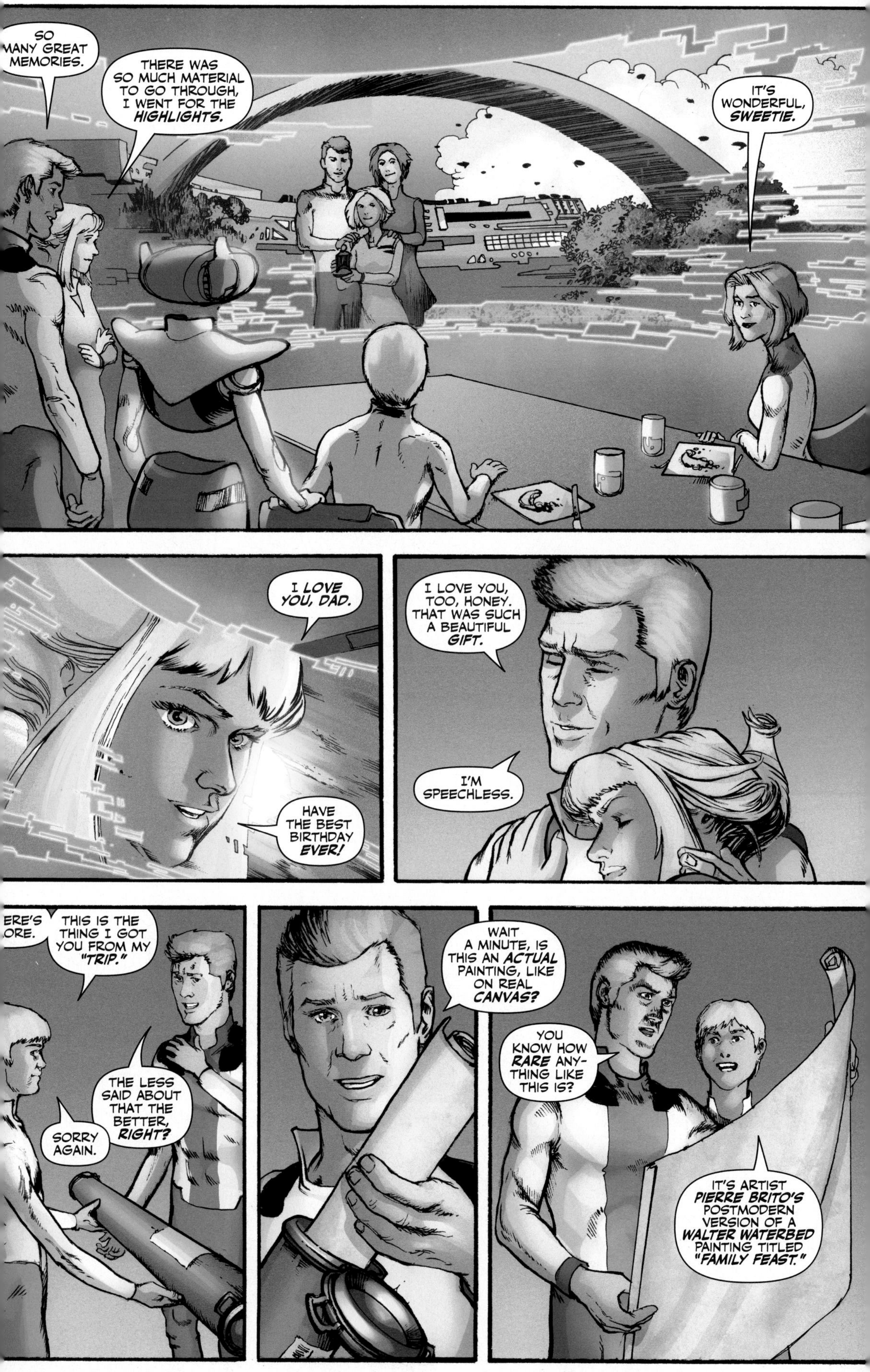
SO MANY GREAT MEMORIES.
THERE WAS SO MUCH MATERIAL TO GO THROUGH, I WENT FOR THE HIGHLIGHTS.
IT'S WONDERFUL, SWEETIE.
I LOVE YOU, DAD.
HAVE THE BEST BIRTHDAY EVER!
I LOVE YOU, TOO, HONEY. THAT WAS SUCH A BEAUTIFUL GIFT.
I'M SPEECHLESS.
ERE'S ORE.
THIS IS THE THING I GOT YOU FROM MY "TRIP."
THE LESS SAID ABOUT THAT THE BETTER, RIGHT?
SORRY AGAIN.
WAIT A MINUTE, IS THIS AN ACTUAL PAINTING, LIKE ON REAL CANVAS?
YOU KNOW HOW RARE ANYTHING LIKE THIS IS?
IT'S ARTIST PIERRE BRITO'S POSTMODERN VERSION OF A WALTER WATERBED PAINTING TITLED "FAMILY FEAST."

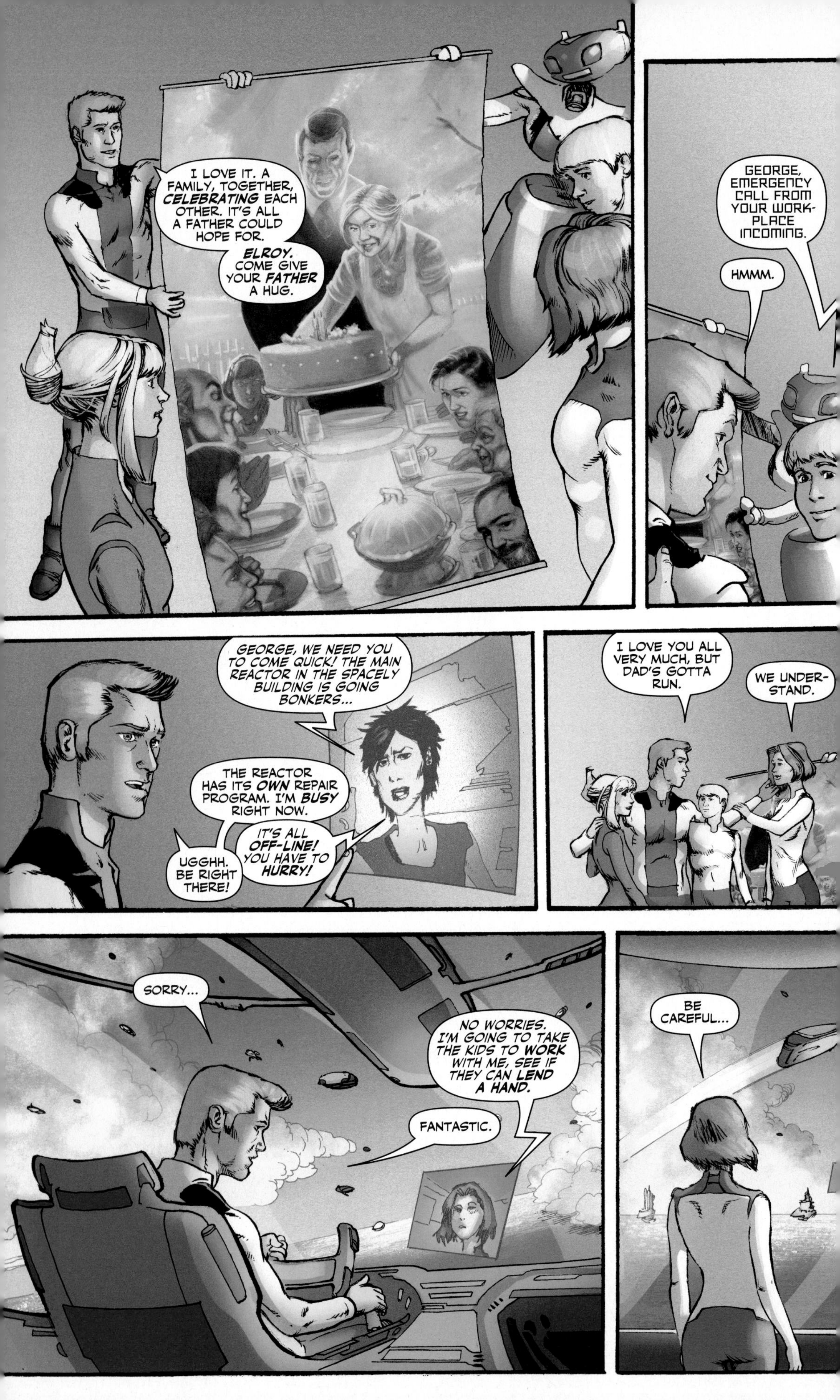
I LOVE IT. A FAMILY, TOGETHER, CELEBRATING EACH OTHER. IT'S ALL A FATHER COULD HOPE FOR.
ELROY. COME GIVE YOUR FATHER A HUG.
GEORGE, EMERGENCY CALL FROM YOUR WORK-PLACE INCOMING.
HMMM.
GEORGE, WE NEED YOU TO COME QUICK! THE MAIN REACTOR IN THE SPACELY BUILDING IS GOING BONKERS...
THE REACTOR HAS ITS OWN REPAIR PROGRAM. I'M BUSY RIGHT NOW.
IT'S ALL OFF-LINE! YOU HAVE TO HURRY!
UGGHH. BE RIGHT THERE!
I LOVE YOU ALL VERY MUCH, BUT DAD'S GOTTA RUN.
WE UNDER-STAND.
SORRY...
NO WORRIES. I'M GOING TO TAKE THE KIDS TO WORK WITH ME, SEE IF THEY CAN LEND A HAND.
FANTASTIC.
BE CAREFUL...

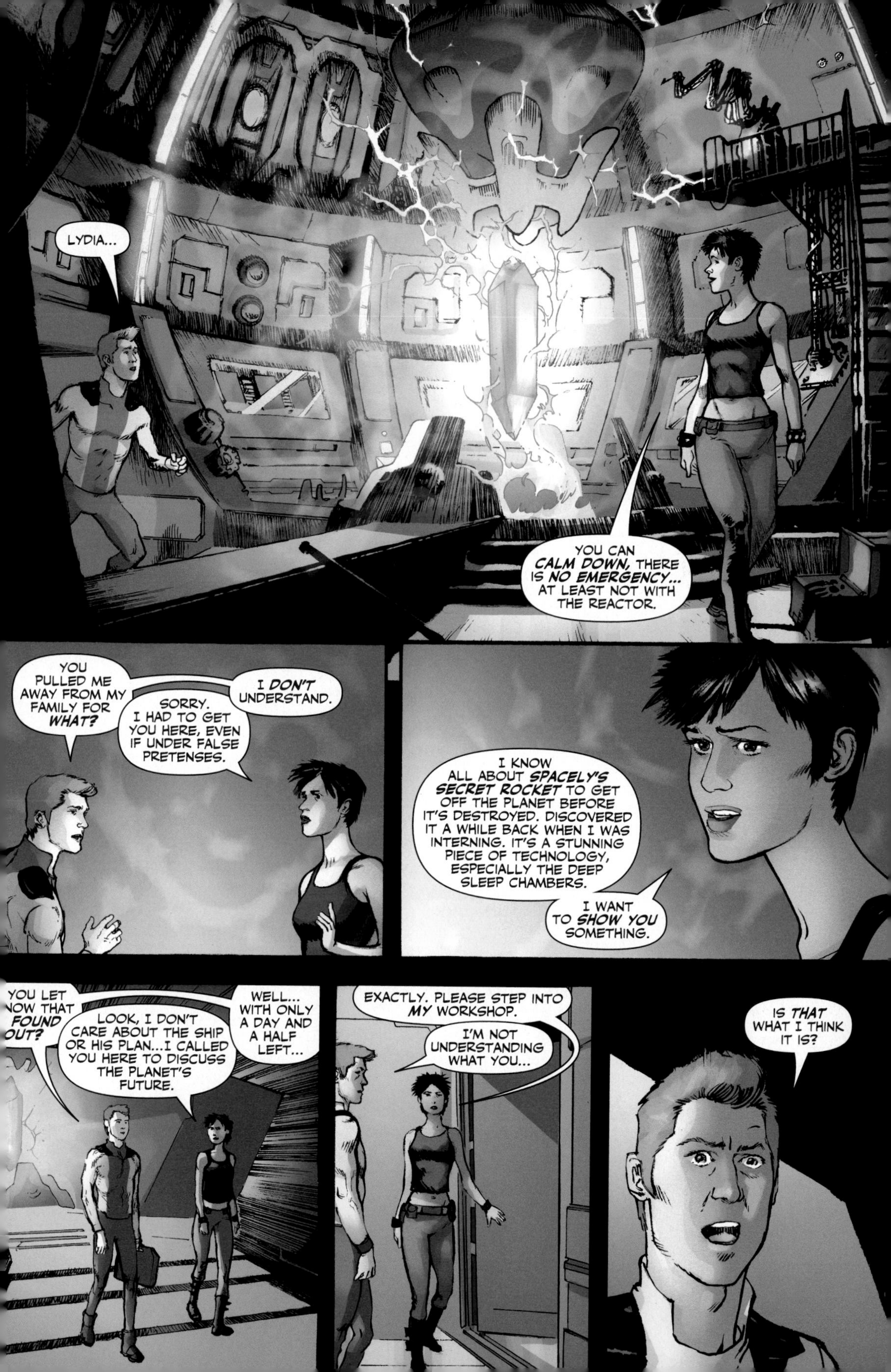
LYDIA...
YOU CAN CALM DOWN, THERE IS NO EMERGENCY... AT LEAST NOT WITH THE REACTOR.
YOU PULLED ME AWAY FROM MY FAMILY FOR WHAT?
I DON'T UNDERSTAND.
SORRY. I HAD TO GET YOU HERE, EVEN IF UNDER FALSE PRETENSES.
I KNOW ALL ABOUT SPACELY'S SECRET ROCKET TO GET OFF THE PLANET BEFORE IT'S DESTROYED. DISCOVERED IT A WHILE BACK WHEN I WAS INTERNING. IT'S A STUNNING PIECE OF TECHNOLOGY, ESPECIALLY THE DEEP SLEEP CHAMBERS.
I WANT TO SHOW YOU SOMETHING.
YOU LET NOW THAT FOUND OUT?
WELL... WITH ONLY A DAY AND A HALF LEFT...
LOOK, I DON'T CARE ABOUT THE SHIP OR HIS PLAN...I CALLED YOU HERE TO DISCUSS THE PLANET'S FUTURE.
EXACTLY. PLEASE STEP INTO MY WORKSHOP.
I'M NOT UNDERSTANDING WHAT YOU...
IS THAT WHAT I THINK IT IS?

THAT'S A *650-ATOMIC BOMB!* THAT MONSTER GENERATES OVER *FIVE HUNDRED MEGATONS* OF EXPLOSIVE FORCE!

ACTUALLY, I MODELED IT AFTER ONE, BUT IT'S ONE-SIXTH THE SIZE AND *DOUBLE* THAT FORCE.

YOUNG LADY, IF ANYONE *KNEW* YOU WERE MESSING WITH...YOU KNOW ANY KIND OF *WEAPON* HAS BEEN *BANNED* SINCE...YOU WOULD BE *PUT AWAY...*

COMPUTER, FULL SCREEN, AND RUN THE *420 SEQUENCE,* PLEASE.

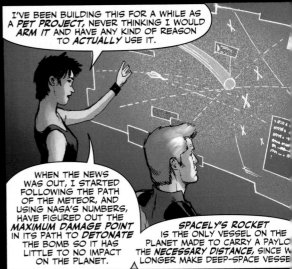

I'VE BEEN BUILDING THIS FOR A WHILE AS A *PET PROJECT,* NEVER THINKING I WOULD *ARM IT* AND HAVE ANY KIND OF REASON TO *ACTUALLY* USE IT.

WHEN THE NEWS WAS OUT, I STARTED FOLLOWING THE PATH OF THE METEOR, AND USING NASA'S NUMBERS, HAVE FIGURED OUT THE *MAXIMUM DAMAGE POINT* IN ITS PATH TO *DETONATE* THE BOMB SO IT HAS LITTLE TO NO IMPACT ON THE PLANET.

SPACELY'S ROCKET IS THE ONLY VESSEL ON THE PLANET MADE TO CARRY A PAYLO THE *NECESSARY DISTANCE,* SINCE W LONGER MAKE DEEP-SPACE VESSE

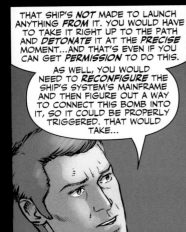

THAT SHIP'S *NOT* MADE TO LAUNCH ANYTHING *FROM* IT. YOU WOULD HAVE TO TAKE IT RIGHT UP TO THE PATH AND *DETONATE* IT AT THE *PRECISE* MOMENT...AND THAT'S EVEN IF YOU CAN GET *PERMISSION* TO DO THIS.

AS WELL, YOU WOULD NEED TO *RECONFIGURE* THE SHIP'S SYSTEM'S MAINFRAME AND THEN FIGURE OUT A WAY TO CONNECT THIS BOMB INTO IT, SO IT COULD BE PROPERLY TRIGGERED. THAT WOULD TAKE...

ABOUT A *DAY AND A HALF...* I KNOW.

IT'S WHY THE SHIP WILL HAVE TO BE MANNED AND TRIGGERED *MANUALLY.* MY CALCULATIONS SHOW THE SHIP WOULD HAVE TO LEAVE THE PLANET WITH THE PAY-LOAD IN ABOUT *FORTY-EIGHT MINUTES* AND COUNTING.

FORTY-EIGHT MINUTES?

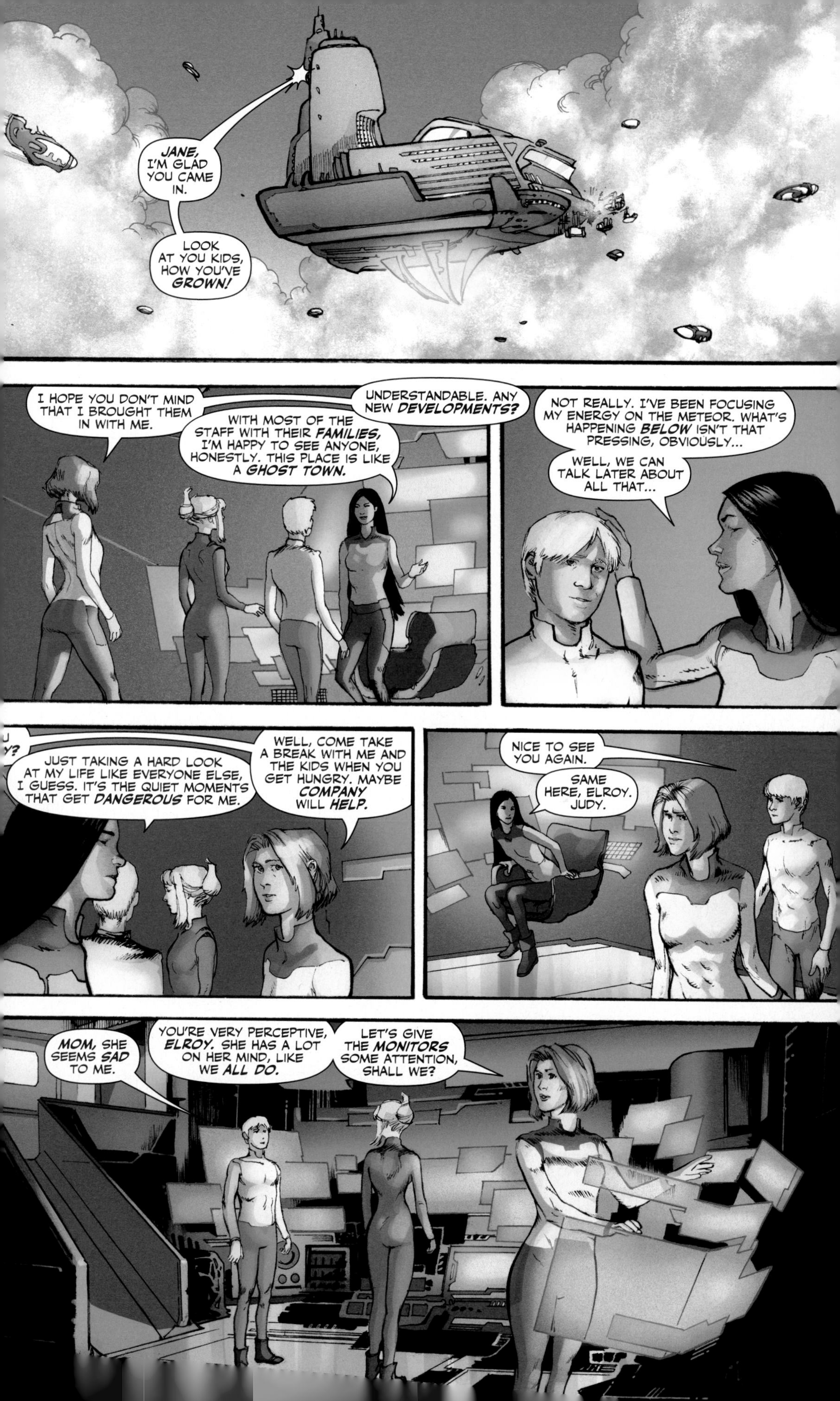
JANE, I'M GLAD YOU CAME IN.
LOOK AT YOU KIDS, HOW YOU'VE GROWN!
I HOPE YOU DON'T MIND THAT I BROUGHT THEM IN WITH ME.
WITH MOST OF THE STAFF WITH THEIR FAMILIES, I'M HAPPY TO SEE ANYONE, HONESTLY. THIS PLACE IS LIKE A GHOST TOWN.
UNDERSTANDABLE. ANY NEW DEVELOPMENTS?
NOT REALLY. I'VE BEEN FOCUSING MY ENERGY ON THE METEOR. WHAT'S HAPPENING BELOW ISN'T THAT PRESSING, OBVIOUSLY...
WELL, WE CAN TALK LATER ABOUT ALL THAT...
JUST TAKING A HARD LOOK AT MY LIFE LIKE EVERYONE ELSE, I GUESS. IT'S THE QUIET MOMENTS THAT GET DANGEROUS FOR ME.
WELL, COME TAKE A BREAK WITH ME AND THE KIDS WHEN YOU GET HUNGRY. MAYBE COMPANY WILL HELP.
NICE TO SEE YOU AGAIN.
SAME HERE, ELROY. JUDY.
MOM, SHE SEEMS SAD TO ME.
YOU'RE VERY PERCEPTIVE, ELROY. SHE HAS A LOT ON HER MIND, LIKE WE ALL DO.
LET'S GIVE THE MONITORS SOME ATTENTION, SHALL WE?

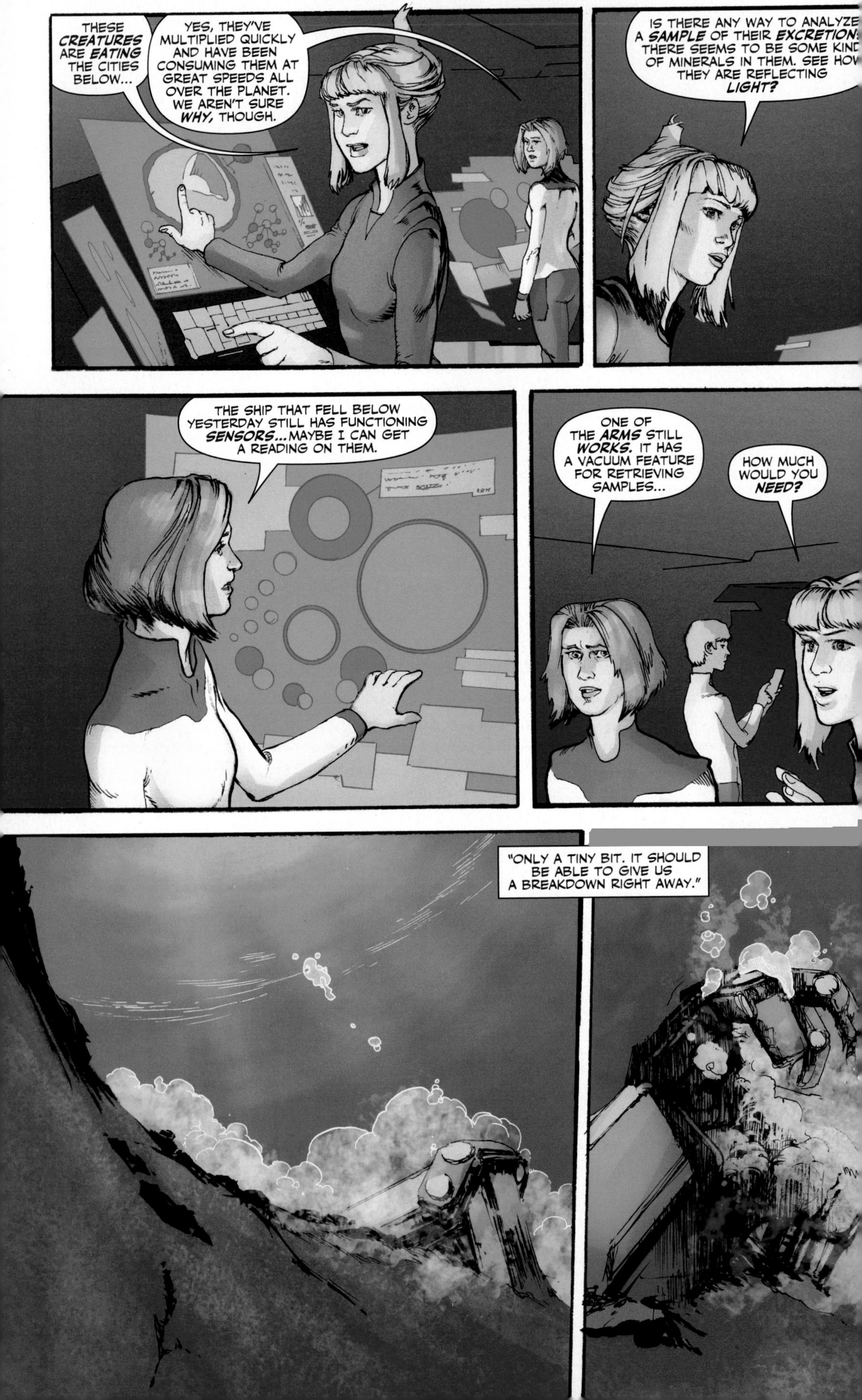
THESE CREATURES ARE EATING THE CITIES BELOW...
YES, THEY'VE MULTIPLIED QUICKLY AND HAVE BEEN CONSUMING THEM AT GREAT SPEEDS ALL OVER THE PLANET. WE AREN'T SURE WHY, THOUGH.
IS THERE ANY WAY TO ANALYZE A SAMPLE OF THEIR EXCRETION? THERE SEEMS TO BE SOME KIND OF MINERALS IN THEM. SEE HOW THEY ARE REFLECTING LIGHT?
THE SHIP THAT FELL BELOW YESTERDAY STILL HAS FUNCTIONING SENSORS... MAYBE I CAN GET A READING ON THEM.
ONE OF THE ARMS STILL WORKS. IT HAS A VACUUM FEATURE FOR RETRIEVING SAMPLES...
HOW MUCH WOULD YOU NEED?
"ONLY A TINY BIT. IT SHOULD BE ABLE TO GIVE US A BREAKDOWN RIGHT AWAY."

IS THAT WHAT IS *INSIDE* IT?

YES, AS IT'S LOADING...LOTS OF *MINERALS*, QUARTZ, CALCIUM, MAGNESIUM, SULFUR, COPPER, ZINC, BORON, CHLORINE, MOLYBDENUM, NITROGEN AND OTHER ORGANIC MATTER STILL TO BE FIGURED OUT.

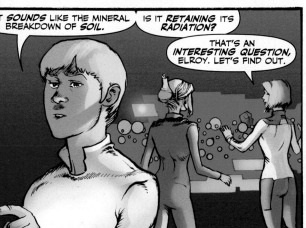

IT *SOUNDS* LIKE THE MINERAL BREAKDOWN OF *SOIL*.

IS IT *RETAINING* ITS *RADIATION*?

THAT'S AN *INTERESTING QUESTION*, ELROY. LET'S FIND OUT.

THE COMPUTER'S BREAKING IT DOWN NOW. IT'S GOING TO TAKE ABOUT TEN MINUTES.

KEEP LOOKING TO SEE IF YOU CAN SPOT *ANYTHING ELSE* FROM THE CAMERAS UNTIL THEN.

ELROY? ARE YOU IN HERE? WHAT'S SO *IMPORTANT*?

LAKE?

MOM?

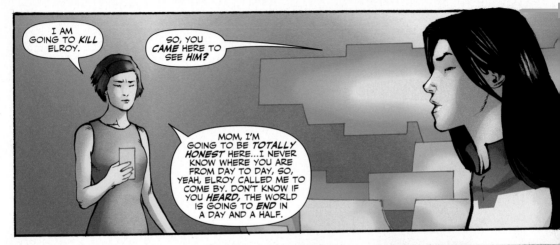

I AM GOING TO *KILL* ELROY.

SO, YOU *CAME* HERE TO SEE *HIM*?

MOM, I'M GOING TO BE *TOTALLY HONEST* HERE...I NEVER KNOW WHERE YOU ARE FROM DAY TO DAY, SO, YEAH, ELROY CALLED ME TO COME BY. DON'T KNOW IF YOU *HEARD*, THE WORLD IS GOING TO *END* IN A DAY AND A HALF.

VERY FUNNY. YOU KNOW HOW *BUSY* I HAVE BEEN TRYING TO FIND A WAY TO CHANGE THE SITUATION WE ARE IN.

CAN YOU JUST BE MY *MOTHER* FOR ONCE AND GIVE ME A *HUG*?

OH, MY...

OH, MY, *WHAT*?

I SHOULD HAVE BROUGHT YOU KIDS TO WORK *SOONER*...

WHAT? TELL US!

THERE IS NEXT TO *NO RADIATION* LEVEL PRESENT. THESE CREATURES ARE ABSORBING THE EXISTING RADIATION CONTAINED IN THE EARTH BELOW AND PROCESSING IT, CREATING A CLEAN SOIL-LIKE MATERIAL...

YOU MEAN...

THEY ARE *TERRAFORMING THE PLANET*.

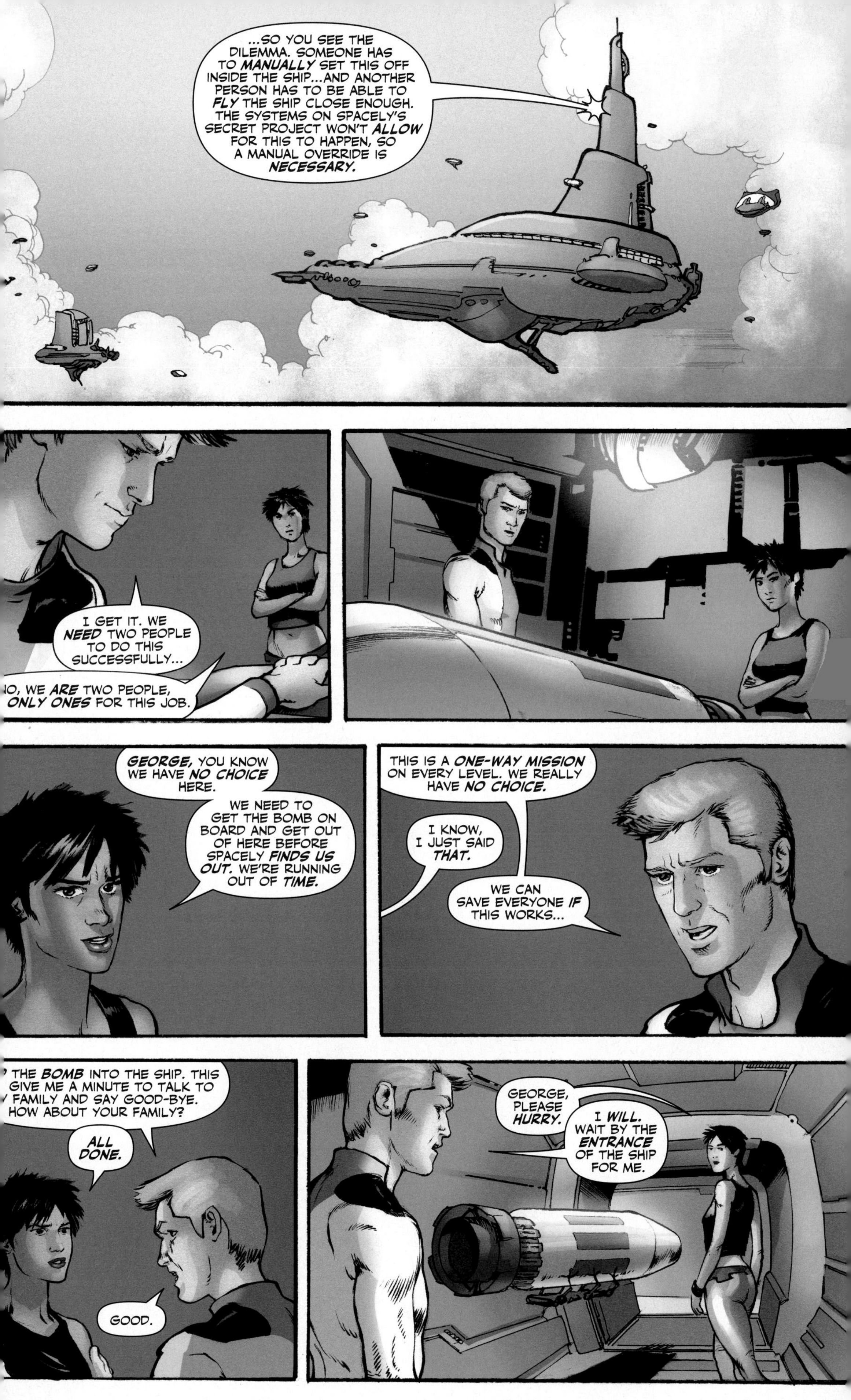
...SO YOU SEE THE DILEMMA. SOMEONE HAS TO MANUALLY SET THIS OFF INSIDE THE SHIP...AND ANOTHER PERSON HAS TO BE ABLE TO FLY THE SHIP CLOSE ENOUGH. THE SYSTEMS ON SPACELY'S SECRET PROJECT WON'T ALLOW FOR THIS TO HAPPEN, SO A MANUAL OVERRIDE IS NECESSARY.
I GET IT. WE NEED TWO PEOPLE TO DO THIS SUCCESSFULLY...
IO, WE ARE TWO PEOPLE, ONLY ONES FOR THIS JOB.
GEORGE, YOU KNOW WE HAVE NO CHOICE HERE.
WE NEED TO GET THE BOMB ON BOARD AND GET OUT OF HERE BEFORE SPACELY FINDS US OUT. WE'RE RUNNING OUT OF TIME.
THIS IS A ONE-WAY MISSION ON EVERY LEVEL. WE REALLY HAVE NO CHOICE.
I KNOW, I JUST SAID THAT.
WE CAN SAVE EVERYONE IF THIS WORKS...
THE BOMB INTO THE SHIP. THIS GIVE ME A MINUTE TO TALK TO FAMILY AND SAY GOOD-BYE. HOW ABOUT YOUR FAMILY?
ALL DONE.
GOOD.
GEORGE, PLEASE HURRY.
I WILL. WAIT BY THE ENTRANCE OF THE SHIP FOR ME.

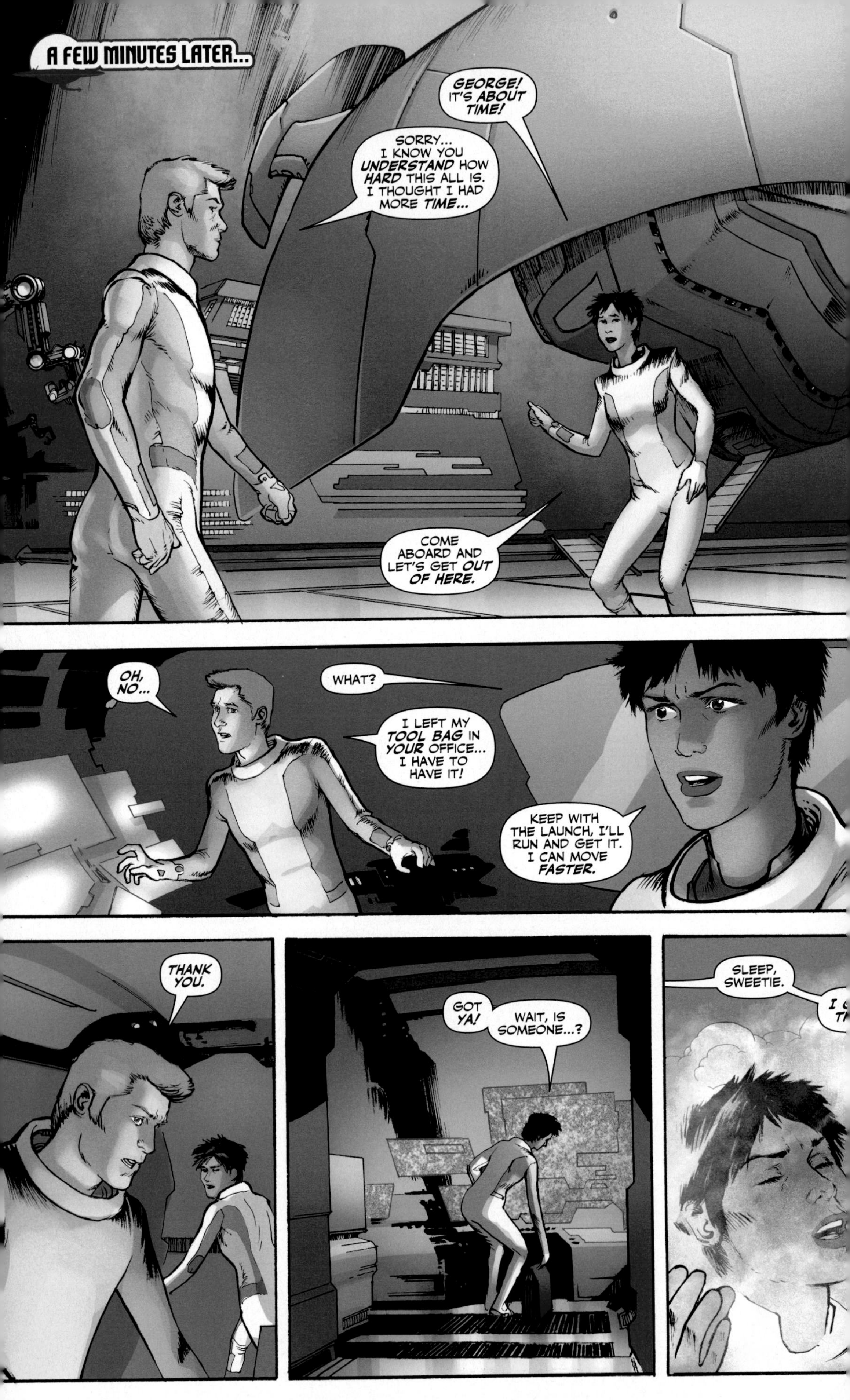
A FEW MINUTES LATER...
GEORGE! IT'S ABOUT TIME!
SORRY... I KNOW YOU UNDERSTAND HOW HARD THIS ALL IS. I THOUGHT I HAD MORE TIME...
COME ABOARD AND LET'S GET OUT OF HERE.
OH, NO...
WHAT?
I LEFT MY TOOL BAG IN YOUR OFFICE... I HAVE TO HAVE IT!
KEEP WITH THE LAUNCH, I'LL RUN AND GET IT. I CAN MOVE FASTER.
THANK YOU.
GOT YA!
WAIT, IS SOMEONE...?
SLEEP, SWEETIE.

'S THAT
MBLING
UND?

Fooosshhh!

MY SHIP!

SOMEONE IS STEALING MY SHIP!

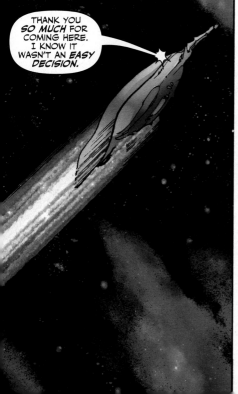

THANK YOU SO MUCH FOR COMING HERE. I KNOW IT WASN'T AN EASY DECISION.

ACTUALLY, IT WAS. I'M SO GLAD YOU THOUGHT OF ME.

I THINK IT'S ABOUT TIME YOU CALLED YOUR FAMILY AND LET THEM IN ON WHAT IS HAPPENING.

I AGREE.

I'LL LEAVE IF YOU LIKE.

MOM, PLEASE... DON'T.

I WANT YOU HERE FOR THIS.

OKAY, SON.

THIS IS *AMAZING!* GOOD NEWS AT THE *WORST* TIME...

YEAH, BITTERSWEET, FOR SURE. IMAGINE THE FUTURE FOR OUR PLANET IF WE ONLY HAD THE TIME...

INCOMING MESSAGE FOR *JANE JETSON,* *ELROY JETSON* AND *JUDY JETSON.*

WHO FROM?

GEORGE JETSON.

ACCEPT.

HEY, YOU'RE ALL IN THE SAME PLACE. THIS WILL MAKE IT *EASIER,* THEN.

ZELDA, LAKE, NICE TO SEE YOU BOTH.

HELLO, *GEORGE.* WE WILL GIVE YOU SOME *PRIVACY.* COME ON, *LAKE.*

PLEASE, N[O] NEED TO. T[H] CONCERN[S] EVERYON[E]

JA[NE] DARL[ING,] PLE[ASE,] DON'[T] MAD[AT] M[E]

WHAT WE SPOKE ABOUT L[AST] *NIGHT,* WELL...T[HAT] HAPPENED.

IN A NUTSHELL, MY NEW ASSISTANT, LYDIA, CREATED A BOMB STRONG ENOUGH TO *DESTROY* THE *JACOB METEOR,* BUT IT HAS TO BE DELIVERED IN *PERSON* DEEP IN SPACE, SO I LIBERATED *SPACELY'S* ESCAPE *ROCKET* AND AM HEADING THERE WITH MY *MOM* TO SET IT OFF.

I'M SORRY I DIDN'T TALK TO YOU *FIRST,* BUT THE TIME FRAME DIDN'T ALLOW ME TO DO EVERYTHING I WANTED TO DO...I HAD TO ACT *QUICKLY.* IF I LEFT A *MINUTE* TOO LATE, IF SPACELY HAD *STOPPED* ME, ALL THOSE THINGS...THE CALCULATIONS GAVE ME SUCH A *SMALL WINDOW* TO WORK WITH.

*ZELDA, LAKE...*IF I CAN BE WITH MY *FAMILY* NOW.

GEORGE, WHAT YOU ARE DOING... *YOUR SACRIFICE...*

COME ON, *MOM.* LET'S GO.

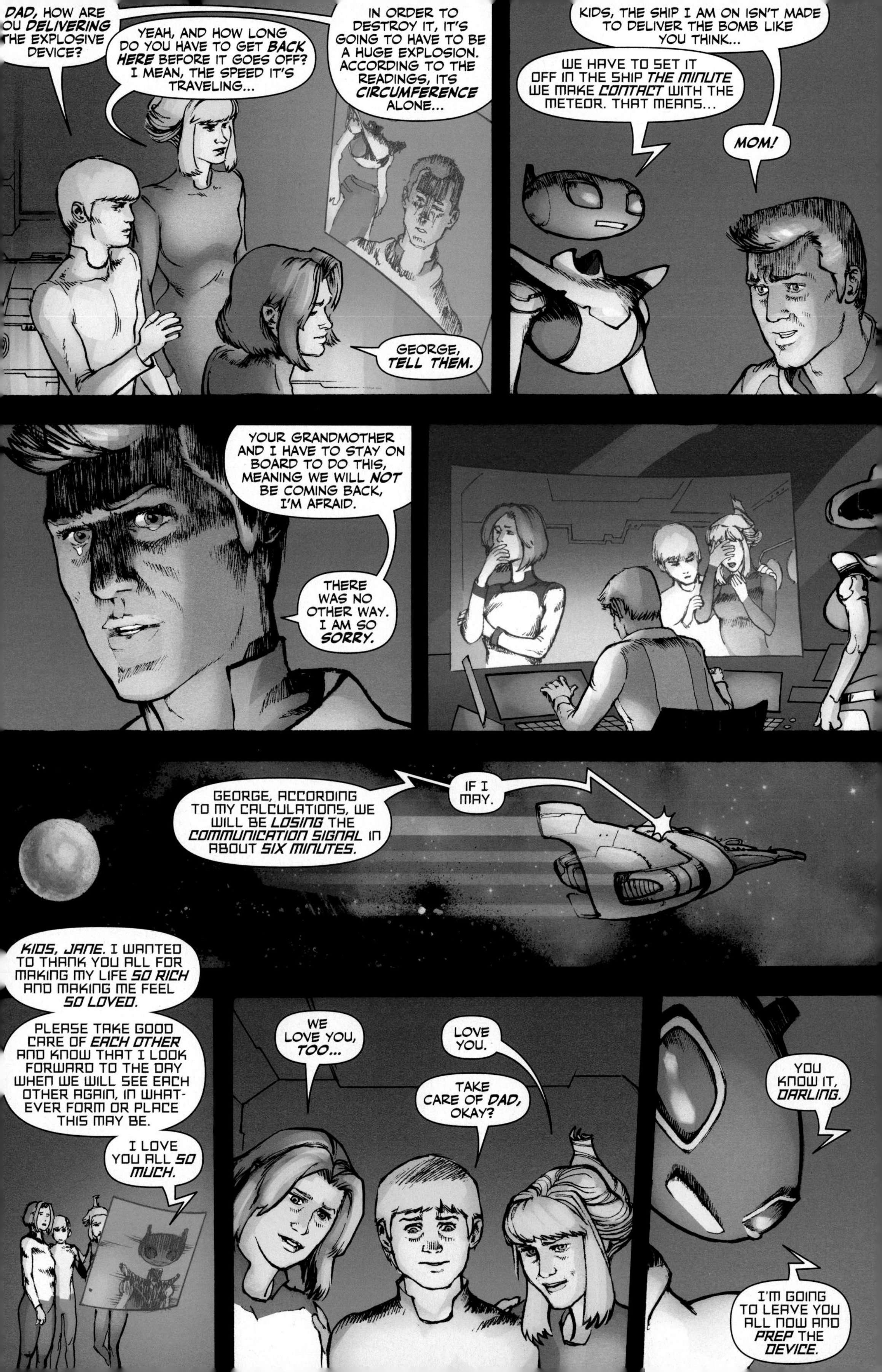
DAD, HOW ARE YOU DELIVERING THE EXPLOSIVE DEVICE?
YEAH, AND HOW LONG DO YOU HAVE TO GET BACK HERE BEFORE IT GOES OFF? I MEAN, THE SPEED IT'S TRAVELING...
IN ORDER TO DESTROY IT, IT'S GOING TO HAVE TO BE A HUGE EXPLOSION. ACCORDING TO THE READINGS, ITS CIRCUMFERENCE ALONE...
GEORGE, TELL THEM.
KIDS, THE SHIP I AM ON ISN'T MADE TO DELIVER THE BOMB LIKE YOU THINK...
WE HAVE TO SET IT OFF IN THE SHIP THE MINUTE WE MAKE CONTACT WITH THE METEOR. THAT MEANS...
MOM!
YOUR GRANDMOTHER AND I HAVE TO STAY ON BOARD TO DO THIS, MEANING WE WILL NOT BE COMING BACK, I'M AFRAID.
THERE WAS NO OTHER WAY. I AM SO SORRY.
IF I MAY.
GEORGE, ACCORDING TO MY CALCULATIONS, WE WILL BE LOSING THE COMMUNICATION SIGNAL IN ABOUT SIX MINUTES.
KIDS, JANE. I WANTED TO THANK YOU ALL FOR MAKING MY LIFE SO RICH AND MAKING ME FEEL SO LOVED.
PLEASE TAKE GOOD CARE OF EACH OTHER AND KNOW THAT I LOOK FORWARD TO THE DAY WHEN WE WILL SEE EACH OTHER AGAIN, IN WHATEVER FORM OR PLACE THIS MAY BE.
I LOVE YOU ALL SO MUCH.
WE LOVE YOU, TOO...
LOVE YOU.
TAKE CARE OF DAD, OKAY?
YOU KNOW IT, DARLING.
I'M GOING TO LEAVE YOU ALL NOW AND PREP THE DEVICE.

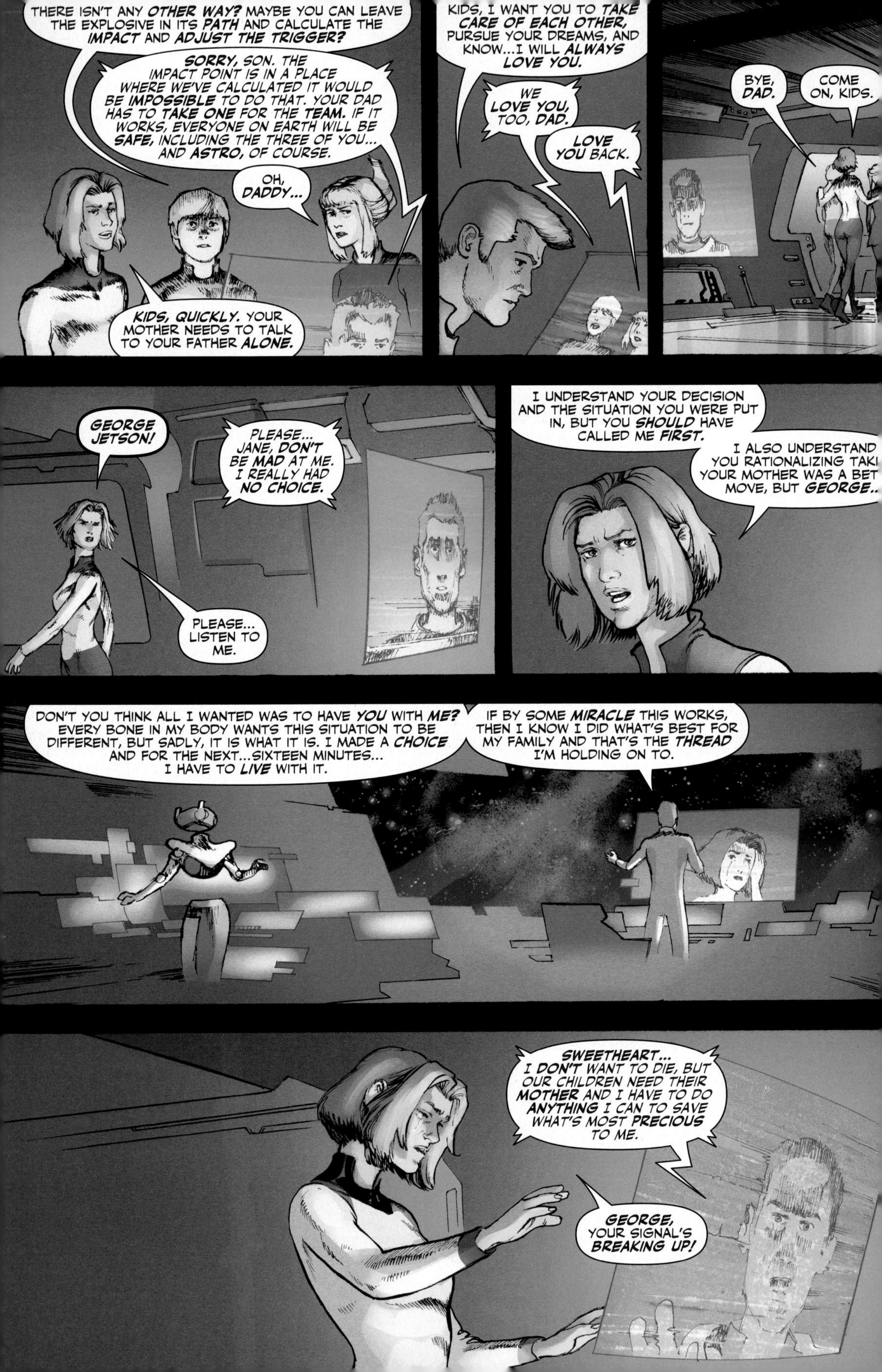
THERE ISN'T ANY OTHER WAY? MAYBE YOU CAN LEAVE THE EXPLOSIVE IN ITS PATH AND CALCULATE THE IMPACT AND ADJUST THE TRIGGER?
SORRY, SON. THE IMPACT POINT IS IN A PLACE WHERE WE'VE CALCULATED IT WOULD BE IMPOSSIBLE TO DO THAT. YOUR DAD HAS TO TAKE ONE FOR THE TEAM. IF IT WORKS, EVERYONE ON EARTH WILL BE SAFE, INCLUDING THE THREE OF YOU... AND ASTRO, OF COURSE.
OH, DADDY...
KIDS, QUICKLY. YOUR MOTHER NEEDS TO TALK TO YOUR FATHER ALONE.
KIDS, I WANT YOU TO TAKE CARE OF EACH OTHER, PURSUE YOUR DREAMS, AND KNOW...I WILL ALWAYS LOVE YOU.
WE LOVE YOU, TOO, DAD.
LOVE YOU BACK.
BYE, DAD.
COME ON, KIDS.
GEORGE JETSON!
PLEASE... JANE, DON'T BE MAD AT ME. I REALLY HAD NO CHOICE.
PLEASE... LISTEN TO ME.
I UNDERSTAND YOUR DECISION AND THE SITUATION YOU WERE PUT IN, BUT YOU SHOULD HAVE CALLED ME FIRST.
I ALSO UNDERSTAND YOU RATIONALIZING TAKI YOUR MOTHER WAS A BET MOVE, BUT GEORGE..
DON'T YOU THINK ALL I WANTED WAS TO HAVE YOU WITH ME? EVERY BONE IN MY BODY WANTS THIS SITUATION TO BE DIFFERENT, BUT SADLY, IT IS WHAT IT IS. I MADE A CHOICE AND FOR THE NEXT...SIXTEEN MINUTES... I HAVE TO LIVE WITH IT.
IF BY SOME MIRACLE THIS WORKS, THEN I KNOW I DID WHAT'S BEST FOR MY FAMILY AND THAT'S THE THREAD I'M HOLDING ON TO.
SWEETHEART... I DON'T WANT TO DIE, BUT OUR CHILDREN NEED THEIR MOTHER AND I HAVE TO DO ANYTHING I CAN TO SAVE WHAT'S MOST PRECIOUS TO ME.
GEORGE, YOUR SIGNAL'S BREAKING UP!

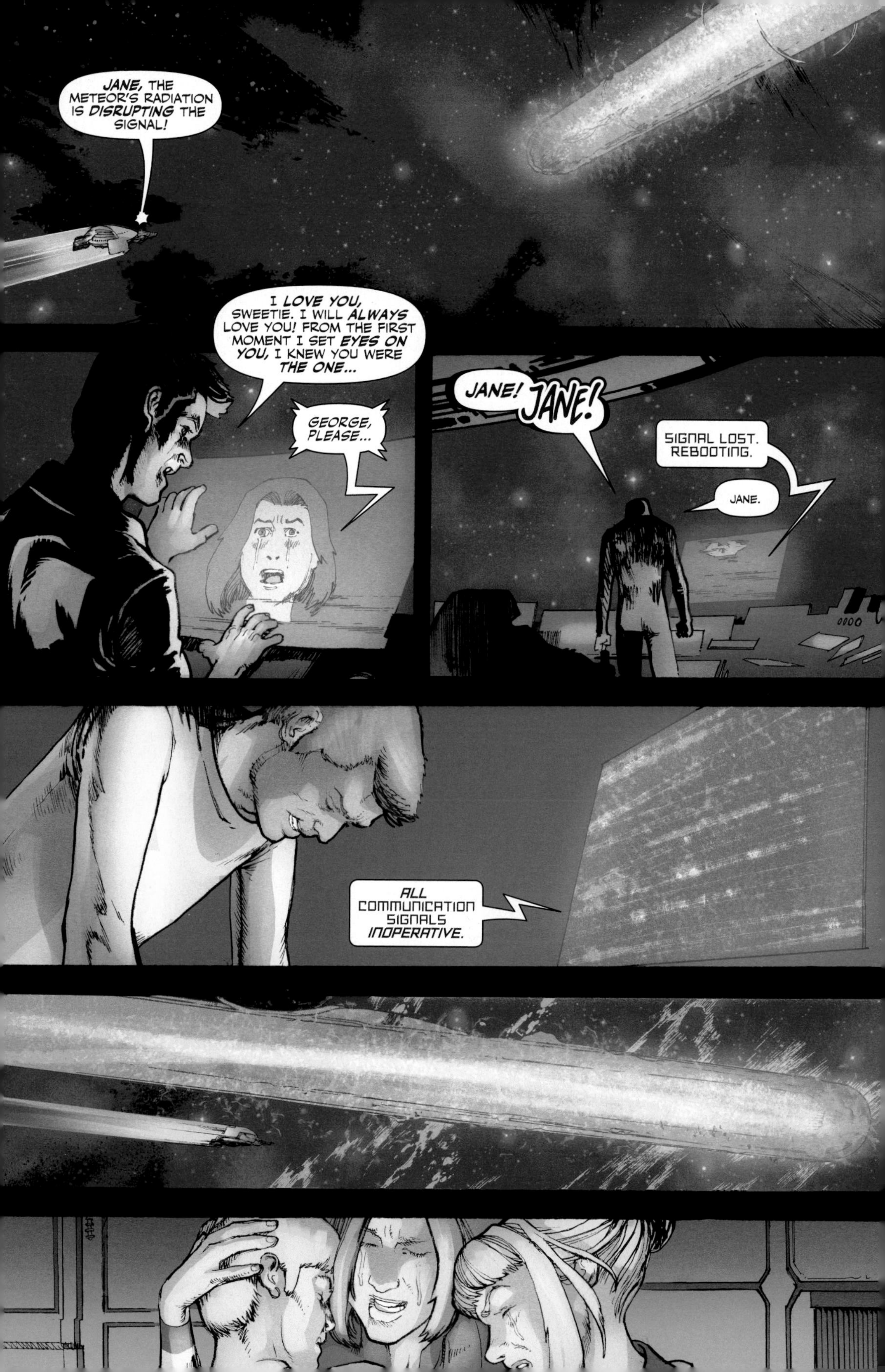
JANE, THE METEOR'S RADIATION IS DISRUPTING THE SIGNAL!
I LOVE YOU, SWEETIE. I WILL ALWAYS LOVE YOU! FROM THE FIRST MOMENT I SET EYES ON YOU, I KNEW YOU WERE THE ONE...
GEORGE, PLEASE...
JANE! JANE!
SIGNAL LOST. REBOOTING.
JANE.
ALL COMMUNICATION SIGNALS INOPERATIVE.

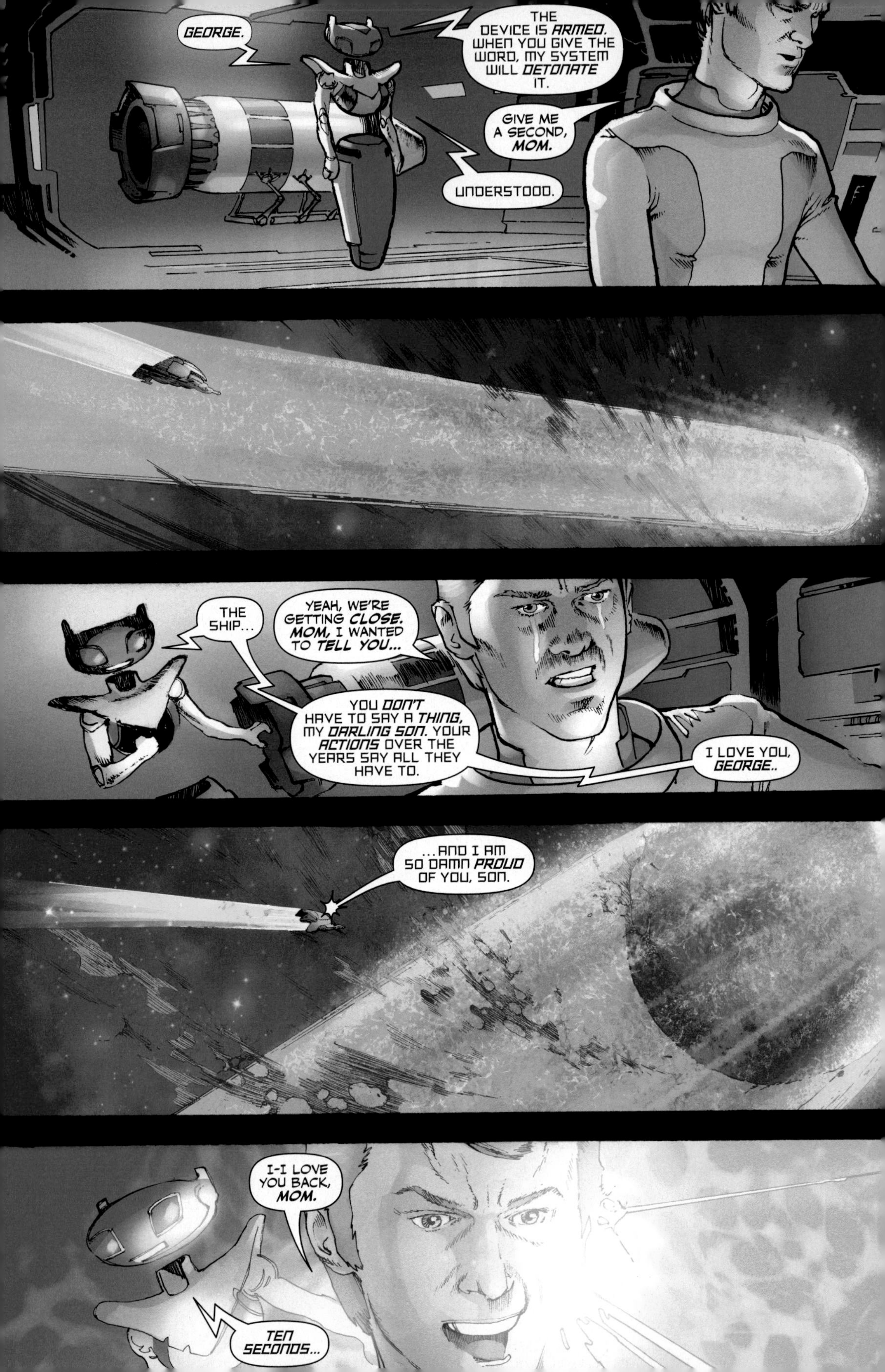
GEORGE.
THE DEVICE IS ARMED. WHEN YOU GIVE THE WORD, MY SYSTEM WILL DETONATE IT.
GIVE ME A SECOND, MOM.
UNDERSTOOD.
THE SHIP...
YEAH, WE'RE GETTING CLOSE. MOM, I WANTED TO TELL YOU...
YOU DON'T HAVE TO SAY A THING, MY DARLING SON. YOUR ACTIONS OVER THE YEARS SAY ALL THEY HAVE TO.
I LOVE YOU, GEORGE..
...AND I AM SO DAMN PROUD OF YOU, SON.
I-I LOVE YOU BACK, MOM.
TEN SECONDS...

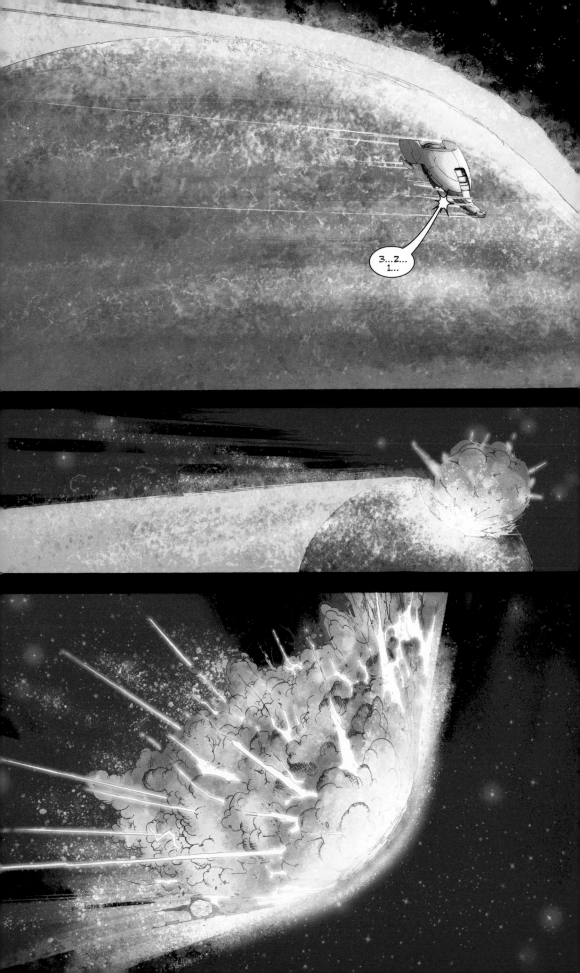

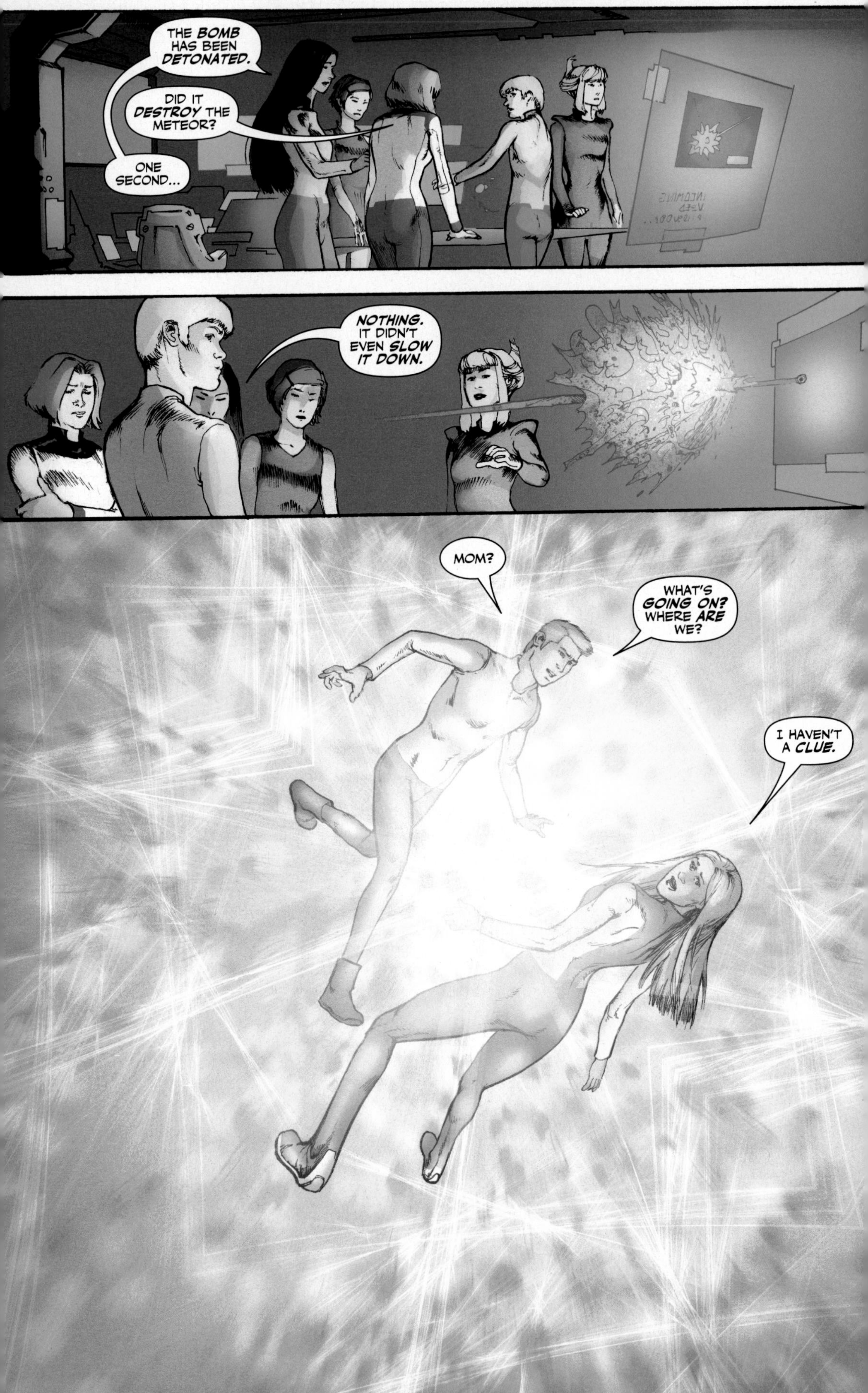
THE *BOMB* HAS BEEN *DETONATED.*
DID IT *DESTROY* THE METEOR?
ONE SECOND...
NOTHING. IT DIDN'T EVEN *SLOW IT DOWN.*
MOM?
WHAT'S *GOING ON?* WHERE *ARE* WE?
I HAVEN'T A *CLUE.*

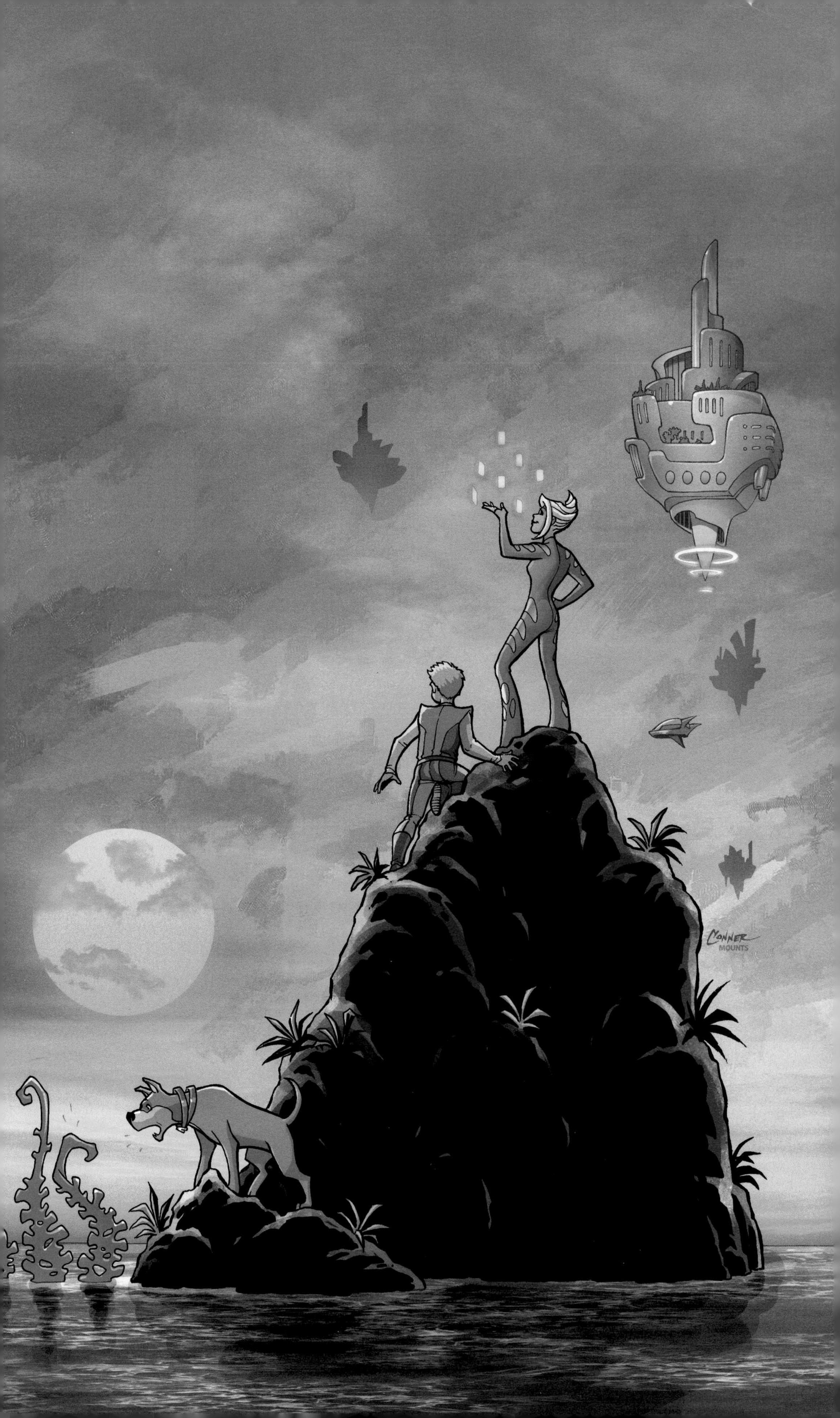
CONNER
MOUNTS

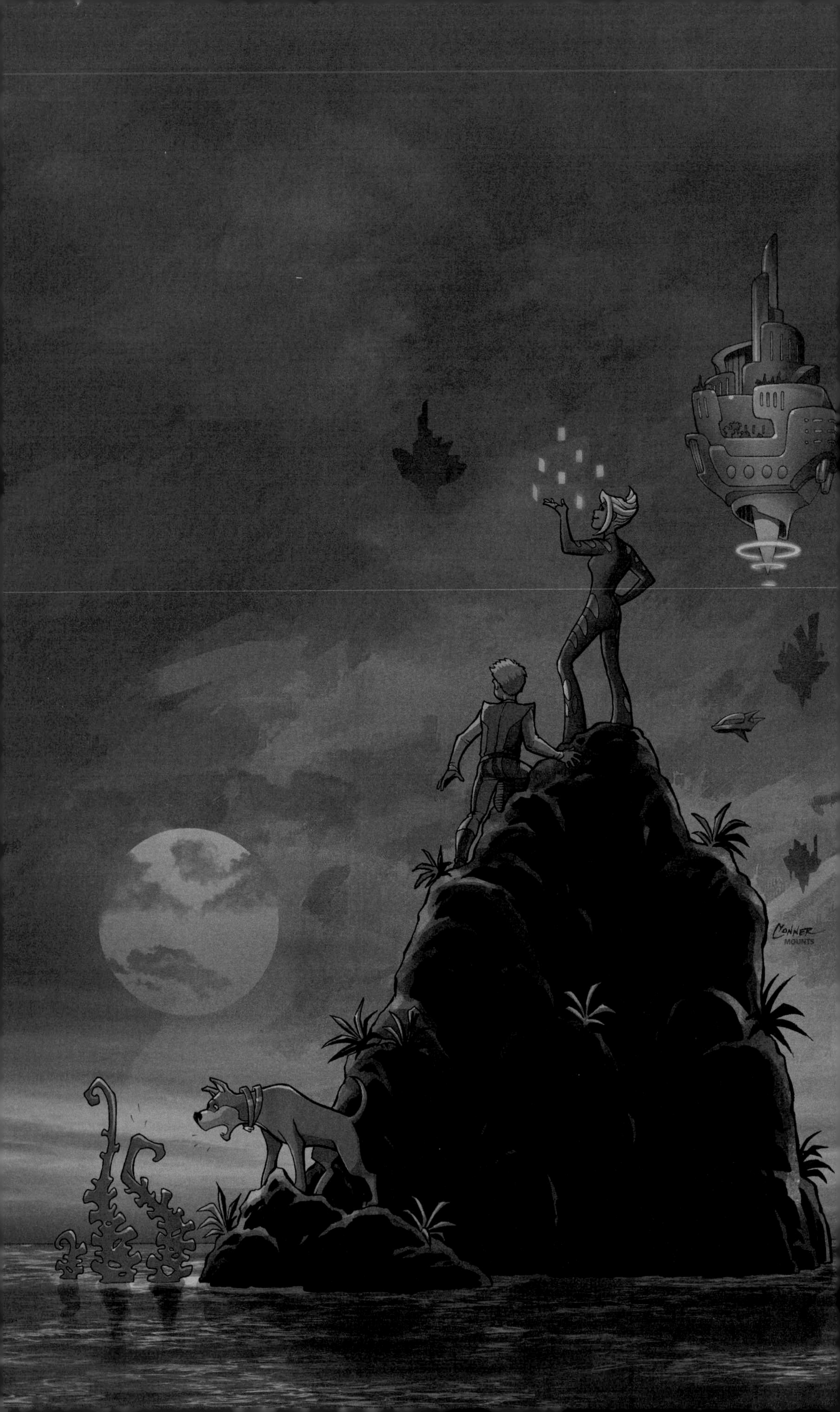
CONNER
MOUNTS

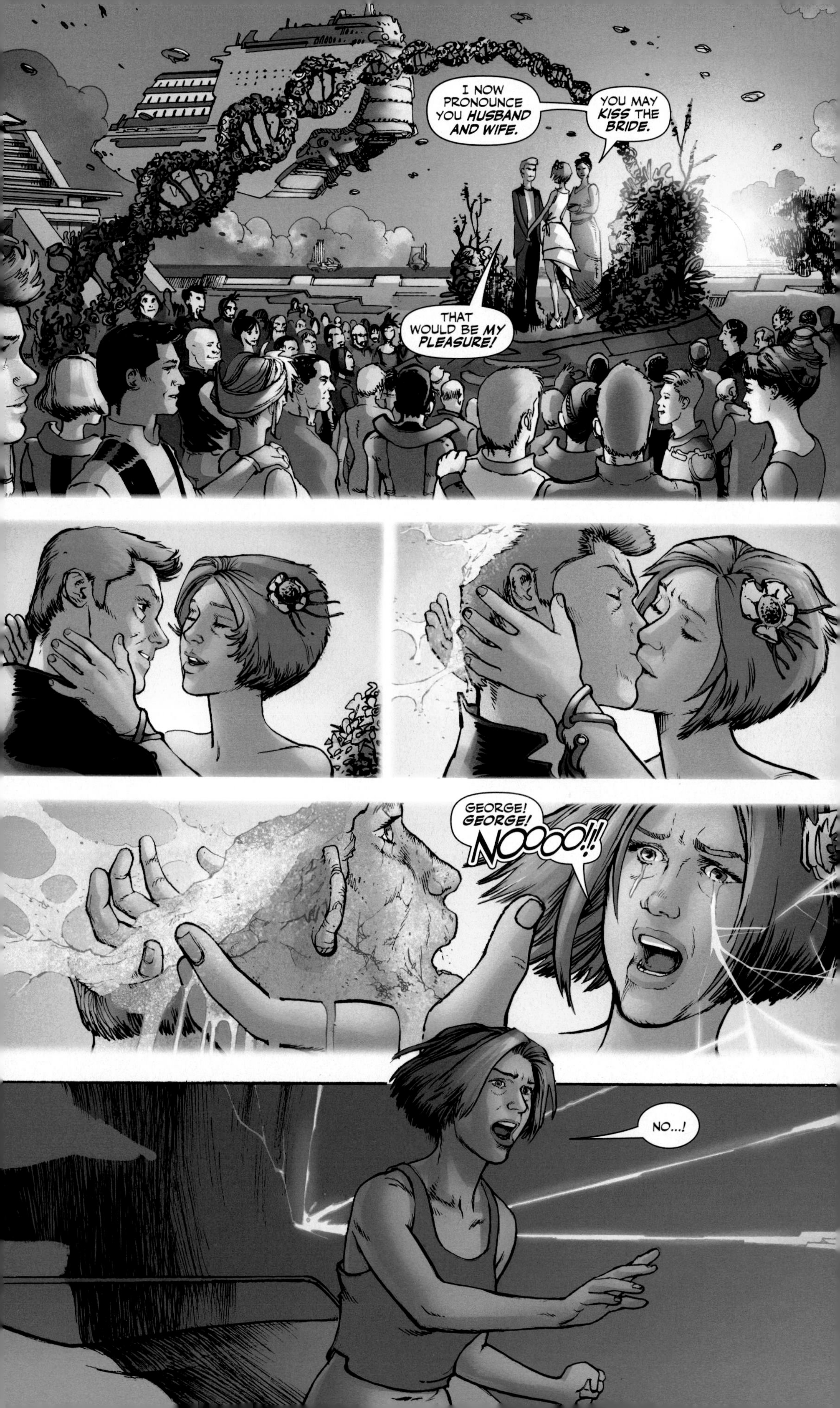
I NOW PRONOUNCE YOU HUSBAND AND WIFE.
YOU MAY KISS THE BRIDE.
THAT WOULD BE MY PLEASURE!
GEORGE! GEORGE!
NOOOO!!!
NO...!

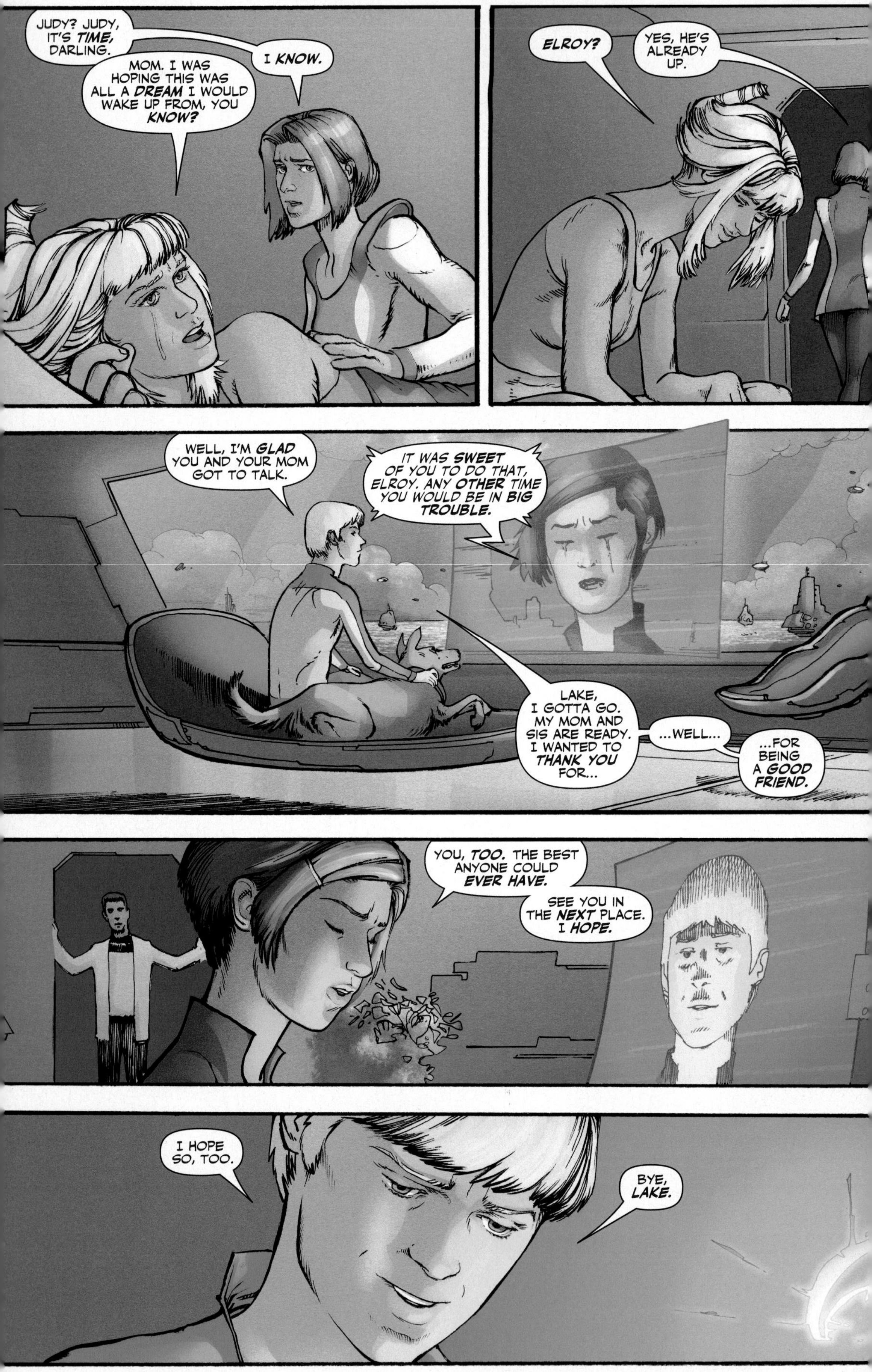
JUDY? JUDY, IT'S TIME, DARLING.
MOM. I WAS HOPING THIS WAS ALL A DREAM I WOULD WAKE UP FROM, YOU KNOW?
I KNOW.
ELROY?
YES, HE'S ALREADY UP.
WELL, I'M GLAD YOU AND YOUR MOM GOT TO TALK.
IT WAS SWEET OF YOU TO DO THAT, ELROY. ANY OTHER TIME YOU WOULD BE IN BIG TROUBLE.
LAKE, I GOTTA GO. MY MOM AND SIS ARE READY. I WANTED TO THANK YOU FOR...
...WELL...
...FOR BEING A GOOD FRIEND.
YOU, TOO. THE BEST ANYONE COULD EVER HAVE.
SEE YOU IN THE NEXT PLACE. I HOPE.
I HOPE SO, TOO.
BYE, LAKE.

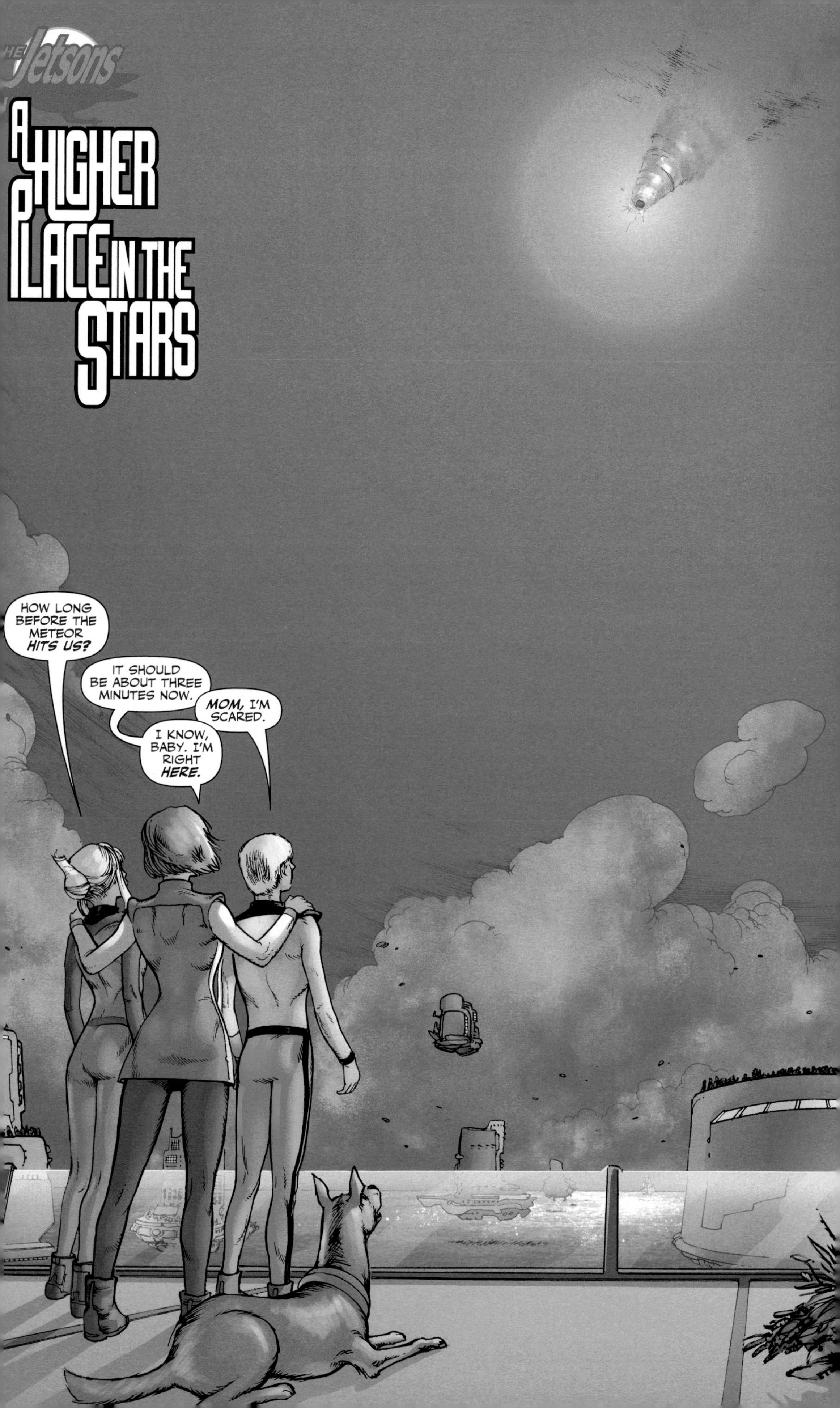
THE Jetsons
A HIGHER PLACE IN THE STARS
HOW LONG BEFORE THE METEOR HITS US?
IT SHOULD BE ABOUT THREE MINUTES NOW.
MOM, I'M SCARED.
I KNOW, BABY. I'M RIGHT HERE.

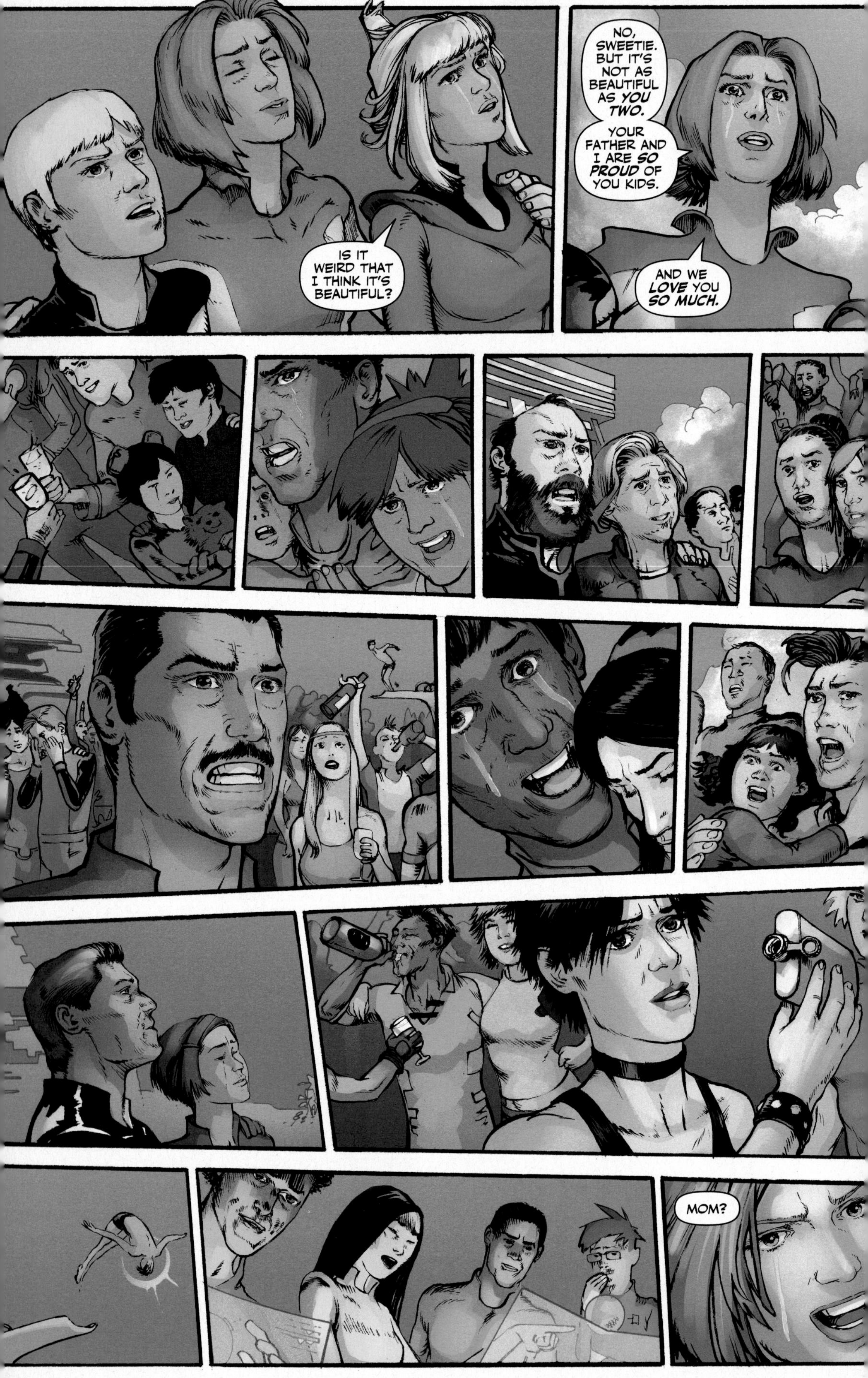
IS IT WEIRD THAT I THINK IT'S BEAUTIFUL?
NO, SWEETIE. BUT IT'S NOT AS BEAUTIFUL AS *YOU TWO.*
YOUR FATHER AND I ARE *SO PROUD* OF YOU KIDS.
AND WE *LOVE* YOU *SO MUCH.*
MOM?

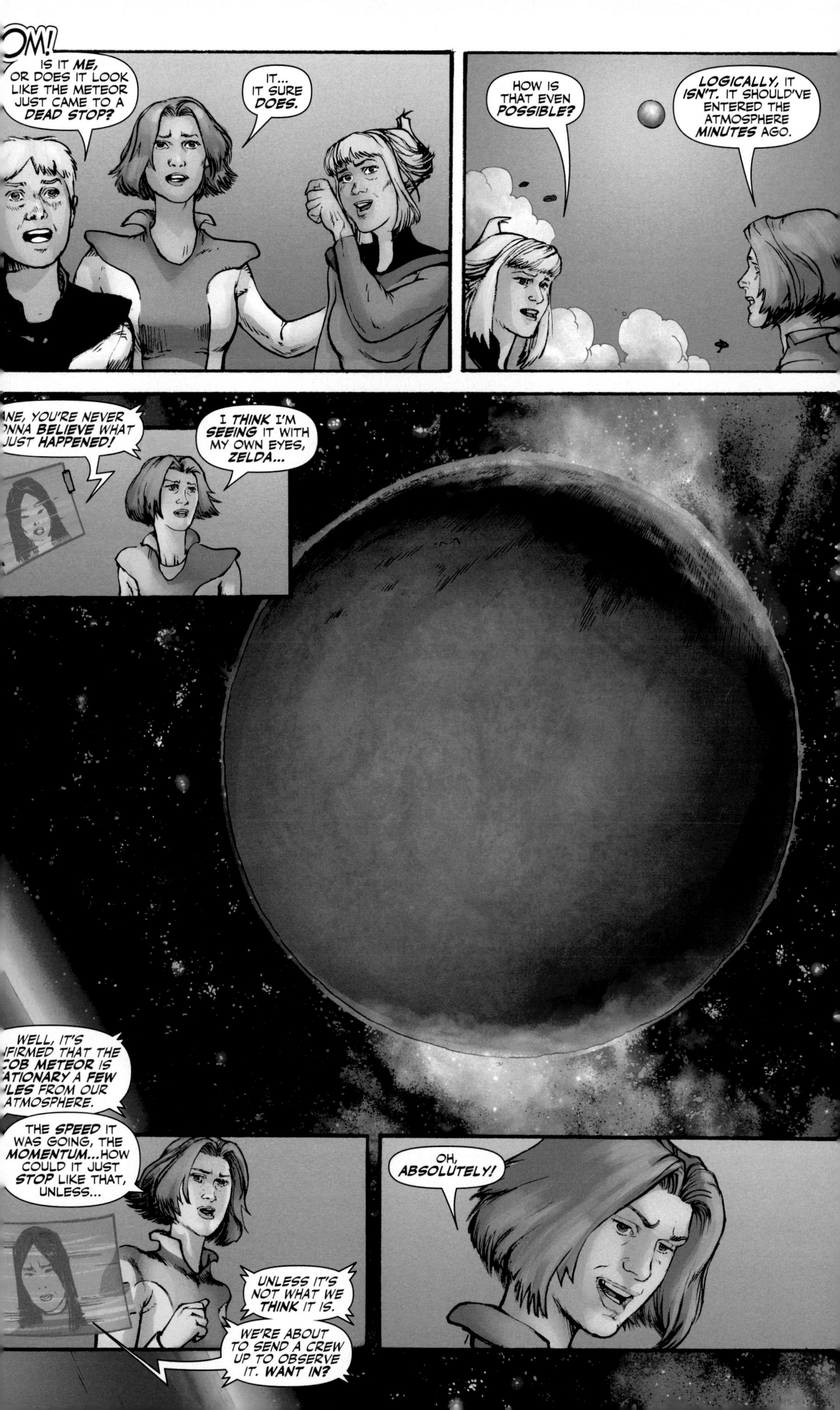

OM!
IS IT ME, OR DOES IT LOOK LIKE THE METEOR JUST CAME TO A DEAD STOP?
IT... IT SURE DOES.
HOW IS THAT EVEN POSSIBLE?
LOGICALLY, IT ISN'T. IT SHOULD'VE ENTERED THE ATMOSPHERE MINUTES AGO.
NE, YOU'RE NEVER ONNA BELIEVE WHAT JUST HAPPENED!
I THINK I'M SEEING IT WITH MY OWN EYES, ZELDA...
WELL, IT'S IFIRMED THAT THE COB METEOR IS ATIONARY A FEW ILES FROM OUR ATMOSPHERE.
THE SPEED IT WAS GOING, THE MOMENTUM...HOW COULD IT JUST STOP LIKE THAT, UNLESS...
UNLESS IT'S NOT WHAT WE THINK IT IS.
WE'RE ABOUT TO SEND A CREW UP TO OBSERVE IT. WANT IN?
OH, ABSOLUTELY!

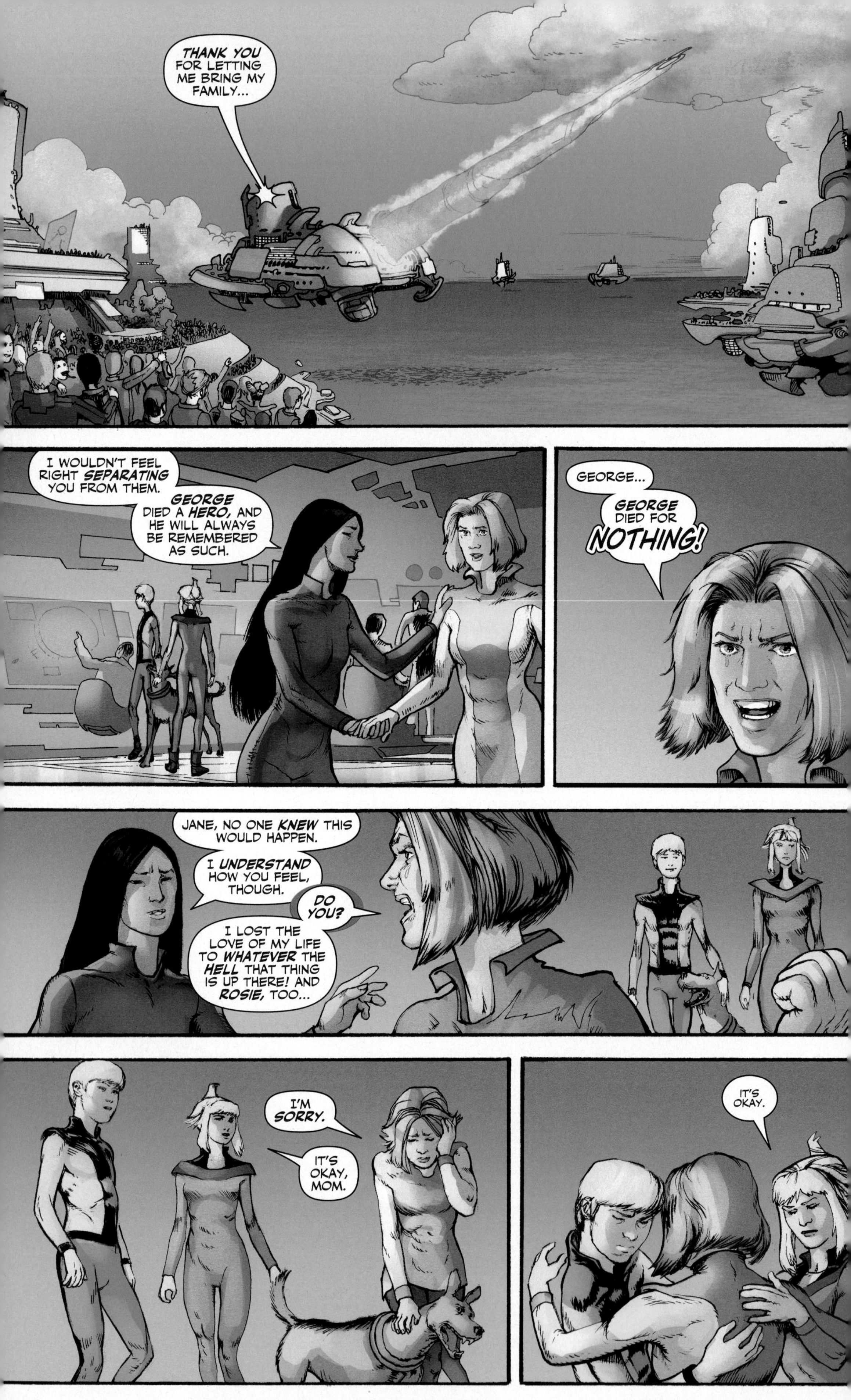
THANK YOU FOR LETTING ME BRING MY FAMILY...
I WOULDN'T FEEL RIGHT SEPARATING YOU FROM THEM.
GEORGE DIED A HERO, AND HE WILL ALWAYS BE REMEMBERED AS SUCH.
GEORGE...
GEORGE DIED FOR NOTHING!
JANE, NO ONE KNEW THIS WOULD HAPPEN.
I UNDERSTAND HOW YOU FEEL, THOUGH.
DO YOU?
I LOST THE LOVE OF MY LIFE TO WHATEVER THE HELL THAT THING IS UP THERE! AND ROSIE, TOO...
I'M SORRY.
IT'S OKAY, MOM.
IT'S OKAY.

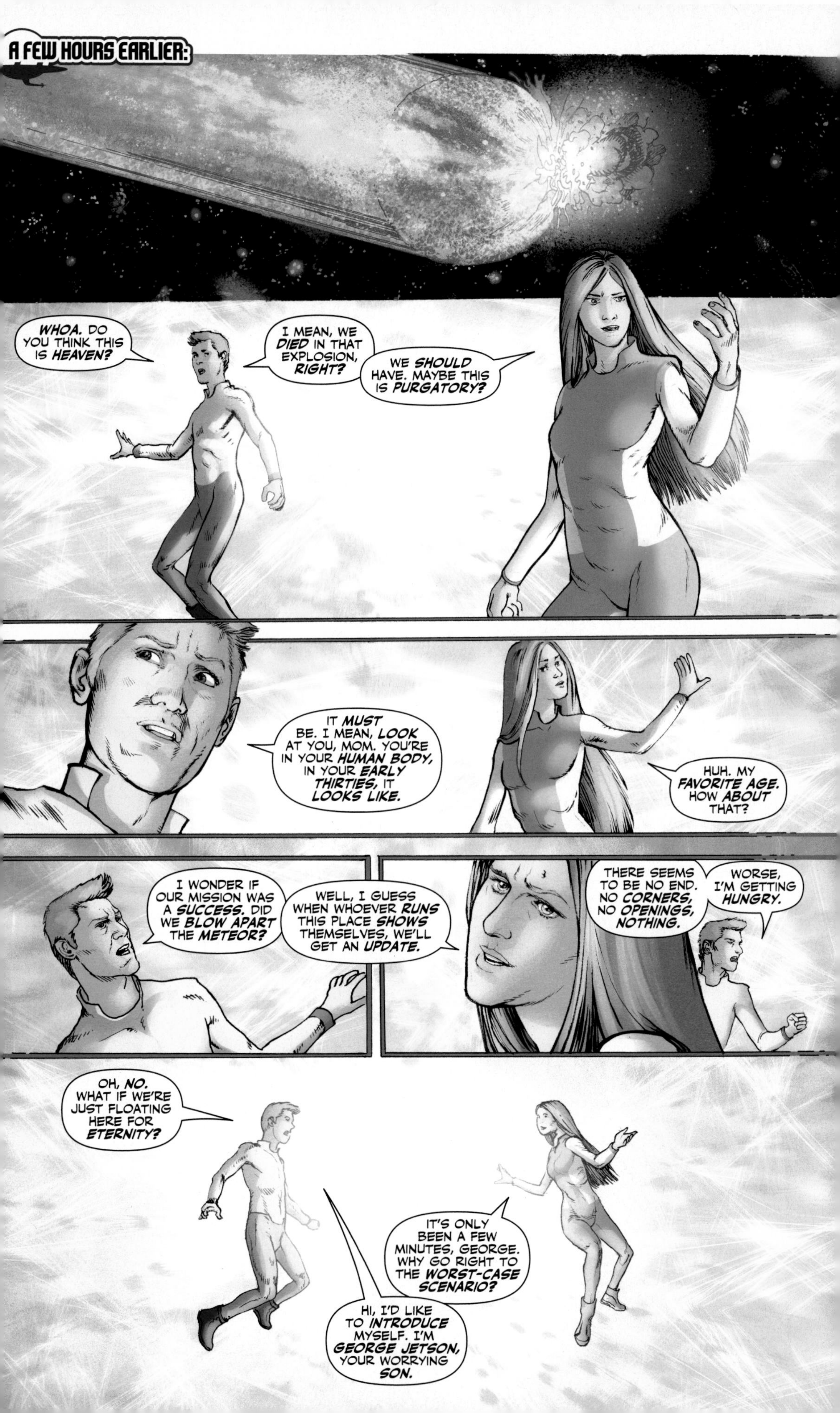
A FEW HOURS EARLIER:
WHOA. DO YOU THINK THIS IS HEAVEN?
I MEAN, WE DIED IN THAT EXPLOSION, RIGHT?
WE SHOULD HAVE. MAYBE THIS IS PURGATORY?
IT MUST BE. I MEAN, LOOK AT YOU, MOM. YOU'RE IN YOUR HUMAN BODY, IN YOUR EARLY THIRTIES, IT LOOKS LIKE.
HUH. MY FAVORITE AGE. HOW ABOUT THAT?
I WONDER IF OUR MISSION WAS A SUCCESS. DID WE BLOW APART THE METEOR?
WELL, I GUESS WHEN WHOEVER RUNS THIS PLACE SHOWS THEMSELVES, WE'LL GET AN UPDATE.
THERE SEEMS TO BE NO END. NO CORNERS, NO OPENINGS, NOTHING.
WORSE, I'M GETTING HUNGRY.
OH, NO. WHAT IF WE'RE JUST FLOATING HERE FOR ETERNITY?
IT'S ONLY BEEN A FEW MINUTES, GEORGE. WHY GO RIGHT TO THE WORST-CASE SCENARIO?
HI, I'D LIKE TO INTRODUCE MYSELF. I'M GEORGE JETSON, YOUR WORRYING SON.

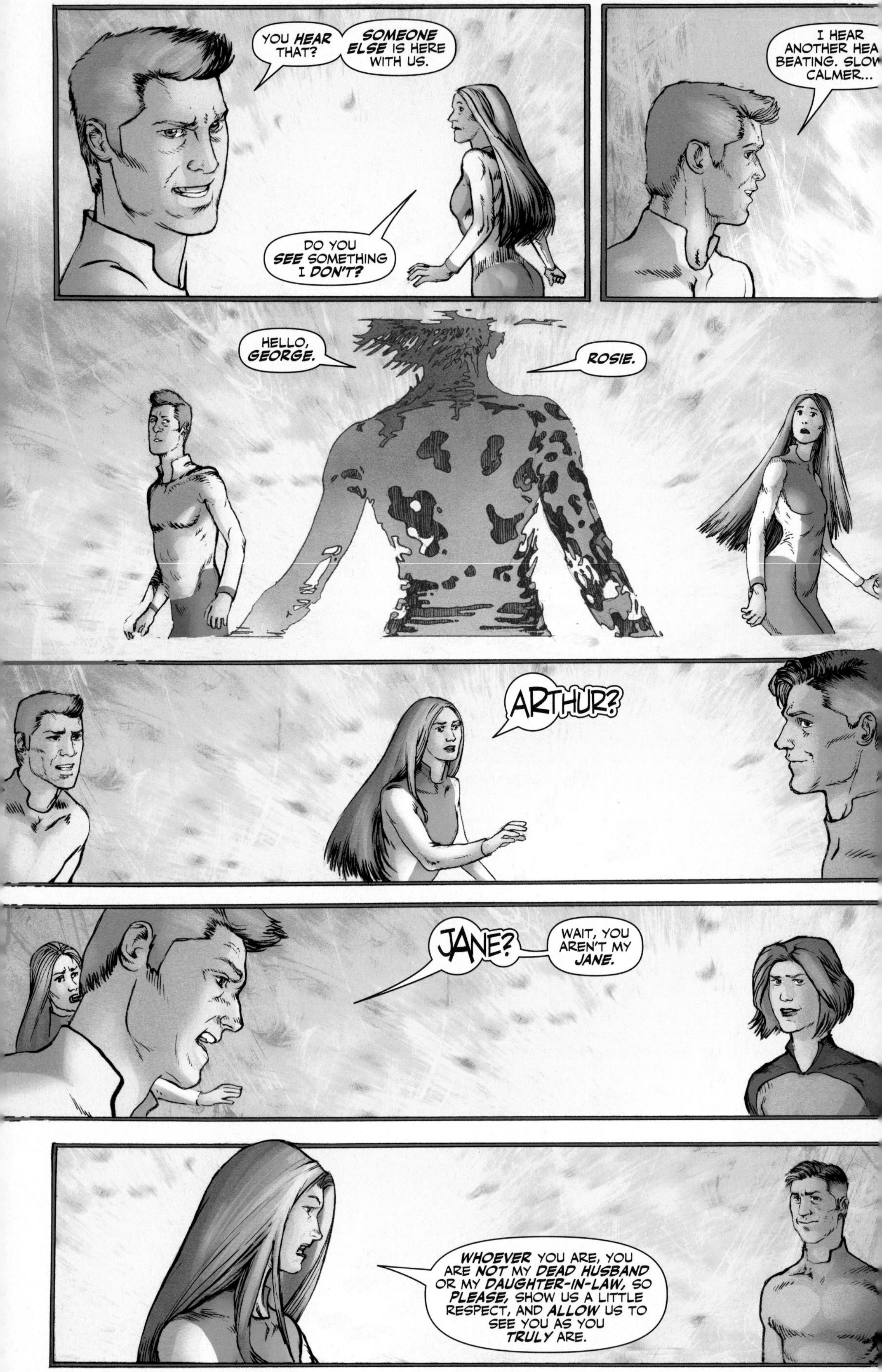

YOU **HEAR** THAT?
SOMEONE ELSE IS HERE WITH US.
DO YOU ***SEE*** SOMETHING I ***DON'T?***
I HEAR ANOTHER HEA BEATING. SLOW CALMER...
HELLO, ***GEORGE.***
ROSIE.
ARTHUR?
JANE?
WAIT, YOU AREN'T MY ***JANE.***
WHOEVER YOU ARE, YOU ARE ***NOT*** MY ***DEAD HUSBAND*** OR MY ***DAUGHTER-IN-LAW,*** SO ***PLEASE,*** SHOW US A LITTLE RESPECT, AND ***ALLOW*** US TO SEE YOU AS YOU ***TRULY*** ARE.

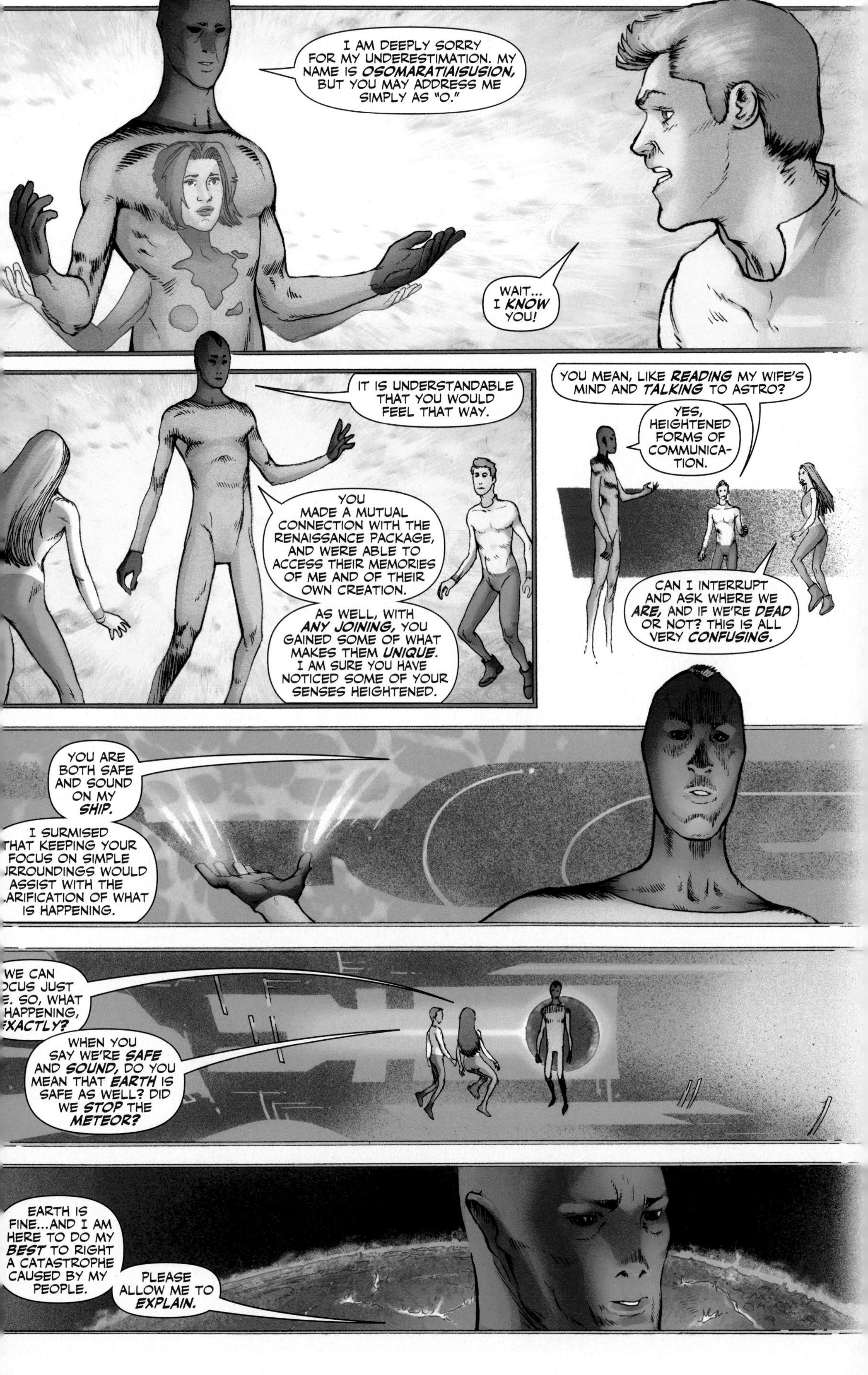
I AM DEEPLY SORRY FOR MY UNDERESTIMATION. MY NAME IS *OSOMARATIAISUSION,* BUT YOU MAY ADDRESS ME SIMPLY AS "O."
WAIT... I *KNOW* YOU!
IT IS UNDERSTANDABLE THAT YOU WOULD FEEL THAT WAY.
YOU MADE A MUTUAL CONNECTION WITH THE RENAISSANCE PACKAGE, AND WERE ABLE TO ACCESS THEIR MEMORIES OF ME AND OF THEIR OWN CREATION.
AS WELL, WITH *ANY JOINING,* YOU GAINED SOME OF WHAT MAKES THEM *UNIQUE*. I AM SURE YOU HAVE NOTICED SOME OF YOUR SENSES HEIGHTENED.
YOU MEAN, LIKE *READING* MY WIFE'S MIND AND *TALKING* TO ASTRO?
YES, HEIGHTENED FORMS OF COMMUNICA-TION.
CAN I INTERRUPT AND ASK WHERE WE *ARE,* AND IF WE'RE *DEAD* OR NOT? THIS IS ALL VERY *CONFUSING.*
YOU ARE BOTH SAFE AND SOUND ON MY *SHIP.*
I SURMISED THAT KEEPING YOUR FOCUS ON SIMPLE URROUNDINGS WOULD ASSIST WITH THE ARIFICATION OF WHAT IS HAPPENING.
WE CAN OCUS JUST E. SO, WHAT HAPPENING, *EXACTLY?*
WHEN YOU SAY WE'RE *SAFE* AND *SOUND,* DO YOU MEAN THAT *EARTH* IS SAFE AS WELL? DID WE *STOP* THE *METEOR?*
EARTH IS FINE...AND I AM HERE TO DO MY *BEST* TO RIGHT A CATASTROPHE CAUSED BY MY PEOPLE.
PLEASE ALLOW ME TO *EXPLAIN.*

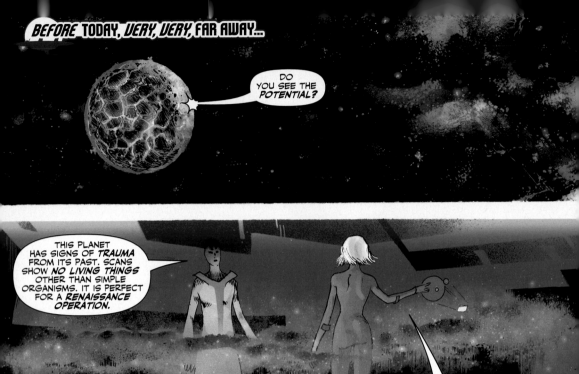

BEFORE TODAY, VERY, VERY, FAR AWAY...
DO YOU SEE THE POTENTIAL?
THIS PLANET HAS SIGNS OF TRAUMA FROM ITS PAST. SCANS SHOW NO LIVING THINGS OTHER THAN SIMPLE ORGANISMS. IT IS PERFECT FOR A RENAISSANCE OPERATION.
THE ORGANISMS DISCOVERED, WHAT ARE THEIR CHANCES OF EVOLUTION OVER TIME?
EXTREMELY LIMITED. THE PLANET HAS NO GROUND SURFACE. IT IS ALL FLUID WITH A CORE THAT IS CONTAMINATED FROM THE PREVIOUS AND NOW EXTINCT LIFE-FORM THAT DOMINATED IT.
SO, YOU'RE TALKING ABOUT OUR PLANET, EARTH?
NO. NOT EARTH. BUT ANOTHER PLANET THAT WAS ONCE LIKE EARTH IS NOW, MINUS THE EXISTING DOMINANT LIFE-FORMS.
WE HAVE DOCUMENTED EXPERIENCE THAT MOST SPECIES OF HIGHER LIFE-FORMS INEVITABLY CAUSE THEIR OWN EXTINCTION IN VERY SIMILAR WAYS.
ALLOW ME TO CONTINUE. I WILL EXPLAIN IT ALL.

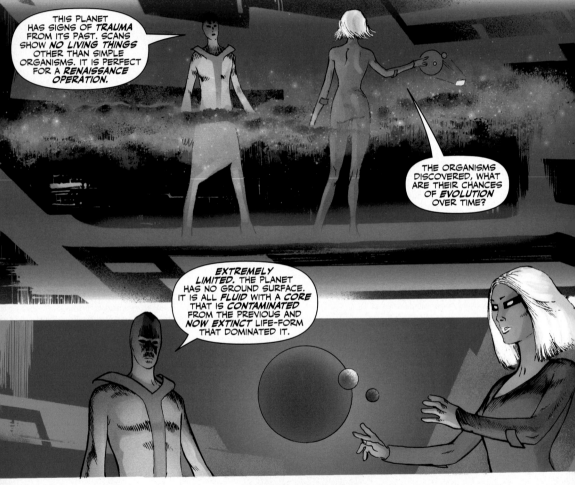

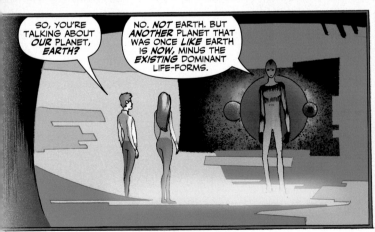

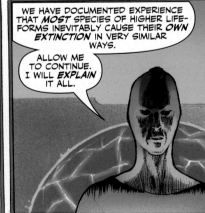

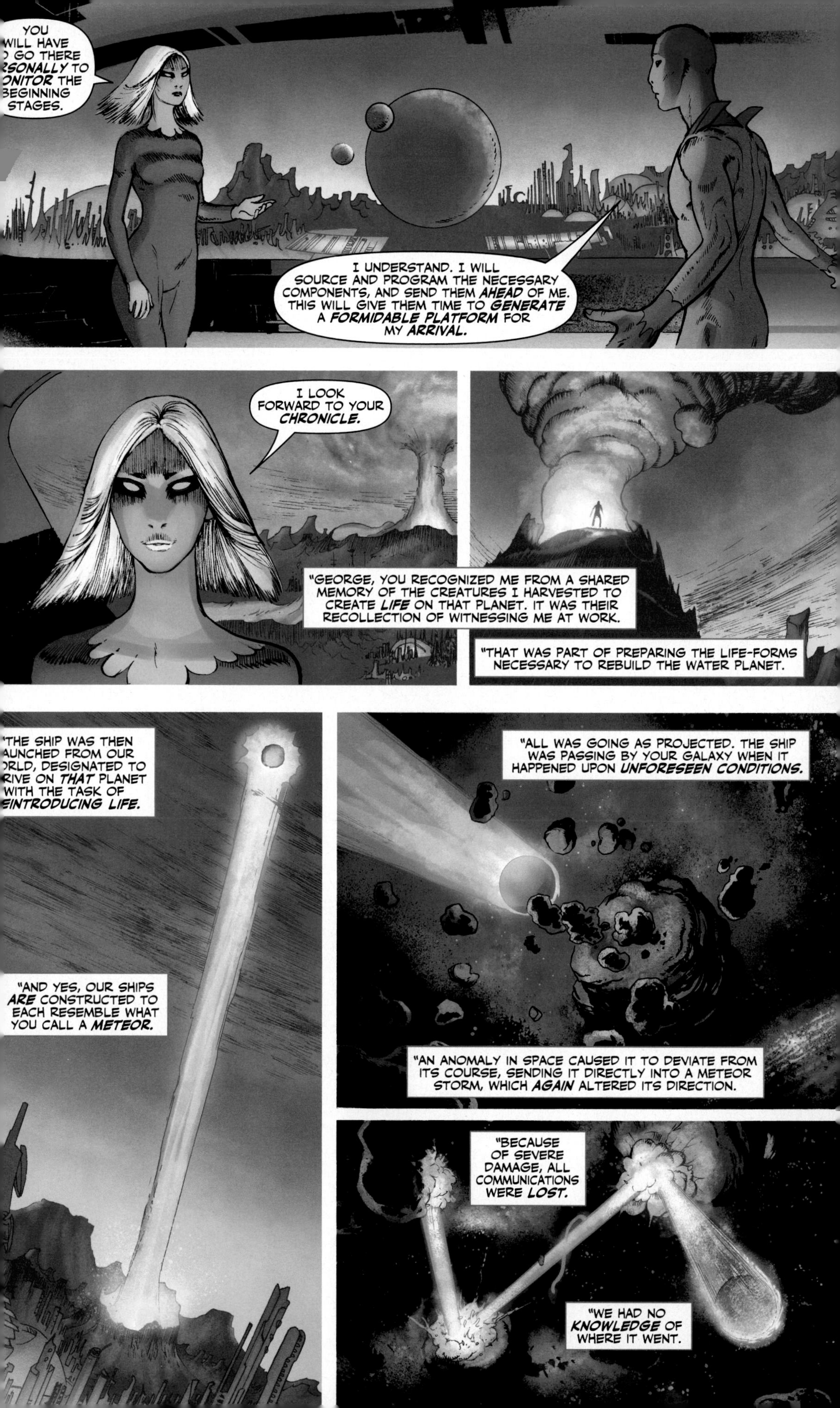
YOU WILL HAVE O GO THERE RSONALLY TO ONITOR THE BEGINNING STAGES.
I UNDERSTAND. I WILL SOURCE AND PROGRAM THE NECESSARY COMPONENTS, AND SEND THEM AHEAD OF ME. THIS WILL GIVE THEM TIME TO GENERATE A FORMIDABLE PLATFORM FOR MY ARRIVAL.
I LOOK FORWARD TO YOUR CHRONICLE.
"GEORGE, YOU RECOGNIZED ME FROM A SHARED MEMORY OF THE CREATURES I HARVESTED TO CREATE LIFE ON THAT PLANET. IT WAS THEIR RECOLLECTION OF WITNESSING ME AT WORK.
"THAT WAS PART OF PREPARING THE LIFE-FORMS NECESSARY TO REBUILD THE WATER PLANET.
"THE SHIP WAS THEN AUNCHED FROM OUR ORLD, DESIGNATED TO RIVE ON THAT PLANET WITH THE TASK OF EINTRODUCING LIFE.
"AND YES, OUR SHIPS ARE CONSTRUCTED TO EACH RESEMBLE WHAT YOU CALL A METEOR.
"ALL WAS GOING AS PROJECTED. THE SHIP WAS PASSING BY YOUR GALAXY WHEN IT HAPPENED UPON UNFORESEEN CONDITIONS.
"AN ANOMALY IN SPACE CAUSED IT TO DEVIATE FROM ITS COURSE, SENDING IT DIRECTLY INTO A METEOR STORM, WHICH AGAIN ALTERED ITS DIRECTION.
"BECAUSE OF SEVERE DAMAGE, ALL COMMUNICATIONS WERE LOST.
"WE HAD NO KNOWLEDGE OF WHERE IT WENT.

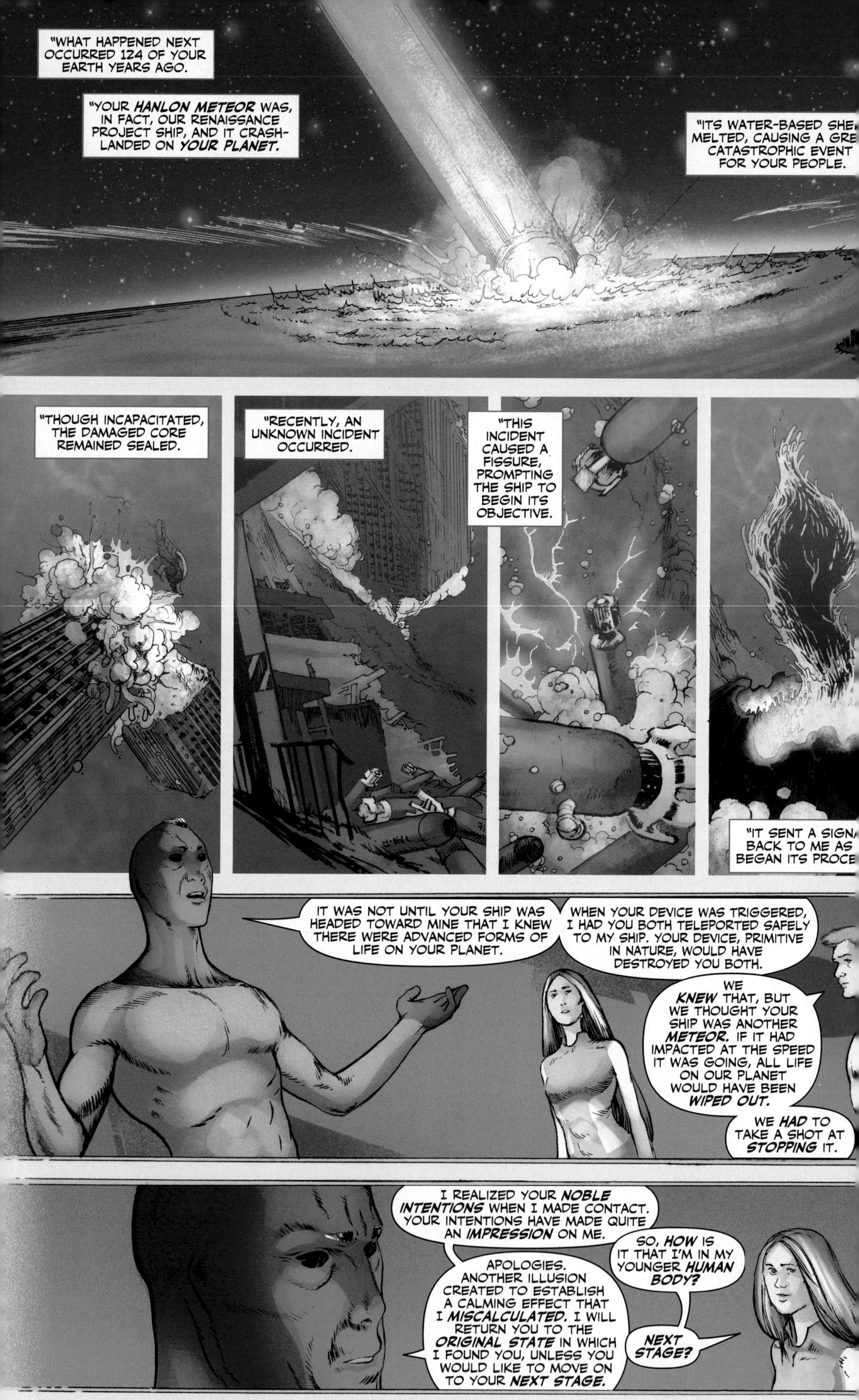
"WHAT HAPPENED NEXT OCCURRED 124 OF YOUR EARTH YEARS AGO.
"YOUR HANLON METEOR WAS, IN FACT, OUR RENAISSANCE PROJECT SHIP, AND IT CRASH-LANDED ON YOUR PLANET.
"ITS WATER-BASED SHE MELTED, CAUSING A GRE CATASTROPHIC EVENT FOR YOUR PEOPLE.
"THOUGH INCAPACITATED, THE DAMAGED CORE REMAINED SEALED.
"RECENTLY, AN UNKNOWN INCIDENT OCCURRED.
"THIS INCIDENT CAUSED A FISSURE, PROMPTING THE SHIP TO BEGIN ITS OBJECTIVE.
"IT SENT A SIGN BACK TO ME AS BEGAN ITS PROCE
IT WAS NOT UNTIL YOUR SHIP WAS HEADED TOWARD MINE THAT I KNEW THERE WERE ADVANCED FORMS OF LIFE ON YOUR PLANET.
WHEN YOUR DEVICE WAS TRIGGERED, I HAD YOU BOTH TELEPORTED SAFELY TO MY SHIP. YOUR DEVICE, PRIMITIVE IN NATURE, WOULD HAVE DESTROYED YOU BOTH.
WE KNEW THAT, BUT WE THOUGHT YOUR SHIP WAS ANOTHER METEOR. IF IT HAD IMPACTED AT THE SPEED IT WAS GOING, ALL LIFE ON OUR PLANET WOULD HAVE BEEN WIPED OUT.
WE HAD TO TAKE A SHOT AT STOPPING IT.
I REALIZED YOUR NOBLE INTENTIONS WHEN I MADE CONTACT. YOUR INTENTIONS HAVE MADE QUITE AN IMPRESSION ON ME.
SO, HOW IS IT THAT I'M IN MY YOUNGER HUMAN BODY?
APOLOGIES. ANOTHER ILLUSION CREATED TO ESTABLISH A CALMING EFFECT THAT I MISCALCULATED. I WILL RETURN YOU TO THE ORIGINAL STATE IN WHICH I FOUND YOU, UNLESS YOU WOULD LIKE TO MOVE ON TO YOUR NEXT STAGE.
NEXT STAGE?

THE *NEXT* STAGE OF YOUR JOURNEY. *PAST* THE BODY YOU OCCUPY.

HAVE YOUR PEOPLE NOT *DISCOVERED* WHAT THIS *IS* YET?

IT'S THE *BILLION-DOLLAR* QUESTION.

APOLOGIES AGAIN. OUR PEOPLE HAVE INTERFERED *ENOUGH*.

WHAT?! DOES T MEAN YOU'RE OT GOING TO *TELL* US?

TIME WILL ANSWER THIS QUESTION FOR YOUR PEOPLE.

FIGURES.

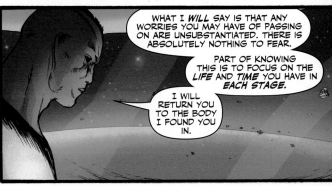

WHAT I *WILL* SAY IS THAT ANY WORRIES YOU MAY HAVE OF PASSING ON ARE UNSUBSTANTIATED. THERE IS ABSOLUTELY NOTHING TO FEAR.

PART OF KNOWING THIS IS TO FOCUS ON THE *LIFE* AND *TIME* YOU HAVE IN *EACH STAGE*.

I WILL RETURN YOU TO THE BODY I FOUND YOU IN.

HMMM.

I DON'T KNOW HOW I FEEL ABOUT THIS.

SO, *NOW WHAT?* DO YOU REMOVE YOUR CREATURES AND LET US LIVE *OUR LIVES?*

I MEAN, YOU CAUSED OUR PLANET TO BE IN THE SHAPE IT'S IN.

I AM WELL AWARE OF THIS, BUT YOU HAVE TO UNDERSTAND THAT THE PROCESS HAS *STARTED...*

...A PROCESS I *CANNOT STOP.*

FORGIVE MY DISTRACTION. IT APPEARS WE HAVE COMPANY HEADING THIS WAY.

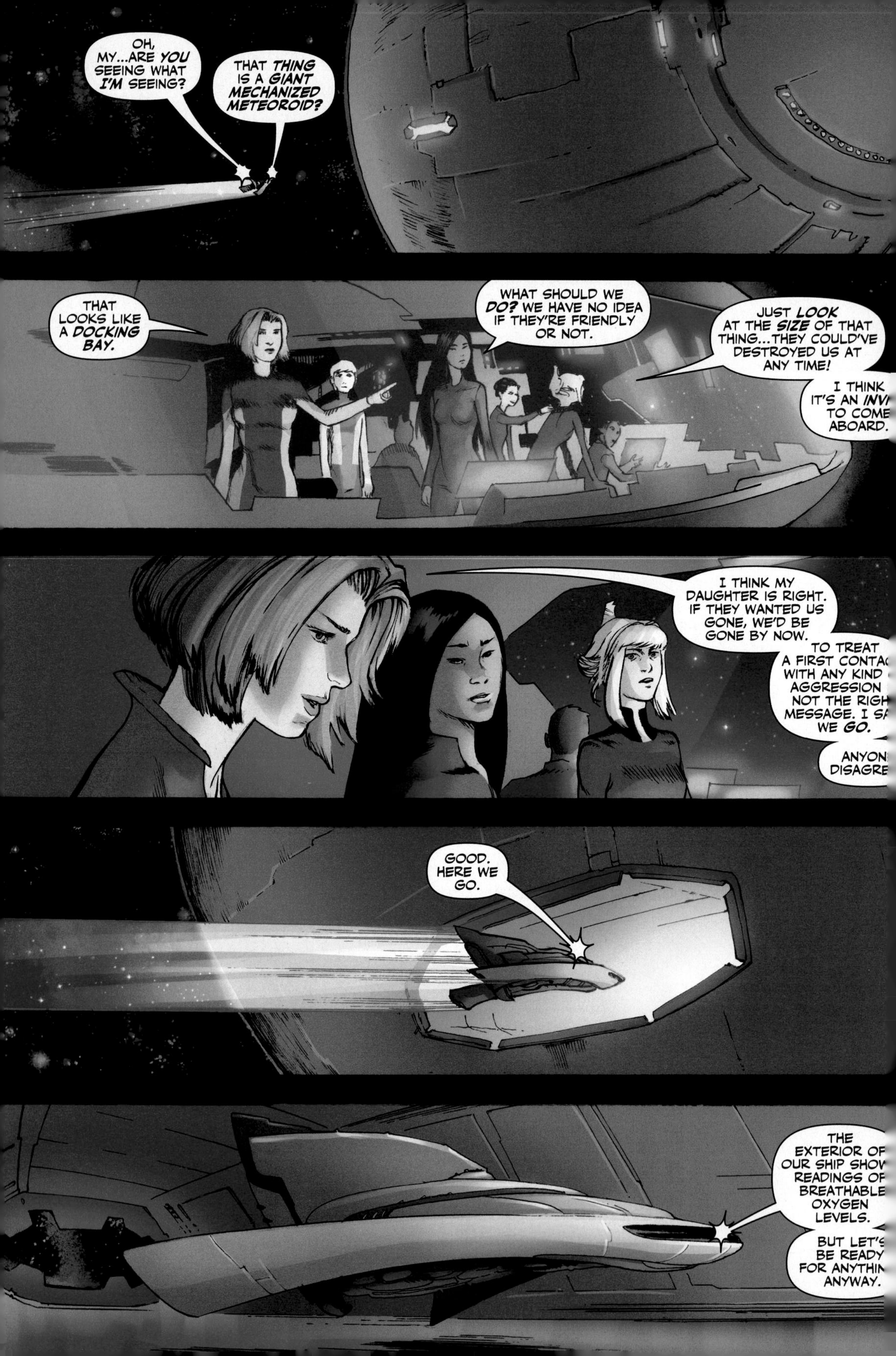
OH, MY...ARE YOU SEEING WHAT I'M SEEING?
THAT THING IS A GIANT MECHANIZED METEOROID?
THAT LOOKS LIKE A DOCKING BAY.
WHAT SHOULD WE DO? WE HAVE NO IDEA IF THEY'RE FRIENDLY OR NOT.
JUST LOOK AT THE SIZE OF THAT THING...THEY COULD'VE DESTROYED US AT ANY TIME!
I THINK IT'S AN INVI TO COME ABOARD.
I THINK MY DAUGHTER IS RIGHT. IF THEY WANTED US GONE, WE'D BE GONE BY NOW.
TO TREAT A FIRST CONTA WITH ANY KIND AGGRESSION NOT THE RIGH MESSAGE. I SA WE GO.
ANYON DISAGRE
GOOD. HERE WE GO.
THE EXTERIOR OF OUR SHIP SHOW READINGS OF BREATHABLE OXYGEN LEVELS.
BUT LET'S BE READY FOR ANYTHIN ANYWAY.

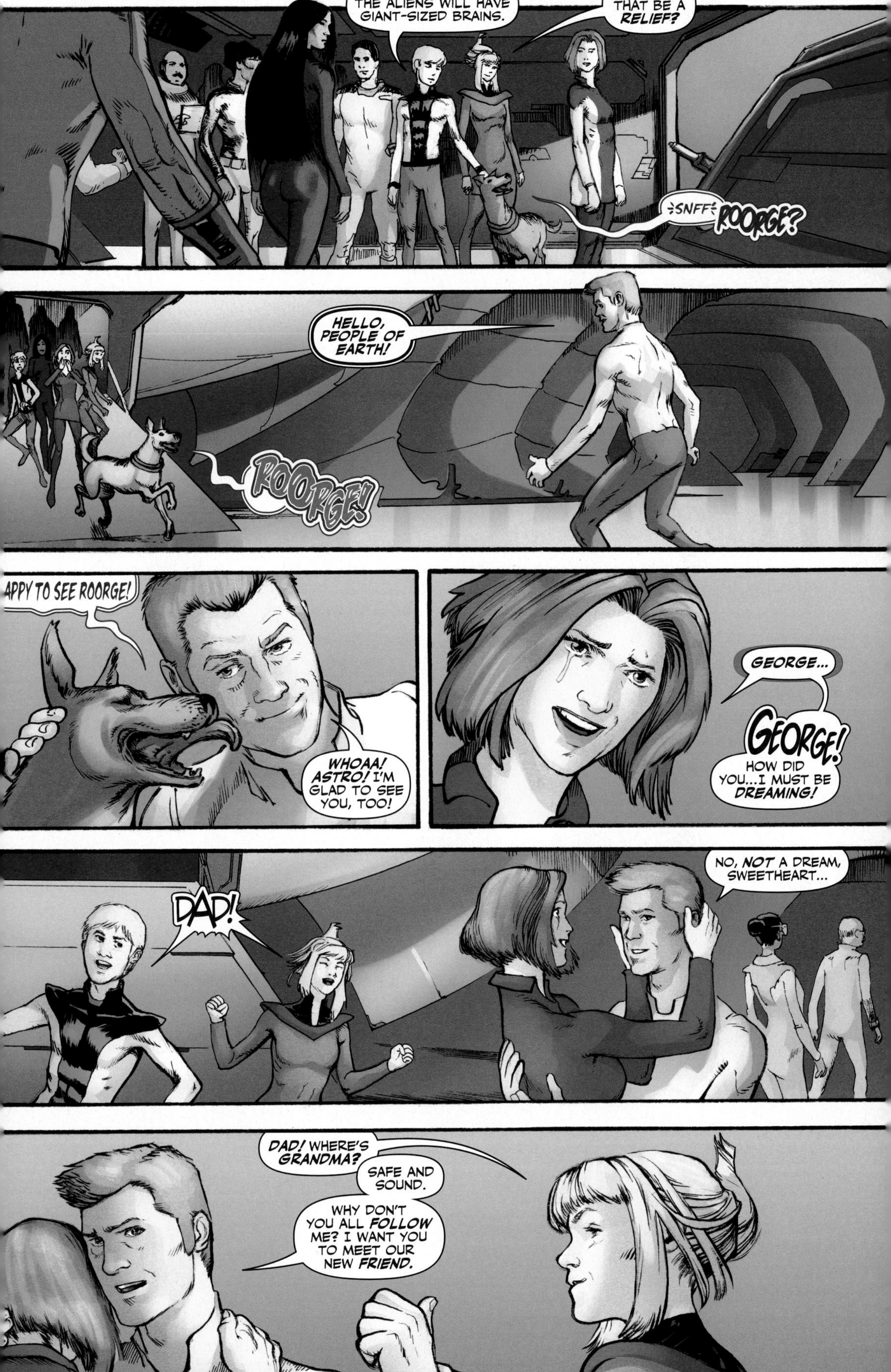
I WONDER IF THE ALIENS WILL HAVE GIANT-SIZED BRAINS.
WOULDN'T THAT BE A RELIEF?
SNFF
ROORGE?
HELLO, PEOPLE OF EARTH!
ROORGE!
APPY TO SEE ROORGE!
WHOAA! ASTRO! I'M GLAD TO SEE YOU, TOO!
GEORGE...
GEORGE!
HOW DID YOU...I MUST BE DREAMING!
DAD!
NO, NOT A DREAM, SWEETHEART...
DAD! WHERE'S GRANDMA?
SAFE AND SOUND.
WHY DON'T YOU ALL FOLLOW ME? I WANT YOU TO MEET OUR NEW FRIEND.

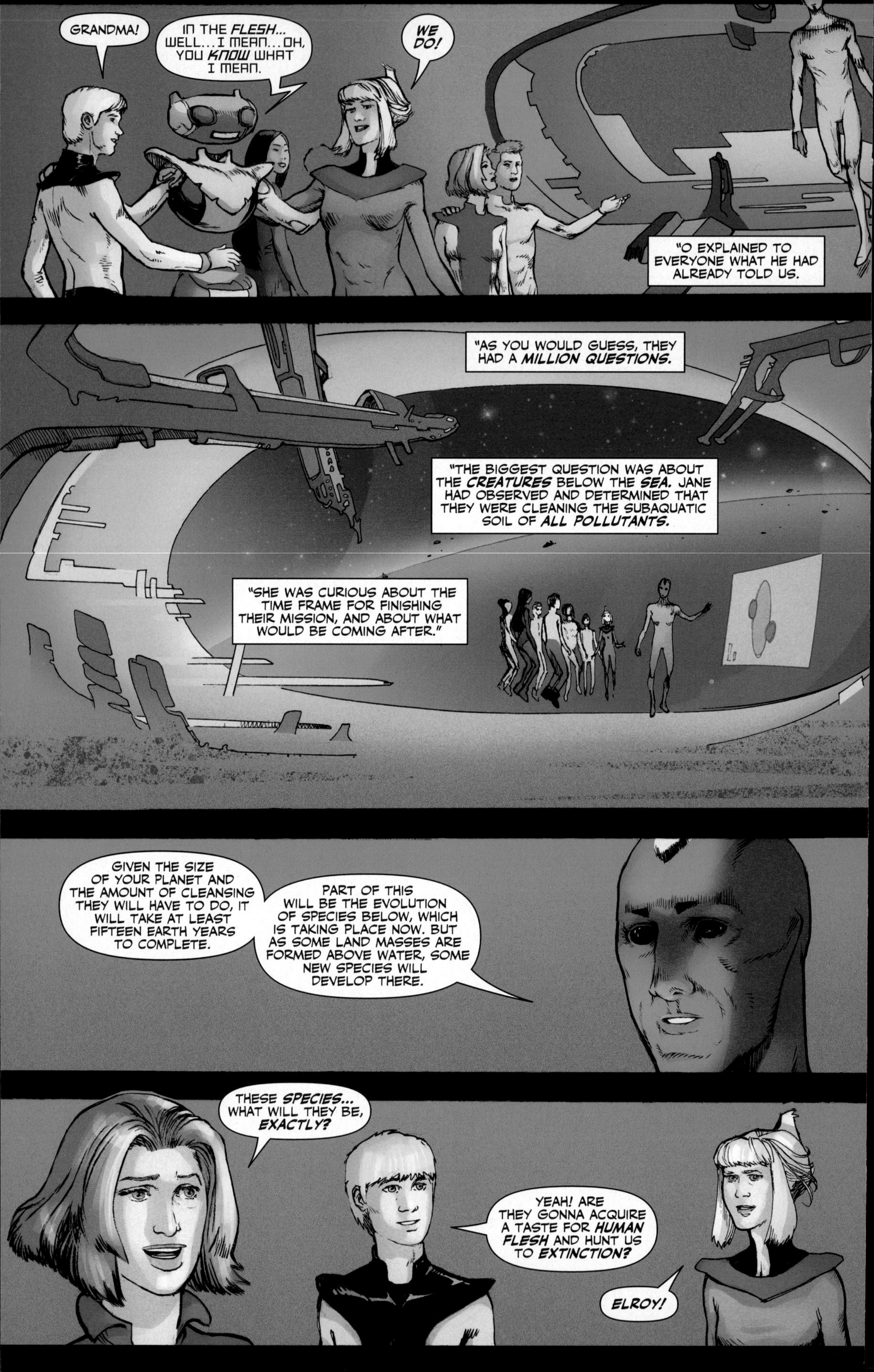
GRANDMA!
IN THE FLESH... WELL... I MEAN... OH, YOU KNOW WHAT I MEAN.
WE DO!
"O EXPLAINED TO EVERYONE WHAT HE HAD ALREADY TOLD US.
"AS YOU WOULD GUESS, THEY HAD A MILLION QUESTIONS.
"THE BIGGEST QUESTION WAS ABOUT THE CREATURES BELOW THE SEA. JANE HAD OBSERVED AND DETERMINED THAT THEY WERE CLEANING THE SUBAQUATIC SOIL OF ALL POLLUTANTS.
"SHE WAS CURIOUS ABOUT THE TIME FRAME FOR FINISHING THEIR MISSION, AND ABOUT WHAT WOULD BE COMING AFTER."
GIVEN THE SIZE OF YOUR PLANET AND THE AMOUNT OF CLEANSING THEY WILL HAVE TO DO, IT WILL TAKE AT LEAST FIFTEEN EARTH YEARS TO COMPLETE.
PART OF THIS WILL BE THE EVOLUTION OF SPECIES BELOW, WHICH IS TAKING PLACE NOW. BUT AS SOME LAND MASSES ARE FORMED ABOVE WATER, SOME NEW SPECIES WILL DEVELOP THERE.
THESE SPECIES... WHAT WILL THEY BE, EXACTLY?
YEAH! ARE THEY GONNA ACQUIRE A TASTE FOR HUMAN FLESH AND HUNT US TO EXTINCTION?
ELROY!

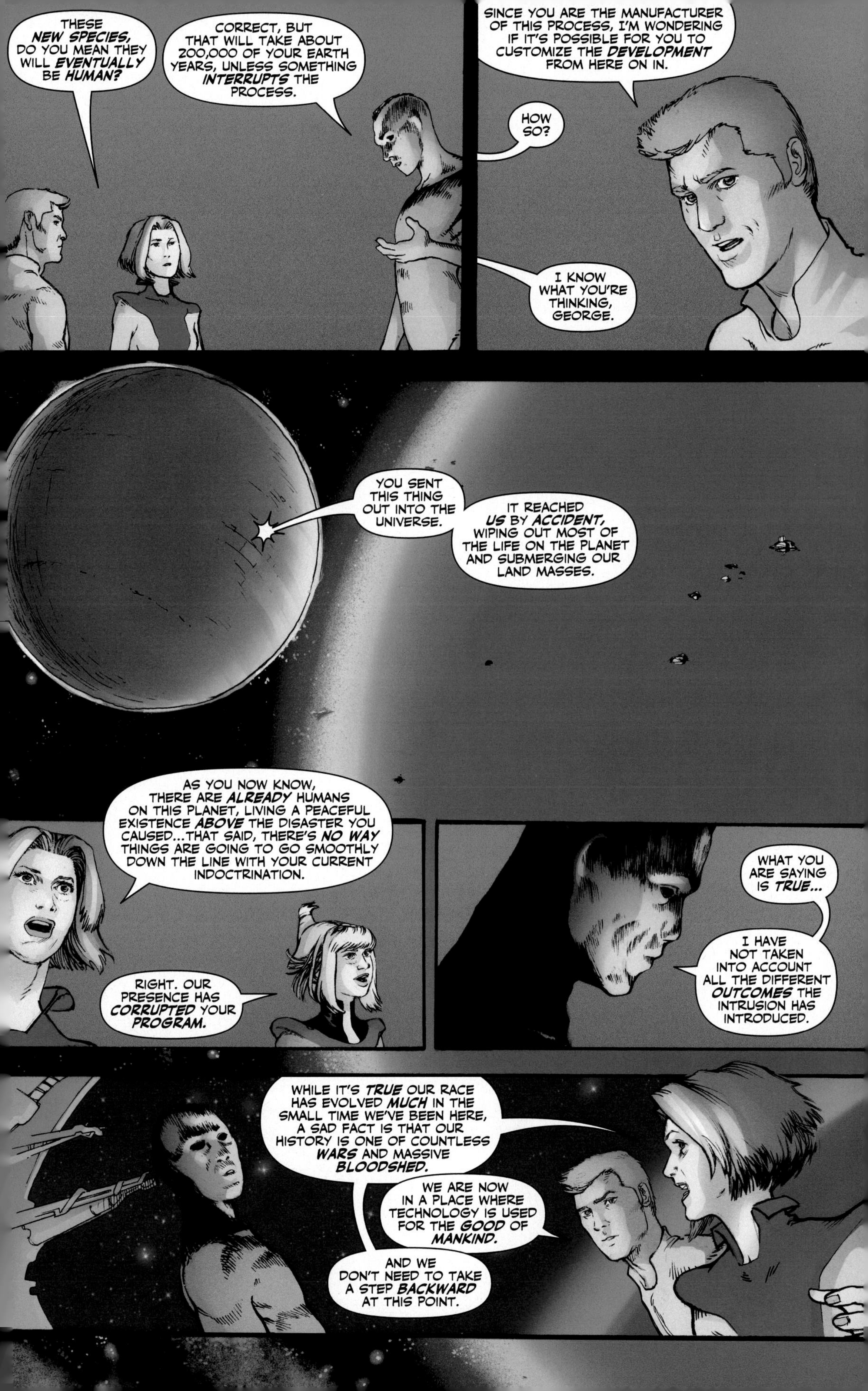
THESE NEW SPECIES, DO YOU MEAN THEY WILL EVENTUALLY BE HUMAN?
CORRECT, BUT THAT WILL TAKE ABOUT 200,000 OF YOUR EARTH YEARS, UNLESS SOMETHING INTERRUPTS THE PROCESS.
SINCE YOU ARE THE MANUFACTURER OF THIS PROCESS, I'M WONDERING IF IT'S POSSIBLE FOR YOU TO CUSTOMIZE THE DEVELOPMENT FROM HERE ON IN.
HOW SO?
I KNOW WHAT YOU'RE THINKING, GEORGE.
YOU SENT THIS THING OUT INTO THE UNIVERSE.
IT REACHED US BY ACCIDENT, WIPING OUT MOST OF THE LIFE ON THE PLANET AND SUBMERGING OUR LAND MASSES.
AS YOU NOW KNOW, THERE ARE ALREADY HUMANS ON THIS PLANET, LIVING A PEACEFUL EXISTENCE ABOVE THE DISASTER YOU CAUSED...THAT SAID, THERE'S NO WAY THINGS ARE GOING TO GO SMOOTHLY DOWN THE LINE WITH YOUR CURRENT INDOCTRINATION.
RIGHT. OUR PRESENCE HAS CORRUPTED YOUR PROGRAM.
WHAT YOU ARE SAYING IS TRUE...
I HAVE NOT TAKEN INTO ACCOUNT ALL THE DIFFERENT OUTCOMES THE INTRUSION HAS INTRODUCED.
WHILE IT'S TRUE OUR RACE HAS EVOLVED MUCH IN THE SMALL TIME WE'VE BEEN HERE, A SAD FACT IS THAT OUR HISTORY IS ONE OF COUNTLESS WARS AND MASSIVE BLOODSHED.
WE ARE NOW IN A PLACE WHERE TECHNOLOGY IS USED FOR THE GOOD OF MANKIND.
AND WE DON'T NEED TO TAKE A STEP BACKWARD AT THIS POINT.

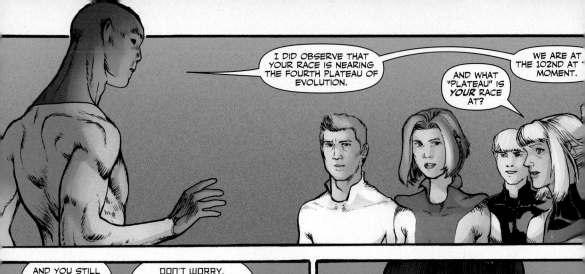

I DID OBSERVE THAT YOUR RACE IS NEARING THE FOURTH PLATEAU OF EVOLUTION.

AND WHAT "PLATEAU" IS *YOUR* RACE AT?

WE ARE AT THE 102ND AT MOMENT.

AND YOU STILL MAKE *MISTAKES*. IT'S A MIXED BAG, EVOLUTION, *ISN'T IT?*

DON'T WORRY, YOU'RE ONLY *HUMAN*. WE *ALL* MAKE BLUNDERS, BUT AT *YOUR* LEVEL, YOU MUST HAVE A BETTER UNDERSTANDING OF HOW TO *FIX* THEM.

AM I *RIGHT?*

YES.

YES, YOU A

GOOD MORNING, EVERYONE. TODAY IS A SPECIAL DAY INDEED, AS WE HAVE THE EXCLUSIVE FIRST INTERVIEW WITH THE MAN WHO PUT HIS LIFE ON THE LINE, AND ALMOST MADE THE *ULTIMATE SACRIFICE* TO SAVE ALL OF US.

LADIES AND GENTLEMEN, I WOULD LIKE TO WELCOME TO OUR WORLD STAGE, THE ONE AND ONLY *GEORGE JETSON!*

GEORGE, ~~ANTED~~ TO PERSONALLY ~~NK YOU~~ FOR DOING WHAT ~~I~~ DID ON THAT BRAVE DAY ~~OVER~~ A MONTH AGO. ~~T~~ WAS IT LIKE, KNOWING ~~T~~ YOU WERE *NOT* GOING ~~TO~~ COME BACK FROM THE MISSION?

AND THEN, IF YOU WOULD TELL EVERYONE...WHAT WAS IT *LIKE* MAKING *FIRST CONTACT* WITH AN *ALIEN SPECIES?*

WELL, THAT'S A *LOT* TO ANSWER, BUT I WOULD LIKE TO TAKE THIS TIME TO PROPERLY THANK THE *REAL HEROES* WHO MADE IT ALL POSSIBLE.

FIRST, MY WONDERFUL BOSS, *MR. COSMO SPACELY,* THE MAN WITH THE *BRILLIANT FORESIGHT* TO SEE THAT ONE DAY WE WOULD HAVE A NEED TO CREATE TECHNOLOGY TO TAKE US PLACES *BEYOND* OUR OWN SOLAR SYSTEM.

I HAVE WORKED FOR HIM MOST OF MY ADULT LIFE, AND A SMARTER, KINDER AND MORE FORGIVING PERSON JUST *DOESN'T EXIST.*

THAT'S MY BOY!

TAKE A NOTE TO GIVE JETSON A *BIGGER* OFFICE AND A *SUBSTANTIAL* RAISE.

MR. SPACELY! DID YOU TAKE YOUR *MEDICINE* TODAY?

~~EXT,~~ I WANT TO THANK MY ASSISTANT AT SPACELY SPROCKETS, *LYDIA CEE.*

HER UNDERSTANDING OF HISTORIC TECHNOLOGY CREATED THE PAYLOAD THAT I WAS ABLE TO SUCCESS-FULLY DELIVER.

I OWE HER A PUBLIC ~~APO~~LOGY FOR MISLEADING HER, BECAUSE ~~ORI~~GINALLY, SHE'S THE HERO WHO CAME ~~UP~~ WITH THIS IDEA...AND WAS SUPPOSED ~~TO~~ *ACCOMPANY* ME ON THE MISSION.

I OWE HER SO MUCH. *THANK YOU, LYDIA.*

YOU'RE WELCOME, *YA BIG SNEAKY JERK.*

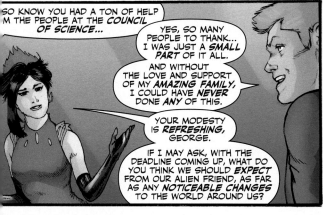

~~I AL~~SO KNOW YOU HAD A TON OF HELP ~~FRO~~M THE PEOPLE AT THE *COUNCIL OF SCIENCE...*

YES, SO MANY PEOPLE TO THANK... I WAS JUST A *SMALL PART* OF IT ALL.

AND WITHOUT THE LOVE AND SUPPORT OF MY *AMAZING FAMILY,* I COULD HAVE *NEVER* DONE *ANY* OF THIS.

YOUR MODESTY IS *REFRESHING,* GEORGE.

IF I MAY ASK, WITH THE DEADLINE COMING UP, WHAT DO YOU THINK WE SHOULD *EXPECT* FROM OUR ALIEN FRIEND, AS FAR AS ANY *NOTICEABLE CHANGES* TO THE WORLD AROUND US?

YOUR GUESS IS AS GOOD AS MINE. IT'S JUST *WAIT* AND *SEE* AT THIS POINT.

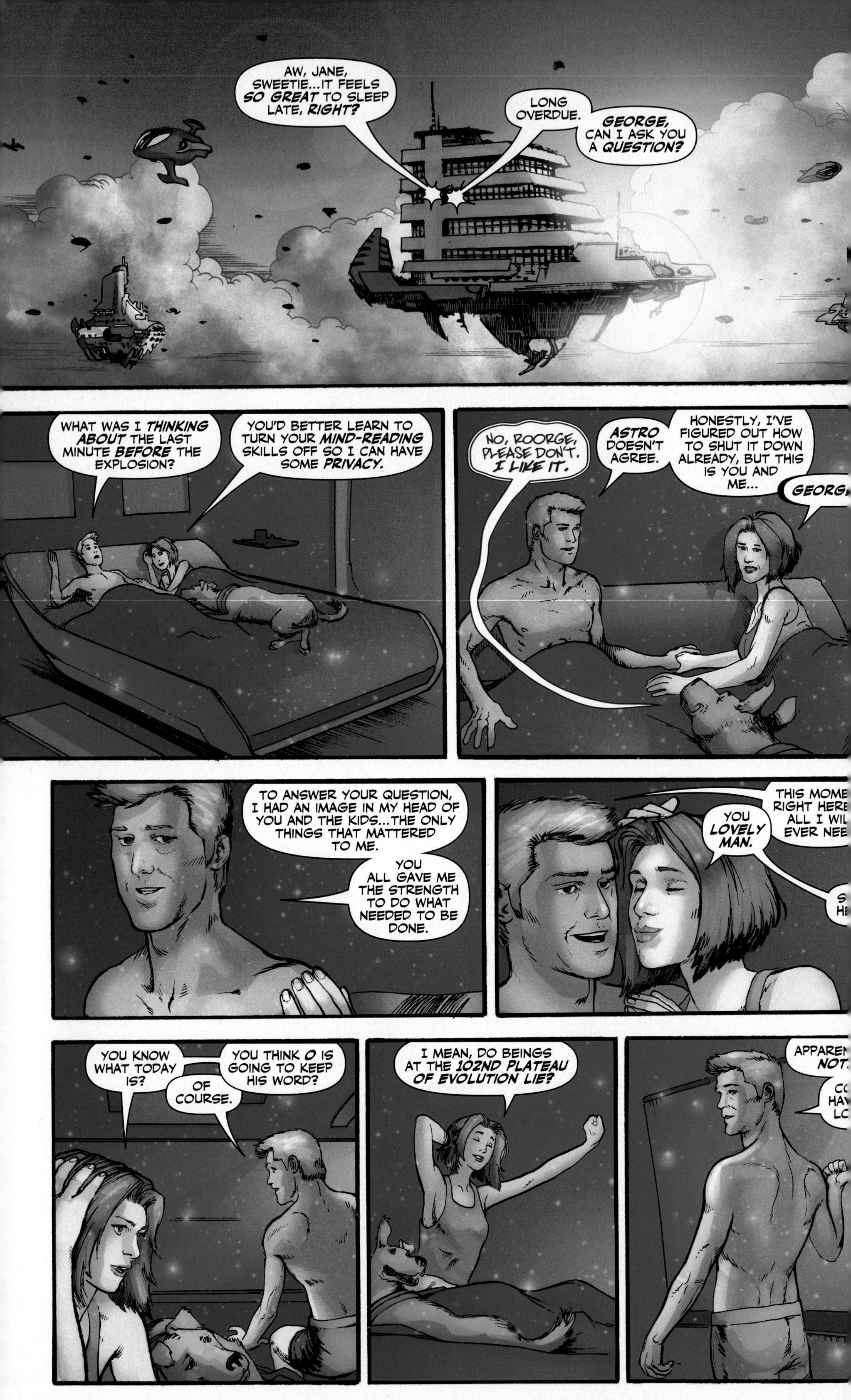
AW, JANE, SWEETIE...IT FEELS SO GREAT TO SLEEP LATE, RIGHT?
LONG OVERDUE.
GEORGE, CAN I ASK YOU A QUESTION?
WHAT WAS I THINKING ABOUT THE LAST MINUTE BEFORE THE EXPLOSION?
YOU'D BETTER LEARN TO TURN YOUR MIND-READING SKILLS OFF SO I CAN HAVE SOME PRIVACY.
NO, ROORGE, PLEASE DON'T. I LIKE IT.
ASTRO DOESN'T AGREE.
HONESTLY, I'VE FIGURED OUT HOW TO SHUT IT DOWN ALREADY, BUT THIS IS YOU AND ME...
GEORG
TO ANSWER YOUR QUESTION, I HAD AN IMAGE IN MY HEAD OF YOU AND THE KIDS...THE ONLY THINGS THAT MATTERED TO ME.
YOU ALL GAVE ME THE STRENGTH TO DO WHAT NEEDED TO BE DONE.
THIS MOME RIGHT HERE ALL I WIL EVER NEE
YOU LOVELY MAN.
YOU KNOW WHAT TODAY IS?
YOU THINK O IS GOING TO KEEP HIS WORD?
OF COURSE.
I MEAN, DO BEINGS AT THE 102ND PLATEAU OF EVOLUTION LIE?
APPARE NOT.

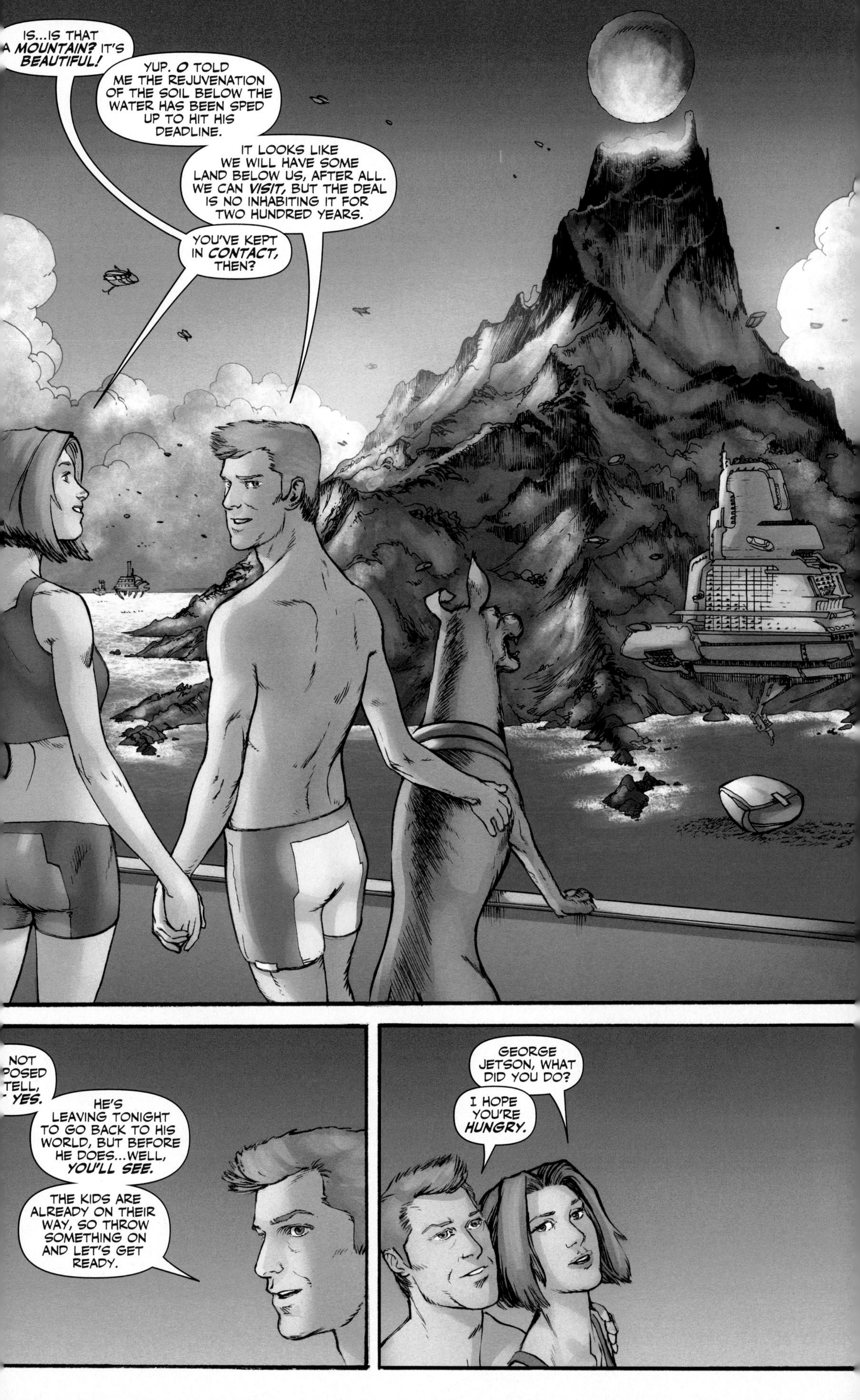

IS...IS THAT A MOUNTAIN? IT'S BEAUTIFUL!
YUP. O TOLD ME THE REJUVENATION OF THE SOIL BELOW THE WATER HAS BEEN SPED UP TO HIT HIS DEADLINE.
IT LOOKS LIKE WE WILL HAVE SOME LAND BELOW US, AFTER ALL. WE CAN VISIT, BUT THE DEAL IS NO INHABITING IT FOR TWO HUNDRED YEARS.
YOU'VE KEPT IN CONTACT, THEN?
NOT POSED TELL, YES.
HE'S LEAVING TONIGHT TO GO BACK TO HIS WORLD, BUT BEFORE HE DOES...WELL, YOU'LL SEE.
THE KIDS ARE ALREADY ON THEIR WAY, SO THROW SOMETHING ON AND LET'S GET READY.
GEORGE JETSON, WHAT DID YOU DO?
I HOPE YOU'RE HUNGRY.

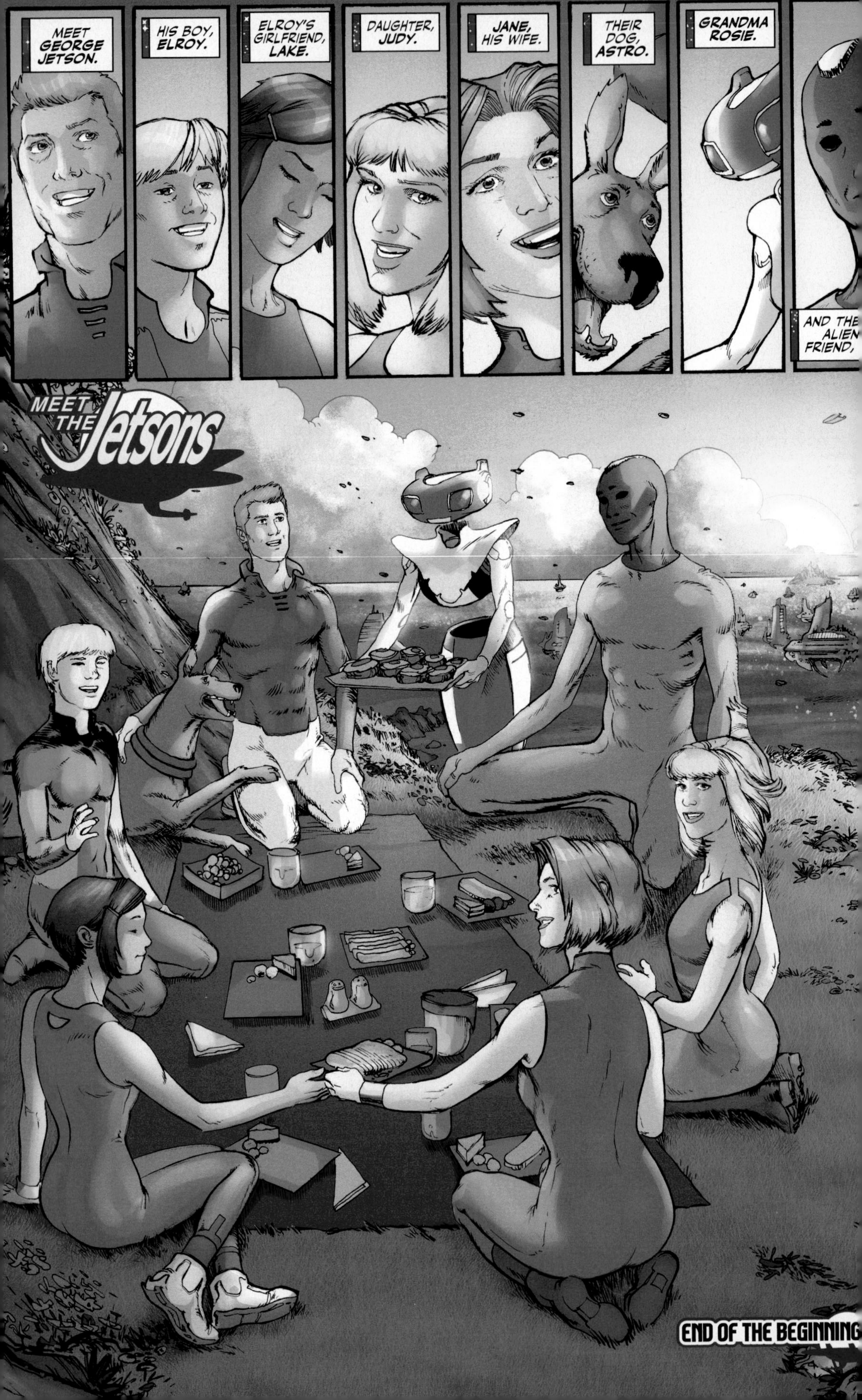
MEET GEORGE JETSON.
HIS BOY, ELROY.
ELROY'S GIRLFRIEND, LAKE.
DAUGHTER, JUDY.
JANE, HIS WIFE.
THEIR DOG, ASTRO.
GRANDMA ROSIE.
AND THE ALIEN FRIEND,
MEET THE Jetsons
END OF THE BEGINNING

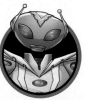

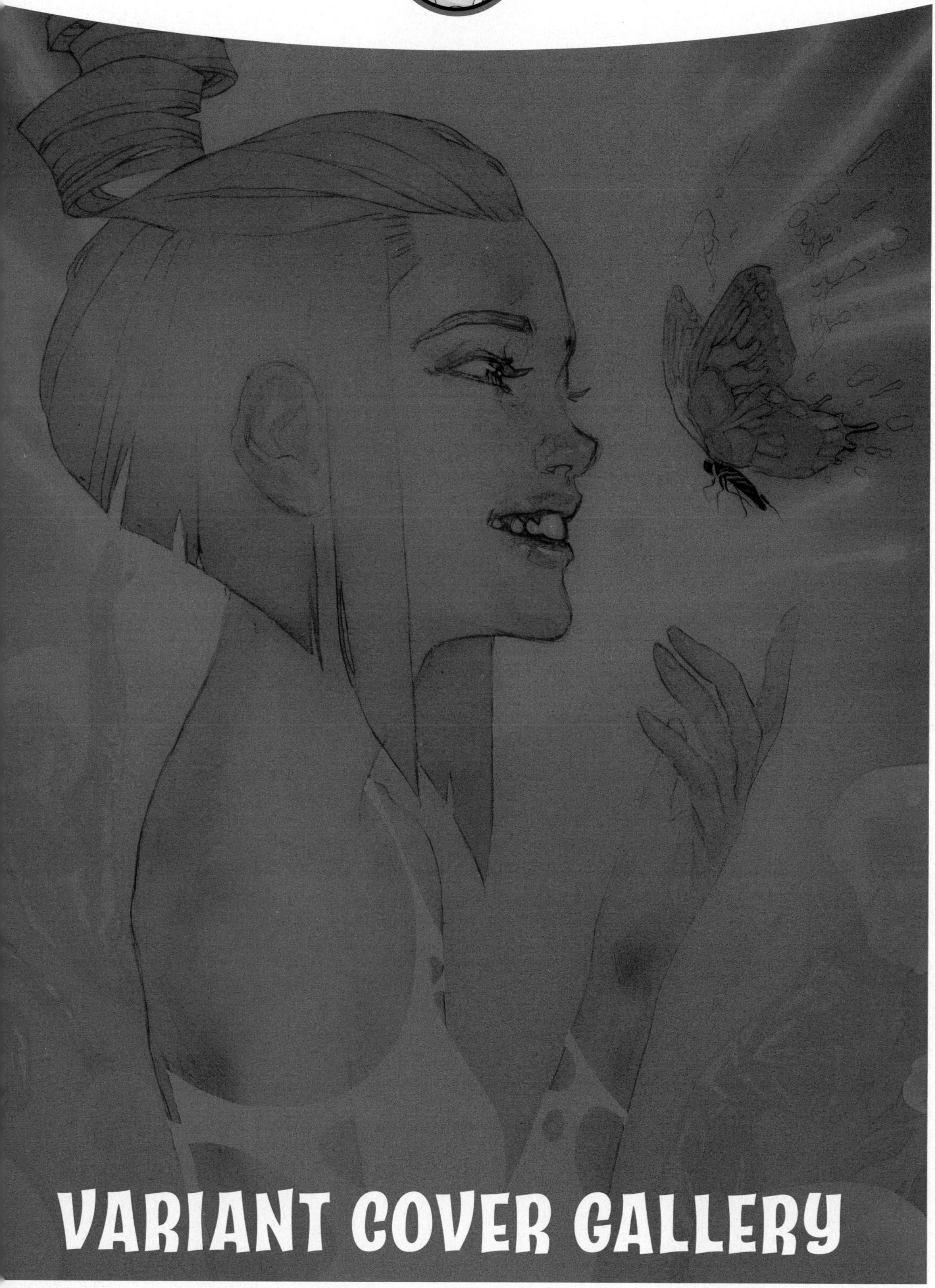
VARIANT COVER GALLERY

THE JETSONS #1 variant cover
by DAVE JOHNSON

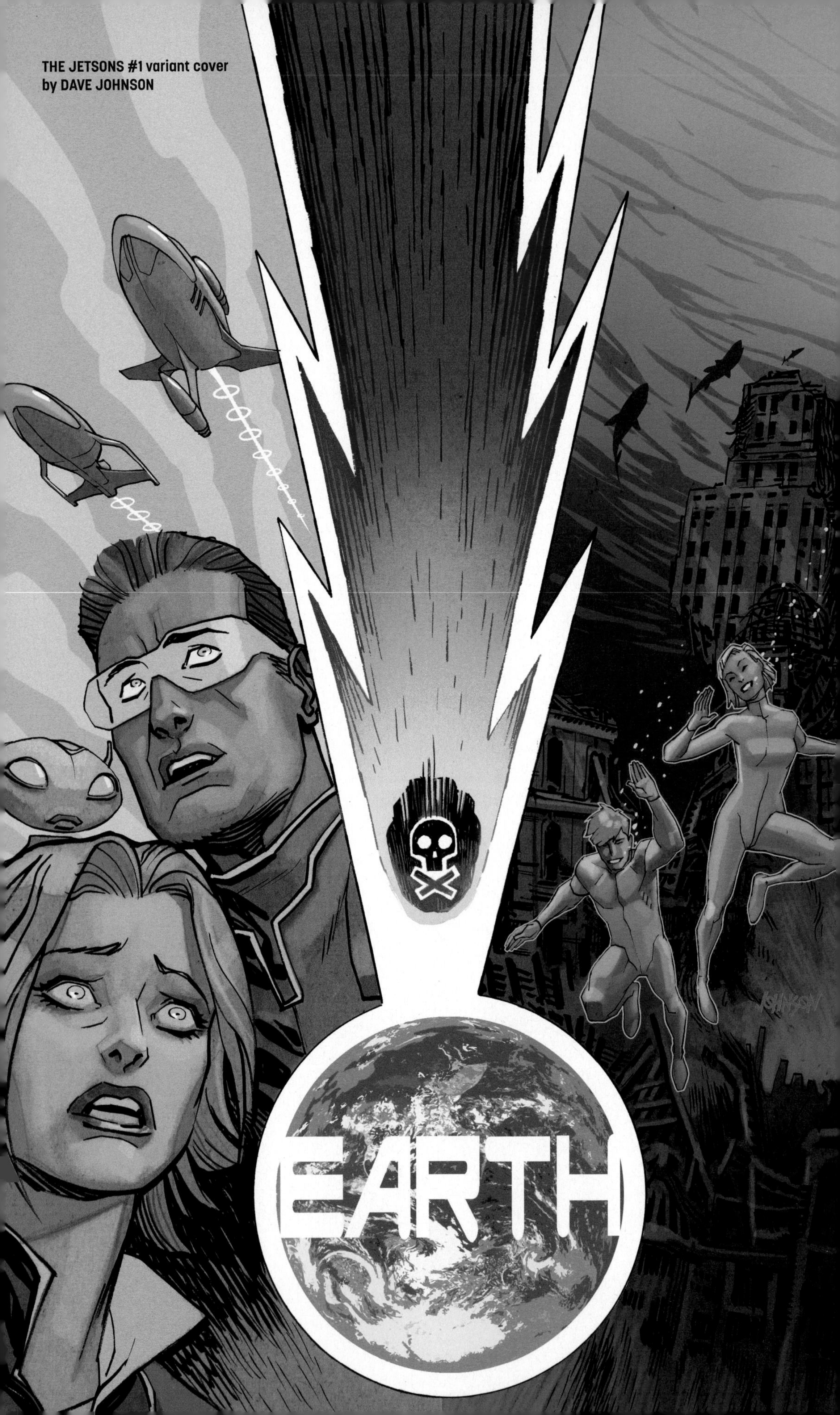
EARTH
JOHNSON

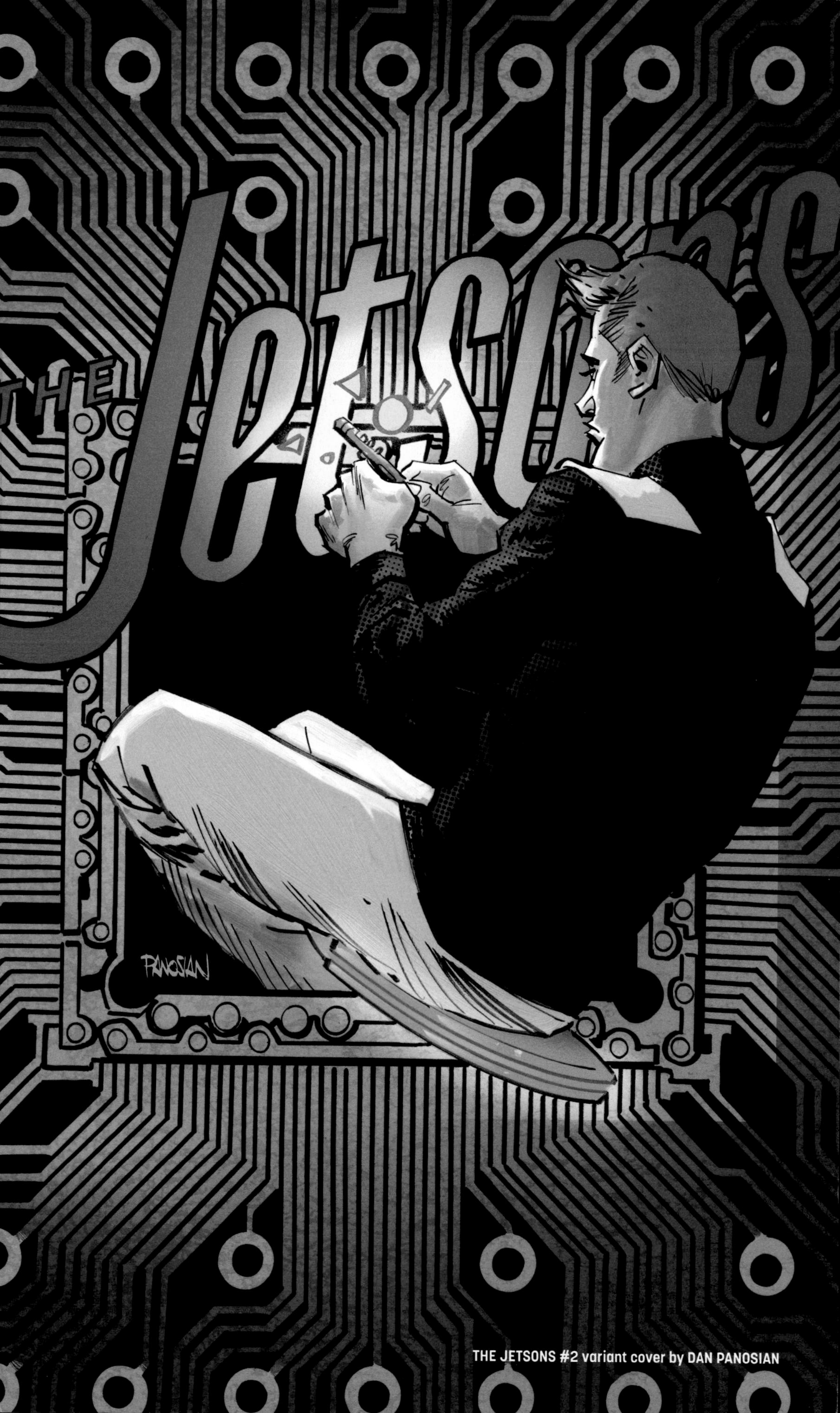
THE Jetsons
PANOSIAN
THE JETSONS #2 variant cover by DAN PANOSIAN

THE JETSONS #3 variant cover by MICHAEL KALUTA and DAVE STEWART

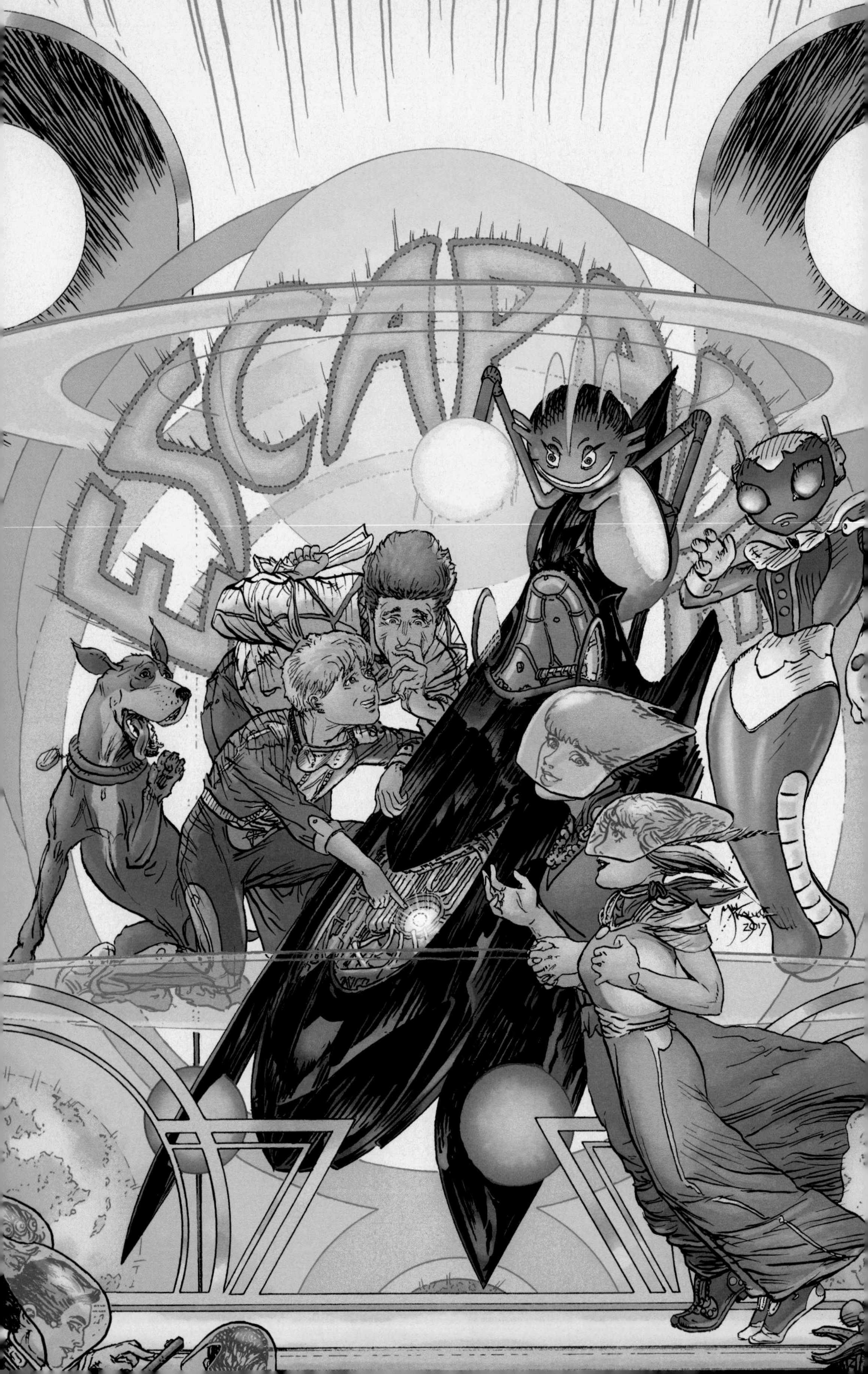

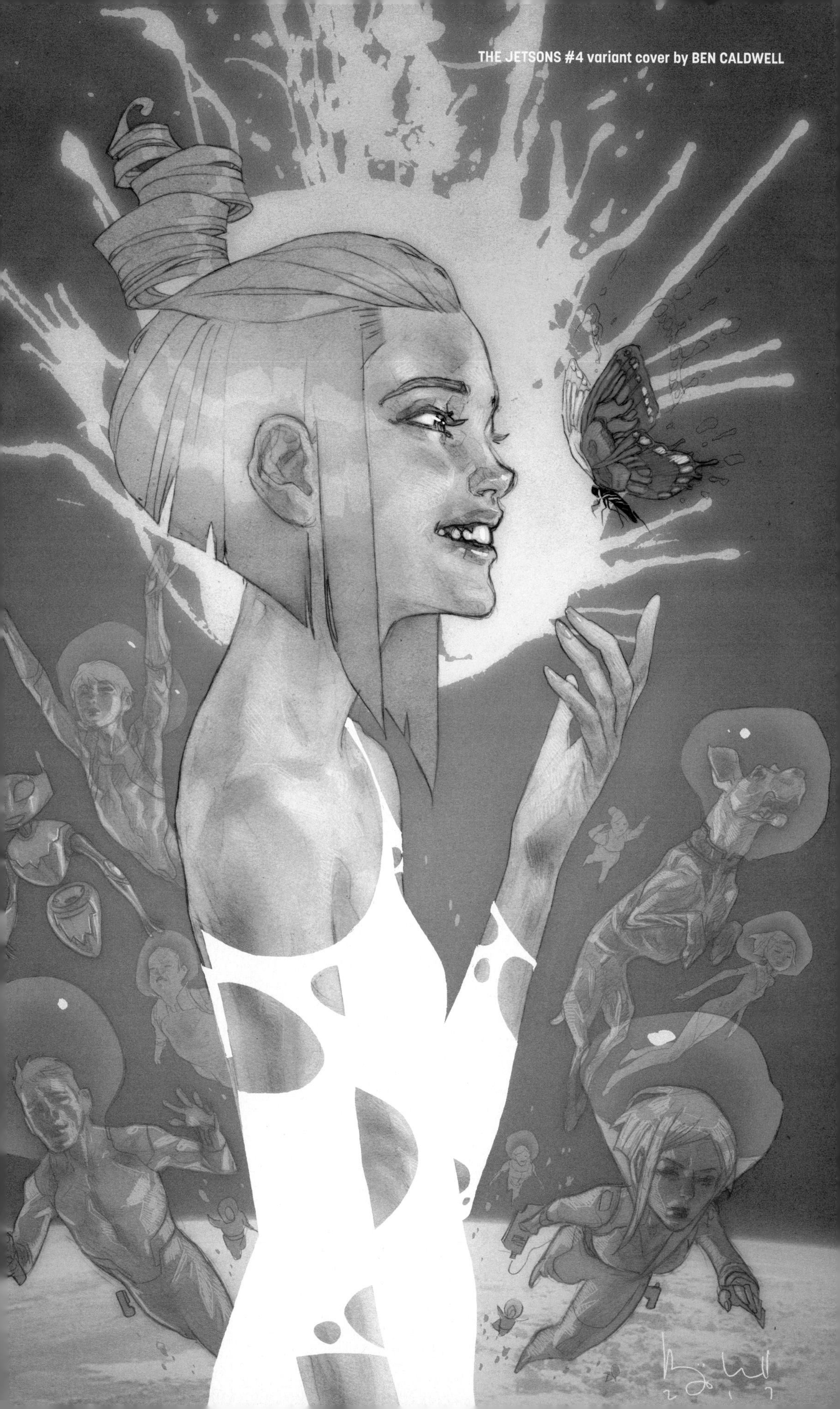

THE JETSONS #4 variant cover by BEN CALDWELL

THE JETSONS #5 variant cover by SANFORD GREENE with PAUL MOUNTS

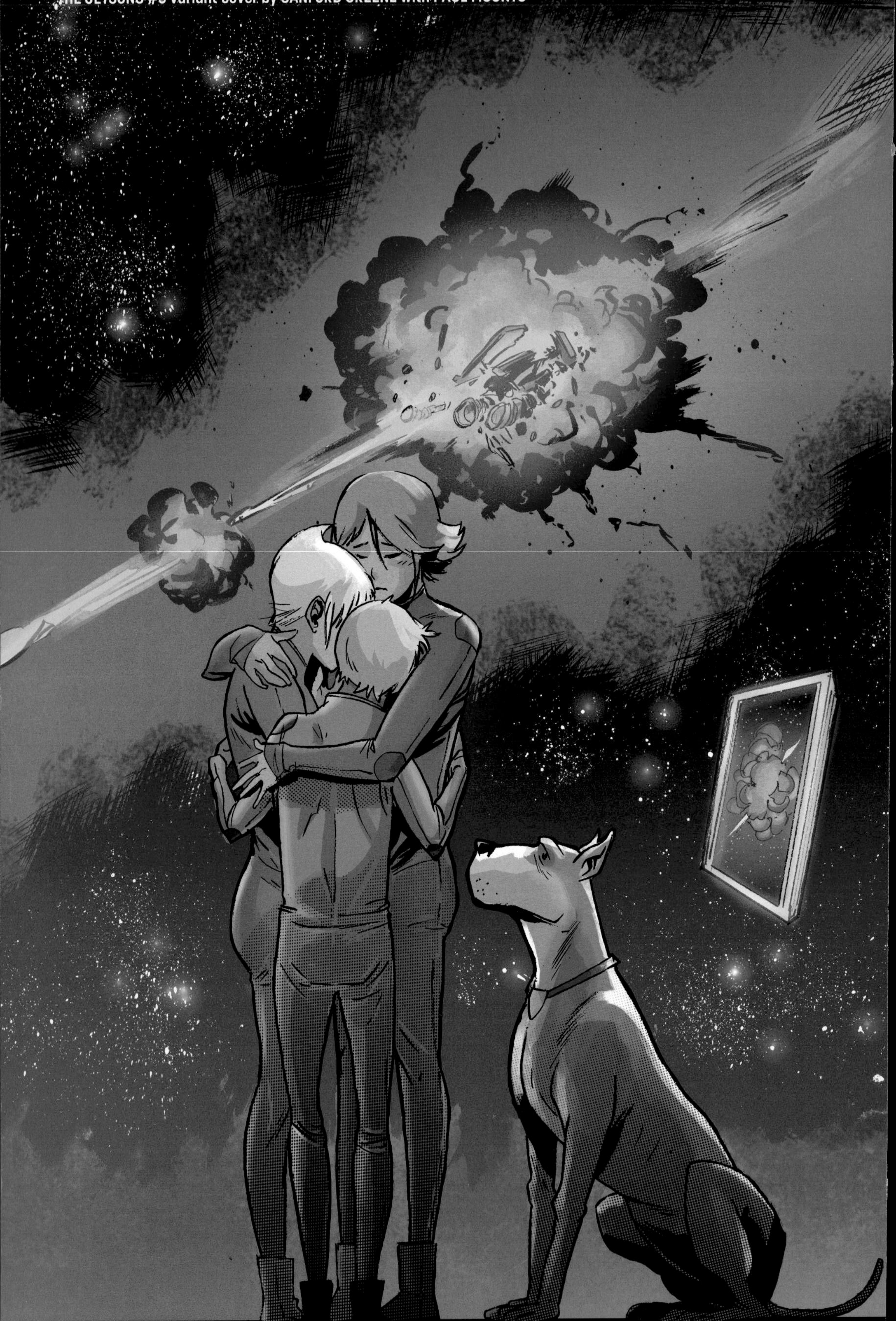

THE JETSONS #6 variant cover by RYAN SOOK

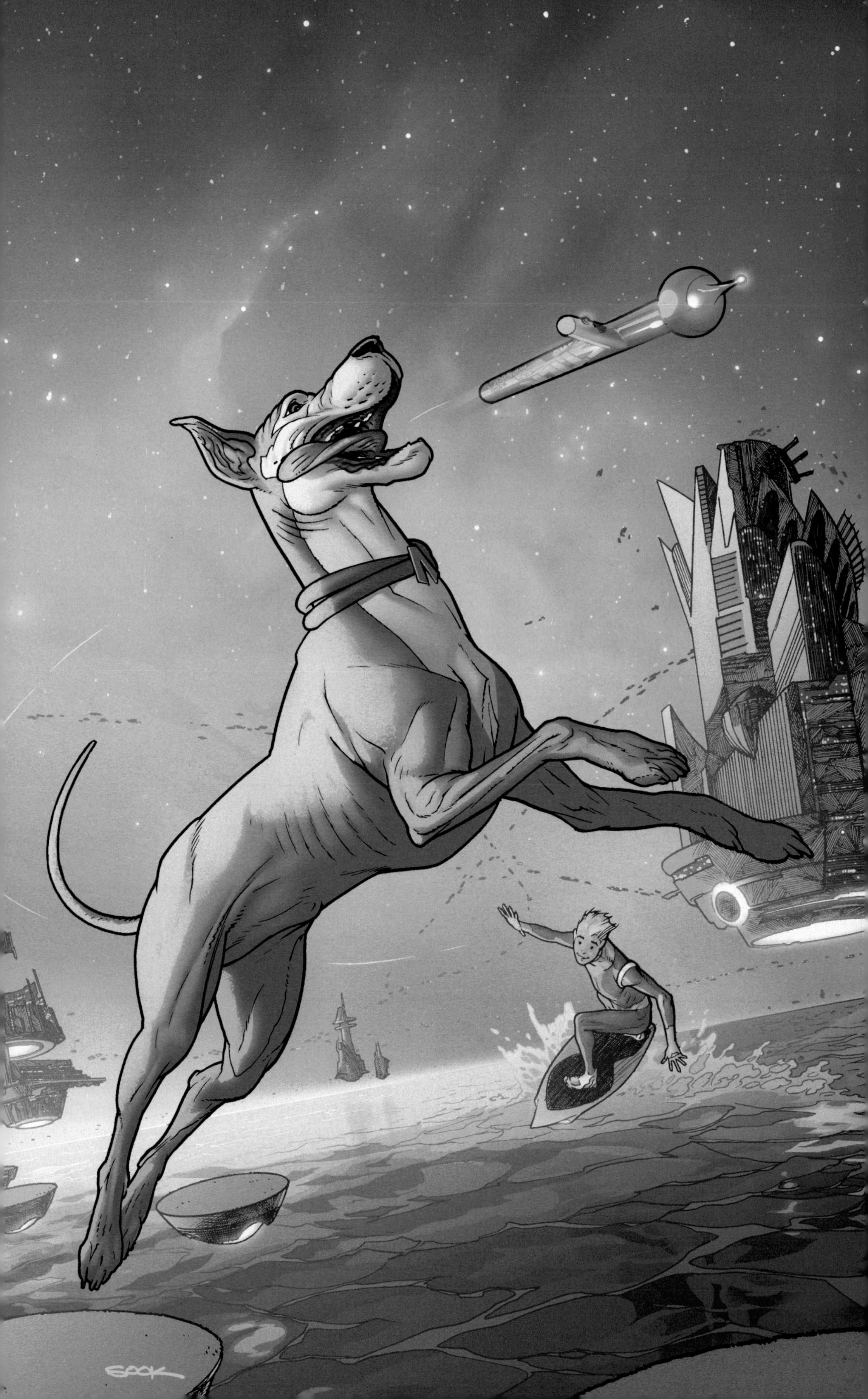
SOOK

THE JETSONS character sketches
All character sketches by PIER BRITO

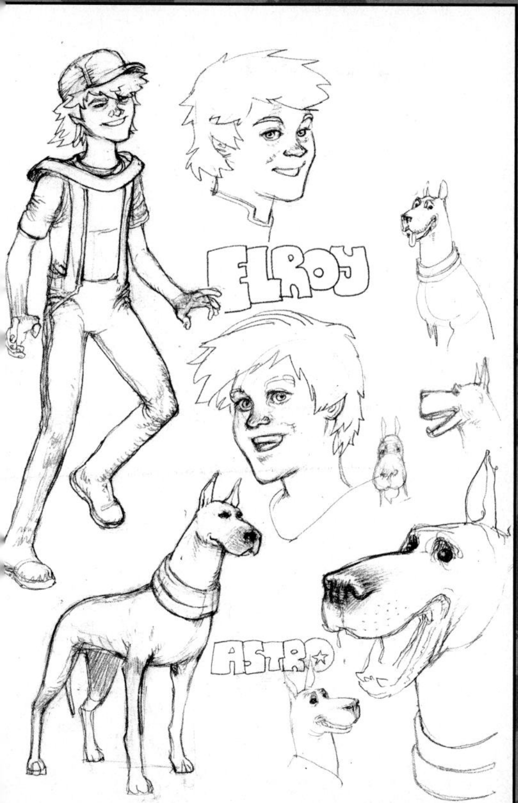
ELROY
ASTRO

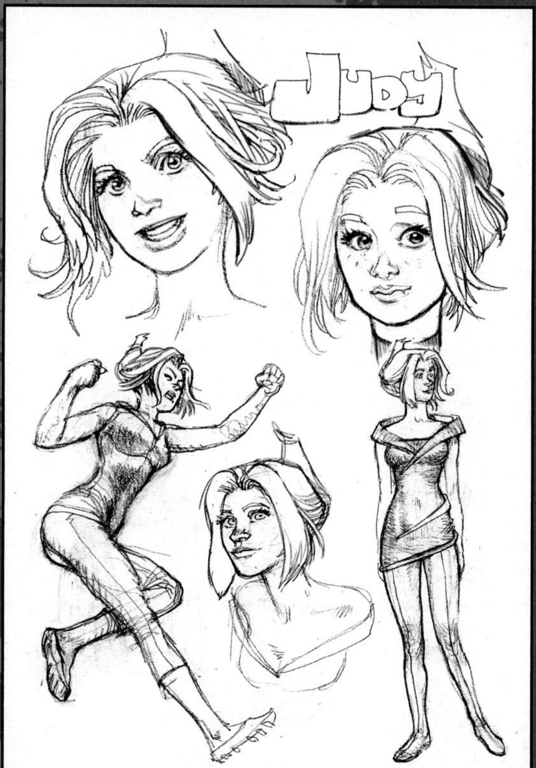
JUDY

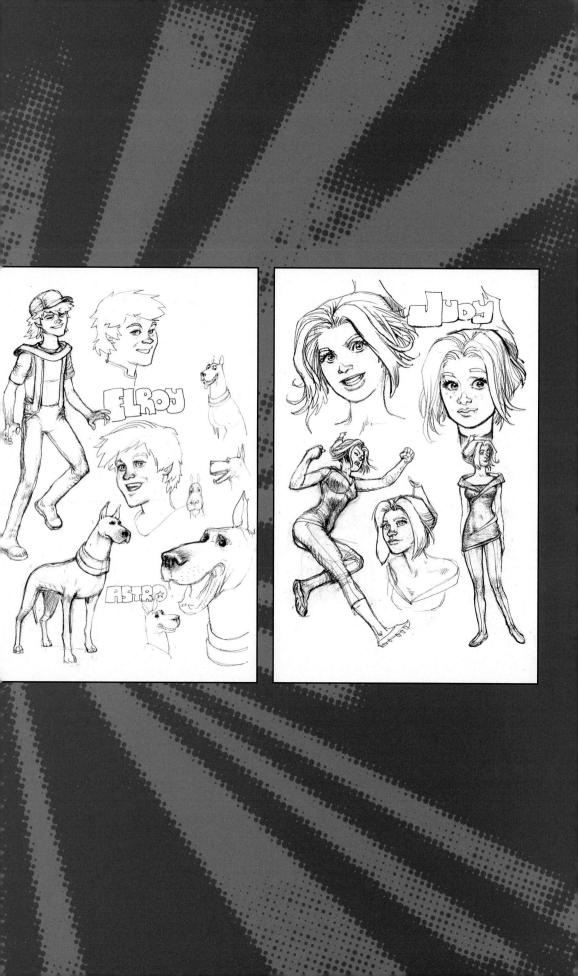

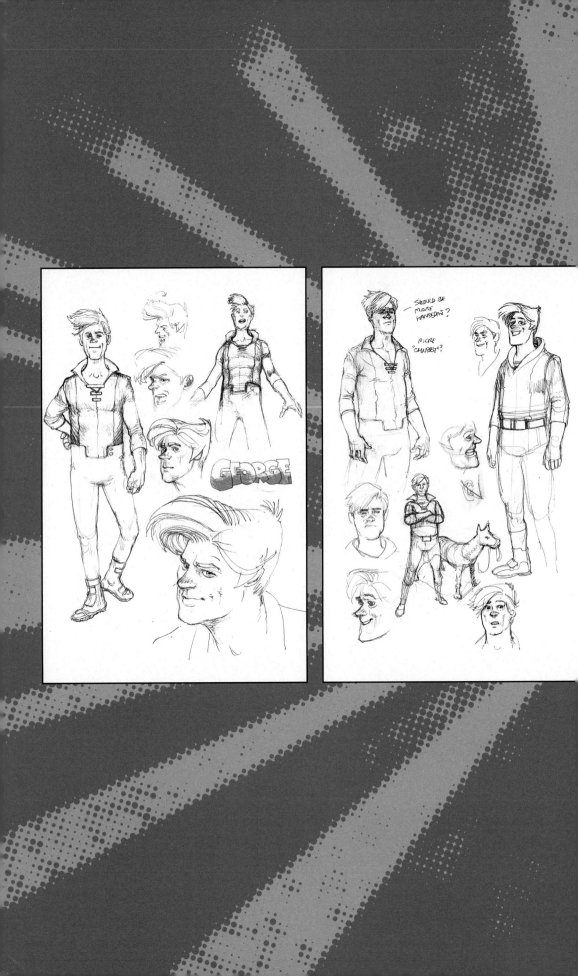

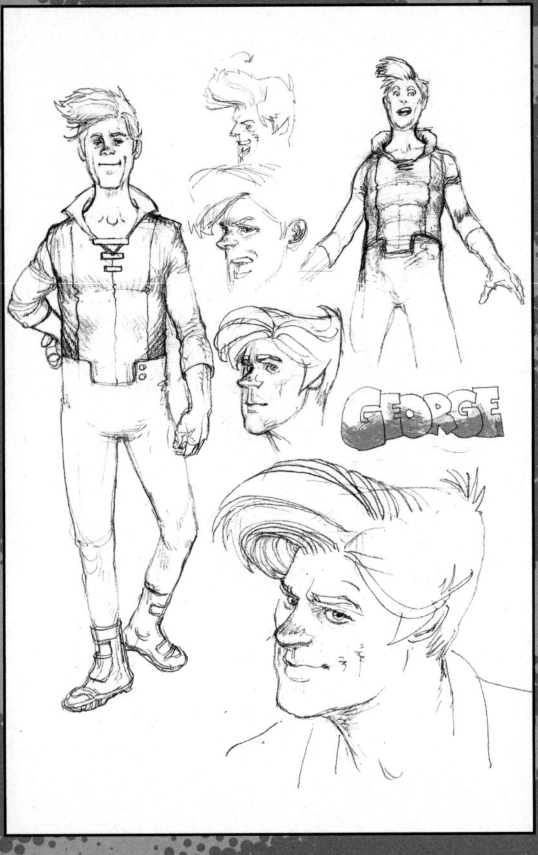
GEORGE

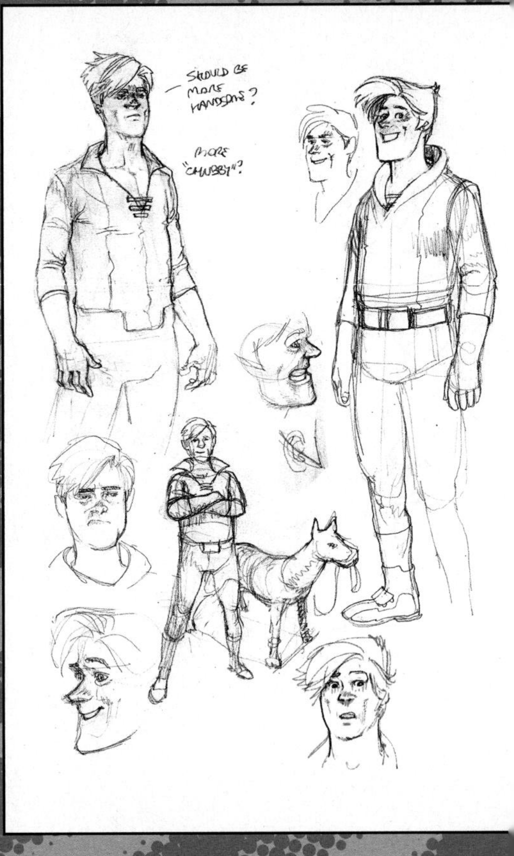
SHOULD BE MORE HANDSOME?
MORE "CHUBBY"?